PS: Love Me?

The War Memoirs of Flight Sergeant Ed Gallagher

Diaries, Letters and Sonnets

of

Edward Bernard Gallagher

~

Australia & Britain

1941-1943

Compiled and Annotated by Tricia Timmermans

ISBN-10: 1492310603
ISBN-13: 978-1492310600

Cover Design by Tricia Timmermans

Front image of a Sunderland over the Bay of Biscay is from the cover of the
scrapbook kept by my mother, Molly, when Ed served with the RAAF

In Memory of my Parents: Ed and Molly Gallagher

All things, of Man's endeavour built, decay,

And dying, of their passing leave no sign,

Save where the Master's hand assigns the clay

A lasting beauty, - tinged with the Divine:

And, Dear, when all things else we loved are gone,

Our Love, - deep born of God, - will linger on!

E.B.G. 1942

Edward Bernard Gallagher, 1915-1986

CONTENTS

Molly and Ed, Brisbane, 1941

Foreword

When I began reading my father's wartime diaries many years ago, I had no forewarning of the long journey I was about to set out on. I became immersed in his story of love and separation, one that was perforated with the sorrow of losing his *mates* and of his own uncertain future. The intensity of his story was reinforced, when, after my mother died in 1997, I came across letters he had written to her during his training in Australia and while serving with the Royal Australian Air Force in Britain from 1941 to 1943. Hitler's forces were threatening to separate my mother and father permanently, and, on a few occasions, almost did.

When war broke out in 1939, my father, Edward Bernard Gallagher, was working for the Australian Post Office in Brisbane. He was living in a boarding house in New Farm, where he met and fell in love with my mother, Mary (Molly) Thomson. In 1940, he joined the RAAF in an effort, as he put it, "to be doing something to give Adolf a smack in the eye". He was first stationed at Amberley in Queensland, and in March 1941 he began his training as a Wireless Air Gunner at No. 1 Air Navigation School in Parkes, New South Wales, where his letters to my mother begin.

His war journey took him across the Pacific to the USA and Canada, and on to England, where, as a result of an agreement made in Ottawa in November 1939 between Great Britain, Canada, Australia and New Zealand, he became a member of the Empire Air Training Scheme and was posted to Number 10 Squadron at Pembroke Dock in south-west Wales. His letters home ended in New Zealand in June 1943, where he awaited a ship to take him to Australia and home to Molly. He had been, as he described it, "put out of the flying game ... the result of a bit of a crack up", which was double-talk for a severe head injury caused by a plane accident in the waters off Mount Batten, near Plymouth, UK. Without his pen over those few short years, we, his family, would never have understood just how funny, smart and delightful a man he really was ... but then, Molly knew that already.

In acknowledging my father for his honest writings, I also give thanks to my mother, who courageously raised their children in the shadow of her invalid husband, and who, for more than fifty years, kept his cherished letters tied up with blue satin ribbons in a couple of old shoeboxes.

The words in this book are entirely my father's. Nothing has been altered, not even what would be considered, by today's standards, politically-incorrect terminology. I have added notes in parentheses for descriptive information where I felt it was useful.

Thanks to my family and friends who have urged me to complete this work—may we all be richer for Ed's words. I have a feeling, Dad, you would have had a smile on your face at seeing them in print.

Tricia Timmermans, Victoria, BC, Canada　　　　　　　*September, 2013*

Dear, that I could but hear a fleeting while,

Those loved lips speak, or see those shy eyes smile …

Ed Gallagher

Wireless Air Gunner Training
Parkes, New South Wales

No. 1 Air Navigation School, R.A.A.F. Station, Parkes, New South Wales.

Miss M. Thomson
137 Moray St.,
New Farm, N.1.
Brisbane Qld.

March 4, 1941

Darling, I miss you terribly! You've no idea what a rotten trip to Sydney I had. I couldn't sleep because we were jammed together like sheep, and every mile I could only think that it was a mile further away from you. There were times when I felt like jumping out and catching the next train back. I love you so, dear. The crowd in my compartment helped to make the trip a bit more bearable, – they are great chaps – we sang through most of the night. As soon as the train started we changed into shorts to try to keep our uniforms a bit clean. Mine got so dirty though that I had to wash it myself tonight. We arrived in Sydney at about 8 o'clock and had breakfast and a wash and shave on the station. I took Les Main, who had never been to Sydney before, on a quick tour of *the sights. We went out to Bondi, over the Bridge and round the city in the morning. Then we called on Jeanne who greeted me like an old friend, (Gee! did I have a guilty face until I saw that she treated our old "Romance" as a thing of the past) and took her to dinner. In the afternoon we had a ride on the harbour and saw the zoo. We caught a train to Parkes* at 5 to 8 and after an uncomfortable ride reached here at 7.30 in the morning. The country we saw after dawn was lovely. Orchards and wheat fields and rolling plains. No mountains as far as the eye could see.* *[Parkes is famous for the Parkes Observatory which was one of several radio antennas used to relay signals to NASA during the Apollo 11 moon landing on July 20, 1969.]

The town of Parkes is a rather nice place. Something about twice the size of Nambour. It is very neat and clean. Les and I got leave yesterday afternoon and went for a swim in the best baths I've ever seen. The dressing rooms are separated from the baths by about 100 yards of gardens, lawns and trees. You can lie and sunbake on the lawns, and the water is as clear as crystal. Leave is very easy to get here. We have every night off up to midnight and the week-end lasts from 12 on Saturday to Sunday midnight.

This is the best station in Australia. The officers are all great chaps from the C.O down to the Corporals. They all yarn to you like old friends and although there is discipline and plenty of it, it is never overbearing, like it was at Amberley. The course I'm on is very interesting, even the Morse. Tell Ken I'm sending already. We have a wireless in the hut and it is always on. It seems funny to be listening to 2PK Parkes.

The weather here is beautiful. The air is crisp and cool. You feel wonderfully braced, but the flies are awful. I got a letter from Alan Broadhurst today, readdressed from Ipswich and he starts off with "The weather is lovely but the flies are 'b' awful." Townsville must be like Parkes.

Well, darling girl, that's enough about unlovable me, – except I'm now given the title of L.A.C. when spoken to. Alan has been made a Corporal – good news eh?

How are you keeping, love? Missing me a little I hope. Don't forget that 6 o'clock. – I've got no chance of forgetting, I think of you all the time, except in the Morse periods when no one can think of anything but "di' dah." I hope your folks and the boys at Burstows* are all well. – Give my regards to them all – and to Nev,

2

Ken, Dick and the rest. *[Mrs. Burstow ran a boarding house at 137 Moray Street in New Farm, Brisbane, where Ed and Molly both boarded, and first met.]

How is work going? No more rows or trouble I hope. Did you go to dinner with Joan on your birthday? – I hope they didn't hurt her dragging out the stitches from her tonsils. I can shut my eyes and picture you, – and the picture makes my heart ache with longing just to see and kiss you once more. – Oh! Darling! I miss you. – and love you!

I have one bit of good news. – We get eight days leave in three month's time and will be up like a shot to see you. – How those three months will crawl by!

Please write soon and tell me the news. – And, dear, tell me you love me, – just a bit. – It will make me very happy. – happier than anyone else has ever been, I think, because I love you – darling.

My address now is as I show below and we have been instructed that all mail must be addressed this way.

No. 405206, L.A.C. GALLAGHER, E.B.,

No. 2 W.A.G.S., "E" FLIGHT, R.A.A.F.,

PARKES, N.S.W.

It is getting near "lights out" now so I'll have to finish off. –

I adore you, darling girl, Ed xxx

Gosh! I miss you, dear! – Pray for me whenever you can. – I have good news in that respect. – We can go to Church every Sunday here. So I'll be keeping my promise on Sunday.

I love you.

Ed.

No. 2 W.A.G.S. Parkes N.S.W.

March 17, 1941

My Darling Girl,

I love you. It was the greatest thrill I've ever known, except when you first said you loved me, to hear your voice last night. You've never been so dear to me, and you know how dear to me you were, as you have been these past two weeks when I have been so darn far away from you. I adore you, dearest.

It was a great thrill to get your letter and wire on Friday. – You know, dear, that I've never been able to believe that you love me. – You see, I know my merits. – So you can imagine how I felt when I read that you know that you loved me. – and were even a little jealous. – I was so happy I could hardly eat any dinner. You are silly, dear, to feel sorry for any imagined hurt you caused me. Anything I got I deserved – and a lot more.

Things have been very quiet here lately. The novelty has worn off and there is not much to do but walk up and down the main street, have a "jug" or two and go home to bed.

We have a lot of fun in the camp. – Every night there's a muck-up on; beds are tossed. Last night one chap's was put up on the rafters. He had a devil of a job getting it down. Tonight they took a fellow's flying kit and made it up into a man. Then they rigged up a girl with mosquito nets to look like a bride and hung them both from a rafter. Dozens of photos were taken of them. I'll try to get one and send it to you.

They have a Catholic Club in town for the Air Force. My cobber and myself met a Father Kelly there on Thursday night. He's a great fellow and played billiards and ping pong with us. He wasn't bad either.

Tell Len not to be long in sending down my clubs, because it's the only thing I'll be able to do of a weekend down here. The course is rotten, sand greens etc., but it's better than nothing.

Morse is getting more and more monotonous. I go to sleep now nearly every session. It's a great life – eat, sleep, and think of you, and how much I miss you. Whew! I thought that blighter was flying so low he would take the roof off the hut, but I'm still here. They're doing night flying tonight, but luckily I'm out of that – too cold up there this time of year. Rod Macdonald and your boy went on a hike this afternoon to a farm house we can see on the far horizon. After what seemed a week, we reached it, and by managing to look on the point of collapse, got invited in and given a cool drink of fresh milk. Then we staggered back to the

4

camp. I'd sleep well tonight if only blighters wouldn't act the goat.

Darn it. I just found my watch had stopped, and when I tried to wind it the winder came out in my hand. A few bob to get it fixed, drat it.

I miss you so, darling. It is hard to be so far away from you. But I still have that last kiss you gave me at your gate to remember. I'll remember it all my life.

I'm counting the weeks till I see you again. Only ten now – keep loving me, dearest.

How is the work going? Are you still a bit fed up with the place? Still having a headache over registrations?

I was glad to hear all the family at Yandina were well. I wish I had been with you last Sunday. Give them my love darling.

I'll be ringing you again next Sunday. I hope the lines are better then than last night.

Give my regards to the crowd when you see them.

Lights are about to be put out, so I'd better finish off. – I adore you, my darling. –

Please write soon.

Ed. XX

Flight "E". No. 2., W.A.G.S. Parkes, NSW

March 24, 1941

My Sweetheart,

I can't tell you how I felt when I opened up the parcel from you and found that wonderful photograph of you. Oh! Darling! It made me the happiest and proudest man in the camp. I'm looking at it now. It's on the ledge next my bed and the photographer has made a marvellous job of it. It's you to a "t." But even then I don't think Simmonds has done you justice. He would have to know you like I do – know what a lovely person you are and perhaps love you, like I do, to make a really perfect photograph. All the boys in the hut have admired it, and are full of congratulations for my good taste. Tomorrow, the C.O. will probably admire it, for he'll be inspecting the hut I'm in, and as my bed is the first next the door he can't fail to notice it. He'll probably promote me on the spot.

The last two days have been very happy ones for me – although the happiness has been tinged with a little sadness because you're so far away – because last night I heard your voice, and today your picture arrived. And last night you said you still loved me. I suppose you think I'm a silly sentimentalist, writing in this fashion, darling, but I can't help being so much in love with you – that's your fault.

I hope the Sonnet arrived O.K. I tried to tell you, in it, how much I miss you, but I'll never be able to do that. I hope you haven't forgotten our promise about 6 o'clock each day. Last week has been pretty dull, as usual. Study has been very heavy. I sat for an exam the other day and passed fairly well – 83%. A few of us were promoted from the Morse class we were attending (12–15 w.p.m. receiving and sending) to 15–18 w.p.m. I'm finding that speed a bit tough. I suppose Ken will be going in to camp shortly. I hope he enjoys it. And I hope he never becomes a W.A.G. – the course is enough to drive you mad. We "RC's" in the camp were delighted to find we had our own Padre in the camp. He arrived last Thursday and carries the rank of a Flight Lieutenant. We had Mass in the Gymnasium on Sunday morning. Last Sunday night, it being the National Day of Prayer, all the camp was taken to just outside the town. There we formed up in all the various Religions, and marched through the town to our separate Churches. There was great cheering, cat-calling (from the town urchins), etc. Our Padre conducted the service at the Church. It was an impressive sight to see all the boys marching along. (And although I say it as I shouldn't) We can march. I got a letter from

Mollie* today. She's her usual bright self, and all the family are well. She tells me all about Joan's* holiday, and I suppose you've heard about it from Joan herself ere this. *[Joan, Mollie and Rita (Margaret) were Ed's younger sisters.]

I'm looking forward to getting your letter to me, tomorrow, darling. If you look forward to mine as much as I do to yours, I'll post one on Sunday and Wednesday night in future, and you'll get them on Thursdays (takes a long time, doesn't it?) and Mondays. We've just finished cleaning the hut out and it looks like a new pin. Or does it? – C.O.'s inspection tomorrow. Reason for energy. How are your Mother and Dad, and Alice and the boys? Remember me to them, when you can. It must have been great, going up there for the week-end. It's only 8 weeks and 4 days before I'll be on leave and will be able to see you again. I count the hours.

I hope all the boys are well. It was great to hear old Nev's voice the other night. I suppose they still patronise "Rundel's" Fridays and Saturdays. It's nice of them to keep in touch with the Burstows.

Have you heard anything about being made permanent yet? And how is the job going? I couldn't see any gray hairs in the photo – and I went over it very carefully – so work can't be getting you down yet. Like it did me, and made a blinkin' hero (?) out of me.

They call us W.A.G.s the "suicide squad" but I think it's the safest job in the plane – you just sit there, listening to d'dahs and firing off a few guns now and then. When things get too tough you crawl into a corner and when they get very bad you jump out, pull your parachute cord, and hope for the best.

I loved the frame on your photo. It's a good idea isn't it?

Of course I remember you in my prayers. You are my prayer – every time I take out my Rosary beads – your rosary – I think of you. And the prayer I always offer is that we will soon be together, forever. Do you pray for that, too, darling?

Well some of the blighters in the hut are calling out for "lights out" – and unless I want to be scragged I'd better finish off.

I love you with all my heart, my sweetheart. I adore you, and I miss you terribly,

– Ed xxx

Keep loving me, darling, or you'll break my heart.   Ed

Sonnet to M.

I sought through all the limits of my world

A shrine secluded, where deep silence drowned

The snarling dogs of war, and still were furled

The blood-red flags of Mars: – And oft I found

A place that seemed ideal, – a valley veiled

With trees, – a cool clear creek, – a hidden Church

Stilled by the spell of Age: – But Peace I failed

To find, and I grew weary of the search.

I thought I'd known Love, – but found it brought

No lasting calm of soul, – and saw it pass

Without a tear, – and oft I vainly sought

Fool's solace in the bottom of a glass:

But came a day, when in a flash I knew

My quest was ended: – That day, I met you.

Flight E, No. 2 W.A.G.S., Parkes,

29 March, 1941

Sweetheart,

Your letter arrived today, and, of course, made me very happy. I had such a struggle (a delightful one) to make you admit you loved me, that when I read it in black and white I find everything in the world O.K., – except the fact that we're so far apart. Eight weeks now, darling. I hope you enjoy your week at Wynnum; it'll be good to be away from that ding-bat Bonnie, whom I dislike immensely for trying to pair my Darling off with a Gob. I'll be ringing you at Wynnum tomorrow night.

I'm sorry I couldn't write you on Wednesday, dear; I haven't been out of the camp since Sunday because one of our most important exams came off this morning – Radio Science – and I've been studying each night up to lights out. If I don't pass they might chuck me out and make me a mess-steward or a cook (for one meal anyway), but I think I did pretty well. (Pride cometh before a fall!)

I'm worried to hear that your Mother and Dad are not so well. I wish I was near you so I could try to cheer you up a bit, sweetheart. Damn this rotten war – but for it we could be together and share our worries. They're not so bad when you've got a good shoulder to lay your head on. It'll be over some day, though, and that day can't be too soon for me.

Did you like the Sonnet? I was feeling extra lonely when I wrote it and would have given anything just to see you for a second. Your photo is just in front of me as I write and – oh Darling – I love you so! – Do you love me very much, sweetheart? – Enough to make me the happiest man in the world by saying "Yes" – some day?

How are Ken, Nev, Dick and the rest of the gang? I suppose Ken will be in Amberley by the time you get this. I hope he likes it more than I did.

I'm glad you like your new room-mate. It would be awful to be landed with some crabby blighter or such like.

Have you seen the Kildare crowd lately? Don't forget to invite yourself out there some time. You know they love to have you out. I suppose Uncle Jim is now a gentleman of leisure. I wish I were. If you see my unworthy cousin Leonard, tell him he owes me a letter. I wrote him and all the boys about a fortnight ago, but haven't heard from anyone but you and Joan and the Townsville folks since I've been here. When I finish this letter I'm writing a few lines to Patsy. I asked Len to send down my golf sticks – but so far they haven't arrived and I'm dying to have a game.

Have you seen Joan, lately? – I told her to look after you for me, darling, and I hope she has.

Nearly all the camp is going to Orange for the day tomorrow, but as I have a few things to do, and also a very important 'phone call to put through to a certain very lovely girl, at 2030 hours tomorrow night, I'm staying here. It is to be a gala day there – procession through streets etc., flag flapping and flappers – so I'm glad to be out of it.

Mass will be at 0930 tomorrow morning. Our Padre also looks after the R.A.A.F. station at Narromine* and after he says Mass there he flies here and says Mass here. Wally Johns, who sleeps in the next bed to me, and myself, are great favourites of his. He's a wonderful chap. You can yarn away to him by the hour. I'll be losing Wally soon, though. His wife is coming here to stay and he's going to live out. Only came here for the classes in the day time. Some fellows have all the luck. I wish my darling were coming here. *[Narromine Airfield, 100 km north of Parkes, was requisitioned by the RAAF in July 1940 for the establishment of No. 5 Elementary Flying Training School as part of the Empire Air Training Scheme (EATS).]

Is the Bribie Club still going strong? Give my regards to Kev, Laurie, "Doc.", Ronnie and Neil when and if you see them. I wish the old days were back again. I miss all the old gang. I wish they were here with me. I'll address this letter to you at the office, dear, in case you won't be at the "B's" for the week.

Why didn't I kiss you a thousand times more while you were near – and worse still, why was I such a fool as to quarrel with you then? Darling I'd give all the world for one kiss from you now. "X's" marked on paper are very poor substitutes for the real thing – but keep putting them there, dear. I've a fairly good imagination and it's great to know you love me. Darling, I wish I could tell you what that means to me.

I love you with all my heart, my sweetheart. I always will.

Ed xxxx

P.S. *Love me? Darling? I adore you, you know.*

Ed.

April 2, 1941

My Sweetheart,

It was wonderful to get your letter today, and to read the last sentence that told me you loved me. I think I read that part of your letters a hundred times every time one arrives – because I love you, darling, more that all the world. I'm glad you're enjoying your stay with Mollie, who seems a very nice person. Mollie (or Molly) seems to be a name that's only given to the best of people. I know three of them, and one of them, at any rate, is the nicest girl this world has ever seen – and I love her. Your friend must miss her husband. Do you miss me, Darling?

I gloated for hours over my usual Sunday night thrill, which seems better every time, because it means that another week has passed, and brought the day when I'll be seeing you again, closer. I heard today that it would be the third of June when our leave starts, which means that I'll be with you on the 5th – those three days in Brisbane will seem like three seconds, sweetheart.

When I rung you I had just returned to the camp after having the best day's fun I'd ever had, so far as sport was concerned. I went with my two pals from the camp in a car to the foothills that surround the camp. Wally Johns was one of the pals. His people live in Parkes and his three brothers came with us. We had six guns, two of them shot guns, and the others 22's. We split up into two parties: three of us went to the top of the hill and waited while the others separated and walked up from the bottom, yelling and shooting off their rifles. The two with me had shotguns, but I had a 22, as I thought the bunnies ought to have a chance. Suddenly, over the top came a horde of rabbits and hares running everywhere. The shot guns were banging, bullets from the three coming up the hill were buzzing around, and I was letting off bullets like a machine gun. When the hub-bub had subsided we found we had about 6 rabbits and two hares between us. I had got one hare, and was very proud of my shooting, though the boys said I missed one that almost ran between my legs.

We "drove" about three drives in this fashion during the afternoon, taking turns to be drivers and waiters, and came home to Wal's place with about 24 altogether. We had tea there, and as I missed the 8 o'clock bus I had to wait for the 9 o'clock and just got "home" in time for my call. I'd have cursed rabbits, buses, Wal and Parkes generally if I'd been late for that.

On Monday morning I got good news. I got 90% exactly in that exam and became the apple of the C.O.'s eye. So brilliant is the boy who loves you that he has now been promoted to 11 "A" flight, and letters must be addressed him thus in future. Don't forget the 11 (eleven) part of it as there are two "A" flights, 11 "A" and 12 "A", darling.

I got a letter from Joan today and she is doing well.

You were right about Dad* coming down, Molly. His father, Joan tells me, is not expected to live more than a few days. Joan is well and says she has been too busy with Dad or Grandfather or something or other to see you lately. I'm a bit crooked on her, though, for not bringing him out to meet you – and must tune her up for it. But perhaps she was worried about his father. You'd have liked each other, I know, dearest.
*[Ed's father, Bernard Gallagher, was Comptroller of Queensland Railways in Townsville during the war.]

Mollie advised me on Monday that she and all the Townsville crowd were well. And that Dad had gone to Brisbane for a day or two. I hope you like the so called "sonnet" I enclose, dear. I wish I could write something that would be good enough for you. I wish I could see you now to give my approval (I can imagine you saying "To billy o! with your approval") of the new hair style. Will I love you as much sans much hair as I did with much hair, sweetheart? ("Of course you will, you dope!")

So that Brassington* chap has been trying to go under my neck again? I sent up a postal note for the old Labour Party but am not sure whether it got there or not. I see they didn't need it anyway. I'm pleased to see Sam got in again – as I suppose Mat is too. *[Sam Brassington was the Labour member of the Queensland Legislative Assembly representing Fortitude Valley in Brisbane from 1927 to 1932, and 1933 to 1950.]

Give my regards to all the gang when you see them, darling, and I hope Ken is enjoying his "Rookies" course at Amberley. It's a hole of a joint.
I was shifted to a faster Morse class today. Aren't you proud of your sweetheart?

I went swimming this afternoon as the weather has become warmer, and am now feeling as fit as a fiddle. (How fit is a fiddle?) We had another dose of needle last Friday, but I never felt it. Tough eh?

Regarding my promise, dear, I kept it the second Sunday we were here. Wally Johns and another of the crew who sleep within snoring distance of me are extra good "Micks" and they dragged me off on the Saturday afternoon to see Fr. Maxwell. (I had the name wrong when I said "Kelly") and it wasn't as hard as I thought. I felt as if a ton weight had been lifted off my shoulders. I won't ever let it go so long again. Lent is very hard to keep up here. Even on Fridays, sometimes, there is only meat, but I think it's O.K. to eat meat if it's the only thing offering. Anyway I've given myself an indulgence on a couple of occasions.

I hope your Mother and Dad are well again, Sweetheart. Damn this war. If I were only there to help you forget your worrying about them!

I enclose a couple of snaps one of the boys took. Aren't I handsome?

Dearest, I wish I could tell you how much I love you – and how much I miss you, and how much I want to hold you in my arms again. Please keep on loving me, and try to answer the question I asked you in my last letter the way I want you to.

Ed. Xxxx

Now for the famous "Sonnet.

To M. on Receiving her Photograph.

Dear, that I could but hear a fleeting while,

Those loved lips speak, or see those shy eyes smile

For me, as once they did, – a thousand years

Ago! – (So long it seems) – If I could dry the tears,

Again, that trembled on those cheeks that night

I said good-bye! When harsh pain blurred my sight,

– Dimming the distant stars as though with rain,

– And unbelieving anguish numbed my brain.

~

"A thousand years!" I said, – "so long it seems!"

Dear Heaven! – The days have dragged like fearful dreams,

Where seconds are as years, since I caressed

That dear dark hair, and softly pressed

My lips to that wide brow: – And Time will drain

Like clogging oil, 'till I'm with you again!

Ed   2.4.41

Flight 11 A, No. 2 W.A.G.S., R.A.A.F., Parkes, NSW

April 4, 1941

My Darling,

I got a brilliant idea today. I can almost hear you say you could hear a sound like wheels turning. I'm going to write a part of a letter every night at 6 o'clock (remember our promise re 6 o'clock Sweetheart), and I'll post the letters on Sundays and Wednesdays; and I'll do this every night until I see you again. So you'll know what I'm doing every night at that time.

Regarding our promise, dear, have you kept it? I know it must be awkward at times, when you are doing something important. It's been easy for me, because I think of you all the time – and we have tea at 5.30 every night, which means I'm in my hut, lying on my bed by six and it's easy to think of you and of how much I love you.

I hope your Mother and Dad are better, darling girl.

Yesterday was pay day here – and there has been so little to do that I was able to shove a pound in the bank – which, (as in 1066 and all that) is a good thing.

I hope you liked my second effort at poetry. I know it's crook – (nothing I write now seems any good. I think I feel that way because I know that even if I were a second Bill Shakespeare, what I wrote wouldn't be good enough for you) but at least I try to tell you how much I love you, which at any rate is aiming at the impossible.

I went into town last night with one of the boys – Arthur Smiles – who lived down the road from the Mulligans*, and we had a few jugs together, after which we visited some relation of his in Parkes. Then went to the dance and I came home, after a few more pots, to bed. Some of the boys who went to the dance tried to sneak back about four in the morning and were landed for being A.W.L. *[Pat, Aileen and Len Mulligan were Ed's first cousins; they lived in Lutwyche, Brisbane.]

Today has been its usual monotonous self, but as usual, we managed to kid ourselves it wasn't so bad by acting the goat, etc. I started another Sonnet in the first Morse period, which I'll inflict on you in good course (or should I say "due time"?)

Tonight I'm going to iron my shorts and shirts and drop a line to Dad, and to Joan's boyfriend, Eric Jones, who is overseas with the A.I.F.

[Australian Imperial Force] *so until tomorrow night, sweetheart, I'll leave you - at least so far as pen and paper are concerned. I adore you, my darling. Love me?*

April 5

Had pork 'splosheges' for tea and backed up for a second issue, with the results that I have a very comfortable feeling of fullness in the old tum – and feel very satisfied with the world.

Today, up till 12 o'clock when I knocked off, was just as other mornings here, except that Morse absolutely refused to register on what I use for a brain, so I finished off your Sonnet. I think it's one of the best I've ever written. I hope you like it. You'll find it at the end of this letter darling.

After dinner, I was pleased to find a letter from Len waiting for me. He must have had a whale of a time batching while the family was on holidays. He and Graham had tea together in town nearly every night, so you can imagine the life they led. Have you seen anything of old Graham, lately? He's a great guy, Molly, so serious, and worried all the time, yet full of dry humour. Len says he's sending me the clubs this week-end, so I'll probably be playing next Saturday.

I went into town as soon as I was dressed and had a haircut and bought a pair of drab socks. While I was buying the socks I saw something I thought you might like, so I got it and posted it to you. Do you like them, darling? I hope you'll find them useful. When I came home I did the washing and ironing I said I was going to do last night. Lazy blighter that I am, after I wrote the letters to Dad and Eric last night, I crawled into bed and wrote most of the beautiful sonnet – (?). The weather has again taken a decided turn to the cold side and tonight it is just about freezing. Thank the powers that be they give you plenty of blankets. I've got two singlets on and am still shivering. I think "grey winter" has really come at last. We have snow here, you know, in the middle of Winter. Brrrr.!

I am becoming adept at the washing and ironing game, sweetheart. Hope to qualify for the Station Championships shortly. Gosh! – You'll have a marvellous husband in me, although my memory is notoriously bad. Shouldn't be surprised if I forget the whole art as soon as this darned war is over.

Talking of wars, Adolf got a smack in the eye from Yugoslavia, didn't he? But nothing to what he'll get when Flight 11 "A" hits him.

Strange to say, although it is so cold, the "mossies" are frightful here. If I didn't have a net the cursed blighters would carry me off in the night.

It's a wonder I can write at all tonight. There's an awful row going on. Les Main, at the other end of the hut, is rending, in a horrible baritone "Stay in my arms, Cinderella", despite sundry objections, such as cat-calls, boots and other articles of sufficient weight to cause damage. Other blokes are rushing here and there getting pretty for the dance – borrowing my shoe polish, razor blades and hair oil, drat 'em. When all is quiet I'll try to iron the stuff I washed this afternoon, if it's dry, which will mean the second lot of washing for me in today's bout of ironing fever. However I must get some practice in for the Championship – if we hold one.

I feel good-oh now. I've just had a lovely hot bath and feel a nice clean man again. Have been thinking over the ironing question while under the shower, and was overjoyed to find my washing "not quite dry enough" to iron. It may be dry enough in another half hour, but I'll be much too tired then. Anyway I have all day tomorrow. ("Lazy blighter," you say? But I love you just the same.)

I suppose Nev and the boys (or are they in camp like Les and Jack again) are down at Bribie just now – probably sinking a noggin at John Goodwin's celebrated pub. Don't forget to give my regards to Mrs. Burstow, Nev, Ron and Laurie, every time you get a letter from me, even if I forget to mention them, darling.

I'm being talked into making a four for a game of 500 at the moment. Suppose I'll give way. I adore you, dear.

Dear. Another day has gone and brought the time I'll be seeing you closer. I'm lying, or half lying, on my bed at the moment, and the time is just 6 o'clock. In another three and a half hours I'll be talking to you. In exactly six weeks I'll be with you again. I expect to be back on the Sydney Express, which arrives in Brisbane at half past two on Sunday 25th May. Keep loving me darling.

We had bad news last night. Some of the boys who were going into town late were told to try to find a chap named Johnson, who sleeps in the next hut, and tell him to come back to camp at once. When he arrived the C.O. broke the news to him that his wife had been killed, and his two children seriously injured in a car accident. The chaps tell me he nearly went off his head with the shock and was looking for a gun to shoot himself. I can't blame the poor fellow, for I know how I'd feel if anything happened to you. The C.O. was very decent. He ordered a plane to fly the chap to the town where his kiddies were.

We had no Mass here this morning, because the Padre couldn't get over from Narromine, so we had to go into town. All the boys in the camp seem to have got holy. They all go to their various services, Meths., C. of E., Pres., etc., of a Sunday now. Some of the sects provide free suppers for their adherents after the service; perhaps this is the reason for some of the piety.

I plucked up energy, and did that ironing this morning after Mass, and then, wearied with my journey into town and the horrible exercise of wielding a heavy iron, I slept till dinner. Wonder of Wonders, we had fruit salad for dessert. Cookie must have gone mad. After dinner I also slept.

Well, darling, I must do some study, or else there'll be no 90% next exam. I hope your Mother and Dad are well again; have you told them we love each other, dear?

I miss you terribly, darling girl, Ed xxx

Hear you in three hours – Ed.

To M. 5.4.41 Parkes, N.S.W. – Because I love her. –

Oft, in the drowsy hours of silent night,

I lie awake, – half dreaming – while the light

Of magic moonbeams makes gay mysteries

The places where it falls: – And sometimes, through the trees

That cloak the gleaming pathway, low I hear

The North Wind whispering its tales of fear

And hope to all the world; – singing of wrongs,

– Of joy, and grief, and love, in sad-sweet songs.

And when I know this same white clouded moon

Has smiled on you; – this wind has sung its tune

In your dear ears, and kissed your soft dark hair,

– And laid caressing fingers on the fair

Shy beauty of your face, – deep envies seize

My soul, – and I grow jealous of the moon and breeze!

Parkes, Monday April 7, 1941

My Dearest,

I miss you terribly. I think I need you more, and feel being parted from you more tonight than ever before. I don't know why it should be so hard this particular night, but somehow it is. If I had even less intelligence than I have, I'd go into town and get drunk with the foolish idea of drowning my longing, but past experience has shown me the stupidity of that course. I'll try to bury myself in some study when I've finished writing, and Radio Theory is deep enough to bury anything in. Perhaps the fact that today, when I read your letter and came to realise, for the first time, that you really love me, has made me so lonely. You know, dear, I have never been able to realise that you could ever love me; I've always had an inferiority complex where your loving me is concerned, and rightly so. (Perhaps that's why I asked you so often if you did). Can't see any reason why you should, so you will know how happy and proud it makes me to read in your letter that you mightn't be able to "take it" if I ever ceased to love you. You have no need to ever fear that, Sweetheart.

I hope you don't think I'm a sentimental idiot, writing in this fashion. Perhaps I am, darling, but I love you and miss you so much. I used to argue once with Len and Mat, in the days before I met you, that this love business was a bit of highly publicized bunkum. They used to laugh at me. Now I laugh at myself. I wish I could get home for Easter, like Mollie's husband. It would mean all the world to me to see you again and to be able to see your Mother and Dad and Alice and the boys. Give them my love when you get up to Yandina, my darling, and tell them I'll be able to see them before I go away. If I miss you so much now, I don't know how I'll be when I go overseas. No wonder poor old Bill was so cut up when he had to leave his Molly, and Eric when he had to go away from Joan.

You must be looking forward to next Friday. I hope your Mother and Dad are their old selves again when you see them.

It's great to see you so pleased with the change in your job. It will probably mean that you'll be made permanent any time. I hope so, dear – although I also hope you won't be needing a job, (at least an office one) – as soon as this damned war is over. Darling, if only that could happen tomorrow.

Today has been terribly exciting. We had sausages for breakfast – then Radio Theory, Morse, Radio Theory, Morse, Roast Pork, Baked

18

Potatoes and Cabbage, Radio Theory, Morse, Drill, Morse and Stew. Leaves one breathless with excitement.

One of the boys who is a bit slow on the uptake has asked me to give him a hand with the Radio Theory tonight, and he's sitting on the bed waiting for me – so I'll say "Good night" Darling mine. I love you.

Tuesday April 8

Here I am, darling, at the end of another day. We changed our Sports afternoon from Wednesdays to Tuesdays this week, and I have just returned from the baths. Lord! Was it cold! Girl, I'm still shivering. I think that all through my life I'll shudder whenever I think of that water. I covered two lengths of it in a time that no Champion has ever equalled and dashed thence as blue as a lizard. Afterwards we had to run to the nearest inn and warm ourselves up. Some of the lads bet the Corporal one pound he wasn't game to jump in from the high board. As he was fully clothed, and had no togs, the quid looked safe; so you can imagine their sick feeling when he took off his shoes and dived in clothes and all.

I think it was worth a fiver as he had to come "home" in the tender wrapped in towels. But he refused the quid. These N.C.O.s here are great chaps. There was a grand celebration here this afternoon. A crowd of Navigators had finished their course and were presented with their wings. A big crowd of civilians was there and all the planes were doing acrobatics, etc. However I missed most of it while I was swimming (or rather freezing). There'll be some show when we leave. All the gang here are joining in a chorus of "Somewhere in France" and it doesn't sound too bad at all, although some of them couldn't sing in tune for a fortune. It's rather a nice song, that. –

Today saw the start of our practical Radio work. That means we commenced pulling wireless transmitters and receivers to pieces and trying to put them together again, mostly unsuccessfully.

I've got over my "down in the dumps" feeling I had last night – which doesn't mean I don't miss you as much, but that I have a better hold on myself than I had then. Dear Darling, do you ever get those horrible lonely spells, too, about me? I hope so, and yet I hope not. They're rotten. They make the whole world seem not worthwhile.

They've changed the name of my flight from the beginning of this week. Please address your letters in future, sweetheart, to Flight 2"A", instead of 11"A". Soon you won't know where I am, if I keep changing about like this. But, if you should happen to forget, any of the old addresses will find me.

I'll miss being able to hear your voice next Sunday – though it will make it seem all the better (if that were possible!) when I can speak to you on Monday night. I was thinking of ringing you at Yandina on the Sunday night as usual, but thought it might interfere with some plans you had made. We had early tea tonight, being a half day, and it's just six o'clock now. I hope you're thinking of me, dear. You're all the world to me.

A wire arrived for me today from Uncle Jim, wishing me a happy Easter and telling me he had railed my clubs to me. Decent of him wasn't it?

I'll be on the study again tonight. Even with all this swatting, Radio Theory is too much for me. I hope you say a few prayers for me, mentioning my exams, dear; otherwise I'm sunk. I had better get on with the brain work - even though I hate the blankety blank stuff. Good night- Darling.

Ed with his sister Joan at the PO Ball

Wednesday April 9

Another weary day has dragged by. After I've finished this letter tonight, I'll post it, and it should be waiting for you when you come home to Burstows on Monday night. I'll be waiting impatiently just about that time for my phone call to go through. I was thinking of ringing you at Yandina on Sunday night but I thought I might clash with some plans you might have made. I wish I could be with you up there. As I said before, damn this war! I would have liked to have been with you at the dance on Friday night. I suppose you had a wonderful time. I can imagine all the old gang there. Len – Lou (in all his sartorial splendour – the life of the party) – Ces and Mrs. Cec. – Joan – all the boys with a slight sting acquired from Mr. Johnson of the "Royal George." I wish I could be in Brisbane for the Post Office Ball. This year's will be the first I've missed. As the boys and Joan will tell you, it's the Ball of the year.

However, I expect to be in Brisbane for some time waiting to go overseas so we may be able to go to some together. The couple of dances I've been to here have given me a hankering for the old "light fantastic" again. You'll be able to undergo the torture of having your feet mangled by the worst dancer in (or out of) Christendom. By that time I'll be such a vision that even your beauty will pale beside me – with my wings, Sergeant's stripes (at least), etc., and my chest thrust forth as set down in Air Force Order 300 A.

I hope you liked the handkerchiefs darling. I hope they keep you thinking of me now and then. I got a letter from Mollie today. When she wrote it, Dad had not yet returned to Townsville. She told me about my Grandfather's dying.

Well, I've just about exhausted my very poor stock of news. I'll go and do a bit more fag. – I'm going to be very impatient to hear your voice until Monday night. I love you, with all my heart, Darling Girl.

– Ed xxxxx

P.S. Did you like the Sonnet?

P.S.S. Please give my regards to all the Kildare Push and Mrs. B. and Nev, Laurie, Ron, and Neil.   Ed.

P.S.S.S. Love me?

R.A.A.F. P.O. Parkes, NSW Australia

Flight 2 "A", No. 2 W.A.G.S., R.A.A.F., Parkes

April 10, 1941

My Darling,

Your letter arrived this morning and so, for the while, everything seems right with the world. It makes me feel very happy that I can be a reason for your happiness – and a little proud, too. The only sour note about it is that I should never have caused you any worry in that particular direction in the first place. I suppose laziness is the only excuse I can offer, or worse – indifference. But I've got over that now. I don't think I'll ever fall into the old ways again. Especially if I keep knocking about with Wall and Jack, and since I know it means so much to you. But, dearest, you'd better keep up the prayers on my behalf; my carelessness in all things – except where you, and loving you is concerned – is notorious.

According to latest bulletins, the correct date of our arriving in Brisbane is Sunday 1ˢᵗ June – but no one can guarantee anything here – not even our next meal. I suppose the exact date will be announced on our last week. Whatever day it is, it'll be the best day of the year for me. I'll be able to see you again. Sometimes, when I think on how far off it is, (six weeks seems a lifetime) I feel like chucking up the whole business and catching the first train home. I wish the war would end, but, instead of that, it appears to be growing worse. I suppose this being parted has all happened for some good reason – (although I can't see it). It may mean that we'll appreciate each other all the more when we can be together always – (although, here again, I fail to see how it could possibly increase my appreciation of you.)

A letter arrived from Aileen today. She told me you were coming out for tea on Tuesday night. I hope you were able to find your way there. How are they all?

Since writing the last I have been up at the Radio room working on my own little set. It's only worth about £80 - £90. You can get any station in the world. I've been listening into nearly all of them. It's a great thrill. Ray Connolly would go off his head with glee if he were let loose in that room. There's everything you can use in Wireless in there. Some of the news I heard is not the very best, although it contains a lot of welcome stuff.

How are your eyes lately, dear? I'm very worried about those darn headaches you used to get. Remember how I used to worry about whether you had brought your glasses every time we went to a show? I hope you're looking after them, my darling. Today we had our first experience in a plane. It was an Avro Anson *and I was surprised at all*

the gadgets we have to know about. Sending from a plane is a very hard thing to get used to. Whenever you strike a bump you're liable to send out an unwanted "dit" or a "dah".

*[In the early days of the British Commonwealth Air Training Plan, the Avro-Anson was selected as the standard twin-engine aircraft for the training of pilots, observers, wireless operators, and bomb aimers. More than 20,000 aircrew received their training on Ansons.]

I wonder if Ken will be coming down here? I expect not – he's too tall. It's very decent of Sam Brassington to do what he did. When you see him remember me to him, but I doubt if he will remember my name. So good old Laurie has been looking after you for me. Give him and Carmel my best wishes, darling. I haven't seen a picture since I went with you. I soon won't know the stars' names.

I hope your Dad and Mother are not so ill after all when you see them. They may be just a little off colour owing to the change of season. The "kids" may have the same trouble. I'll say a few prayers for them darling, though I very much doubt the efficacy of my prayers.

Re that question, darling. – Don't you remember? – You said "yes" to it once before – I hope we'll both be asked it by a third person some day. And I hope your answer then will still be in the affirmative. If it is I'll try to make you very happy, darling.

It's just about "Lights Out" so I'll have to finish. Oh, I nearly forgot to tell you I underwent a major operation here today. I went to the M.O. and had a corn that had been driving me mad, removed. No complications ensued, so I'm still above the daisies.

Don't forget to love me a little. No! Darn it! – a lot!

Please, sweetheart – I adore you.

Ed.

Instead of my previous decision - I'll post this tomorrow and from hence forward will inflict three letters on you a week – will you like that, my dear? Although I would love you to, you needn't send me three a week. You have so much more to do than I have.

I adore you, my darling (I said that before, but I'll never tire of saying it)

Ed   xxxxx

P.S. Love me? Ed. X

Ed playing cricket at home in Brisbane. He was an A-Grade cricketer.

Flight 2 "A" No. 2 W.A.G.S., R.A.A.F., Parkes, NSW

April 11, 1941

Darling, -

This has been the strangest "Good Friday" I've ever known. The rest of the boys think so too. None of us, except one, has ever worked on this day before, and our having to work has been the subject of discussion and "cussin" all day long. Even the one who worked one Good Friday said he had to work for a garage keeper, and he (the g.k.) was "pinched." To make matters worse we had to go back after tea and do another lecture on account of the exam tomorrow. Anyway Someone had to undergo a lot more than we on the first Good Friday.

We had "Hot Cross Buns" on the menu for tea. They were good. I ate quite a few – I fear more than my Lenten allowance. They had fish on every meal, which was another surprise.

I won't have time to write you much tonight, sweetheart. The exam tomorrow has got me scared. I don't know why it should because the blighters can't do very much to us except throw us out, which would mean I'd be back with you; but I've taken on a job and it's up to me to finish it. So I'll say "Good Night", darling. – I love you.

April 12, 1941

It's about 4 o'clock and I've been enjoying a well deserved siesta. The exam this morning was even worse than I expected but I'm pretty sure I managed to get a fair pass. Here's hoping.

I suppose at the moment you're enjoying yourself with all the folks at home. Darling I wish I were there with you.

We had quite a thrill a little while ago. Arthur Smiles' girl friend has come up from Sydney for the Easter and is staying at Parkes. He got a permit to show her over the camp and aerodrome; he brought her along to the hut and, as some of the boys were in a considerable state of undress, quite a deal of excitement was occasioned. Some of the boys are still blushing!

I got an Easter Hamper from Mother today. It was a wonderful surprise. In it was a huge Easter Egg – nuts, muscatels, Biscuits, cigarettes and tobacco. The gang have been tucking into it all afternoon with me. – I'll have to hide what's left if I want anything for tomorrow.

I have a line full of washing outside, all my own work. I plucked up some energy and got stuck into it after dinner. Gee! It's a rotten job. If I were a laundress I'd want £10 a day.

When I get over the tired feeling, I'll have a shave and bath, get dressed, go along and see the Padre to get rid of a bit of a load; and then, after tea, I'll go to town to see if my golf sticks are at the station, and perhaps down a noggin or two of ale with Jack.

I've lost Wally from today. His wife has come to live in Parkes in a house he managed to rent, after trying since he's been here, so he'll be "living out" from now on. This means he'll only be on the station from 7.15 in the morning 'till 5 at night. He's as pleased as punch. Some chaps have all the luck.

April 13, 1941 Easter Sunday

It seems strange, my darling, to be sitting here, in the Church Hut, writing to you. Every other Easter Sunday I can remember, I have been lounging on a beach or with Len and the boys somewhere.

Last night, after I had finished writing to you, I went into town and  *tried to get my golf sticks from the Railway Station, but the darn things weren't there. On the station I met Wally who was waiting for his wife to arrive from Broken Hill on the "Silver City Comet" - a diesel-engine train that runs between Parkes and Broken Hill. (About this train I attach a cutting I came across today.) I thought his wife was already in Parkes but it appears she was here only for a day or two and then went to Broken Hill to collect some things. I was able to give Wal a hand with some of the stuff she'd brought. She's a nice girl – old Wal is very lucky. Not as lucky, though, as a friend of his hopes, someday, to be.*

After seeing them settled, I met Jack Jackson, who used to work with Edna Beirne in the Defence Department, to see Fr. Maxwell. (I can never remember his name when I have to, I always to go call him Fr. Kelly for some reason) our own Padre not being at the station. However, we found him (the Padre) at the Parkes Church giving Fr. Maxwell and the parish Priest a hand with the big crowd lined up there. On Easter Sunday here, everyone must go to Communion.

Later – much later, I've still got the marks on my knees – we went, and, alas, again started our vicious career of crime, by downing a few jugs of the vile beverage they call beer here, and reeled, (only slightly though) to the bus and thence to camp. I pursued investigations at the Guard House re my recalcitrant golf sticks, and though I bribed the Corporal of the Guard and his crew with some chips and scallops we had bought, thus endearing myself to them – they were shivering around a fire – I could elicit no information ("Grandma, what big words you use!") but that they had <u>not</u> been brought from the station to the camp in one of our tenders. I suppose the Easter Holidays have held them up somewhere.

I was asleep by half past ten, but was woken up at every hour by blighters staggering in late. We had mass this morning here at 7 a.m. This is an awkward time, in a way, as breakfast starts then, and we R.C.s come in for a lot of abuse from the cooks, who have to cook a separate breakfast for us. Some of them get very cheeky. One of them yelled out this morning, "What would you so and so's do if we Cooks all went to Church?" The reply from Jack – who is scared of nobody – shut him up. Jack called out, "We'd cook ourselves a decently cooked meal for once."

I hopped into a stack of ironing after breakfast – and then washed my drab uniform. It's a gin of a job, sweetheart, washing it.

After dinner (which was a beaut) I read and dozed until about half past three, when I got a fit of energy and ironed my now dry uniform. This is also one heck of a job.

I suppose, just now, you are enjoying yourself at Yandina. I hope you are, darling, and that the family are all well and having a great time at the old homestead. I suppose you'll have been to Mooloolaba and Maroochydore. Remember the last time we were there and I was in my right place, as I said to Alice*, in the Dog Box? *[Alice Holden, nee Thomson, was Molly's younger sister.]

That ride home was one of the worst I ever had in my life – with you, not speaking to me on one side, and old Sid on the other. It will never happen again, though, dearest, will it? I love you so much.

I'll miss not speaking to you tonight. I'm still half tempted to ring you at Yandina. But I'm taking a philosophic outlook on it. – If I ring you

27

tonight, I'll have nothing to look forward to tomorrow night.

I'll have to stop writing now, darling girl. The C. of E. Padre has just come in to prepare his altar for an evening service.

It's a very high C. of E. The altar is covered with flowers and there are statues, a crucifix and holy pictures – it looks beautiful. It's good to see people so devoted to their religious beliefs that they go to so much trouble, even though their beliefs are wrong. He's a decent chap this C. of E. Padre. Only a young man and rather good looking. He evidently has a sense of humour, for on the walls of this Church Hut, which is also used as a writing room, he has tacked such notices as "Do not use the ash trays, they are only ornaments." "If you throw your rubbish on the floor at home, by all means do so here" etc. His flock call him "Father" just like we "Micks" do our padre. Both of them (they get on very well together, which is nice to see) carry the rank of Flight Lieutenant. From now on we'll be having Mass every morning at 6, but as we get our breakfast then, I won't be able to go.

I'll have the results of the exam tomorrow. Gosh! I hope you prayed hard!

I'd better finish off now or I'll find myself guilty of the sin of attending the service of a non-Catholic religion. I adore you dearest, and I miss you terribly.

Ed. xxxxx

P.S. Love me? Enough to marry me some day, soon, when all this madness is over? Please say "yes" to both questions, dear – they mean so much to me. Ed.

Parkes,

April 14, 1941

Darling,

An hour's excitement has just subsided, the hurry and scurry that comprise our weekly "Panic" night has ceased, and things have returned to normal. And so I'm sitting here trying to find something to write you about, but am not meeting with much success. All I can think of to say is "I love you," – I'd like to tell you that a thousand times, but you know it already.

"Panic" night is not, as it suggests, a night of terror with enemy bombers dive-bombing overhead, etc., but the weekly clean out of the Barracks. After tea, every Monday night, everyone grabs a broom or a bucket or something and tries to look as if he were working like a Trojan. That is, everyone except the - - (I can't tell you what the boys call them) who sneak off and dodge the work. They take a risk those blokes. The rest of us make life a hell for them whenever we get a chance.

I've just been up and booked my call to you. It's about 7.40 now, which means I have nearly two hours to wait before I can hear your voice. Seems a lifetime. I don't suppose you'll be in the best of moods either, tonight, Sweetheart, after being up at home for four whole days and having to come back to Brisbane. Dear Darling, I hope your family were O.K. when you left them. I have been very worried.

Do you still miss me as much as ever? I miss you more, and if it is possible, I think I love you more. It was the most wonderful thing in the world, to me, your falling in love with me. I must have been very good at least one period in my life for the angels to have been so kind to me. I hope I never do anything that will make you sorry you love me, Sweetheart. I don't think I ever will, if I can help it – I love you too much.

Today has been a bit of a change from the usual. We had three hours' practical Radio work, and as this is very interesting, the day seemed much shorter. The exam papers haven't been marked yet, so I'm still on tenterhooks about whether I passed or not.

Don't forget to look up Joan now and then, dear, and look after her a little for me, will you? I can hear her laugh if you tell her I suggested such a thing as – "She needs looking after." Did you go to any dances in Yandina? I hope so, and I hope you had the time of your life, though I can't help feeling a bit jealous of any gay young blade who dared to dance with you. Lucky blighter. Sometimes I wish I'd never joined up for this bally war; but I suppose some nit-wits have to do it or old Adolph would get everything his own way; which wouldn't be at all the right thing. I get very lonely sometimes, not only because I'm away from you, which is hell, but I miss the boys very much. Jack, Wal, and Rod Macdonald are great guys, but they'll never be able to fill the gap that being so far away from Len, Les, Mat, and Cec and Graham has made in my life. I wish you'd rouse them up and get them to write to me a bit more often. I've only heard once from them (from Len) in the six weeks I've been here. Get Mat on the job next time you see him. (Bit of a whinge, ain't I?)

I suppose all of them and Mrs. B. have done a purse on the nags over the Easter. A few of the boys cleaned up a bit of dough on the Sydney Races today and have gone into town to celebrate.

I've just got a book out of the library. Some blood and thunder yarn, and I think I'll curl up in bed and read it until it's time for our call. I hope when I ring you, you tell me you still love me, and have not found anyone among your numerous admirers at Yandina, Maroochydore, or Mooloolaba who'd cut me out.

Please tell me that's not possible. I also hope the darn telephone service is better tonight. If it isn't, I'm glad I got out of the old Telephone Dept. I'm ashamed to have been associated with such a place.

Another worry I'll have 'till I hear your voice – I've been imagining you and the family careering along the road in the truck in the capable, but reckless hand of "Mick." Like the priest in Anjo Banjo Patterson's "Father Mulligan's mare,"* I've prayed you over every bump and over every inch of the way there and back. Dill, aren't I? Well - until 9.30, Sweetheart, so long. X *[Ed may be confusing Andrew (Banjo) Patterson's "Mulligan's Mare" and "Father Riley's Horse": I've prayed him over every fence – I've prayed him out and back! And I'll bet my cash on Father Riley's horse!]

Tuesday April 15, 1941

It's raining cats and dogs outside and the Mercury is down to about zero. Gosh it's frigid, darling! We're nearly too cold to dare to uncover our noses, and as for venturing out of the hut, it's just not done. I may don overcoats and pullovers and dash to the "Prac." Room to do a bit of dial whirling later, if I'm game enough.

By the way, Sweetheart, I found, after I had posted your last letter, I had forgotten to include that cutting about the "Silver City Comet." Mug that I am. So, in case you were wondering what it was, I'm including it this time – if I don't forget again, doggone it!

It was wonderful (as it always is) to speak to you again, last night. I was glad to hear you say you had such a good time over the Easter. Wish I'd been with you – and to hear that your family are not too bad.

> to England, in His Majesty's ship 'Renown'."
> – "E."
>
> BRITAIN'S railways made a great fuss when the "Coronation Scot" travelled at 125 miles per hour, but you have to dig into the depths of the New South Wales railway timetable to discover that the "Silver City Comet," running between Parkes

September 1, 1938.

> and Broken Hill, averages 180 miles an hour over one 9-mile stretch. The timetable shows the "Comet" as leaving Kinalung (662 miles from Sydney) at 4.9 p.m., and arriving at Wahratta (671 miles from Sydney) at 4.12 p.m.! Surely a railway timetable wouldn't exaggerate.

My golf sticks arrived this morning, so I was able to get in some practice this afternoon, it being "Sports Afternoon". You should have seen the way Uncle Jim had it tied up! I thought it would take me hours to undo, but no, Unc shares with me the cunning hand of a sailor in the matter of knots; it came undone quite easily.

The rain has stopped so I think I'll dash up to the Radio Room while the going's good. I wonder how long this enthusiasm will last?

Here I am, back again after a dash through what was either snow, sleet, rain, hail or a combination of all. Brrr! When I've finished writing I'll hop over to the showers and try to thaw myself out under a hot one. 'Fraid it will be no good though.

I had some fun, tonight. I fluked the frequency of the N.S.W. Police force and was able to hear their instructions to the various Police Cars. I only found out the other day that a chap who used to work with Joan is one of my cobbers here. When you see her, darling, ask her does she remember Jack Macdonald. He's a real decent chap.

I think I'll turn in now and try to sleep the sleep of the just – and try to dream of you. If I concentrate on you hard enough just before I pass out, perhaps I will. (Dilly, aren't I?) Love me, dear? Know what? I sort of adore you.

April 16, 1941

Another day wiped off the slate. Another 24 hours nearer seeing you, sweetheart. Some of the lads have started counting the time between now and leave, by the number of meals left. I have just been informed that there are now 108 meals to go. That's how Morse Madness gets you in its first stages. It's when you go around biting people they put you away. Your letter and Alice's arrived today and as usual put a new

31

complexion on things. I was glad to hear from Al. I must write to her tonight.

The exam results came out today. The bloke what loves you got 89% and has a swelled head. Seeing the average of the class was 53% I think I'm a corker. Seriously, though, dear, you must have prayed very hard. Thanks, sweetheart.

The day has been much the same as the last two. The night is different. There's no rain tonight. In fact there's not a cloud in the sky – and our bombers are kicking up a din overhead – blast 'em.

I've just been listening to the B.BC – the news is much the same as ever. I've been trying to get the famous (or infamous) Lord Haw Haw's station, but with no success.* ***["Lord Haw-Haw" generally refers to William Joyce who was German radio's most prominent English-language speaker.]

Please give my love to all your family, dearest, and my regards to I B. and the crowd. Look after your eyes, darling mine. I hope Joan is going to play tennis with you. Trust old Nev to get as much leave as he can.

Those three days will be the most wonderful I'll ever have spent. I wish I could have been in Yandina with you that night; it would have been Good Friday night indeed. However, it is good to think on what we might have done – where we might have gone. Perhaps we'd have strolled arm in arm – not saying much – to the bridge over the old river; and we'd have stood there a while watching the moonbeams mirrored in the water. (It was a lovely moon that night.) And I'd have told you, a thousand times, as if I were afraid you mightn't believe me the first time – that I love you. And maybe you would have let me kiss you. And then I'd have asked you, as I have so often done, if you loved me; and you'd have said, with the shy smile in your eyes that made me love you first, that you didn't. And we'd have laughed, remembering how you used to tease me on the old strolls we used to take. Then I'd have asked you again, holding you tight and making you look me in the eyes; and, darling, you might have been kind to me and said "Yes", – and kissed me. It would have been a wonderful walk, my sweetheart.

I wish I hadn't thought so much on it now. It's heaven when I let the old imagination run riot, but it's hell when I come back to earth.

I thank God for you, my darling, He has been too good to me.

Ed. XXXXX

Pray for me when you can, dearest. X

32

Flight II "A", No. 2 W.A.G.S., R.A.A.F. Parkes

April 17, 1941

Darling Molly,

Pay day today, so am very happy, and financial. I think, after I've told you all the exciting (?) things that have happened, I'll take a run into town with Jack for an hour or two to have a game of billiards and a few jugs.

In exactly five weeks time I'll be starting my leave! I've taken to counting the meals now, like the others. Dear, if only I could tell you how much I'm looking forward to that time! I think I'd go mad if I didn't have it to look forward to.

Slight change in today's routine. I have passed a sufficient number of tests in the Morse speed I was doing and have been promoted to a faster class. As a few of us are now over six weeks ahead of the others, some of whom are still doing only 8 to 10 words a minute, we are having a great loaf. Which is very good, as I have a naturally tired disposition. This will explain, probably, why I am able to turn out my brain-children, the famous Sonnets. I'm glad you liked them darling.

Jack is wandering around giving me a series of looks which may be interpreted as "Hurry up! Darn you!" So I'd better get into my glad rags – washed and ironed by my own lily white hands.

Friday

Sweetheart,
Your letter arrived today, and, as usual caused the old heart to flutter. It's a wonderful thrill to come in from dinner and find a letter from you waiting for me.

I hope your friend in the Mater is not seriously hurt. I must look up that chap in Parkes when I get a chance.

I'll be playing golf on the Parkes Course on Sunday with some of the boys. Hope I haven't forgotten how to play. I'll probably take about 150 for the round.

I received a wire from Jeanne today. I was very sad to hear that her mother had died suddenly this morning. She was a great friend of mine and I was very cut up. I must confess that Jeanne and I have exchanged two or three letters since I've been here, but there's no need to be jealous (though I hope you are a bit, for my sake) darling; we're only "old friends" now. I think she has a boyfriend with whom she's very much in love. I hope he's a decent chap, because she's a very nice girl. (Although I know a much nicer one!)

I'd like to meet that boyfriend of yours, "Dick." It would be handy to learn a few points from him on how to "handle you." Unless I do, you'll probably lead me to distraction when we're married. (As I hope we will be, someday soon, my darling.)

So old Laurie has joined the Navy. Good on him! Give my congratulations to the old blighter, please Molly, and tell him I hope we'll "sink a few" both by H.E., and in the usual manner, with bent elbows, together. Bonny doesn't seem too popular with you, sweetheart; I trust the new maid is not like her namesake.

How are old Pearle and Bob doing? I bet you two will have a great old yarn, or rather had a great old yarn last night. (I was forgetting how long the old P.O. takes to deliver our letters.)

You say, darling, you're a queer person in lots of ways. I say you're the most wonderful person in the world, and it's heaven to know you love me! And, dearest, I love you more than all the world, and I'd give my life to make you happy.

Don't forget to take care of your eyes darling. Does Dick advocate a stern attitude in "handling you?" Should I wag my finger in your face and growl "Now, then, young lady! None of this 'ere goin' to pictures or readin' without your glasses!" in best policeman manner.

I think I'll do a bit of study tonight. This Radio Theory business is getting deeper and deeper.

I love you, dearest – If only I could hold you close and try to tell you so. In five weeks, I'll be able to. Pray for me sweetheart. Thank heavens the telephone exists – I'll be able to talk to you in two more days, anyway.

I'll post this tonight and it should get to you on Tuesday morning. Please give my love to all your family, my darling (you <u>are</u> <u>my</u> darling, aren't you, dear?) And remember me to Len, Nev, Ron and the others.

All my love, Ex.

XXXXX

P.S. Love me?

April 19, 1941

Dearest Molly,

All the boys are out tonight – gone to the dance, the pictures, and/or the pubs, and blessed quiet reigns. I have just been to the canteen and (don't tell the boys or I'll never hear the end of it!) sunk a lemonade. It was good, too.

I forgot to tell you I received a letter the other day from Bill Moffatt, a cobber of mine in the Telephone a/cs. He gave me the good news that a chap who used to work with me in the same office is now in camp at Amberley and has been made a W.A.G., so he'll be down here in a week or so. I'm looking forward to seeing him.

There was great fun in the hut this afternoon. The boys went mad. If you were to walk into it, now, you'd get the shock of your life. You'd imagine that a bomb had hit it. Not a bed is standing. Some are even on the rafters. Never have I seen such a mess. I hope sincerely I never do again – although I think I caused more havoc than anyone else – heel that I am.

Tomorrow night I'll be able to speak to you again. My darling, you'll never know how much it means to me to hear you say you love me. I love you so much, darling girl, that it hurts. We must be going to have such happiness later on, to make up for the unhappiness this being parted is causing. Pray that we'll always be happy, sweetheart.

I missed the Padre this afternoon; owing to the muck up we were having I forgot all about it. (You see, you'd better keep up your prayers for me – I'm horribly forgetful.) However I'll be able to go in the morning before Mass.

We're having the monthly church parade in the morning. As usual, we Catholics will have to go on parade and drop out when they call out "Conscientious Objectors, fall out!" We'll have two Masses in the morning, one at 7 and one after the parade.

After Mass (I am getting good, going to two! But, unfortunately, I can't claim too much credit, the second's compulsory, and it's too long to fast 'til) Arthur Smiles and I will attack the Parkes Golf Course and make the welkin* ring with curses and the divots fly with missed shots. Remember the time we went to Clontarf, sweetheart, and we were so darn awful you were disgusted? I enjoyed that day. *[A *welkin* is an archaic English word referring to the sky or the heavens]

News is just about non-existent, so I'd better stop writing or I'll bore you to distraction by recalling a thousand occasions I've been with you. I don't think I'll ever forget one of them. I miss you my darling. I love you more than I can ever tell. I'll let you know all about the round of Golf tomorrow. Goodnight dear.

20.4.41

Here is your wicked boy-friend back again, with head hung low in shame because of the bad language he hurled at an inoffensive little ball this afternoon at the Golf Club. It's a lovely course and the crowd there, a real country crowd, made us very welcome. The greens, instead of being grass, are of sand, rolled hard like a tennis court, and are very peculiar to play on. I played the game of my life – I only took 92 for the round, which was excellent (for me.) The funniest part of the game was the local rule, which reads: "If the ball lies in or near any hole dug by a miner, it may be lifted and dropped without penalty." You see, all around the course are gold miners all industriously panning for gold. It was interesting to stop and watch them at their digging. None of the holes are more than four or five feet deep. The secretary of the club said they weren't getting much gold or I might have "resigned" from the R.A.A.F. and pegged a claim.

On the way "home", we were stopped by the urgings of a terrific thirst and had a pot or two at the Exchange Hotel. There we ran into "Mac," one of my particular cobbers in the hut. Seeing he was looking very sad I asked him what the matter was. He told me that three urgent telegrams had arrived at the station since Friday, and not one of them was delivered to him. They were just left to rot in the Guard Room. The first, which arrived on Friday afternoon was to say that his father was seriously ill in Sydney, the second, which came last night was to tell him his father had died, and the third was from his sister at Broken Hill, telling him to meet her on the train which went through last night and be ready to go to Sydney with her. He wouldn't have known until tomorrow if his family (worried enough already) hadn't thought something must have happened to him and got the Police in Parkes to come out to the Station for him. The Padre broke the news to him this morning and he left for Sydney on tonight's train. If he had been given the first wire he could have gone to Sydney on the Friday night's train and seen his dad before he died. It was a horrible bit of laxity on someone's part, and there'll be an awful row about it. I hope the blighter responsible, who was too lazy to walk 100 yards and give the wires to poor old Mac, gets it well and truly in the neck. The C.O. is as mad as – about it.

When we got back to camp I booked our call. Darling, it's just half past eight, now. Another hour I've got to wait to hear you - I hope it goes quickly.

Mass this morning must have given the Padre the shock of his life. You see, it was a compulsory parade, and the lazy blighters who used to dodge going, had to go. The Gym, which usually has a roll up of about 30 of us, was packed to overflowing. The Padre made a few heart to heart remarks, and I, who was attending my second for the day – like the Pharisee – threw out my chest in pride and looked around, as if to say "Thank the Lord, I'm not like thee!" I didn't really, though, darling mine. I was worse than anyone before your prayers, and Jack and Wally's example, woke me up.

The hut looks funny tonight. It's so tidy, after the mess last night.

I think I'll do a bit of reading while I'm waiting to talk to you. If I can concentrate on any book while I'm thinking of you.

I hope all the family are well. Give them my love, please, darling.

I love you so, Sweetheart, I'll go on loving you more and more all through my life, and, please God, dear, forever afterwards.

Ed. XXXXXX

P.S. Love me, darling girl?

Flight II. A., No 2 W.A.G.S., R.A.A.F., Parkes

21 . 4 . 41

My dearest,

Once again "Panic" night is over, and I'm another week nearer a period in my life which will be the happiest I've ever known – the time when I'll see you again. When I look back, the time appears to have flown. I can hardly believe it's seven weeks since I kissed you goodbye; but when I look ahead the days seem to be crawling by like sleepy snails. I miss you, darling!

Your letter arrived today, and one from dad and Mollie. I wish Bob were being transferred to Parkes, not Wagga. It would be great to have him and Pearle here. I bet you two got through some "scandal mongering" that night.

Do you know what Ken has been classified as, sweetheart? I hope for my selfish sake he's been made a W.A.G. I'd like his company down here. I expect I'll be seeing Dick soon. How are he and Mrs. Cohen doing? Are they still at Burstows?

Dad told me about his father's death. He had a very happy one. My uncle came every day and gave him the last Sacraments. He actually died in dad's arms while he was lifting him up to adjust his pillow. I hope I die like that.

Dad also says Len is getting as fat as a house – and that it doesn't suit him. Tell Len he'd better get rid of the "corp" before I see him. It must be too much beer.

Mollie tells me Alan and Peg are often out at our place and the family love them. Alan is always doing something around the house, putting oilcloth on tables and sharpening knives etc., and every time Peg goes there she makes scones, etc. (and you know how Peg can cook!)

Life has been monotonous as ever, since last night when I spoke to you. You know, darling, that service is rotten. I never understand more than a few words you say. I have to fill in the gaps with my imagination. I hate yelling out "Can't hear you" all the time, but it's heaven just to hear your voice, and perhaps hear you say you love me. That's all I ask of any Telephone. Nothing else in the world could make me so happy!

I'm steadily working my way through this miserable course here. I can't imagine how I'd have been if I hadn't met you. I suppose I'd go off my head with Morse Madness. Morse code wasn't meant for people with lively imaginations. The duller you are in that respect, the more chance you have of becoming good at Morse.

That about concludes things as far as news is concerned. I love you, my sweetheart. Goodnight.

Tuesday 22.4.41

Darling, after I finished writing you last night I dropped a line to my uncle in the Redemptorist Monastery at Oxford Park. You know, the one that gave the Sermon at New Farm at the Mission last year. [Ed's uncle, Father Eddie Gallagher, was appointed the Australian Provincial of the Redemptorists in 1943.]

Today we have been delving into the depths of direction finding. It's all very interesting but very deep. If you are tuned into a station you can tell by a certain type of aerial from what direction the wireless waves are coming, and hence where the Station is; so that, if you were lost somewhere near Alice Springs you'd know in what direction to fly to get to 4QG* *or any other station in the world. The working of the apparatus is very simple, but the theory of why it happens is something for Einstein to ponder over.* *[4QG was the first A Class station in Queensland, set up in 1925 and nationalised in 1928 when the Australian Broadcasting Company (ABC) was formed.]

I've just been washing a shirt, shorts, socks, singlets, etc. Depressing toil. After I got them Persil white, when I was hanging the shirt on the line I dropped it in the dust. Girl! You should have heard the dreadful language! But in the middle of my tirade I had to laugh, because Mac, who was laughing at me, shook so much that he dropped all his washing! I pray he may be forgiven for the words he uttered. (There are about a dozen "Mac's" in our flight – it's very confusing.)

I just knocked off for a minute to exchange a book at the Library – "White Face" by Edgar Wallace – I took out. I still have the same low taste in literature for murders and lots of blood.

We had sports afternoon today and I got in some Golf practice I sadly need.

There were rumours current today that our leave is to commence four weeks from this Friday instead of five. I hope it does. Fancy seeing you in a month. Sweetheart it will be heaven – I love you.

A letter from Joan arrived today. She gave me all the news and told me she was shifting to Langshaw St. *and is thinking of joining your tennis club. I hope she does.* *[In New Farm near Molly and Ed's boarding house on Moray Street, close to the Brisbane River.]

Well, wearied by my terrific exercise of this afternoon, I think I'll curl up in bed with "White Face." Lord! I'll have to do some study soon!

Wednesday 23.4.41

Sweetheart, I love you. Gosh! How I love you. Glad?

I've just had a glance at my washing on the line, and shuddered at the sight of so much promised ironing. Think I'll put it off until the week-end.

The C.O. informed us that our leave is to commence on the 23rd of May, today. It's straight from the horse's mouth this time. I've got my leave all planned out already, until I see you, then you can have a go at the planning. On the 23rd (a Friday) I catch a train which gets me to Sydney at about 8 a.m. on Saturday morning. Then I'll have to moon around like a lost sheep until about 8 p.m. when the Kyogle* leaves. From then on, every mile we travel brings me nearer to the Sunday afternoon - and you! *[Kyogle is in the Richmond Valley, about 90 km west of Byron Bay in northern NSW. It is the centre of a rich dairy and farming area. During WWII, twenty-five trains a day took troops and supplies north. Today Kyogle is promoted as the *Gateway to the Rainforests.*]

I'll have Sunday afternoon, Monday, Tuesday, Wednesday, and Thursday in Brisbane (with you) and then I'll have to leave, curse it, on the Friday morning's train which gets – No! Whacko! I have Friday in Brisbane. I don't have to catch the Kyogle until Saturday. This gets me to Sydney on Sunday, and I'll be back at camp on the Monday morning (Drat it!). This gives me 5½ days to be near you. I'll imagine I'm in Heaven, I think. Will you be glad of me, darling?

I think this completes the news, dear, except that they've sprung another exam on us for Friday. Say a prayer for me.

I adore you, my sweetheart,

Ed. XXXXX

P.S. Love me? Ed x.

Parkes,

24.4.41 Thursday

Darling,

Your letter arrived today, and things took on a brighter hue immediately. I was worried, a little though, dear, by your thinking Les and Mat are a bit "crooked on" you. I think you must be only imagining it. I know them too well to think that they'd ever feel that way about you, and I know you'd never give them a real reason to be. If, however, they think they have some obscure reason for being that way, it's their worry, not ours; and they'll soon get over it.

You're too lovely a person to be "crooked on" for very long. Tell me, though, darling, why you think they may be. In my best Dorothy Dix manner I might be able to laugh with you about it, and point out the fact that you're only the victim of imaginitis.

One of the reasons I like Len so much more than any chap I've ever known is his "easy-goingness." Nothing ever seems to worry him much, and he rarely has a row with anybody. Mat and Les and the others often imagine they are mad at somebody, but not for long.

You ask me if I ever think a person can be too happy. As far as we are concerned, definitely not! (With knobs on!) The only unhappiness loving you can bring me is this darn being parted from you; and I can find some solace even in that if I only concentrate on the time when we'll be together. Only a month, now! (Only a month! Seems like a year sometimes.)

A letter also arrived from Pat. She tells me about the Dance, and a night they had at the Oasis*. It seems to have been a "great time was had by everyone" and she suggests that we have a similar night while I'm on leave. It sounds good to me. *[The Oasis was a popular tourist attraction famous for its strict rules: no picnics, no bare feet or backs, no strapless togs (swimsuits) or bikinis, and more. It was developed in Brisbane's Sunnybank area and consisted of seven acres of subtropical gardens, four swimming pools and rockeries. It is now a housing development.]

The news of the day is about the same as yesterday's. Nothing ever happens here, except that I go on loving you a bit more every day; and seem to want you more with each day's passing bringing nearer the day I'll be seeing you. Do you feel that way, a little, too Sweetheart?

Pat told me of the sudden death of an old cobber of mine, Eddie Shannon. It seems impossible to believe I'll never see him again, in this life. As he was a particularly good Catholic I don't think sudden death

41

would hold any terrors for him. These things show you the necessity of keeping on the straight and narrow, don't they?

Your family must have forgotten you, not having written for so long, but you know what sisters are like – Alice may have been too busy, little heart-breaker as you call her, with her numerous beaux to write. Anyway, no news is good news, isn't it? So cheer up, old sweetheart; I bet a letter will have arrived by the time you get this, and things won't seem half so blue, and the erring family will have been forgiven. Just as well you forgive easily, or I'd never have been able to worm my way into your heart. I am there, aren't I, dearest? (Like myself, don't I?)

No wonder everybody has been talking about the wonderful service at the Main Roads on Monday. So it was you on the switchboard! No wrong numbers were connected and everybody was happy! I bet you were 100% on the girl that used to put me through to every number but yours whenever I rang you there. You mentioned little Audrey the other day. I was wondering how she, Lal and "Stacey" were flatting. Or has there been the expected split up? Don't suppose you worry much about them, though.

Old Ken must have been letting his head go the other day at the races. Remember his terrific plunges? I wonder if he had a win.

Remember me to Toni and Al when you write, darling, and give 'em my love.

I don't feel very confident about tomorrow's exam. Hope I fluke another pass – but this is very doubtful, very, very doubtful. I'll need a lot of your prayers, so out with the Rosary Beads, darling. I'd better help myself, too, by doing a bit of study, curse it!

I wish I were near you, just now, my darling, I'd be so happy. Sometimes this longing for just one kiss from you drives me nearly crazy. I love you, sweetheart, more than I'll ever be able to tell or show you. Try to love me always, because you're all that this world holds for me.

Ed. X

P.S. Give my love to your family, please, my darling, and pray for me.

Ed X.

Flight 11 A., No 2 W.A.G.S., R.A.A.F., Parkes, N.S.W.

25.4.41 Friday

Sweetheart,

There is great excitement at the moment. Two blokes from another hut have paid us a visit and are being greeted in the usual manner. About a dozen have collared them, taken off their shoes, and at present they are gyrating between heaven and earth in, or mostly out of, a blanket. I've copped this treatment more than once, as has about everyone in camp – and it's great fun, unless you're unlucky enough to hit the roof. The boys have finished with the visitors and, being in the mood, are bent on more prey. I think the Corporal looks like being the next victim unless he flees while the going's good.

The exam went all right today, I think, or rather, hope. The paper was very long and I had to move to get it finished. Unless they can't read my writing, I think I got at least a pass.

The direction finding business occupied all the rest of the day, apart from the inevitable Morse. Sometimes it's jolly hard to get a bearing, owing to interferences and the movement of the Heaviside Layer* (though I don't think you'll be very interested in that.) I will be though, sometime, if we get lost and I can't get a bearing on the station's oscillator to bring us home. *[A region of the ionosphere, roughly 90–150 kilometers up, that reflects radio waves of medium length.]

The course that started a month before us commenced their eight days' leave, today, lucky blighters. I suppose they're all happy as Larry now, on their various ways home. Wish I were on my way to home, and you. I miss you so, darling, and I love you more than life.

26.4.41 Saturday

Week end at last, and a whole 36 hours away from lectures. We spent most of the morning at Direction Finding, which I like very much; you have to take as many bearings as you can on all the stations you are able to get. I spent a glorious half hour listening to a programme from 3AR, in Victoria. Heard Bing Crosby sing "Whistling in the Wildwood," and a few other items. Gosh! I like Direction Finding.

I have been doing a spot of washing, and my hands have become as wrinkled as a piece of tripe. Makes writing a job and a half.

The boys reckon I'll stagnate if I don't go out more often, and have talked me into going to a show tonight. I haven't seen a picture now for over two months. I wonder if I've forgotten what they're like.

The Golf Club sent me an invitation to a dance there tonight. I've heard they're the best and wildest dances ever heard of, so would like to go, villain that I am, darling, but decided against it. Some of the boys are going, and I have been promised a partner if I should go, but, unfortunately for her, some poor girl will be done out of the brilliance of my company, and the sparkle of my wit, not to mention the weight of my foot on a pet corn. Still, she won't know what she's missing, so I suppose my sympathy is misplaced. I hope there's a dance on while I'm in Brisbane. I think I'll have a bath and shave and spruce up for the pictures.

27.4.41 Sunday

Darling, in exactly a month from now, I'll be with you. It's wonderful to be able to look forward to a time when I'll be the happiest man in the world. When I'll be able to see you, to hug you again. You'd better get into strict training because this camp has made such a terrific brute out of me that I'm liable to hug you to death. I love you so, darling.

The pictures weren't bad, dear, although Eric insisted on going to sleep half-way through the first, waking up for a smoke at interval then going to sleep for the rest of the show. If he'd stayed at home he'd have saved 2/-.* These darn N.S.W. pictures; I'd forgotten they don't allow you to smoke and was calmly rolling a cigarette when Jack pointed out to me the error of my ways. "Hullabaloo" with Frank Morgan, and "High Sierra" – Humphrey Bogart were the two films and they were rather good, or so I thought. *[2/- = two shillings or more informally, two bob; other coins of the day were crowns (5/-), shillings, sixpences, threepences, pennies and half-pennies. Today, a sterling silver Florin (two shillings), in absolute mint condition and uncirculated, could fetch approximately $100AUD.]

I slept in beautifully this morning, missed breakfast, and just made nine o'clock Mass. Jack hadn't time to dress and had to go in shorts. But, then, as there are only the lads here to look at you, he didn't mind.

After Mass I went back to bed and read until eleven, when I summoned up sufficient will-power to do the ironing waiting for me on the line. Then I had dinner, and did I eat?!

After dinner I curled up again and read and slept all the afternoon. What a life!

Now, darling, you mustn't think the reason for all this apparent laziness is laziness. The temperature last night and today is almost freezing. In the short breaks when I quitted the safety of the blankets I wore two pairs of pants and two pullovers. Lord! It's cold. Yesterday morning the mist around the camp was like pea soup and the cold seemed to get into the marrow of your bones. And today hasn't been much better. Everywhere you go, you run – not walk – to warm yourself up.

After tea tonight I booked our call and am now waiting to speak to you. Dear Darling, I look forward to this so much every Sunday night and it makes me very happy to read that you do too. You do love me very much, don't you, my sweetheart? There are no doubts, now, are there? Please tell me if there is anything of doubt, darling girl, because it means everything to me to know that you love me, as I love you,

Ed XXX

PS. Pray for me, dear. Ed.

Parkes N.S.W.

28.4.41

Dearest,

Another "Panic" night has come and passed, and I can safely count another day gone. And, dear, what a day it's been. Luckily we've been out in the sun all the time, otherwise we'd have froze. In all the lecture rooms huge fires have been kept going, and even they couldn't keep out the cold. The wind seems to be able to blow round corners, sneak in through keyholes, and generally make a darned nuisance of itself. Wish I were back in good old Brisbane.

The phone behaved rather well last night and I was able to hear you fairly clearly for the first time. I wish I could tell you how happy you make me when you tell me you really love me.

Results of the exam came out today. You must have worn your Rosary to the links because I got 84%, which was one of the best recorded efforts. Gosh! I'm brainy. Sometimes my own cleverness almost frightens me. (My lack of cleverness frightens my instructors.)

All the gang are now getting more and more excited as the promised leave draws nearer. You know, darling, the time since I saw you last, although it has crawled by, seems only yesterday, instead of over two months.

I can still picture every little thing you did that last night. Still hear everything you said. And I can still picture you the way you looked that morning when I called in to see you. And can still remember how I cursed to myself those damned people in the office who made it impossible for me to kiss you just once more before I went. I suppose I am, as I suggested before, a sentimental dill, but, darling, I wanted to more than I have ever wanted anything.

I wrote to Graham last night; the letter I got from him was "Gorm" all over. Even if I hadn't read the signature I'd have known who the author was. He's one of the best.

I think I'll drop Joan a line tonight. So, until tomorrow, darling, dream of me a little.

29.4.41 Tuesday

Noting of note to report tonight, Sweetheart, except that it was sports afternoon this "arvo" and a few of us frightened the worms around the Drome with glorious golf shots. I fear golf was not cut out to be my game. Think I'll take up marbles again.

I instituted a game of cricket in the hut after tea tonight with a Radio Theory book, a ruler and a ping-pong ball. Judging by the enthusiasm (hope I've got that word right) displayed, it bids fair to become a national pastime. When I left them just now to come up to the hut to write they were still at it.

The cold spell ceased suddenly about midday today and now it is almost warm. I was wondering if Ken will be one of the new batch arriving here tomorrow morning. There are a couple of chaps coming down whom I knew – including one that used to work with me.

Your letter arrived today, darling, and, as usual, I rushed to the end, to find out if you still love me. Dill, aren't I, I know you do, but I'll always be unable to understand the miracle that you can.

I hope that darn tooth is not troubling you still, dear. If it is I'd go back and see the dentist about it, if I were you.

You are lucky blighters having holidays. We never get one here. I wonder how I learned to ride that motorcycle you dreamt about – and where was I going. It's terrible of your Dad to commit sacrilege like he was doing. I hope his thumb has healed up all right. He must have been in some pain with it.

No, darling, I never think for hours and hours on this darn war. As a matter of fact I hardly ever think on it, except to curse it now and then, because it has parted us. I've got tired of it and all I do is pray it will end soon. I've no ambitions to act as target for A.A. guns. Never had, but I suppose I'll come through it O.K. I must, for our sake. I've too much to live for now, with you to love and be loved by. Don't think of it too much, dear. It hurts so, if you do. I try, (and I think I've succeeded) to think of it as something apart, intangible, that cannot affect us. I bet I'll be causing you a lot of worry, and putting gray hairs on your lovely head, fifty years from now. Your loving me, sweetheart, has made me awfully proud of myself. I feel as if nothing can hurt me now. And nothing ever will very much, so long as I can keep your love.

You were never "nasty" to me, Molly, darling. If you did tell me off now and then, it was less than I deserved, and I don't think I'll ever give you cause to be unhappy again, on my account.

I think I'll drop a line to the folks at work, if I can think of anything to tell them. Good night, dear. I love you.

30.4.41 Wednesday

We must be kindred souls, all right, Sweetheart. It seems as if everything that happens to you must happen to me. I was sitting inoffensively at Morse today, when along comes some blighter with a chit for me. It read "Report to the Dentist at 1530 hrs (half past 3)." So along I toddled at the appointed hour, shaking like an old Ford, and was shoved into a chair where some ex-inquisitor tortured me with various drills. He has also promised to drag one out on Friday. I hope, darling mine, that yours is right again.

Apart from this visit to the torture chambers, the day passed pleasantly enough, except that I was disappointed to find that the chap I was expecting hadn't come down after all.

One thing the dentist saved me. It appears that, while I was experiencing the torture business, the boys started a muck-up in the Morse and were copped. All of them have to go back tonight to do "Battery fatigues," which consists of recharging batteries. I'd have been in the fun if I hadn't been away, so was lucky – "it's an ill wind."

I hope all your family are well, Darling. Give them my love, please, and don't forget to let me know how your Dad's hand is getting on.

Say a prayer for me, dear, and keep loving me always. I will always love you – I always have.

Ed. XXXXX

Parkes

Thursday May 1, 1941

Sweetheart,

I'm still likely to start shaking with laughter any minute. The funniest thing for years has just happened to me. I've been up for a bath – (No, that's not the funny part) – taking, as usual, my cake of soap in my pocket. When I arrived, I (as I thought) took out my cake of soap and sharked some poor blighter of a Corporal for his position. I bathed luxuriously, using plenty of soap, under his baleful glare, while he waited. I put my soap on the ledge while I dressed, then turned around and caught him using it to bathe with. I picked it up when he replaced it on the ledge, looked at him scornfully and walked out. His eyes popped out and I could see him trying to utter words that wouldn't come. When I got back to the hut, still carrying my soap in my hand, I put my hand in my pocket and (Dear Molly pray for me) found my soap in my pocket. I've been bursting into uncontrollable laughter ever since. I'm wondering what he thinks I am. I pinch his position, use his soap, and then, adding insult to insult, calmly walk off with it under his nose. As I walked back to the hut I was wondering why he looked at me so peculiarly. – Now I know.

They sprung a surprise on us today. A couple of buses rolled up about half past three and took us in to see a picture showing at the Parkes Theatre. "A March of Time"* about the R.A.F. It wasn't bad either and saved us doing some darn Morse. *[A 1935 documentary co-produced by the British Air Ministry and the Admiralty which chronicled the British RAF training program.]

Your letter arrived today and I was, of course, very happy to read you were well and that you love me. I am worried about your tooth. I hope it's better now dear. My own bit of drilling hasn't given me any trouble since, but I'm living in dread of my next bit of torture, which comes off tomorrow morning.

Three weeks exactly from tomorrow I start out on my way to you. The journey, which is about 1,000 miles, will seem short, then, but, darling, how darn long it will seem on the say back! But I won't even think of that yet.

So that was what you were trying to tell me last Sunday! I thought you were saying that there was someone talking on the line. Aren't I a mug? No wonder I can't understand why you love me!

It must have been a surprise to see Ev again. Is she still working at

Woolworths? She was rather a nice girl, I used to think. Remember when you got her to go to Con. With you?

Fancy old Nev going for his stripes! I thought he looked on the army as a real pain in the neck, and I thought they'd give him three months for not turning up those nights, instead of three stripes.

The place must be packed if I B. couldn't find any room for Ev. You never mention Hazel in your letters. Is she still staying there? What is "her nibs" (Bonnie the "Quig") doing these days. Is she working?

The really cold spell is over for the moment, but it's still like an icebox down here. Worse – there's no wind in an icebox. I am looking forward to a few days of Queensland weather, but that's only a very small reason why I'm so anxious to get to the old home town. I think you know the real one – don't you darling?

Well, that's about all for tonight – except that I must let you into a secret. Did I ever tell you, sweetheart, that I love you? It's a fact.

Goodnight, darling

X.

Friday May 2, 1941

Here's the weekend on us again, thank the powers that be. Only four hours work tomorrow and then we can do what we like for 36 hours. Whoopee!

There was a bit of a weeding out in our flight, today. Some of the boys who haven't been able to pass the exams have been told they must either choose between being discharged or re-mustering as ground-staff. Sometimes I wish I were among them. It would mean I'd be back with you, and we'd be able to make such wonderful plans, but then I think that all through my life, I'd feel I'd failed in something big, and, therefore failed you, so I'd feel that I wasn't much good, and be never really happy. Not even though I knew I still had your love.

If they should happen to throw me out, I think I'd try to re-muster as an ordinary Air Gunner, or something. Things are so bad now that I think that every chap who is able should be either in the R.A.A.F. or the A.I.F. or the Militia. But that's only my opinion, and I'm usually wrong.

Morse Madness hits us all, now and then. At present the boys have a Gymnastic craze for the moment. They are indulging in various forms of swinging from the rafters – carrying each other. Someone will break his neck soon.

They didn't pay us yesterday, because of the picture show, so last night we were very poor. However, they came across today and tonight we are rich. Later I'm going across to the road house they've opened down the road to have (don't laugh, it's true) a couple of milkshakes.

I think I'll finish off now, Darling. The dentist didn't cause me any torture today, he merely polished up the filling he'd one. I hope your tooth is right, now. Please keep loving me, sweetheart, because you mean all the world to me.

Ed. xxxxx

P.S. Don't forget to give my love to your family, dear, and my regards to all the crowd. I love you so much, darling, Ed.

Parkes May 4, 1941

Darling, –

Another weekend is over and I'm looking forward, glumly, to work again in the morning. However, there's one great consolation. I'm another two days nearer to you. I wish every day would pass as quickly as Saturday and Sunday.

I had a good time at the Roadhouse on Friday night. Each of us bought a quart of milk and when we'd drunk it, felt as bloated as a football. We also had apple pies and cream which were delicious. After this gorging we gathered round the pianola and sung or shouted to our heart's content. I don't think I've ever enjoyed myself so much since I've been down here.

I felt so darn tired after all this gaiety that I slept like a log for the first time in years and had to be dragged out of bed in the morning.

Mother sent me some books and a pair of socks she'd knitted on Saturday morning, so I spent the afternoon reading.

Last night I took a stroll into Parkes with Mac for tea. It was great to get steak after the muck we've been having served up to us here. When we'd gotten through this we had a few drinks and a sing-song at one of the hotels, then came home to sleep off the effects of our guzzling.

Our Padre was away at Narromine this week, so we had to catch the tender and go into Parkes for Mass.

I've been a bit off-colour all day, sweetheart – somewhat squirmy in the tummy, but I think it's only a mild hang-over. That's what the boys tell me is wrong with me anyway. No one gets any sympathy here. I feel very sorry for myself and wish more than ever that you were here to comfort me, darling, like you used to when I was crook (or thought I was) before. I think that the possibility of my passing away is very remote, though.

I have just been up to book our call, and this has made me feel ever so much better. I mustn't forget to tell you I love you tonight, just in case you don't know. I do love you, darling girl. I think I always have, even before I met you. Because I have always, more subconsciously than consciously, been in love with an ideal, and you are that ideal. And, dearest, I always will love you, more than all the world.

I hope that the old tooth is not giving you any trouble, dear. They can be darn nuisances at times.

When does Laurie enter the Navy? I suppose the time for his call up is getting close now. How does his girl like his joining up?

There seems so little to write about tonight. I'm in one of my very despondent (if I ever could feel that way) moods today. Feel very annoyed with all the world, because you are so far away – and inclined to think that I have been very badly done by – which I have been. Do you ever get that way, my darling? And feel that our being apart is the worst thing that has ever happened in this world. I get very selfish sometimes, and think we are the only two people that matter in this old life, which, perhaps, is correct, as far as we are concerned. At any rate you are the most important person in the world so far as I am affected. No one could make me quite so happy as you have, and, I think, no one possesses the power to hurt me quite so much. All of which I could have said in three words "I love you." Do you mind very much, my loving you, darling?

Give my love to your family, sweetheart and my regards to all the boys and I B. –

Say a prayer, for me, please, Molly, I adore you, darling, Ed xxxxx

P.S. It's just 6.30 which means I have to wait another 3 hours before I can speak to you.

Love me? Ed.

Parkes

May 5, 1941

My Darling,

Your letter arrived today, and I wish I could tell you how happy it makes me to read that you are so thrilled about my leave.

I hope the wogs at work aren't getting too much on your nerves just now. I wish I were there to give you a bit of moral support. A good "sticker" is always handy. And that darn old tooth must be worrying you, too. Those sorts of fillings are always painful, when they have to remove the nerve. It makes me mad as a hatter that the incompetence of some glug is causing you so much trouble. Is he very big, that dill of a dentist? If not, maybe I'll dong him when I come up on leave. But don't worry, if the worst comes to the worst, and it has to be hauled out before I come up, it won't worry me – I love you, not your teeth.

Last night was about the best service the Telephone Dept. has ever given us – I could hear every word you said, for once, especially your "yes' in answer to my last question. I love you too, darling, you know. ('s a fact.)

I was surprised to hear of Mat's posting to Townsville. I wonder how he feels, being so far away from the boys? Just like I do, I suppose. One thing, though, he hasn't anyone like you to leave behind, so it shouldn't be so hard in his case. It will be tough for him to have to do his own washing and ironing. He used to bring it home of a weekend and get it done there. I can't imagine Matthew bending over a tub, and I bet everything he scorches will be everything he tries to iron. I can see him going about with lovely holes burnt in his pants.

I still think you are mistaken about him and Les, dear. If he had only one day's notice, and, you know how excited he gets about anything, he'd probably forget to say "Goodbye" to his Mother, and then forget his bags etc. I can imagine the circles he'd be running around. I wish you'd tell me why you think they are "snaky" on you, sweetheart. It worries me, a bit – as you know it must; I love you more than all the world, and Mat and Les, although neither of them could ever mean as much to me as Len, have knocked about with me for the greater part of my life, ever since we were kids, so a quarrel between you and them worries me. I know you are mistaken, darling, but tell me, please, what is worrying you and I bet I can show you where you're wrong.

I think I'll do a bit of study, tonight. I was reading through a bit, tonight after "Panic" and discovered how very little I know. When I read your letter, and you mentioned "Butch" and his posting the letter for you, it made all the old times come back to me and, although the memories were all happy ones, they made me a bit sad. However, in only another 20 days, (60 meals) I'll be up there, and though it's only a short visit, I'll have to make up for that by the good time we can cram into it, and the thrill of being with you. I love you, darling, with all my heart – and I always will. "Goodnight, dear" X

Only another 19 days now, dearest. Three meals have been gobbled up, and now only 57 remain. Wish I could get them over in one sitting.

My Morse must be improving. I handed in a paper to the C.O. the other day, and became puffed with pride when it was returned today with no mistakes and marked "Excellent work." As it was 10 minutes at 22 words a minute, I think I'm entitled to a bit of a head.

I'm going over to the "Roadhouse" again tonight for a bit of music, milk, and apple tarts. I'm trying to feed this darn cold I've got.

Speaking of that cold, it's a beauty! I have a fit of the shivers every now and then. My eyes are bunged up, and I sniffle every second breath. Lord, I'm sorry for myself! I look the picture of misery. But nobody feels sorry for me, except me. You'd better be sorry for me, darling, or I refuse to love you so much in the future.

I'm looking forward to seeing Dick in three weeks time. Where is I Cohen staying now? I bet she was cut up when Dick went to Bradfield Park.* He'll be a champ here, with his wireless training and ability at Morse. But before I see Dick, I'll be seeing you. He'll arrive here while I'm in Brisbane, so the fact that one of my old cobbers will be waiting for me here when I get back will soften the blow of having to come back, just a little. *[RAAF Bradfield Park was an RAAF station built in Lindfield (a Sydney suburb) in 1940. During World War II, more than 200,000 members of the RAAF and the WAAAF (Women's Auxiliary Australian Air Force) received training there on their way to service in World War II.]

I hope Alice has written you in time to prevent the weight of your ire falling on the family. You know, sweetheart, your wrath can be a most terrifying thing. I know; I've copped some of it at times.

Please give my regards to Butch and Laurie and the others at home. Tell 'em I'm half crazy with the anticipation of my leave, when I can see them all again.

The best place to give that erring sister of mine a ring is at the A.M.P., darling. She owes me a letter, too.

Give my love to your family, dear, and dream of me a little, because I love you so much – and I miss you terribly.

Ed. xxxxx

P.S. Love me? Ed. X.

You'd better be prepared for more substantial ones than these (xxxx) on the 25th.

Ed.

Ed, left, with Ralph Moores (who married Ed's cousin Aileen Mulligan), and on right, one of his closest friends, Mat Donovan. The women are unidentified.

Parkes

May 7, 1941

My Darling,

Each time I sit down to write means another day has passed, and the day when I'll see you again is considerably nearer, so you can understand why I feel a bit excited, and more than a bit happy.

There was a bit of excitement here today. One of the boys forgot to land his plane how it should be landed, with the result that they don't think they'll be able to put it together again. Like "Humpty Dumpty and all the King's Men." The chap wasn't hurt much, but is doing a spell in hospital. If they give him another chance, I bet he won't make the same mistake again. I'm very glad I wasn't with him when he did his little act. The wind was a bit tricky today, and, just after he'd make his mess, another fellow tried the same stunt, and we watched goggle eyed as he bounced along like a jack-in-the-box, but by the biggest fluke in the world he rolled to a standstill still right way up. Sort of put us off work for the rest of the afternoon.

My cold is still keeping up its attack on poor innocent me. I sneeze about once every three minutes and each time it seems as if my head were coming off. Hope I recover.

I had a good time at the Roadhouse last night. Mac (the one who used to work with Joan) is pretty good on the piano, and, as we had the place to ourselves, we sang and played to our heart's content, and doubtless to the distraction of the proprietess. I got stuck into a huge apple pie with about a pint of fresh cream. It was great. I can still taste it.

The silence of this writing room seems louder than the row outside. You can hear a pin drop. As I look about there are twenty or thirty chaps all heads down and writing as though their lives depended on it. All that can be heard is the scratch of pens, and every time I sneeze all heads lift and I become the centre of a hundred baleful glances. If I could only stay here long enough I'd cure this cold; soon I'd become too scared to sneeze, like the Chemist's customer that the raw assistant attended to.

I hope your old tooth is not giving you too much "heck." I had an insult hurled at me today. Rod Mac told me I am getting fat. Perish the thought! I still look like a rake, and a skinny rake at that.

I achieved a record today. For the first time since I've been here, two days in succession there has been no mail for me. I feel I'm being harshly treated by all my pen friends. There'd better be one tomorrow from one of the gang or else. Anyway yours generally arrives on a Thursday, so it will surely get me over my unhappiness.

The study here gets "worser and worser" every day. We get crammed so much these days that I don't know whether I'm coming or going. But, with the aid of your prayers, I think I'll struggle through somehow. (A bit of luck is necessary, too, I fear.) But just so no one can say, when I fail, "you didn't study", I think I'll wander up to the "Prac" hut and get stuck into the "TRHB" – one of the transmitter-receivers we use – and of which I know very little. I'm glad the C.O. didn't see the Morse I did today. I had about 15 mistakes. Must have been my day off.

I'll be glad to hear from Ken. I wish he'd have come here instead of to Cootamundra*. However I may be able to give him a ring when I go to Brisbane, as he won't have left Sandgate by then. *[Cootamundra, about 400 km south-west of Sydney, housed No 1 Air Observers School and No 2 Recruit Depot during World War II, in addition to Nos. 60 and 73 Squadrons.]

I think I'll post this letter to you tonight, darling, instead of waiting until tomorrow. It means that it will arrive on Saturday instead of Monday. I hope you are pleasantly thrilled by its arrival. (Got tickets on myself.)

Give my love to your family, sweetheart, and my best wishes to all the gang. I love you (although I don't think you need to be told that) and I'm looking forward with all my heart to the 25th May. Till then, darling, don't forget to pray for me. I need all your prayers, unhappy villain that I am. Keep loving me, dear.

Ed XXXXX (Remember what I said last letter about these. – Ed.)

I'm a little 58neeze, I am. Darn it. I wish some of the horses I once backed were as good as my nose. I've just ruined my umpteenth handkerchief. Wish your shoulder was here for me to cry on, darling. Anyway, whether I've a cold or not, I still love you.

Ed.

May 8, 1941

Sweetheart,

It was my flight's turn to be last for lunch today, so, with ten flights of about forty each, you can understand the wait we had – and you can understand how pleased I was to be handed a letter from you. There was one from Uncle Ed (the Redemptorist) too. A "little bird" must have been telling him about us for his letter reads in one part "With 'someone' praying for you, and with a constant memento for you in my Masses we can hope for our Lord to watch over you", – and in another part, "we may be able to arrange a meeting when you're on leave, but I suppose "someone" will take up all your time. I wonder who's been talking?

They changed our Sports afternoon again (today, instead of last Tuesday) and we started on our usual golf around the 'drome. We'd only had about two or three hits when the worst dust storm I've ever seen blew up. We were nearly choked and had to beat a retreat back to the hut. Now everything is covered with red dust, and the sunset looks wonderful through the haze. That's how I come to be writing to you now, instead of after tea. I've also done all my washing, though I fear I'm a mug, hoping that I can get anything clean with all the dust about. I left it soaking, hoping the dust clears away by tonight.

I'm going up for tea, now. I hope the old cook has something worthwhile on – but he won't.

I B's finances must be well up, with all that crowd staying there. Trust Audrey to win the stockings. She must have quite a collection of prizes, now.

As I said before, we must be kindred spirits, all right. You get something wrong with a tooth – I tail off to the Dentist; I get a cold in the head – you get the sniffles. We were made for each other. You can't deny it!

Back from tea, and it wasn't bad, for once. The quality of the tucker has fallen off sadly lately – or maybe we're getting too fussy.

I'd save my breath, too, if I were you, darling. Dill pot isn't worth wasting it on. If you don't like anyone, then I hate them. (Good sticker aren't I?)

There's one of the boys comes from Broken Hill. He used to work in one of the mine's offices. The boys are "having him on" at the moment – he bites easily. They are telling him that clerks work harder and undergo more risks than miners and he thinks they mean it. I'd better go up and finish up that washing, (darn it, I hadn't thought about the ironing 'till I made that mistake.) Know what, darling? I love you. I'll continue telling you this uninteresting drivel when I get through. Love me?

Thank heavens that's over. I've just finished, and Oh! Darling, just as well you've reformed me. It's started to rain. You can imagine the mess my pour washing will be in, with all the dust. It will probably rain mud.

Uncle Ed says that he's giving the retreat to the Brothers at Nudgee in a few weeks and asks me if I can suggest some point to stress. It's pretty hard to think of a point to stress to a Christian Brother, isn't it?

You were worried because you thought you had nothing interesting to write about. Darling, you gave me the most interesting of news (although you could hardly call it news). You wrote – "Keep on loving me, as I love you, dear." Do you think anything more could be desired by me than that? Dear Darling, I always will love you. Even if by some impossible chance I should ever want to stop loving you, I couldn't, you're part of me, dearest.

The boys are braving the rain and going across to the Roadhouse. I've commissioned one of them to bring me back an apple pie. Hungry thing, aren't I? Don't you dare say yes.

Friday, May 9, 1941

Just about this time in a fortnight exactly I won't be sitting here on my bed, writing uninteresting drivel to you. I'll be sitting in a Railway carriage, averaging about 40 M.P.H. towards you. There'll be about 40 of us, all intent on getting back to Brisbane as quickly as we can, and cursing the train for not speeding up a bit. But none of the others will have such good reason as I to curse. No one can have anyone just like you waiting for him. And that's not flattery either.

Surprisingly enough, this week hasn't been as slow in passing as I expected. It must be because our most important exam will be coming off a few days before our leave; that makes the time go fast.

Today has been just like any other day here. Darn monotonous. But the boys are a grand crowd, and we generally find something to make the time pass. Things get so dry that happenings that wouldn't raise a feeble grin anywhere else, cause uproarious laughter here, and every joke is a good 'un.

My "code in the node" is still running well (Hope Eric's "Gainwee" is doing as good.) but, thank heavens, has left my eye. I hope yours is better, sweetheart.

Like you have so often accused yourself of being, I'm a little funny. (Jack Jackson just walked past and said "Har! Writing to Molly, eh? Give her my love." A great chap, Jack; remember I told you he was instrumental in my "Reformation"). But to get back to the subject after the rude interruption. Ninety percent of all my happiness has been in anticipation – except for one thing – where you are concerned. I look forward to things so much that often, when they happen, I'm left with a sour taste in my mouth. But, where you are concerned, all the anticipation in the world can't equal the happiness I'll know when I can actually see you, and hold you again. That's why I'm so sure I love you. The joy you give me is on a higher plane altogether than any other happiness I've ever known.

We'll I'd better not write like that too much, or I'll be getting "sentimental" again, but it's true.

The next thrill I can look forward to is ringing you on Sunday night. It has been a great idea that, and I think you're wonderful, always being there on a Sunday night when I ring. Do you look forward to it too, dear?

I hope all your family are well. Please give them my love, sweetheart, and my regards to all the gang. Only a fortnight now. It will be less, by the time you get this.

I love you, darling.   Ed.   XXXXX

Love me? Pray for me, dear.

Ed x

Parkes, NSW

May 10, 1941

Sweetheart,

I've been working as if I liked it for the last couple of hours. I did my ironing, washed out a few things, and spring-cleaned. I must have been overcome by a fit of energy, and now the inevitable reaction has set in and all I want to do is sleep. But there's no rest for the wicked. So the boys say, and so they're kicking up such a rumpus that sleep is impossible. The wireless is blaring out the races, so I'll wait for the Brisbane one to come on before I seek my rest.

Tonight I'll go into town with Rod and "Smiler" for a few drinks and to buy some things I'll need for the trip to Brisbane. It shows you how close that is now, doesn't it, darling? I wish it were nearer, though. I'm going to ring Mother after I've rung you, tomorrow night. Thanks for the reminder about Mother's Day, though I had no chance of forgetting. Nearly everyone in camp has been reminding everyone else for the last week.

After tonight I'm going to settle down to some really heavy study for the forthcoming exam. It's going to be tough, I fear – and if I don't do some work soon, it'll be getting beyond me. (Better take out your Rosary for me again, darling girl.)

This looks as if it will be a horribly short letter, this time, unless something exciting happens before tomorrow night. I can't think of anything else to write, just now, but "I love you" and you know that already.

Sunday May 11, 1941

I have just returned from eating a dinner consisting of – you'll never guess – Turkey and Ham. I wonder what's got into the cook? Must be letting his head go. I didn't do much last night; Smiler and Rod and I had a few drinks, and ran into another chap from the station and his wife. They invited us up to their place and we sat in the darkness around a roaring fire eating chips and sipping beer, each one trying to tell the most eerie experience of his life. There were some pretty tall ghost yarns. You'd have enjoyed yourself if you'd been there. I wish you had been. I'd have seen you.

We just got to camp before lights out. I bought some collars, etc. for my leave. This morning we had to go into town again for mass, as the Padre is still at Narromine.

We've had a busy morning this morning, washing out the hut. I grabbed the easy job of water carrier – lazy blighter that I am. The hut looks like a new pin now. Afterwards I sewed ("This is a Man's Job" Har! Har!) and did such a good job that I'm thinking of taking up sewing as an occupation if this war ever ends. How do you like the idea of marrying a seamstress? Soon I'll be stuck into a bit of ironing. A man's (?) work is never finished.

Before dinner I booked two calls – one to you, sweetheart and one to Mother – so I have a good night ahead of me.

At this time, exactly, in 14 days I'll be with you, darling. Are you going to meet me at the Station? If you can, and I hope you can, darling girl, we'll go out to Aunt's for tea – then we can go somewhere, afterwards. Oh, darling if you only knew what it will mean to me, being able to see you again.

I'd better do something about that ironing – I'll finish this tonight. Maybe something will happen by then that is interesting. I love you, dear.

We had a fight with about a dozen tennis balls just before tea. There were about twelve of us in it and the pills were flying everywhere. As soon as you had your shot at one of the opposing six, you ducked for your life with balls whizzing around your ears. It was great while it lasted. After all our good work this morning the place looks like a shambles, now.

I'll do a bit of study, now, to try to make the time pass quicker until I can hear you. It's half past five, now, and that means I have four hours to wait. It will be grand talking to Mother, too – and I think she'll be excited. – I wish she could get down to Brisbane – you'll love her when you meet her, I know.

I read in the paper that Bill Fleming is missing – hope he's O.K.

Remember me to Nev, Laurie, and Butch and the rest, please, sweetheart.

I love you, darling, and I miss you terribly; pray for me, dear.

Ed. xxxxx

P.S. Love me? Ed. X

Parkes,

May 12, 1941

Sweetheart,

The telephone department must have been in a very generous mood last night. I must have had easily six minutes talk to you, and so I was in an extra good mood when the call was over. I'm glad you're going to meet me on the Sunday, darling – it will make the trip up, which is usually a horrible ordeal, very pleasant because I'll know that every hour that passes will be an hour nearer to you.

Mother and dad and the girls were all excited by my call. I had quite a long yarn to all of them, and the line was as clear as a bell. Mother is going to try to come down for the week that I'll be there. I hope she can manage it.

Your letter arrived today, also one from Len.

I hope, darling, you are not staying at home so much, just because of me. It makes me very glad to know that you miss me and love me so much, but you should go out and enjoy yourself. As you used to say whenever I asked you if you loved me, you're only young yet, and while you're young is the time to enjoy yourself. Don't ever give up loving me, though, it would break my heart.

Aldis Lamp

Today passed very pleasantly, although I was (and still am) feeling a bit seedy. We had work in the open for part of the day on the "Aldis Lamp". You know that light they blink at one another from distant hilltops. I found it pretty hard to get used to, but am hoping for improvement. It's very hard on the eyes. If I shut mine now I can still see the light flickering.

I must drop Len a reply, and then do a bit of study. It's only thirteen days now, darling. I love you so much.

May 13, 1941

Another day gone. Whacko! 25–13=12 – only 12 days, 36 meals, 288 hours (which seems a lot; wish I hadn't thought about the hours apart.)

A letter from Ken arrived today, darling. He seems to be enjoying camp. Did he tell you about his attempt to arrest W/C Rigby and P/O Evans? I can easily imagine old Ken dashing up waving his rifle around his head and shouting "Halt! Or I fire!" He must have done a lot of talking to get the night off for the Mater Ball.

I think I'll just miss him, up there. I think he'll have left the day before I get to Brisbane.

I'm going across to the "Roadhouse" tonight, to indulge in some more apple pie and cream and a spot of singing. All the boys here must suffer from tone-deafness. They think I can sing.

There seems very little to write to you about in this letter, dear. I'm looking forward to the 25th so much that other things that have happened seem very unimportant and I can't remember them. Anyway, the days don't seem to be passing as slowly as I feared. It doesn't seem like 48 hours since I was talking to you – but I bet next week drags. I don't mind, though, I can stand anything so long as I know you are waiting for me at the end of the week, and still love me.

Len told me all about Mat's going away and the news re the boys in general. He hardly ever sees them himself, now, with Les and Jack and the others in camp – and he is eagerly awaiting my leave. I suppose I'll be seeing a lot of Uncle Jim during the day, now that he's a gentleman of leisure. I'm looking forward to seeing old Nev and Laurie again. They are great chaps. Although I lost Mother and Dad by their going to Townsville, I certainly met some great friends. (Not to mention yourself of course.)

It's funny the way things work out, isn't it, darling? I wonder what I would have done if Dad hadn't got that transfer. I'd have been here, because I'd joined up before they left, but I'd never have known such happiness as I have; I'd never have met you.

Pray for me, dear, and please keep loving me. I love you so much, that nothing else seems very important.

Ed. XXXXX

P.S. Love me? Ed. X

Parkes,

Wednesday May 14, 1941

Darling,

Another day gone, and now I am getting excited. I may execute an improvised song and dance any moment, now. You can see the effect of the nearness of the leave on all the flight. All moroseness and worry seems to have lifted like a cloud, and all that remains is an inclination for mucking up. If they keep it up I wouldn't be surprised if some of them lost their leave.

However, with the approach of the 25th, each day brings nearer the 21st, on which day we have our final and most important Radio Theory Exam. It's one we have to pass or else. I don't know what the "or else" is, but it must be something pretty drastic. So I'll be off to the Science Hut any old time, now, and, sweetheart, please say a few prayers for me.

We had some fun, today. A new lot of "Rookies" have come in and as our Flight has the reputation of being the best in the station we were dragged out to put on a show for them. The Bosses must have been disappointed. Every time they gave us a "Right Turn," some dills would turn left, and all the other orders were the same. I've never seen such a mess. Our reputation is now mud, and malodorous mud at that.

Have you anything you'd like to do, or any particular place you like to go to, some show or anything, while I'm up there, darling? We have to fit a lot into six nights, you know.

I hope the old tooth is not giving you too much trouble and your cold, like mine, is a thing of the past, and may now be thought of only with the memory.

Your dad must have had a ripper splinter in his hand to be so proud of it. Why, I once had a bridge pylon removed from my little finger, and I've never said a word about it, hero that I am.

That darned ball chucking has started again, drat it. I wish they'd go to ... (billyo). They just crowned me. I'll have to hit some blighter now, and so the game goes on. Ah! Har! (twirling my moustache) that was a good shot. I connected with that part of Les Main that he uses for sitting purposes, generally. However, it did me no good. As I said, the game goes on. I'm keeping one eye on him, trying to write, while he is manoeuvring for a favourable position to retaliate. He's missed me three times now, and I've made many disparaging remarks on the quality of his aim. (That part of this letter sounds like a description of a gun fight.)

I'm going while the going's good. I love you, darling. But that won't do either of us any good if I get my skull knocked off by Les Main. Please keep loving me, darling.

To escape my threatened fate, I hied me to the "Ablution Huts" as our D.W.O calls them and indulged in the luxury of a hot shower. (No penny in the slot.) Now I'm nice and clean again, the battle here has ceased, and everything in the garden's lovely – except that you're not here; so, really, nothing's right, but I'm kidding myself it is. I'm enclosing a fairly horrible photo of myself next letter, if the photographer develops it quickly enough.

You seemed so pleased at getting an extra letter from me last week that I posted one to you today which should have arrived on Saturday morning. Gee! Sweetheart, it's great to know that you love me so much.

I'll start on the study, now, dear. Keep a place in your heart (the best place) for me.

Thursday May 15, 1941

Sports afternoon, again. Gee! I'm surprised at the speed with which this week has gone. I was expecting it to drag, yet it seems no time since I was hitting a golf pill around the 'drome, to the imminent danger of fitters, etc.

Rod Mac seized me when I got to the "etc" and dragged me off to tea. It wasn't bad, but an apple dumpling is sitting heavily on my tummy.

Owing to a certain amount of mucking up, all our flight who are in the 18–22 w.p.m. class in Morse have to go back tonight and do an hour's Morse. Makes you think you're back in school again – they treat us like kids. "Discipline must be maintained" and all that Bovril. I don't mind the going back, because I had already intended studying all night, but I think the instructor's attitude is a bit childish. Anyhow, what do I care? I'll be with you soon, and, till I have to come back, nothing can touch me. I'll have to go now, dear, or be A.W.L., so Goodnight, darling, I love you. I may have time to finish this letter afterwards; if so, I'll post it tomorrow.

Just a few lines before "Lights Out." The Morse passed pleasantly enough. I did Science instead.

Your letter arrived today, dear. Of course I want you to meet the train on Sunday. I was afraid something might turn up and you mightn't be able. It will be great those last few miles, knowing you will be waiting on the station for me. I hope Joan's foot isn't very bad. If you post me a letter on Tuesday night it will get here before I leave. It only takes two and a ½ days. Please do, dear.

Trust Nev to land an easy job. I didn't expect his girlfriend to be as "hot" as he said. None of his "gf's" ever are. (Don't tell him I said this or he'll want to tie me in knots.)

Well, I'd better put out the darn lights. I'm looking forward to seeing you in 10 days, dearest. Till then keep loving me, darling.

Ed. Xxxx

P.S. Love me? Ed. X

Ed in Brisbane.

May 16, 1941

Darling,

We were paid first thing this morning, which considerably improved the day. And at dinner time your letter arrived, so things have passed very happily today. I'm off to Parkes with Rod and "Smiler" shortly to celebrate. In exactly a week from now I'll be on the train to Sydney, feeling very happy.

I passed the highest Morse test today that we have to pass, so I'm through with worrying about it as far as exams are concerned.

I see you still have the same old habit at B's of ransacking the cupboard for supper. Your letter made me think of the good old days, and wish I were there again.

May 17, 1941

A letter from Pat that arrived today told me about your visit there the other night. You seem to be very popular there.

While you're at the dance on Friday night, darling, think of me on the train, probably shivering like a leaf, and thinking how, in two days, I'll be with you again. I hope you enjoy yourself at that dance, sweetheart; I wish I could be there with you. It would be swell.

In the middle of writing you last night, I was rudely dragged away by Rod and "Smiler" who were scared we might miss the bus. When we got to the gate, I found I'd left my pass behind and had to race back like a hare to get it. Then we sat in the bus, like dills, for ten minutes.

I'm going into Parkes tonight for tea – and to get a haircut. I need one, so the boys say. This will be my last fling in Parkes before my leave, and it won't be much of a fling, I can tell you. I'll be back by 7.30 and get stuck into Theory.

I've been up to my old Saturday tricks again – Washing – I'm trying to write now with fingers all shrivelled up – it's an awful sensation.

I must drop Ken a line, now, darling. Gee! I love you!

Here I am back at camp, with my hair looking just lovely. (Pansy!)

I'm shivering like a leaf, now, and sneezing between the shivers. Lord! I've got a cold, darling! Think I'll see the M.O. about it on

Monday. It would be awful if, when I met you on Sunday, I had to sneeze like a hyena every time I opened my mouth. I hope yours is right now, dear. They're a curse, aren't they?

This is the last page of the pad, but, thoughtful as ever (like myself, don't I? – Well why shouldn't I, with you loving me?) I've bought another in town, so I'll inflict more of this awful attempt at letter writing on you tomorrow. Now I'm getting stuck into Radio Theory, if I can read between the sniffles.

I've never felt so cold as I do now. In the mornings it is possible to see frost as thick as billyo everywhere, and, during the night we are often woken up by the cold. Our hands are so cold in the morning that it is hard (and this is fair dinkum) to pick up a knife and fork to eat with. They stand us "easy" on parade so that we can keep rubbing our hands together to keep the circulation flowing. I don't think you'd like it here, sweetheart. I'll be seeing you in a few days. That this is my second last letter to you until I see you makes me so happy, darling. Are you as pleased, too?

As I promised, I'm sending you a couple of snaps of a few of the boys and your handsome sweetheart in working dress. In case you can't recognise me (I've grown so beautiful) I'm second from right in front row in both photos. Ain't I 'lervley'? – The boys reckon I spoil the rest of the show. They're wrong, of course.

May 18, 1941

Just a week from now, and I'll be wondering if I'm dreaming, with you to see (and [may I?] kiss) near me. If only I could tell you what it will mean to me, dear.

It was Station Church Parade, today, and we went to Mass at 9.30 – in a body. It must break the heart of the Padre, when he sees the gym full on the Sundays when everyone has to go, and only a few of us there on the days when there is no compulsion.

Tonight will be our last phone call before I'm able to talk to you without the aid of a thousand miles of wire. Whoopee! I've just booked the call and now all I have to do is wait. That waiting is a curse, as always. I'll try to fill in the time by studying.

Goodbye, until tonight, Sweetheart, I love you so much that it will take me until the end of my life to tell you – Pray for me, dear,

Ed   xxxxxx

P.S. Love me? Ed x

May 19, 1941

Sweetheart,

You can imagine what I feel like, now that I know this is the last letter I'll be writing you before seeing you. Gee! It makes everything seem right with the world, especially now I feel pretty confident I have this exam on Wednesday just where I want it. I went for the study in a big way yesterday and managed to clean up a lot of things that had me worried. I hope I did anyway – However with your praying for me, and Uncle Ed remembering me daily in his Masses, I should be a cert.

As ever, it was wonderful to have a yarn with you last night, darling. I'll try to find out tomorrow whether there is one or two divisions and, if so, which one we'll be on. Oh! Girl! You can't know how much I am looking forward to seeing you on the platform next Sunday! All I can think of to write is "whacko!" which sounds a bit goofy, but is the only word I can find to express my feelings.

You must have been glad to get the letter from Toni. I wonder when we'll be seeing them again? It would be good to run into old Mick again while I'm up there – and to down a couple with him for old times' sake.

My cold seems to be mending gradually. I no longer sneeze every three minutes. The average has dropped to about once an hour. I'm glad to hear yours is practically gone. The Governor is paying us a visit on Thursday, which is a good thing, because it means we'll have a couple of hours off. As we already have a few hours off on Thursdays, that should be a pretty fair day for us. After the Exam on Wednesday I'm going to have a bit of a rest on Thursday and Friday.

I'm enclosing a photo of a part of my hut after the boys had been playing games the other night. The whole hut looked like a shambles. Horrible goings on. Of course I had nothing to do with it.

I had some more fun with the Aldis Lamp, this afternoon. I was picked out to send to the rest of the flight and spent an hour telling them what a lot of dills they are. I was savagely greeted when I returned and I fear my bed may be tampered with tonight.

Despite my swelled head, I better get on with some study. Gee I love you, darling.

Tuesday May 20, 1941

Another day gone, dear, only 4½ more to go – and my spirits have sunk again. I've found I know less about Radio Theory than I thought I knew yesterday. I'll be even more down in the dumps tomorrow. Alack!

71

Alack!

Today hasn't been too bad. I loafed most of it – spending Morse periods studying Radio Theory, in dire dread of being found out any minute. However I got away with it and hope to profit a bit by my results tomorrow. I suppose, though they won't give us anything I went through today. It's always the way.

I can hardly realise that when I finish writing tonight I will have written to you for the last time before I'm able to see you. I'm afraid, sometimes, that it is only a dream.

It says little for the patriotic spirit of Brisbane men that only seven responded to the recruiting March. I think most of those who are not in uniform in Brisbane (excepting, of course, those who can't be released from their work, and those with responsibilities) are too damn scared. I was once the most ardent opponent of conscription, but when I see some of the chaps loafing round street corners and in pubs, while jokers like Bill and his brother and Eric and other pals of mine are risking their necks to fight for them, my blood boils. Well enough of that, maybe I talk too much, but still. At any rate those sort wouldn't be any good in a scrap. Probably be more nuisance than they're worth. That seems to be the opinion of everyone here, at any rate.

Well dear, I think I'll go and get stuck into the Radio Theory. Please meet me on Sunday. I haven't been able to find out on which division I'll be coming up on, but if I can find out I'll wire you from Sydney on Saturday night.

Pray for me, sweetheart – I love you, you know that I always will.

Ed. xxxxx

P.S. Love me? Ed. X

405206   Flight IIA No. 2 W.A.G.S. R.A.A.F., Parkes, N.S.W.

June 3, 1941

My Darling,

I've had many a long train journey, and each one has been like a little private bit of hell, but I've never spent such a time as I did between Brisbane and Parkes. I could have howled when I saw you gradually disappear and finally merge in the sea of faces and waving hands on the platform; I've never felt so much like deserting before.

Arthur, who was quite happy in the prospect of seeing his fiancée in Sydney, found me a very poor travelling companion for a good part of the journey. He could hardly raise a mumble from me. I was as savage as ---. And I still am – Oh! Darling! – I've been in the dumps the last two or three days. Nothing seems to go right. I've been finding fault with everything in this God-forsaken dump of a camp.

The rest of the boys are much the same, so you can imagine the happy family we are.

Before we got to Sydney, Arthur, who was growing brighter with every mile, as I grew more sour, had changed his mind and decided to stay overnight in Sydney instead of going through to Parkes. Perhaps the prospect of spending another night in my glum company influenced him more than the thought of being with his girl. When we got to Sydney I sent you a wire to let you know that I was still on top of the daisies, and then I met Jeanne. I took her to dinner, then we went out to her place to meet the rest of her family. Her brother, Russell, who used to work with me in the G.P.O., perhaps noting my despondent condition, dragged (???) me off to the local inn where we imbibed a few pots. The prospect of going back to Parkes that night and spending a miserable day on my own, seemed to loom with awfully dark proportions, and finally I succumbed to his pleading to stay at his place for the night.

I had tea at their place and then we went to see a show at the St. James – Mickey Rooney and Judy Garland in some show or other that must have been crook or I'd remember it. The others seemed to have enjoyed it, but I wasn't in much of a mood to enjoy anything.

I slept in next morning as did all the family except Jeanne's sister, Dorothy, the married one who is keeping house for the others. Her hubby is a traveller or something, and is only home occasionally. There was High Mass at Randwick Church on Sunday, so I was able to hear my old choir going full out. I don't think it is as good as when I was in it (???). However, it was good to meet some of the old crowd again after Mass.

It rained heavily all day after we got back from Mass, so we had a bit of a sing-song, with Russ and Jeanne playing until dinner – I was in as bad a voice as ever.

I had another sleep during the afternoon. I had quite a lot to catch up, but the Jepsen's must have thought I was terribly lazy.

Jeanne came in to see me off on the train on Sunday night. It would have been funny being a disinterested spectator, looking at the sad expressions on the boys' faces, there, but mine was longer than any of the others. I was wishing, very hard, that I had carried out my original intention of coming up on the Saturday night's train. We clanged out of the station with Jeanne and Arthur's girl doing a little private weep on each other's shoulders. I am still worried about Jeanne, dear; she is very keen on me. I don't know what to do. I can only pray that time will fix things up.

Ed and Jeanne in Sydney

Every mile nearer Parkes seemed a league nearer hell. Darling, the train seemed to be travelling at an incredible rate of speed. I tried to compose one of our famous sonnets, but inspiration refused to come. All I could think of was that I wouldn't be seeing you for four darn months, and every month seemed to be like a year. I tried to console myself with the thought that I'd be hearing your voice on Monday night, but a voice 1000 miles away seemed a poor consolation.

As we got nearer Parkes, especially as we climbed the Blue Mountains, the cold got so bitter that it chilled your very bones. I had a glance at a thermometer in one of the stations (Mt Victoria) and it was just hovering about freezing point. If it had rained there'd have been snow.

74

When we got off at Parkes, (drat its name) – we hopped into buses, because to stand out in the wind was impossible, as quick as we could, and were bundled off to the Station. There they had a good breakfast waiting for us; we changed, and then hopped straight into the Morse again.

Oh! Darling Girl! It was cold! I shivered, although I had three pullovers and a pair of pants under my overcoat as well as my overalls, for minutes on end. I've never known such bitter weather. A slight drizzle was falling and the puddles, early in the morning, were filmed with ice.

I don't know how we got through that day. Some of the boys fell asleep during lectures, much to the annoyance of the lecturers. However tea time came, and after that, my call to you; Sweetheart, it was great to hear your voice, and to know you missed me, and loved me. But it hurt, terribly, to be able to hear you, and yet not be able to hold you in my arms. Did you feel that way, too?

Today was as bad as yesterday. When we woke up, a big canvas-covered marquee was one sheet of ice. So you can imagine how we were. Maud Millikin must have known about Parkes when she made me that Balaclava. It certainly came in handy.

I learned I got 70% in the surprise exam they gave us on the day we left. Only 25% of the course passed the exam, so I feel very pleased with myself.

This about brings me to the end of my news. Did you say, dear, that you wrote to me last Friday night? I thought you did, but you know how the reception is on my 'phone. I was waiting, like a child for a lolly, when our mail was handed out, but none arrived. I was terribly disappointed. I suppose I was a mug thinking the darn telephone ever acted like it was originally intended to.

Perhaps one will arrive tomorrow. Don't forget Sunday night, darling. – I've only that to look forward to these days. And it's a wee bit of heaven to hear your voice.

Pray for me, Sweetheart, I need your prayers very badly.

All my love, Ed xxxxx.

P.S. Love me? Ed xxxxx

June 5, 1941

My own Darling,

It was wonderful of you to write to me on Friday night; it makes me very happy and proud to know that someone as wonderful as you can love me so much – to know that the girl I love is in love with me. Dear, darling, I miss you terribly.

They are shoving the work on to us these days. We have to work at night as well as all day, so I may not be able to inflict so much drivel on you as I have been doing, but I must write to you at least twice a week or perhaps you'll not write so often, and that would hurt like the dickens. Please write as often as you can, dearest.

What with the extra work and the intensity of the study, the camp, since we came back from leave, has become a nightmare.

Soon we'll be spending eight hours a day on Morse alone, and the five hours we do now are bad enough. – Alack! Alack! –

I have to go up to the "Prac." Room soon and do three hours work, and the cold and this muck heap of a place, it's a wonder I don't go off my rocker. So please pray for me, sweetheart.

It is bad news about your dad, dear, but I suppose he knows what is best. I hope everything goes all right with him.

Fancy thinking you were a bit mad writing to me so soon! It was one of the sweetest things I've ever known – because it certainly removed any fears I might have had that you didn't really love me. And to <u>know</u> that is heaven.

You're right about my having a swell sister in Joan. I couldn't wish for a better one. We used to fight like billy-o, but were always each other's best stickers, when anyone else started anything. Don't forget to keep in touch with Joan, darling; I want you two to be great friends.

I had a letter from Mat yesterday, and he says he's having a good time in Townsville, and that Mother and the rest are well.

I have a bit of news gleaned from Mollie in a letter that arrived yesterday – (yesterday was a red letter day for me) – getting curious about that news eh? Well, it's like this (Dill, aren't I?) – Alan and Peg have had an addition to the family in the shape of a lusty young son. Lucky blighters, aren't they? Some people have all the luck. Had you heard?

None of the boys has settled down here yet since we were on leave. And I doubt if they ever will. Everyone seems to just tolerate the place because they have to. Perhaps they have sweethearts they left behind, too, but that's not the only reason. An N.C.O who was here when we first came and was such a – – that a sigh of relief went up when he left, has returned worse than ever – and is doing his best to make a Limbo into a Hell – and doing a pretty good job, too. Anyhow it's about time I bucked up and stopped inflicting this misery on you. It's not fair to weep on your shoulder (though 'tis a lovely shoulder) – you've enough worries of your own, but, darling mine, I miss you so – and I love you more than all the world.

I can hardly wait until Friday night to hear you; I don't know how people got on, who were as much in love as we are, before old Bell* (Don Ameché) invented the telephone. *[Don Ameché played the title role in the 1939 movie. *The Story of Alexander Graham Bell.*]

Pray for me, sweetheart, and keep loving me. I love you,

Ed xxxx

P.S. Love me? X

June 9, 1941

My Darling Sweetheart,

I have sneaked away for a few minutes, found an unoccupied Morse Hut and, am writing to you. Nothing much has happened, since I last wrote (except, perhaps, I love you more than ever). On Saturday we had a big Recruiting March for the A.I.F. through the streets of Parkes, and am told we looked grand – which is, probably, a lie. Of Recruits we got practically nil. Later Jack and Arthur and myself had a few beers, sank a few billiard balls, then returned to camp, sadder and wiser men. Just as we got into bed it began to rain like the hammers of Hades, and it grew so cold I got up to see if it were snowing.

Although it didn't snow here through the night, it did everywhere around; and early here, the puddles would have made good skating rinks. A fine drizzle kept up through the day, and, just on tea time a terrific storm blew up. This resulted in my hanging around the phone until nine fifty, because only one line was still standing between Parkes and Sydney; then just as I should have been put through, the last line went. I rebooked the call to tonight. I sent you a telegram today (did it arrive, dear?) and I hope you hadn't anything on, sweetheart, tonight, or, if you had, you didn't put it off. I can ring tomorrow or any night.

I know you must have been disappointed, darling. I missed hearing your voice terribly. It's about the only thing I have to look forward to, now; one good thing, though, if we had have been able to talk last night, I wouldn't be so glad now.

I got a letter from Mollie today, and all the family, (including Mat, now) are well. Peg is well and they are celebrating the Baby at our place this week. He has been christened "Noel John," and Mollie says he's "a lovely kid."

Today has been just the same as yesterday, drizzling and heavy rain all the time – and cold! Lord how cold! Sometimes you feel so darn chilly you wish you'd just pass quietly away. Even to write is an agony and your fingers seem to have no feeling on the pen.

I wish nine o'clock would hurry up and get closer. It will be terrible if they haven't been able to clear the lines.

Well that's about enough of my little troubles. This darn dump is turning me into a professional whinger. I wish you were here so that I could cry on your shoulder. You wouldn't mind, would you, dear?

How about your troubles? I hope they've been treating you O.K. at work and at Burstie's. If not, I'll fly up and bomb 'em. It's only about

78

1000 miles – Nothing to my plane.

Speaking of flying, we begin our flying in two weeks from now, so I hear. Girl! Will it be chilly up there! I shiver at the thought. Please pray for me, darling; I'll need your prayers more than ever before when that starts, especially if the weather gets as bad as it has today.

I hope all your family are well and that something has turned up to cause your dad to change his mind about going north.

Mollie tells me that Dad and Mother will try to get down for Len's wedding; I hope I haven't left Australia by that time.

Whew! Didn't know it was that time. I'll have to dash back and do some "practical." A thousand horrible curses! No! Ten thousand!

Have you had any more trouble with the old tooth, sweetheart? I hope the dentist didn't take his ire out on you for missing the appointment (to see me off) by fiendish manipulation of the drill.

Good night, dear, for two hours. I hope we get through tonight. I love you, darling. I wish some miracle could happen and I could be back with you once more, to live again the most wonderful week I've ever known. We will have more weeks – and it won't be only weeks – again, won't we, darling?

I adore you, Ed. xxxxxx

P.S. Love me? Ed xxxxx

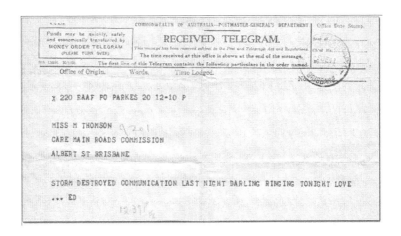

June 11, 1941

My Darling Sweetheart,

We have just received some very bad news, here. They are springing our Final Practical Examination on us tomorrow; first time we knew about it was after tea. Tough, aren't they? But I had to write to you tonight. Your letter arrived today and made me so happy that the exam seems of little importance. After all, what can they do but sling me out, and then I'd be just where I want to be, back with you.

Dearest, you can't know how glad it makes me to know that you love me so. Once I used to spend miserable hours wondering if you ever would, and despairing that such a thing could ever happen. It was hell. I have never known such unhappiness as then. And so, when you write that you are so much in love with ME, you can imagine how I feel. You know, Darling, I've often said I hoped I would always make you happy, and it hurts me to know that you are worried about Jeanne – although it also gives me a sneaking twinge of gladness to know you love me enough to be jealous. You know you needn't be, dearest. If I had not loved you as much as I do, I'd never have told you anything about her. Perhaps, if I'd known it would cause you trouble, I'd have kept quiet.

I'm glad to see you are having a good time up there, and yet miss me enough to think of me, even while you are with crowds of other people. I wish I'd have been able to go to Laurie's party. It would be great to be among the old crowd again. Give Kev my regards when you see him, dear, – likewise Laurie, Butch and Nev and the others.

So someone's ratted Mrs. B's bag again. She's unlucky, isn't she? I don't suppose she'll ever get it back. How is the famous Tommy doing these days? Still the model son?

Hazel will find it chilly at Albury. Give her my regards if she hasn't left before this letter arrives.

I miss you terribly, darling girl. Like you, that week was the most perfect I've ever known, and if other weeks are as good, when we are together again, I don't know how I'll be able to stand such happiness. And yet, I know, we are going to be even happier.

All the others are stuck in to study, so I'd better join 'em. Please forgive me for writing so short a letter, but I want to post this tomorrow air mail, so you'll get it on Saturday. I'm only living for one thing now until Sunday night. – Our weekly yarn. –

It is still as cold (if not colder) as ever. I tried to practice golf this afternoon (it was sports afternoon) but every time I hit the ball, my hands used to sting like billy-o, so I soon gave up the attempt. The weather is still showery, which must be delighting the local farmers. Their land is looking beautiful – miles and miles of perfect green – young wheat about six inches high, and in the distance Mt. Condoblin and others, covered in snow.

Well, I'd better get on with the work. Darn it.

Please write me some more letters like the one I got today, dearest - I have never felt so happy as I did when I received it. I still can't realise how anyone so lovely as you could love someone like me – but please keep on doing so, darling, because it means my only hope of real happiness.

I love you darling,

Ed xxxxx

P.S. Love me?

Ed x

June 15, 1941

My Sweetheart,

It is half past one on Saturday afternoon and I'm lazily lying flat on my back in my bed, trying to think of something to tell you. And when I think (or try to think) back over the last two days, there's not much of interest. On Thursday night, Jack, Arthur, Les and the bloke who adores you went into town and gave the folk a treat by strutting around in our uniforms, white peaks and all.

We all had headaches next day. I don't know what happened to us, darling. I felt, all through that day that I'd have to have a spree – or burst – and the others felt the same way. Remember I told you about this springing a surprise exam on us? Well, I was certain I'd failed, and that, and missing you, and longing to see you, and being forced to stay in this awful dump, all seemed to depress and torment me. Your letter had arrived and it was rotten to read that you loved me so much, and to have to content myself by reading the letter over and over, when I longed to be able to hold you in my arms, and hear you say it. It was a lovely letter, darling. I'm glad you like, and look forward to, our weekly yarns.

You make me very happy, darling. It's only you can make me so happy, because I love you more than anyone, or anything in the world. Nearly three weeks have gone since I last saw you, dearest, and it seems like three years. I thought that time would smooth away the hurt being apart from you was causing, but instead it only made things worse.

This is a whinge of a letter, sweetheart, you'll be wondering what sort of a cry-baby you love if I don't "dry my eyes" – as they say here.

I'm glad you and Margo are sharing a room. She's a great girl, that one. I only saw her on a couple of occasions and on one of those I wasn't in the best condition to form judgements, (why do you love me Darling?), but I liked her very much.

A letter from Eric arrived today and he's well. He gave a very interesting description of the campaign in Greece. Joan was telling me she got a beautiful pig-skin purse from him the other day. He wishes he was back playing golf and knocking around with the boys again. It will be great if I go to some place near him.

Also I got the results of the exam – you must have been praying hard. All my worry was in vain – I got 76% which was one of the best passes. A number of the boys failed and expect to be "scrubbed" – made ordinary air-gunners or discharged. Sometimes I wish I'd failed too.

I'm going into town shortly to see about having my lovely physog taken. There's only one photographer here, and he's pretty good, but he may be too dear. If I get one taken I'll send it to you, and also give one to Mother for her birthday.

Jack is coming along too. By the way, he asks me to be remembered to you. We'll probably drop into Kirk if I know Johnny – and have tea in town. We have to be back for the show I told you about last letter. The serge wanted me to warble, but I very firmly said "NO!" – I'd empty the hall in no time at all.

Although I've reached the fastest speed required in Morse (by the way .. .-.. --- ...- -.-- --- ..- x)*, now we have to practise the actual work – that's the reason for the study. We're getting more and more each day. We start flying, day and night, in about two weeks. *[I love you]

I hope all the family are well, sweetheart; have you heard from your dad? I hope he's getting on all right. If he's anywhere near Townsville, ask him to look up dad. He can give him a ring. I know all the family would be very pleased to meet your dad. They've heard so much about you.

I'll post this "air mail" so it will arrive on Monday. I know you like to get a letter on Monday.

Tomorrow night I'll be ringing you darling – It will be heaven to hear your voice.

I love you,   sweetheart – please keep loving me as much as you do. It is all I want in this world.

Ed xxxxxx

P.S. Love me? Keep praying for me, and us, dear.

Ed xxxx

These "x's" are a poor substitute for something I'd like more than anything in the world.

June 16, 1941

My dearest Darling,

Wonders will never cease! A gasp of awe arose when a notice came round during our second Morse Period this morning that we were to stand down at 1200 hours. More surprise could not have been occasioned had the notice read "The War is Over". This will probably be the only holiday we'll ever have. It's surprising that what is supposed to be a Christian station worked us right through Good Friday and gave us a half-holiday on the King's Birthday. We're supposed to attend some show or other in Parkes, but you said last night (I was in heaven when we were talking) you were staying home and going to write your sweetheart (lucky bloke) a long letter, so I'm going to emulate you.

It's lovely sitting here in the sun, thinking of you. Yesterday and today have been the first two sunny days I've known since I saw you. Whenever I want to think of something to write I can gaze over miles of lovely scenery, and compare its beauty with your smile. I'm a dill I suppose, but just after I'd written the last I ducked inside to get your photograph, and it's now propped up in front of me as I write. Gosh! You're lovely, dear. As I'm the only one left in camp, there's no one to come along and tell me I'm mad, writing with a photograph in front of me. Not that anyone would, or that I'd care if they did. I love you, and I don't care who knows it!

I was writing to Len yesterday and I was telling him that I've never seen such lovely scenery as is around here, just now. High on the plateau, I can see for miles, until the low hills cut off the picture, and beyond them are the mountain peaks, with snow-clad Mount Condoblin in the far distance. The acres of perfect green, young wheat so green that it's hard to tear the eyes away from its restfulness, with shades of brown accentuating the greenness, and the deep red of new mown fields interspersed. You'd never think of war looking at this picture. But drawn up around the hangars are a dozen business-like looking Ansons, and away to my left is a lone Wirraway – stunting – and the illusion of peacefulness is soon shattered.

I wish you were here, my darling. It's times when I'm on my own, like this, that I miss you most. It hurts, with a numb kind of feeling in my heart, to know you and I love each other so much, (more than any two people can ever have done before, I think) and yet have to be separated

84

for so long. It makes me rage a little, inwardly, when I think of the times I wasted, times when I was doing something trivial, out with the "boys", when I could have been with you. Even on the few days leave we had together I practically wasted one whole evening, it was a wonder you still love me, after that episode, my darling. I may have had some excuse, but excuses are poor things at any time. It won't happen again. You were wonderful.

As I told you last night, I've passed the Final Radio Practical exam (written) – the oral one has yet to come. Now remains only monotonous practice. Soon, when we begin our flying, we'll be on the go day and night, and leave will be practically unknown.

A cold wind is beginning to cause shivers to run up and down my spine occasionally – I'll soon have to go inside.

I have gone inside. You have returned to your usual place just alongside my head on Ernie Setterfield's home-made low-boy. Of a night, the moon, (which by the way has been conspicuous by its absence of late) shines on you, and I can see you even after lights-out. (Sentimental blighter, aren't I? But only where you are concerned. You see, I adore you, darling.) It's not only a woman in love that does crazy things. (My old pad ran out, but I [like the boy scouts] was prepared. This one has a picture of Deanna Durbin* on the cover, and Jack, who is one of her fans, has bagged it when this pad's finished.) *[Winnipeg-born singer and actress who appeared in a number of musical films in 1930s and 1940s]

Tonight Herb Gall and myself are going to the "Roadhouse" to guzzle a pie or two, and I will disturb the welkin with bursts of song. Poor old Herb thinks I can sing, so I like him a lot. I miss Pearle, and Joan, to play for me, but I bet they don't miss me.

Ernie Setterfield, Bert Tinkler and Tom Holland are ringed around me, at the moment, begging me to make up a four, at tennis. I thought I had the place to myself, drat 'em, but I'd better oblige. It should be funny – I haven't played for years. And I don't want to play for centuries.

Well, it was good fun, after all. I didn't do too badly because Bert and I won the two games we played in hollow fashion. Maybe I should have written "Bert won the two games."

We had a wonderful concert here on Saturday night. I think I got the best two bob's worth of entertainment I've ever had. One woman, a Miss Saville, who is a well known Radio personality, had the most glorious voice I've heard on a woman. And a soprano, Grace Clark, was amazingly like Gladys Moncrieff* at her best. *[Gladys Moncrieff was a

85

hugely successful Australian-born (Bundaberg) musical comedy singer; she became known as 'Our Glad'.] *We were all sorry when it finished. If you've ever read "The Rosary", you'll remember that the heroine had a glorious contralto voice and that she sang that song. Miss Saville sang it, and a group of girls, often heard here on the wireless, put in a wonderfully arranged background. The audience was so spell-bound, it was quite an appreciable time before they clapped, and when they did, the roof nearly sailed away. By the way, you'd enjoy that book if you've never read it. It's more a woman's book than a man's, but I liked it.*

I'll have a surprise to send you in about a week's time – I'll keep you in suspense (devil that I am) until you get it. Rotter, aren't I. No! It's no use your begging me to let you know, but, Lord! I hope you like it.

I hear tea calling me. I think I could let it go and live on love, but I'm not taking a risk. By the way, can you cook? I'm no good myself without a tin-opener. You'd better get some solid practice in if you can't; I'm going to be no good at all if I develop into a dyspeptic. These camp cooks are doing their darndest to ruin a perfectly good tummy. After this war, everything I eat will have to cooked "just so" or I'll be in the tin, or at the tin.

Not a bad tea. Did I remember, yet, to tell you I love you? I do, you know. 's a fact! Only "love" seems such an inadequate word, and even "adore" is only approaching 1% of how I feel. Love me? You'd better, or else! (Getting cave-mannish!) I don't think I'd have been a great lover in the stone ages; I was never much good at donging a girl on the skull and dragging her off by the hair. I wonder who I can practise* on? What? No offers? (*On reading this over I found I'd spelled the noun with an "s" and the verb with a "c" – awful crime!)

A letter from Ken arrived today, and he expects to go from Sandgate shortly. Great chap, Ken. Wish he was in with me.

I'm glad you and Margo are getting on so well, sweetheart; I think you two are well suited. It must be worrying there with the "Demons," and police buzzing around on the trail of Mrs. B's £8. Hope she finds the blighter who snaffled it.

I don't suppose it would hurt if you were to call on Bill and his family, but with those sorts of families, it is always a bit risky. You may arrive right slap bang in the middle of another quarrel, and family fights are good to be out of. Also, women who have a temporary break with their husbands are apt to wonder what the heck he's been doing while he's been boarding away from her, and lift eyebrows at a strange girl. I think it would be a good place to dodge going to. But I sound like Dorothy Dix. You know best what to do. If I were in your place I'd let him get settled down before accepting to pay him a visit, and then only go if Margo goes too. (Cripes! I am Dorothy Dix!) But you asked for it!

I think I'll drop Ken a reply tonight. He said to reply before the 17th, but he'll hardly get my reply before that date. His was dated 11th and only arrived today (16th) – although it may have been delayed by the weekend. Anyhow, if he's gone before my letter gets there it will be forwarded to his new address.

Have your Mother and the family been well, dear? I hope so, and that your Dad is doing all right. Please give my love to them, sweetheart. Tell Joan, if you see her that I had a letter from Eric and he is well.

The boys are arriving "home" from the fair, and I never missed much. The Parkes' people are the meanest conglomeration of money grabbers I've ever struck – absolutely no concessions are made for men in uniform – on the contrary, prices have gone up 50% since the Air Force Camp was constructed. Especially in the matter of rents – which have been increased 150%. This is especially hard on Airmen who are married and those whose wives board in the town. Yet that utter dill of a Menzies* says "There'll be no war profiteering!" The Parkes Petty Profiteers give him the lie. *[Sir Robert Gordon Menzies (20 December 1894 – 15 May 1978) was the 12th and longest-serving Prime Minister of Australia.] He was the founder of the Liberal Party of Australia.]

Do you know, darling, that all the time I've been here, I have never heard of one man's being "shouted" a drink at an hotel. They just go on putting your money in the till, and never offer you "one on the house." One of the heads here said today, when he heard that we had to pay full price to get into their show (even though we may be "5/6-a-day murderers" as one woman called us) he said we should boycott the town – and I wish the boys would get enough backbone to do so. The local theatre puts up the price on Air Force pay days, and still the fools go to see their darn shows. I know I may sound a bit mean, but I hate seeing these smug Shylocks dragging the money out of chap's pockets who are going away to fight for them – some of them perhaps to lose their lives. (How would I go as a politician? Hot stuff, eh? But I really do get hot around the collar. Even the size of the glasses have been reduced since we came here, and you know how that would hurt me. The miserly skinflints!)

Well, why the billyo, should I inflict political propaganda on you? Have you to share all my burdens? Must I run and weep on your shoulder every time I think something is on the nostrils, as Nev would say?

Give Margo, "the Corp", Butch, Mrs. B. and the rest, my regards, please darling, and all my love to yourself. How can one give oneself anything? Especially something one has already? And you have all my love, already, darling girl, I think you always have had it, even before we met, because you are everything I've ever dreamed about, everything I've ever wanted.

I adore you, dear,

    Ed. Xxxxx

P.S. Love me? Please do, and please pray for us, darling; your prayers have proved pretty hot stuff, so far as I am concerned, and with you praying for me nothing can touch me. Ed.

P.S. I hope you haven't been bored by having to wade through all these pages. Most of them, except the ones where I told you I love you, utter drivel. But when I'm writing you I seem to be closer to you, and I hate stopping to break the spell. I've just been looking at your photograph, darling, and wondering how anyone so lovely can love a dolt like me. But keep it up.

I love you dear,

    Ed xxxxx

Flt. 11A. No. 2. W.A.G.S., R.A.A.F., Parkes.

June 19, 1941

My Darling,

There are some days when right from the time I wake, I feel down in the dumps. When everything seems to go wrong, and Morse an amazingly difficult subject to grasp; when my ears and my fingers seem unable to distinguish the slightest difference between a "dit" and a "dah," and I get well and truly fed up and want to chuck in the towel and remuster as an ordinary air-gunner or ground staff. But when a letter from you arrives on such a day, sweetheart, it's wonderful the change that takes place. The darn old war and wireless and what-have-you seem very unimportant things – which they are – and I kick off again to a new start.

Today was such a day, dear; right up to one o'clock I felt sick of the whole darn business. I don't know why, except that I began my duties this morning as an acting or temporary N.C.O. in charge of all our flight. I don't know whether I told you I'd landed this job. It came out in Daily Routine Orders the other day and was read out on Parade. I got a devil of a surprise. I don't know why they picked me, except I've been doing pretty well in the exams and they want to test my powers to command, etc. It was a pleasant surprise, anyhow, to know I was chosen out of so many. Another result of your prayers, I suppose. I can see your hand everywhere, sweetheart.

If this was the reason for my "blues" it was unfounded, because the day wasn't nearly as hard as I expected. The boys are a good lot, and, with very few exceptions, make the job easy.

Whatever the reason, dear, I was definitely out of sorts, until your letter was handed to me. It was great to get such a long letter from you. Gee! I love you, darling. I'd like to write "I love you" a thousand times, so much do I want to hold you in my arms again and tell you in a language much better than words.

We had a Procedure Test the other day and I topped the course with 96%. Old Knight, the instructor they brought out from the R.A.F. in England to teach us, thinks I'm the ants pants. So do I. – (Conceit has touched me with its sinister fingers – and why not? – I must be pretty good for you to love me.)

You're a lazy one, you are. Fancy lolling in bed until 9 a.m.! And there's no need to rub in that holiday business. Anyhow we had a ½ day off. – See! –

Rain and cold still constitute our major troubles. Speaking of the cold, it's nice of you to want to knit me a pair of gloves, darling. They would be more than handy. We have to send Morse with gloves on. Up in the plane we have sometimes to wear two or three pairs. It's awkward at first but you get used to it.

I wish I could have gone to Corpus Christi with you, dear. You're right. Sheila is a wonderful girl and Len's a lucky chap. Not half so lucky as I am, though. I know a much lovelier girl than Sheila, even.

Don't you go throwing off at these "awful Irish names" – "O'Flaherty" is a real good name. – Anyhow you'll be wearing one, someday not far off, so watch out!

I'm glad to hear that your tooth has ceased worrying you. I haven't heard from the dentist since before I went on leave. Touch wood! You mention that you had a "bit of a headache" on Monday, darling. The old eyes aren't troubling you, are they? When I'm so far away I imagine all kinds of silly things, and even such things as your having a headache worry me.

It's good to hear that your dad is O.K. I've forgotten what it means to be too hot to sleep. At the moment my feet are like two lumps of ice. I have to wriggle my toes now and then to feel if they're still there.

At last the dreaded secret is out! So you captured my heart by dyeing your hair! What were you when your ex-school-mate knew you, sweetheart? A Blonde? A week end at Scarborough seems a good idea. Not a bad place, that, but it's a bit cold for the seaside just now, as far as swimming would be concerned; wouldn't it be a nice quiet week-end, though? – away from the madding crowd at B's. – Why the dickens did I have to mention "swimming?" A cold shiver is still playing up and down my spine, and I can't stop my teeth from chattering, drat 'em.

Yes, Jack Leahy might be the type that thinks a Corporal's stripes are a Field Marshall's Baton. But I always found him quite a decent fellow, a bit soured, I think, by his failure as a potential Priest.

I'm sorry to hear of Laurie's going to Melbourne. I may not see him again for some time, and I was looking forward to seeing him while I was on pre-em in Brisbane. You'll miss him a lot, I suppose. I don't regret the "day-out" we had that Monday so much, now. Give him my regards, please, dear.

I wish I were in Brisbane when Al is down. Tell her she and I will be two N.S.W.-ites for a time and wish her a good holiday for me.

Night-flying has absolutely no attraction for me, sweetheart. I think the only place for a man these days is in bed. But they seem to think here that we need practice for future raids on Berlin, which will necessarily be at night. I hope it's warmer over there. If it's not, I suppose old Jerry will make it hot for us.

If you hate aeroplanes, I loathe them. Nasty noisy things. But there's no need to worry about me, dearest. They build them very strong and safe now-a-days – and we have the best of pilots and mechanics. Not to mention Wireless Operators. But keep on praying for me, dearest. And do worry a little (even though there is no need) because, while you do, I know you love me. And your loving me is the most wonderful thing in the world.

Please give my love to your family, darling girl, and my regards to all at B's. I adore you, dearest.

Ed. XXXXX

P.S. Love me? - Ed. xxxxx

P.S.S. I just had a look at your photo and I think you're the loveliest girl in the world. Ed. xxxxx I miss you so, dearest.

June 21, 1941

My Darling,

Another week gone and it has slipped by like a flash. I can hardly believe that seven days have vanished and will never come again, since I was waiting impatiently to hear your dear voice (the loveliest in the world). I don't know why last week should have flown so quickly, unless the half-holiday on Monday or my new responsibility has contributed. Anyhow I hope the rest of the time here (8 weeks) goes as fast. It will mean that I'll be with you again all the sooner – and no time can go quick enough for that.

My temporary command is progressing pretty well. I've had no trouble as yet, and have made no mistakes. This morning, at out Monthly Church Parade I had charge of a couple of hundred men, and flatter myself that I did a real good job. I hope so, anyhow. The boys make it easy. They're so well trained that I think that even if I did make a mistake in giving an order, they'd do the right thing instinctively.

I took the Flight on a Route march yesterday morning, and Friday morning. On the way back yesterday I ran into our band, out practising, and tacked them on the head of our Flight. We marched back to and through the camp. It's rather good fun being the "boss" – when you've got a Flight like ours to drill.

There has been some talk here that we are going to Pt. Pirie in South Australia for our Bombing and Gunnery (notice we'll be B.A.G.S. instead of W.A.G.S.) practice instead of to Evans Head. I hope not, for I had hopes of managing a week-end in Brisbane from Evans Head.

I love you so much, Darling. As you say, it will be Hell when I can't even ring you. But I will be able to cable you, which will be some consolation (though a poor one) and I know I'll always be safe, while you are praying for me and loving me.

I hope you have been keeping well, dear, and not had any of those old headaches; I think, when I look back, what a fool I was to get annoyed, because you were a bit out of sorts. I was a darn idiot, wasn't I?

A letter arrived from Dad, yesterday, and he tells me that all the family, except Mat, who is "confined to bed (not C.B.) with tonsillitis," are well, and Peg and Alan and their son and heir are the same. Dad says it's a bit like the old days, having Mat there. They go to the League matches on Sunday afternoons and play cards at night.

I'll be sending you that thing I mentioned in my last letter, next week. I hope you like it.

One of our chaps, who went on leave with me has just returned to camp. He broke his leg while he was on leave, and has been on his back ever since.

If I could have seen you for a month, it would have been worth breaking a little thing like a leg.

We have a second Morse Procedure Exam in the morning, and about Thursday is our Final Radio Practical (oral) exam. So please pray for me, darling. I'd hate to fail, after coming so far. Though, if I did, I wouldn't mind so much. It would mean I'd see you again, and that would be heaven. I've just ironed a shirt, and am on my way to feed the inner man, right now. I'll tell you what dinner was like when I return. Gee! I love you dearest.

Not a bad feed. Plenty of Fruit Salad though the meat came off a very ancient Bullock, I fear.

The weather has fined up again. Before dinner it had been very overcast, but now the sun is shining very brightly again. It's funny how it changes hourly. Yesterday was one of the coldest days we've had. Jack and I went to the local show last night and saw "So Ends our Night" and "The Wild Man from Borneo." I liked the first very much; Margaret Sullivan has always been my favourite. Did you see it?

It's lovely to read that you refused to go out with "Twiddles" pal. If he's anything like Twiddles, I wouldn't like any girl (especially my Darling) to be seen with him. However, if he's a nice chap, it's a pity that you didn't sweetheart. I like always to know that you are enjoying yourself, and are happy. I'll never be jealous, in that stupid way I used to be, again. You see, dear, then I did not know you loved me, as you do, and it was fear of losing you, more than jealousy that made me do the stupid things I did. Now that I know you are mine (you are, darling, aren't you?), I feel only envy of the chap who is lucky enough to be able to take you out. And how I envy such a person! Just to be near you, to see you, and to talk to you, I'd give all I ever owned, or ever wanted! – and still count myself rich. I love you, dearest.

Please give my love to your mother, and Alice and the kids, sweetheart, and please pray for me, and think of me, when you can – because I need your prayers, and your thoughts, and you.

Ed xxxxxx

P.S. Love me? Ed x

June 24, 1941

My Darling,

We had our Final Morse Receiving Test today, the whole course in a body. I passed the two 18wpm and the two 20w.p.m. tests easily, and, when the 22 w.p.m. test came on, the one I'd be waiting for – I saw the others around me writing busily, while my phones were absolutely dead. I was in a devil of a mess, wondering what was happening, when I saw that some big useless looking galoot sitting next to me was resting his elbow on the plug connecting my headphones to the set. I gave him a heck of a shove, and Lo! Presto!, everything was right again, except that I'd missed the first five words. I could have killed that dill at that moment! It's not often I really do my block, but when the test was finished I told him all·about himself and his antecedents, beginning from a baboon. To do him justice, however, he explained to the examiner, and, as I had no mistakes in the rest of the message, he gave me a pass. What made me so annoyed was the fact that this dill had touched the plug five minutes before, during the 18 w.p.m. test, but I had been lucky enough to guess the letter, and had told him off then! Pray that I may be forgiven sweetheart, for my burst of ire, but I think it was justified. The results of today's test go into Air Board – and it would have been rotten to have gotten as far ahead of the rest of the class as I have, to have failed on this one exam.

I was very worried, today. The chief Instructor came around and asked a chap named Armour and myself (saying we were the best senders in the class, which is a lie) to work till 9 o'clock tonight, sending to the backward fellows. Tuesday nights I always write to you and I didn't want you to miss your letter. It's wonderful to know you look forward so much to my letters, darling. I'm glad your dad is so interested in us. I must write him a letter over the weekend.

I haven't got the results yet of the Procedure Exam we had yesterday. They asked us a lot of questions about things we've never heard of. If they take that into consideration I may get a pass. On looking back at the last paragraph, I see I forgot to finish it. The instructor came around later and told Bob and I we wouldn't be needed after all. That's how I come to be writing tonight. I want to go up to the Prac. Room to do a bit of work, too, and the darn Morse sending would have interfered with this.

There will be a new batch of chaps here tomorrow, some of them from Sandgate. I wonder if I'll know any of them? I can hardly realise sometimes that it is four months since I first put foot in this dump. Sometimes, when I think of how long we have been separated, it seems four years, and at times, when I think of how much I've done here, it seems four days.

This letter will arrive on Saturday darling – which means that when you get this, I will be thinking "Tomorrow night I'll be able to talk to Molly", and will already be in a mild fever of anticipation. I love you so much, dear, and this darn business of having only your voice to look forward to, once a week, is a distinct pain in the neck, to put it mildly. When I look back at the times we were together, I nearly go mad with the longing to have them over again. I will, some day, though, won't I, darling? And they will be even better than before – if that is possible.

Forgive me for such a short note, dear, but I must go and do some work, in preparation for the big Exam on Thursday. Please pray for me; you've no idea how much I need your prayers, and your love. You are all my world, and most of my heaven. I love you, dear.

Ed. Xxxxx

P.S. Love me, darling?

Ed x

June 28, 1941

Darling Molly,

I have been revolving in my mind the question whether I'd go out or not, and have made the tremendous decision to remain in over the whole week-end. I'm too lazy to resurrect the energy to get dressed. So, just now, at 20 to 2 on Saturday afternoon, I'm sitting in the sun, the only place you can find warmth, thinking of you. Like Cyril Foster – "Dreaming, Oh! My Darling Love of thee! Dreamin' of thee!" It's a very pleasant form of relaxation, I can tell you. Especially when one has someone as lovely as you to dream about.

I have good news to impart, darling. Once again your prayers have proved their efficacy. I've turned the last stage of this darned course. Yesterday I passed the Final Radio Practical (Oral) Exam. No more exams about Radio now. The only tests that we have to pass are in connection with Morse Code and procedure, and studying for them is going to be a headache. We have to do about 3–4 weeks of this, then we do nothing else but fly day and night, and practise like billy-o. We only work 7 hours a day, now, because they say any more than that is liable to send a person off his head. We have the head phones on all day now, and the continuous buzz does get on one's nerves.

I don't know whether I'll stay out here in the sun, it's glare is a bit strong, but I'm lovely and warm. At least I'm warm; there are varied opinions re the "lovely."

Did I tell you I passed a second Procedure Exam the other day, and still retain my position as the apple of the C.O.'s eye? My temporary job has ended now, and I've been reduced to the ranks again. I've been told I made a very good job of it, which is very surprising.

I wish I were really as good as you say I am, Sweetheart; I might approach being worthy of you, then – if anyone can ever reach that standard. Gee! I love you, darling. It's grand, just knowing you, and loving you, but to know that through some inexplicable kindness of God's that you love me, is Heaven. Keep on loving me, Dear, no matter what happens – not that anything is likely to happen, or possible, but to know you love me is the same thing as happiness to me.

I haven't been out of Camp since last Saturday, which is strange. And this has resulted in my having to rack my already Morse crazed brains for news.

The most exciting thing that's happened lately was a concert last night, at which I enjoyed myself immensely. It wasn't so good as the other one I told you about, but it was very good. The last one was perfection.

A game of pitch-penny* is progressing just behind me, and I'm tempted sorely to join in. Darn it, I will. *[A pub game involving pennies thrown into a 2- to 4-inch hole]

I've learned my lesson, darling. Never again will I forsake you for the lure of gambling. I lost 6d, – (one pot). To impose a penance on myself for my lapse I allowed myself to be talked by Mac (remember the chap whose father died?) into going up to one of the outstations and belting Morse at him at about 24 w.p.m., because his receiving is bad. If he can take my sending, he can take anything. Mine is atrocious. I've been getting worse and worse each day. Mac has had a case of oranges sent him from Broken Hill and we've been eating them till we look like oranges. They're beauties. I suppose I'll wonder why I don't like my tea tonight.

I have to struggle out of bed in the morning at 6 o'clock to catch the tender into Parkes, because our Padre is away at Narromine this weekend. This means my resolution to stay in for the week-end is gone already, but I intend coming home from mass straight away in the tender. I have a heck of a lot of mail to catch up with, including one from Alan. Al has now been made a sergeant, and has, so he says, his beer drinking licence. The son and heir is very good (aren't they all?) he advises, and gives no trouble. Our family have practically adopted him.

I forgot to thank you for the Holy Picture Sweetheart. I'll keep it in my top pocket next to your Rosary Beads, always. Gee! I love you. You seem to think of me all the time.

Tomorrow is the best day of the week. I can talk to you tomorrow night. And it's wonderful even to be able to talk to you from such a distance.

I hope for Pearle's sake that it will be longer than 3 months before Bob goes away. Give her my love, if you see her before she leaves Brisbane, dearest.

It's pleasing to see you practising your wifely duties (mending my shirts). I pity the poor blighters that get them though. If I wore them, they won't be too good, even though you achieve a miracle with the needle.

Don't forget to give my regards to Nev, Laurie and the rest and my <u>love</u> to Margo. (Jealous?)

I hope you enjoyed the pictures. Of course I'm better than Ray Milland. Fancy old Scotchie being made a Serge. I bet that he trains the boys in gambling. I haven't heard from any of the boys, including Len, since I came back here. I wonder how he likes camp life? I can't imagine Len in uniform. I'm glad to hear that Laurie's not going South, now, tho' he may not be. I hope he's still in Brisbane when I get there.

Tell Margo I'll look forward to getting a note from her. Tell her she's got a job of spying on you for me. (You see, I don't trust you.) And it's worth a quid a report; if it's a real bad report, I may raise the ante to £2. I think my cash will be safe – (Do you darling?)

Well, tea is on, so I'm off. I'm hungry despite the oranges. I'm always hungry here.

Please pray for me, when you can, Darling, and keep loving me always, no matter where I go, or how far away I am; – I'll always love you, you know that.

Ed. xxxxxx

P.S. Love me?

Ed xxxxxx

P.S.S. I'm working on a Sonnet, just now, that looks too heavy to ever be any good.

Ed X

June 30, 1941

My Darling,

It's funny how the time slips by. It's now exactly halfway through this old year, and I seem to have crowded more into these six months than I've ever done before. First and foremost the loveliest girl in the world has fallen in love with me. That's enough to overshadow all the other things that have happened, despite the fact that they include joining the R.A.A.F., leaving work, living in Brisbane, Ipswich and Parkes, etc. – I wonder what the next six months will bring?

It's a curse having to ring you up in the surroundings I have to ring you from; every Sunday there's always a dozen nincompoops hanging around the 'phone box, and listening with ears cocked to everything I have to say. It's an open box – the 'phone being hung on the wall without any protection except half a partition and I can't say half the things I'd like to tell you. However, it's enough to only hear your voice. I suppose you suffer from the same lack of privacy at B's. A 'phone call there was always as good as a Broadcast. Your letter arrived today, dear. I wish I were worthy of your love. It makes me wonderfully happy to know that you love me so much, Sweetheart. I wish I were going up to Yandina with you for the week-end. I've never had a better week-end than the one we spent last year. Don't forget to give my love to your Mother and the kids and all the friends I met up there. I wonder if we'll be able to manage a week-end up there before I go away? It will all depend on the leave I get.

I did a stupid thing on Saturday night. In the last letter I wrote you, I told you I intended to stay in camp over the week-end except for a trip in and out to Church in the morning. When I'd finished the letter, I decided to make a dash into town to post it, so you'd get it two days earlier. I walked into our Post Office to put the RAAF Stamp on the envelope, stamped it, then, like a goat, dropped the letter into the box. If I hadn't been so well brought up I'd have sworn. (I wasn't well brought up.) As I was dressed, I decided to go into town, and after wandering around with Mac for a few hours, came "home" to bed, to sleep the sleep of the just.

Another game of pitch-penny is in progress at the moment, but once bitten twice shy. I was never cut out to be a penny-pitcher – I have no natural aptitude for the game. It's funny that we boys never tried it on our Friday nights. When this rotten war is over I'll introduce it into the night's entertainment. I wonder if the old days will ever come back again? I hope they will, although we chaps will probably take turn about in bringing our wives along to each of the houses, with Mat and Les the bachelor uncles, in the new days. It will be a good place to live in, Brisbane, when we've cleaned up Adolph.

This afternoon we began a series of strenuous Physical Training periods, to knock us into shape for our flying in three weeks time. We have to be in the best nick for that.

Like you, I have a rotten cold in the head and chest at the moment. With the weather so cold, it's almost impossible to shake it off, darn it. I hope yours is O.K. again, darling. The week-end at Yandina should put the kibosh on it, anyhow.

From your letter it appears as though Burstows is getting madder every month. Twiddles and his ilk would give me the willies to have to live with them. Who are the girls you appear to be so disgusted with? They don't sound as if they are much good, from the way you write. They should be a good match for Twiddles.

Why didn't you go to the Ball at Windsor, Dear? You'd have enjoyed yourself once you got there. I wish I could have been there to take you.

Don't hurry home on Sunday night, darling. I have been talked into visiting some place or other in Parkes – relations of one of the boys. We're having tea there and I don't suppose I'll be able to get home too early, without appearing rude, so I'll ring you on Monday night, instead. I know I'll be a wet blanket at the Smiles; I'll be thinking round nine-thirty "I should be ringing Molly now," and I'll feel rotten.

I have to hop into a bit of work now, darling, so I'll say "goodnight." I love you so much, dear; please keep loving me, and remembering us in your prayers,

Ed. xxxxx

P.S. Love me?

Ed x

I adore you. Ed.

July 3, 1941

My Darling,

If this letter is very short and I seem strange, please forgive me, because I'm trying to write this half-propped up in bed. I've got the 'flu, and how! I wish my nurse of other days was here to sit by my bed and hold my hand, like she did when I was staying at Burstows. Gee! I miss you, darling! It's so darn lonely being crook in camp, although half the boys are showing signs of an attack, too. So far I've refused to miss any lectures, despite the M.O.'s advice. I've come too far now, to have to waste another month here, because I miss a few days. I'm sick of the place already, without wanting to spend any more time here.

They've been feeding me quinine and aspirin every other hour of the day, so, what with them, and the 'flu, and a headache, and Morse Code, you can imagine what sort of a crotchety individual I am.

Just as well your letter (with the enclosure from Margo) arrived today. It cheered me up considerably and now I only feel like a piece of death warmed up. That's enough whinging from me. I'll be talking myself into Pneumonia soon. But Lord! am I sorry for myself. Poor little innocent me!

By the time you are reading this, darling, I'll be waiting anxiously for our 'phone call. I hope you'll have had a great weekend up home, that your Mother and the youngsters are well, and you wish I were with you. I'd rather like to be near you all the time, but especially would I like to visit your Mother with you again.

Morse is becoming increasingly monotonous, especially with the 'flu (there I go again!). I wish I'd been able to go to the dance with you, but there'll be plenty of other dances. Wait till I'm in Brisbane! Will we paint the town red! If Alice and her new boy-friend think they're going to do any painting they'll find they're only amateurs.

I got a letter from Eric today, with some snaps of Palestine and Greece. He tells me Joan owes him a letter, so, if you see that erring one, tell her of it, and also remind her that she owes me one.

Please give my love to all the family, and Margo, and please keep loving me as much as I love you. I'm sorry darling, that I'm not in a more cheerful frame of mind and able to write you a longer and better letter, but I'll try to make it up to you tonight!

I adore you,

Ed XXXXX   *P.S. Love me? Ed x*

July 6, 1941

My Darling,

I've been on my already overworked back all day trying to chuck off this darned dog's disease (or whatever it is) I've got. I've chucked off the 'flu but my throat feels as if some glug had had a go at dragging out my tonsils with a rusty nail-file. My voice is providing amusement for everyone in the hut except me, and even I laugh at it sometimes. It sounds like huge rocks being churned in a concrete mixer. Talk about "Gravel Throat."

Maybe it's just as well I'm ringing you tomorrow night instead of tonight. It's funny; I could be ringing you as usual tonight. The party is (thank the Lord) definitely off. I hope you're having a good time now at home. Oh! Darling! I wish I were with you! I know you wish the same thing, and that makes me feel like doing all sorts of mad things to make our wish come true. I don't know whether you think I'm mad or not, sweetheart, but sometimes at night, when I can't go to sleep for a while, I imagine myself doing all sorts of impossible deeds – pinching Fairy Battles* or Wirraways – and dashing up to Brisbane. It's going to make tomorrow much brighter, anyhow, to know I'll be talking to you that night. *[The Fairey Battle was a British single-engine light bomber built by the Fairey Aviation Company in the late 1930s for the Royal Air Force.]*

Fairey Battle

Being sick of this darn place I wandered into town yesterday afternoon, and, wonder of wonders, remembered to look up Dick's uncle. I was very glad I did. He's a very decent chap and we had quite a long yarn. He knocked off work and shut up shop for half an hour to sink a glass with me - and has invited me to a game of bowls (!) some Sunday morning. He said something about Dick's father or uncle celebrating their Golden Wedding soon and he may be going up for it.

How is the switch board getting on? Do you still like the job as much as ever? By the way, the ancient prophets had a lot to say about you girls. Take, for instance Daniel, who, in between spells of lion-taming, is said to have quoth: "Blessed is the Telly Op, and sweeter than the rose her nature: a thousand times she saith "hello", but never one "O hell" and lo! Wonderful are her works! Add ye together two and two, and subtract ye three and three, yet never will ye get the number thou first thought of" – and other sayings of that ilk.

Jack has been trying to entice me into town tonight, but hasn't even Buckley's chance of getting me out of this bed. It was enough effort to get up for Mass, dinner and tea. Besides, my bark is too bad to risk the rain and chill that seem to fill the outside world. Gee! It's cold! I'm going over for a hot shower shortly if I can pluck up the necessary energy. I think I'd better, otherwise I may become a victim to "B.O." and offend.

Give my love to Margo and tell her to make her next letter much longer; her first report wasn't worth anything. She'll have to do better or I'll be giving her the sack.

Well! The hut's deserted. All the boys, except Jack, Mac (of the crippled leg) and the bloke what adores you have gone in to the bright lights and glittering sin of Parkes. I, true to my love, remain thinking of you, and gazing into the eyes of your photograph, which is propped on my knees. I love you, my darling. God was wonderfully good to me, when He arranged that we should meet, Sweetheart. He had no need to arrange that I should fall in love with you, that was only natural, but He certainly turned on a wonderful miracle when He made you love me. I hope it was a lasting miracle, my darling. (It was, wasn't it?)

We heard a rumour on Friday that we may be getting ten day's leave between here and Evan's Head. If it's true (and it will be wonderful if it is) you know where I'm making for as soon as I can get there. Fancy seeing you, and being able to hold you tight in my arms and kiss you again! and in six weeks time – only 126 meals.

Well, I must go and have that dip. Imagine me, in a few minutes, under the steaming water, trying to sing in a voice like Pop-eye, only worse. Please give my love to your Mother and Alice and the others, and my regards to all the crowd. Please keep loving me, Darling, and praying for me, because I love you more than I have ever loved anyone, or anything.

Ed xxxxx

P.S. love me?

Ed X

P.P.S. I've just been looking hard at your photo again, – you're the loveliest girl in the world – No wonder I'm so much in love with you.

Ed x

July 9, 1941

My Darling,

It was even better than usual to hear your voice last night. I think it must have been because there were not so many eavesdroppers around the box as there usually are of a Sunday night, and I was able to ask you a question I love to hear you answer. You have no idea what a thrill it gives me to hear you say "Yes" or "Of course". I remember the thousands of times in the old days, when the reply was always "I'm not sure" and I used to worry like nothing on earth.

I couldn't make out what was the matter when the idiotic switch crowd tried to tell me that your number wouldn't answer. For a while I was afraid that the phone was disconnected or that one of the dills you have to live with was having a half-hour's yarn. Remember the trouble we used to have before, and Mrs. B. had the five minutes' notice put up? I was certainly in a fix. The call was booked for 9.15, and, by the time we got through it must have been after ten. When they advised me for the fourth time that the number wouldn't answer, I got a bit hot under the collar, because I knew you would be waiting there, and wondering what had happened to me, so I asked them if they were ringing the right number – B3154, and it was remarkable how quickly I got through after that.

We have another Procedure Test tomorrow. We got the results of last week's today – I got 90%, so am still on top. I doubt whether I'll do so well in the next, as it is expected to be much harder. Don't forget the prayers, sweetheart.

I have been swiping a golf ball around all the afternoon. I seem to be hitting the pill more often and further than of yore. When I'm at Sandgate, I expect to be able to have a few games at Clontarf or on the Sandgate links.

I'm enclosing the "sonnet" you asked for, darling, but I wish I weren't; it's about the worst I've ever written, definitely not good enough for you. I think Morse has just about killed any poetry I may have had in me – (if any).

When I'd finished talking to you last night, darling, I felt very happy, because you seemed so glad to hear my voice, and, at the same time, I was terribly lonely. I wanted to be near you so darn much, yet I knew that you were over 1000 miles away. Gosh! That knowledge hurts, dear! Do you feel the same way, sweetheart?

I was glad you had a good time over the week-end, Molly. I suppose

104

everyone was glad to see you there. Lord, I wish I had been with you; it would have been a bit of heaven. I hope we can manage a week-end before I go overseas. It will be grand seeing your Mother and the youngsters again, especially now that I know you love me so much.

How doth the Margo kid? Tell her I refuse to be the sucker in your hatched up plan. As a detective (not a defective) she's sacked, and may consider herself thrust out in the cold cold snow.

My flu, on Monday morning, became a thing of the past. I feel better now than I've felt for years. There's a terrible lot of Conjunctivitis floating round the camp. So much that some of the flights have to disinfect headphones, and wash their hands in some solution, every hour. As we are separated from each other, our Flight have practically escaped the infection. I hope I miss out, anyhow. It's a rotten complaint; you go nearly blind for a week and your eyes become terribly sore.

Rita (my youngest sister) started work in Townsville the other day and appears to be quite thrilled with her job. She's toiling at the E.S.C.A.

I often wonder how Nev and Mrs. B. and Kelly and Laurie and Butch are getting on. Don't forget to give them my regards, will you, darling.

Study calls, and what genius am I that I can disobey. I'd better do a bit. I adore you darling. Lord! I love you. Please keep on loving me, and praying for me and for us.

Ed. xxxxx

PS: Love me?

Ed x

July 10, 1941

My Darling,

Outside the rain is pouring down, (sounds like a song) and the Station is a sea of mud and half-frozen puddles. And it's cold! Lord it's cold. I have got over my flu, thank heavens, or I'd be writing my will instead of this letter. Inside it's not much warmer than outside, so, very shortly, nothing will be seen of your handsome (?) boyfriend except the tip of his Schnoz poking above the blankets.

I've just been up in the Receiver Room taking the Morse from America. It's sent at about 28 w.p.m. and, as I didn't miss a letter, you can see both the improvement I've shown over the last two weeks in "outstations" and the quality of the sender's Morse. There wasn't much of interest. It was all about Japan's economic situation, and left me cold.

I'm sitting here on the hedge of my 'umble bed, and, at the moment I'm looking for the umpteenth time today, at the photograph you sent me. Gee! It's a good photo of you, darling. You may think the chap with the hat on is the best in the bunch, but I have eyes only for the young lady in the middle. (By the way, don't forget to give your dad my regards when you write him, sweetheart.)

It's a nice snap of Alice too, Darling – I suppose you're looking forward to having her with you. Please give her my love. Ask her where she pinched the bike.

I'm glad to hear that Dick approved of your choice, darling. It means a lot to be thought well of by the people you like. I was a bit afraid he mightn't, after the effort I put on that Monday. Do you love me, darling?

I hope Margo is again in the land of the strong and healthy. If she had a touch of the dog's disease I had, gee! I feel sorry for her. It gave me hades. And is your wrist O.K. again, dear?

It looks as if I'd better drop Ken another line – I suppose my letter is reposing on the rack at Sandgate. They used to have a terrible system re the Mail when Sandgate was at Amberley, and I suppose it's just as bad still. They had a system of racks with letters over them, and all the "G"s were supposed to be in the "G" rack, but they were either put in wrongly by the P.O. staff, or some careless blighter used to grab all the letters in the rack, look through them to see if any were for him, then put them back in the wrong place. There were some letters in "G" rack before I came to Sandgate addressed to people, and they were still there when I left. I suppose the addressees had been transferred to other

106

stations months before. It was a very loose system. Ours here is a good one. Each man is handed his letters personally.

I had a letter from Joan yesterday. She's well, and appears to be enjoying herself. She's a great kid.

The old P.O. must have lost that letter of mine, dear. If I'd forgotten to address it, it would have come back to me by now. Though it mightn't, because I never mention my surname in letters to you, do I? In the one to mother that came back, it was written on Y.M.C.A. paper and as it had a special heading with Name – Number – etc. on it, I'd filled in the spaces. I'll have to make it up to you, darling. I'll write you another "Sonnet" tomorrow.

I'd like to meet Betty and Ted again. – (Did I meet Ted?) – I'd like to run into Toni and Alan again, too. I've never heard of the chap you mention. He must be in one of the later courses. I must look up his girl friend when we're in Yandina, though. (Jealous?)

So Twiddles is in hospital. Even though I think he's one of the Glugs of Gosh, I hope he gets well quickly. Appendicitis is no joke.

I passed another Procedure Test yesterday – 88% this time. It was, as I expected, much harder than the last. The next will be harder still, so please keep praying for me, dearest. Thanks for saying the Rosary for me on Monday night, sweetheart. Gee! I love you.

Bed is calling, like the girl across the "sands of Dee." I'll say a Rosary for you, too darling – though lazy me will take a week to say a whole Rosary. One decade a night. I adore you, darling. You are all my world. Please keep loving me.

Ed. xxxxxx

PS. Love me? Ed x

P.S.S. Give my love to Margo. I mean the little bit left over from what you have. Ed x

July 13, 1941

My Darling,

It's about half past two on Sunday afternoon and I'm reclining outside my hut in the brilliant sunshine, watching the Ansons taking off and landing – too darned lazy to look at my watch to make sure if it is half past two or not. Anyhow, who cares about time lolling in the sun, in a place like this, when the only recognisable day is a Sunday, because it's the only day we don't work. When we start our flying, even that differentiation will disappear, for then we'll be flat out every day and nearly every night.

The boys are sitting around, chewing peanuts and chocolates, and reading Ginger Meggs* and Speed Gordon*. Poor old Pop Meggs and Speed and his latest girl-friend appear to be in a spot of bother today. *[Ginger Meggs is the longest-running Australian comic strip about the mischievous escapades of a red-haired, pre-teen boy. In Australia, the character Flash Gordon, of science fiction comic-book fame, was re-titled Speed Gordon to avoid the negative connotation of the word *flash* for which the predominant meaning implied dishonesty.]

You have no idea how cold it was this morning, Sweetheart. The frost was an inch thick on the ground. It looked as though snow had fallen. A pair of overalls that I'd left on the line overnight were frozen solid – so much so that they stood up on their own. One of the boys took a photograph of them, and when I tried to turn on a drinking fountain outside our hut, all that came out was a chunk of ice. It's funny trying to butter bread these days, and you have to eat your meals as fast as you can – even then they are cold before you've half finished.

I hope our dentist doesn't have another go at me before I leave here. Poor old Tom Holland in my hut had six stitches inserted in his gum after a session on Friday.

As a beer drinking party on Friday night, the Ball here was a great success. I decided at the last moment not to go, and went into town instead. However, when I got back to camp about 11, I was talked into going by Arthur Smiles. As I was able to get in "on the nod," I gave in, and regretted my impulse as soon as I got in, because, the mud brought in by a thousand pairs of feet had been ground into dust which floated like one of our pea soups (either fog or cook-house) and I'm still coughing it up. As soon as I got in the door, Les Main asked me to take one of his girlfriends into supper. She had only opened her mouth once when I found I had something on my hands that I detest, a girl 99% under the weather. I had a dance with her praying all the while that she wouldn't pass out altogether, saved her from breaking her darned neck

108

at every turn, dumped her in a corner, then spent the rest of the night dodging her.

It's funny how careful a Catholic has to be, living among a crowd of mixed religions. One of the chaps just remarked that I must be a Saint, getting up for Mass this morning and, before I had time to answer, Bill Isles, a very decent chap, whose bed is next to mine, asked "Don't you ever eat meat on Friday, Ed?", and, when I answered "No," he said, "I was watching you on Friday morning, and saw you pick up a plate of bacon and eggs. I watched, out of curiosity, to see if you'd eat the bacon, but you gave it away to Mac." A bad Catholic (I mean one worse than I am) can do a heck of a lot of harm in a place like this. One thing about the R.A.A.F., I've never heard a word of bigotry uttered since I joined up. On the contrary, everyone is very respectful of another's beliefs. This bears out my old contention that a bigot is the lowest form of animal life. I don't think one of that ilk has the (forgive me, darling) "guts" to fight for his country. Yet you'll find them the best flag-flappers in the world.

I have just been up to the phone to book our call, darling. That's always a thrill for me. Wally John's sister is generally on, on a Sunday, and I only have to say "I want to book a call" when she recognises my voice and says "O.K. Ed, at nine thirty?" and I don't have to say any more. It wasn't she who mucked things up (although I don't think it was anyone's fault but the Brisbane end) last Monday.

I suppose you remember my writing before about Wally. I used to visit his people's place a lot, but he left the station over six weeks ago, now, to become a ground operator. He failed in some of the Radio Theory Exams, so they "scrubbed" him as a W.A.G. He's at Richmond, now.

I can hardly believe that I will only be ringing you five more times from this dump. I wonder how many times we have talked to each other from so far apart? It must be about eighteen to twenty times, which makes five seem small. I hope it is small in time.

There are now only 49 left in our course out of the original 82. All the other have failed in exams or shown no promise at Morse or something. Some have gone as Air gunners, some are studying to be ground operators, like Wally, and the rest have been put back a month into 12 course. I wonder when they'll wake up to me.

Gee this sun is great! I wish night would never fall, but it will.

I hope these last few weeks pass quickly. I'm getting fed up to the back teeth here. I sometimes feel the need of you and your loveliness so darn badly that I want to yell aloud. It's horrible to be so much in love and yet be denied even the sight of you, darling, and even the consoling knowledge that you love me, and want me, only partly makes up for this longing to be near you.

Do you like the photo dear? It looks like anyone on earth but me, but there is only one photographer in this one-horse town and you have to be satisfied with what you get from him. I sent Mother a large sized one, but I bet she thinks it's a photo of Pongo the ape or Wallace Beery and wonders why I sent it to her. She'll probably imagine Morse has addled my brain.

Well, I'd better write Mother a letter now, Sweetheart; please give my love to the family, and Margo and the crowd at B's.

I adore you, darling. If there's no one about tonight, I'll tell you so; I wish I could hold you close and tell you,

Ed xxxxxx

PS Love me? Ed x

July 14, 1941

Dearest Darling,

I must have second sight. Remember my telling you about Tom Holland and his tooth? Well great was my anguish when a small piece of paper was thrust into my hand this morning with instructions to report to the torture chamber at 2 p.m. Slowly my dragging feet bore me thither at the appointed hour, and many were the curses I mumbled re the R.A.A.F., teeth and dentists. There is one aspect about our dentist that appeals, he doesn't keep you waiting, and there are no year-old magazines to bore you (why must I think of such unfortunate similes) to distraction (not extraction!)

My shaking body collapsed into the chair, with its horribly suggestive drill, and the various instruments on the tray. "Open wide," quoth he, and I opened. With an awful chuckle of fiendish glee, he found a tooth that I should have had yanked out months ago. "This one'll have to come out," said he cheerfully. "Must it?" asked I, much less cheerfully. "I've had it such a long time, sir. I've become quite attached to it and it to me."

He jabbed a needle in my mouth in four or five places, and, an hour later, a shaken ghost of the chap you love, fluttered out to the sunlight. I'll say it was attached to me! – He pulled and tugged and twisted, and I lay, bravely, not even uttering a groan. (As a matter of fact I was so full of cocaine that I didn't feel a thing.)

To keep my mind off the jabbing and the tugging etcetera, I tried to compose a sonnet for you. You'll find it on the last page of this epistle. I bet that not many Sonnets have been composed in a torture chamber, so this one should be unique. I hope you like it, sweetheart; I know it's not much good, but – under the circumstances you'll forgive it's weakness.

To further cheer me up, your letter arrived today, darling. Thanks for sticking up for the members of the Air Crew. Frankly, between you and me, I'm rather glad we wear them. This may make us (or me) a bit of a snob as that glug suggested , but I fail to see what some of these young chaps join up the R.A.A.F as clerks or cooks or mess stewards for. Sort of "B" company of the R.A.A.F. Be here to see you off, and Be here to see you come back (if ever). Those jobs could be filled just as well as they are by older men. I'm not referring, of course, to Mechanics or Fitters or such like. I know I'd never have joined up except as Air Crew or a Fitter, unless I were incapable of doing those jobs, in which case I'd have been much more use to the country in my old job at the G.P.O. I know I'd feel kind of ashamed to be as young as I am, and as healthy, pounding a typewriter, or tallying stores, and wearing the uniform of, and basking in the glory won overseas by the men who do the real work in connection with the duties of fighting in, or looking after planes. (Don't I talk a lot of baloney?)

You'll have to forgive the wandering nature of this letter, darling, but my jaw is starting to give me heck. The cocaine has worn off, and you know what these things are like. I enjoyed our talk on Sunday night, but you know how much I love them, don't you?

I'm very sorry about not being there for Exhibition* darling, but we don't finish here till about the 20th August. When I say "we" finish I mean, if I pass this final Examination, and, by the looks of things, that seems touch and go. Our final Procedure Exam comes off on Monday, so say a prayer for me please, dear. *[The Exhibition (or *Ekka*) is an annual Brisbane event. The first show, held in August 1876, was to display agricultural and industrial exhibits.]

How is Al enjoying her stay? Give her my love, please, darling. I wish I were there so I could take you both out. Tell Margo I'm terribly cut up to hear I have a rival. I thought I was her one true love.

We must pay Alf a visit when I come up. I saw his home once, and as Nev said, it is a lovely place. If you remember Toni's birthday in time, darling, wish her "Many Happy Returns" for me, and tell her to give Alan my regards.

This mouth of mine is becoming worse every minute. I wanted to do some study tonight, because we are having a test tomorrow, but what I'll do tonight will be harmless.

Please give my love to your Mother and the rest of the family, and please keep praying for us, darling; I know we will find that everything will come out right in the end (it must, when two people love as much as we do) but a few prayers are always a help.

I love you darling, more than all the world..

Ed xxx

P.S. Love me?

Ed x

To Molly — 14.7.41

I will remember you, though mad intrigues

Of greed-crazed nations set between us leagues

Of empty distances, – and endless years

Of dreary loneliness: – for those shy tears,

You shed to see me go, will be as dew

On dying grass, within the thirsty hell

That sears my soul; – your voice has set a spell,

To fill my drowsy nights with dreams of you.

– Remember you! Could I forget, a while,

The soft touch of your hand, – the tender smile

That trembled on your lips, and lingered there,

– Soft Sunlight on a rose, – your dear dark hair,

Like midnight flecked with stars: – All else I knew

May vanish with my dreams, – but, love,

I will remember you!

Ed

July 18, 1941

My Darling,

I had a bit of bad luck yesterday; we had our final sending test and I expected to be classed at at least 24 w.p.m. However, I got a fit of the nerves, and was lucky to get 20 w.p.m. It was a rotten ordeal, we had to send to the heads, and as we sent we could hear them talking behind us and discussing our merits and demerits. My hand was shaking like a leaf, and I had to grit my teeth and leave an unnaturally large gap in my key to stop sending "dits" I didn't intend. However we only had to do 18 a minute to pass, so I can't growl. It was a disappointment though.

On Monday, we have our final Procedure Exam, and our Final Receiving Test. I hope I don't get the jitters again. Say a prayer for me please, dear.

I was so fed up with myself last night that I couldn't write to you, so this letter will be a day late. I'll tell you on Sunday night, sweetheart, so that you won't be disappointed on Monday night.

It seems fairly certain that I'll be getting leave a month from today. It depends on the weather staying fine enough for us to get our quota of flying hours in. It looks as if it might be fine from now on.

I had a letter from Dad, yesterday, and was very cut up to hear they had to have my old dog, Ted, destroyed. He had the mange. There was a howling match at home when he was taken away. It's funny how we get attached to dogs, isn't it? It seems like losing one of the family.

I hope you liked the Sonnet I sent last letter, darling. At least they show you how much I'm thinking of you. I love you so much, darling, and need you terribly. It's good that this last month will be taken up mostly with flying. That will make the time pass much more quickly, and it can't pass too quickly for me.

How is Alice enjoying her holiday? I suppose she's looking for a job in Brisbane, these days. It would be great for you two if you were both there, but I bet your Mother would be cut up.

My tooth healed up in no time at all. I had hardly any pain, and no trouble with it. That's because I'm so tough. (Oh! Yeah!)

Perhaps, by the time you get this, my hopes may be dashed to the ground re my prospects as a W.A.G. I may have failed in these last two tests, on Monday, or perhaps I may be up about 6000 feet over Wagga or Orange or some place. Whatever it is, you know that my heart will be in only one place.

You must forgive the shortness of this letter, darling, but, for some reason or other, (I suppose these "outstations" are driving me mad) I can't think of anything to write at all.

I could write "I love you" a thousand times, but you'd soon get tired of that, and come down here with a rush, expecting to find me in the local "rat-house".

It was nice of Toni and Alan to ask after me. Please give them my best wishes, dear.

I wish I had a bit of Alice's luck. A few quid is always welcome, even to a plutocrat on 4/6 a day. That's all I get now, what with allotments for keeping up this and that. I won't know myself in a month's time when I become a Sergeant.

I was sorry to learn that Mick had joined the A.I.F. instead of the R.A.A.F. I may be lucky enough to see him while I'm on leave or pre-em. If you see him, give him my regards, please, dearest. He's a great guy, is Mick.

Too blooming right I won't do the wrong thing in a plane. I've been wondering if, should we ever have to use our parachutes (which I hope is never) and it fails to open, if the R.A.A.F. will issue us with another. They're pretty stingy about issues.

Well, I must do a bit of study, dear, or else.

Please think of me often, and keep loving me, like you do. It makes me feel so happy and proud, that nothing else seems to matter.

I love you darling, and I want you more than life.

Ed xxxxx

P.S. Love me?   Ed

-..- -..- *

---

* [Morse for XX]

July 20, 1941

My Darling,

I've just got back from Church Parade, and so am feeling very good, which, so you know, is a rare feeling with me. I've been having a good look at your photograph, and am wondering what you are doing, just at this minute. Thinking of me, I hope, and loving me just a little.

I never left the camp yesterday. In the afternoon I ironed the shirts etc., I washed on Friday night, (thank heavens, that's a job over) and then studied all the afternoon and night. I wish the next few days were over, darling; after then, there'll be no more study, or so I hope; but I've said that so many times, expecting the next part of a course to be easy, and been disappointed. I've got the wind up well and truly re this final receiving test. I'm liable to do all sorts of silly things in a final test, and, if I miss out, I'll have to do another darn month. Say some prayers for me, please, Sweetheart.

One of the boys took a snap of me in all my finery before church parade, and if it turns out O.K. I'll send it to you. It was very dull, though, and I'm afraid it' won't turn out too good.

It seems hard to believe, dear, that I have only a month to go, now, at this station. That is, providing they don't throw me out sooner, or put me back a month. If they do either of those things, they'll be pretty tough, considering the record I've had up to now – but they do things like that, here. Then again I may prove to be no good at all in the air. I need your prayers more than any time before now, sweetness. I don't know why I worry so much, because, if I am thrown out on my ear, I'll be back where I want to be, with you, but my silly old pride would be considerably bruised.

Dad suggested in his letter, that, when I come up on leave, I only tell him now, and then I can walk in and surprise Mother. She'll like that, I think. I can imagine her face, easily, and Mollie and Rita will have a fit. I can't realise that it is only just over eight weeks before I'll see them.

I wish I were certain about that leave in a month's time. There are so many conflicting rumours floating about, that I don't know what to believe. The latest is that we will only have one day over the time it takes to get from here to Evans Head.

I'm dreading my next visit to the torture chamber (alias the Dentist). I fear he'll find a few fillings to insert, but am praying for the best. He even spoke of giving me a plate. If he does, it will never be worn. None of my visible food-crunchers is missing, and the beauty of my smile is still unimpaired – I use Colgates. Has yours given you any further trouble, darling?

I suppose Alice is beginning to dread the day when her holiday will end – I hope she is having a whale of a time. I bet she is, knowing Al as I do. How many hearts has she broken, now? Is Nev going around the place mooning?

Dinner must be early, today. All the boys have cleared out, yet it's only a quarter past eleven, so I suppose I'd better go, or there'll be nothing left. The tucker's been crook lately; I'm wondering if it's worthwhile going up, but I think I will.

I'll interrupt my study this afternoon to pay a visit to the Roadhouse, and wrap myself around a fruit pie and cream. My mouth is watering at the thought.

Gee! I wish I were at Bursties, having dinner, with you across the table from me. I wish these thoughts wouldn't arise in me, because they make me go nearly mad with the longing for you, darling. Do you miss me very terribly?

I haven't heard from the Mulligans since I came back from leave, which is not nice of them. Len owes me a couple of letters now, the hound. How is Sheila doing these days, dear? Have she and Len started to build a home yet? I hope I'm in Brisbane for their Wedding. That would be great.

Well, dinner calls, darling, please remember me to all the crowd, and give my love to your Mother, I love you so much, darling, please keep loving me.

> *Ed xxxxx*

P.S. Love me? Ed x

P.S.S. I adore you, darling.

Ed x

P.S.S.S. Please give my regards especially to Margo, Nev, Butch and Laurie. Ed.

July 23, 1941

My Darling,

We are having a glorious loaf these days, waiting for our flying training to start on Thursday. Tomorrow we have our final receiving Test, and, after that, no more Exams.

The Final Procedure Exam yesterday was so easy that it was an insult to a man's intelligence, so easy in fact that I made an unholy mess of it and I'm frightened that I may have failed. Gee! I did some half-witted things, Sweetheart! And I studied harder for this Exam than I ever did before. If the Exam had been hard I'd have got 100% but they asked us all the easy little things that no one thought of learning. Drat it!

I'm certainly looking forward to seeing your Father's letter, darling; can't you send it to me?

There's a big boxing contest on at the Gymnasium tonight, and if (IF) I can pluck up sufficient energy I'll trot along and have a look at it. The odds are that I'll curl up in bed and read.

Some of the members of 10 flight, who were put back a month (as I will be), shifted into our hut yesterday and brought a huge wireless set with them. It's right alongside my bed, and last night it was lovely to curl up under the blankets and listen to the music, and think of you. I drifted off to sleep with Edward Elgar's "Salut d'Amour" playing softly in my ears. Talk about all mod. cons. It's like home now. There's only one objection: It has to be turned up loud to enable everyone in the hut to hear, and I fear I'll get very sick of it before the month is up, since it's only three feet from me. Your photograph makes an ideal decoration for the top of it, and everyone in the hut knows, now, just what the young lady I love looks like, and all pass very favourable comments, and remarks of wonderment that someone like you can be practically the fiancée of one as unlovely as I.

Maybe I look better in my flying togs. I'll have one of the boys take a snap of me in them, and I'll send it to you. I look as if I weigh 20 stone, which I nearly do, so heavy is the bear skin, etc.

My next letter should be a bit more interesting than this one, my darling, I'll have some flying experiences to tell you, and some funny things are sure to happen up there.

Thanks very much for the medal, darling. There is a little pocket in the flying suit that seems to be made just for the purpose, and the medal is in it now. It's lovely to know you love me so much to worry so, but, dear, these "kites" are as safe as houses. Much safer than the one Jim

Ed flying with friends when living in Sydney before war broke out.

Hucker and I used to tear around the countryside in, and we never struck any trouble, except once on a trip to Sydney, and even then there was no danger. If, and there's no "if", anything should happen, my darling, you know I love you with all my heart, and, after all, we love with our souls, not our bodies, and, this life is only a short one, at any rate; and it will seem nothing in the next life, when we will be together for all time. Only remember this, dear, that I adore you. I always have, even before I met you, because you are the ideal of everything I've ever wanted.

I was sorry to hear that Margo was ill on the Sunday night. The line was so bad that that was about all I did hear. I hope she is well again now and giving plenty of cheek. Give her my love, darling.

My chances of seeing you in a month are rapidly fading into oblivion, darling. However, we can only hope for the best. I'd give a lot just to be able to hold you close again, and kiss you, and hear you say you love me.

I feel sorry for Alice. I know what it's like to have to go back to work after a holiday. I'll say I do!

The visit to 4BH* must have been interesting. I hope that chap is interested in your "baby sister," and not in the girl I love. *[A Brisbane radio station, launched in 1932.]

I hope that picture didn't worry you, sweetheart. Some of those American films about the Air Force flying are ridiculous. If a chap were to do some of the things the "stars" do, he'd not only be "grounded" for life, but he'd be locked up as a menace to the public safety.

Today has been the coldest I can remember, even for Parkes. There's been a fine sleet all day, and it chills you to the very bones. I've had my leather gloves and fur lined boots on all day.

I trust they're not working you too hard at the M.R.C. Don't let 'em, darling. The willing horse always does the most work and some of these Govt. servants are born loafers.

I haven't heard from Ken, yet. I'm worried whether he got my letter or not. I'd like to hear how he's getting on at Cootamundra.

Of course I remember our tea parties at Bursties, when we used to be so unpopular with Mrs. Matthews for creating a din outside her room – and the unholy fear we had of disturbing Alf. It does seem years ago.

It seems I am well loved. I must be even better looking than I think. Thank Alice and Margo for me, darling girl, and keep on loving me yourself.

No matter what happens, dear, or where I go, I'll always love you more than life. Pray for me please, darling.

Ed xxxxxx

P.S. Love me? Ed xxxxx

P.S.S. I'm glad you like the photo, but I am horrible to look at.

Ed x.

July 24, 1941

My Darling,

This will have to be a very hurried letter. I've just got back from flying nearly 1000 miles (I could have reached you if the pilot had flown in a straight line instead of here and there) and I am nearly dead beat and slightly deaf, but I have to be ready in a few minutes to "go upstairs" again if I'm required, and, to cap it all, I have to report to the dentist at nine o'clock. It's six now, so you can see how my time is filled in.

Your letter arrived today and it was lovely (as it always is) to see your handwriting on an envelope, and to read that you are well, and love me.

During this morning's flight we had a bit of fun. The sky was overcast, and, when we got above the clouds, as far as the eye could see was a carpet of gleaming white, with only the shadow of the plane to break its monotony, and here and there a rainbow. Above the clouds rainbows make a perfect circle, and look beautiful. After we'd flown for about an hour, the pilot asked me to get a D.F. bearing. He was lost! He had some idea where we were, but was frightened to come down through the clouds in case there was a mountain peak waiting to make a mess of us. We arrived back about an hour late, and found we had caused a bit of a stir. I came in for a bit of praise, so have a swelled head now.

This afternoon I was up in a Moth* with only the pilot and myself. My Receiver went bung and I never heard a sound after I left the ground, so I had a good rest and admired the scenery. I got all my messages out, because the Transmitter was O.K. but as I didn't know whether they were received I sent them all twice, which was just as well, because there was a lot of static. I was commended again for using my skull, and my head swelled even further – nearly burst my helmet. *[The de Havilland Tiger Moth was a basic trainer for thousands of Australian pilots.]

I met Isobel's brother, last night. You can imagine my surprise, Darling, when I found I know him well – I've been wondering what happened to him. He and the others who came down yesterday had bad luck; their luggage has gone astray; all they have to wear is the clothes they stand up in.

Thanks very much, my sweetheart, for the cigarettes. They were just what I wanted today. I never had time to roll a cigarette. Craven A's, too, are my favourites, Gee! I'm in love with the most marvellous girl in the world!

As I look back, darling at this letter, I don't know how you will be able to read it. But I had to complete it in 15 minutes. And four pages in 15 minutes is hot going.

I'll write you on Sunday and give you much more news. There's the darn Sarge calling for me; I'll pretend I'm deafer than I am for a minute.

I love you, my darling, more than I'll ever be able to tell you, or show you. Please keep loving me; my whole world would collapse if I ever lost you.

Please give my love to Margo, and all the others, especially your Mother and Dad, when you write.

I adore you, Darling.

Ed xxxxx

P.S. I love you, Darling; love me?   Ed x

P.S.S. I <u>hate</u> the Sarge – Ed x

July 27, 1941

Dearest,

Things are now much more interesting here since we started flying. It's a great thrill, especially in the small Moths, when we're absolutely on our own in the front cockpit and have to rely on our own unaided efforts to send and receive messages. The pilots of these Moths are great fellows.

Sergeant Joyce took me up yesterday afternoon (yes, we have to work all day Saturday) and he was a darn nuisance. I was flat out all the while, because things are so cramped in a Moth, and the engine causes a terrible lot of static, but the blighter was continually tapping me on the shoulders and passing messages to me. I got my exercise over in about 12 minutes, so I spent the rest of the hour I was up enjoying the scenery – but the Sarge spoilt that. On Friday I had the doubtful honour and thrill of experiencing my first crash. We were taxiing out to take off, and I had my head buried in the cockpit whirling dials at a furious rate, when there was a bang and I conked my skull on the transmitter. I looked up to find that another plane, coming in, had tangled its wing in ours. No one got a scratch.

We had a beautiful flight in the Douglas yesterday. Nearly four hours, and I saw Orange and Condoblin covered in snow, then Cootamundra, Dubbo and all the places round. There was hardly a cloud in the sky. We took off about eight o'clock, but had to return after twenty minutes, because of a fault in the starboard motor. When this was fixed we went off again, and cruised about four hours. It was glorious. I curse the set, sometimes. It keeps you so busy that you haven't time for much gazing about.

I've done very well, so far, the instructors tell me, and now I have very little fear of being put back a month. If this weather continues as good as it has, we'll be finished our flying in no time. We have only to do about thirty hours, and I have over ten up already, in three days. This puts the matter of leave again in the picture.

Well that's enough about me.

Mother sent me down a hamper, and when I opened it, yesterday, it contained chocolates, biscuits, cigarettes, tobacco and a scarf that she'd knitted me. I was as pleased as punch. I had a letter from Mollie, too, and she told me that the family were thrilled with my photo, and were all well. Rita has a boy friend now. I can't realise those "kids" are grown up. Makes me feel quite old. Do you think I'm old, Darling?

I hope you are well, my sweetheart, and think of me a lot, and love me very much. I think of you all the time, and love you more than life, and no wonder, because you're the loveliest girl in the world. The only girl I want to spend every hour of the rest of my life, with. Do you love me and want me very much, darling. I was glad to hear that your room-mate and my super sleuth was well again. Tell her that washing the hair before going to bed is not supposed to be any good for the 'flu, so not to do it again.

The days are growing perceptibly longer now, and, though the nights and mornings are very cold (below freezing point) the days are quite warm. I hope this keeps up. Flanagan and Allen* are on the air just now, so I'll knock off to hear them. *[Flanagan and Allen were a British singing and comedy act popular during World War II.]

I also heard the time announced and found that, if I didn't go like heck I'd miss out at tea, so I went like a blur of light and just made it. Stew! Ugh! I hate that stuff. Of late we've had stew so often we'll look like stew soon.

It's wonderful to know there's a possibility of seeing you in three weeks, and a certainty in seven – in 21 or 49 days! I'm beginning to feel a thrill already. Gee! I love you, darling!

How are your Mother and Dad, and Alice and the others? I hope they're all in the pink, dear. Please give them my love.

Tell Margo, Nev, Laurie, Mrs. B. and Butch that I'm looking forward to seeing them all soon and give them my regards.

I'll be waiting now, very impatiently, for our call. I hope the line is good tonight, darling, and I wish, more than anything that I'll hear you say you love me. I hope no "glugs" are hanging about, so I can ask if you do.

Pray for me, darling, I keep your Rosary and Medal near me all the while I'm in a plane.

I adore you, dearest.

    Ed xxxxx

    P.S. Love me?

    Ed x

July 29, 1941

My Darling Sweetheart,

I was reconciled to the fact that a letter from you would not be arriving yesterday, so you can imagine how pleased I was when one did arrive; and it wasn't as you thought, a "whinge" of a letter, dear; it was, like all of yours – wonderful. By reading between the lines I could see you were a little, "out of sorts," but you wrote "I love you", and that's enough to make me happier than I ever deserve to be. I was sorry to hear of the death of your friend Molly, though. It is upsetting to lose someone you've known and liked for so long.

Before I tell you any news, I have something important to tell you. I've found out I don't love you. "Love" is too poor a word to describe my feelings towards you, darling, and "adore" is worse than inadequate.

The question of our leave is still a matter for conjecture, but we are still so far ahead of our schedule, owing to the fine weather that I'm beginning to feel very sanguine. Pray I get enough, even if I only have time to see you for a few hours, dear. Please God I will, because I long so much to be near you again. Just to be near you would be enough, but to know that I will be able to hold you in my arms and kiss you will be heaven. (I'd better cut this out or you'll be thinking I'm a sentimental glug).

Yesterday we did a sweep of the countryside for a radius of up to 100 miles. We went hither and thither for nearly four hours, and enjoyed ourselves thoroughly, except a few of the boys who were sick. It was fairly bumpy, but I have never been able to understand people getting air-sick. Flying is too thrilling to have any time for being sick.

Tomorrow we do a six-hour trip in the Douglas, and I'm looking forward to it very much. This will bring my hours above the 20 mark. I have three hours solo to my credit as well as in the Doug. And as our average speed is near the 200 miles per hour, you can see that in five days I've covered a fair bit of countryside. This "solo" doesn't mean we fly alone like it does when it refers to the pilot. It means we go up in the "Moths" with only the pilot in the rear cockpit and yourself in the front with the wireless gear, and you have to rely entirely on the old gumption to get you out of every exercise. The flight Sergeant in charge of us told me today that he was very pleased with me. I am one of the few who has passed every test, up to now. You can imagine this, with the passing my final Morse with the maximum possible marks, has made me the old skull even larger. You must be praying hard for me, my darling. Gee! I love you.

Heavens! That was a long paragraph! Hope I haven't bored you dear.

I had a bosker loaf today. The only work I did was a 50 minutes flight in the Moth with Sergeant Joyce. I worked hard for that 50 minutes, though, because a fault developed in the set, and I had to work like heck to rectify it and get the exercise finished in time. It was different from my last trip, when I was finished in 10 minutes and had a joy-ride for the rest of the time. The Serge, who knows I used to fly myself, called me a lazy blighter and said that if we had been fitted with dual control he'd have had the joy-ride, and I'd have done the work. I wish it had been, myself. I'd have given a lot to have felt the kick of the rudder on my feet again, though I'd probably have broken both our necks.

I'd have been in a mess, yesterday if I'd had to "bail out." Our parachutes fit into clips behind us, and we have to sit on them. The dill who clipped mine on, before I climbed aboard, must have made a heck of a job of the clipping process, because, when I stood up to get out, I found that the "chute' had come adrift from my harness! I'd have been in the well known tin if anything had gone wrong while we were aloft. I'd never have been able to go back for it after I'd jumped, and, I suppose, if, when the plane came to earth, it burned up, the blighters would have made me pay for it! Me on 5/6 a day too!

It was wonderful to hear your voice on Sunday night, my darling, even though the interference was terrific, and it was heaven to hear you answer "yes", when I asked you if you loved me.

Please give my regards to all the folks, sweetheart, especially Margo, Nev, Laurie, Butch and Mrs. B., and please, dear, give my love to your Mother and the rest of your family when you write.

Don't ever, ever for a second, stop loving me, dear, you are all my world, you have all my heart. Pray for me, and us, and our future, please, darling – I adore you.

Ed xxxxxx

P.S. Love me?

Ed x

P.S.S. Gee! you're lovely, – I've just been looking at your photograph.

Ed. X

July 31, 1941

My Darling,

It took me 2½ hours today to go from here to Sydney, circle over the harbour and return, and then go hedge-hopping about the countryside. I left about 8.30 in the Douglas* and was eating my lunch here at about 11.30. I found your letter awaiting me when I'd eaten, and it was better than any dessert or liqueur could ever be. Gee, I love you, sweetheart!
*[This particular Douglas, A30-13, was an ex-Eastern Airlines DC-2. It crashed on January 8, 1943 and was then used for spares. Ten Douglas DC-2 aircraft were in service with the RAAF from 1940 to 1946. *A30-9* is on display at the Australian National Aviation Museum, located at Melbourne's Moorabbin Airport.]

As soon as I'd bolted down my lunch I was off again, this time on a 3½-hour trip to Tamworth. I'm gadding about lately.

Most important thing that happened today was getting the news, straight from the horse's mouth that we're getting 3 more days leave than we expected, and they'll start from Saturday week! That is, if this fine weather holds. Think of it, Darling! I may be able to see you in just over a week. Pray that the weather holds fine, please, dear. I can hardly believe that it will come true, but I'm not worrying about believing, I'm just praying! I love you so much, darling.

We lost a whole day's flying yesterday. Work though the mechanics did, our Douglas refused to take off. It used to sidle across the tarmac like a crab, as one motor was pulling harder than the other, and it's a pretty rotten feeling, moving like a crab at about 90 miles an hour. I had a good old loaf, though, sitting in the plane on a nice plush seat, like Mr. Micawber in Dicken's yarn, waiting for something to happen. I was dead crooked, though, because it was one day of our leave thrown to the winds.

The mechanics and fitters who work on our planes give you a lot of confidence. For instance, when, about 4.30, the Doug. was pronounced O.K., all the fitters and mechanics went up in the test flight, which shows that they are confident of their work.

I had a letter from Mollie, and one from Len, too, today. A few days ago, I got a letter from Mollie enclosing a 1/- share [a one shilling lottery ticket]. *In her letter today she tells me that we each won £1.13.4. I feel rich again.*

Len seems to like the camp life. Strangely enough, he's learning Morse code!

I'm looking forward to a dance with you, darling. I'm an awful hoofer, but I promise not to stand on your toes. If I do, can I kiss you, to make up for my awkwardness, sweetheart?

Hope you enjoy your week-end at Margate, dear, and that the weather's not too cold down there. I bet you will, though. Just think of me now and then while you're there, and say a prayer that I'll be seeing you in a week's time. You'll be able to tell me about it on Sunday night. Don't worry if you can't get back in time, dear. If you're not at home on Sunday night, I'll ring on Monday at the same time.

Tomorrow morning at some horrible hour, I have to do a "flip" in a Moth. You get chucked about so much in the Moths that W.T. operating is always an ordeal. I hope I do as well as I have on previous tests.

Well, darling, I have to enter up my log-book for the month so I'll have to ask you to forgive me for this short letter. Please remember me to Margo, Nev and the others, and give my love to your Mother and the family. And please keep loving me, darling; you're all the world to me,

I love you,

Ed xxxxx

P.S. Love me? Ed x

August 3, 1941

My Darling,

Everything seems right with the world today; in just over a week I'll be seeing you again, and they're playing "Pagliacci" on the Wireless; the only discordant note is that I've haven't your voice to look forward to hearing tonight, but even that can't worry me too much, because, after all, tomorrow will seem all the better. When you get this letter, dear, don't write again to this address, but wait until I get up there, because your letter may arrive after I've left.

Gosh, sweetheart, I'm happy! I love you more than I ever thought I could love anyone, and knowing I'll be seeing you so soon seems a glorious dream. Are you excited, too, Molly, dear? I hope so, because it means that you love me, and I want you to, dear, more than I want to live.

Today, I hope, you're enjoying yourself at Margate, and the weather is as lovely as it is here, without a cloud in the sky. I wish I were with you, but I'm always wishing for the moon where you are concerned. If I keep on wishing, though, one day it will come true, and that day you'll be mine for all time. Would you like that dear?

My Friday's flip in the Moth was the best I've had, so far. I got through my Exercise in no time at all, and this meant that I'm one of the very few who've passed every air exercise so far. Touch wood.

Yesterday morning we were allowed to sleep in until all hours, and then we spent an hour or so tying knots and splicing wire.

It's amazing the way we're treated now. As we have only a week to go, we have the run of the place. Officers and N.C.O.'s treat us like life-long friends. Everyone is called by his Christian name, and the N.C.O.'s fight among themselves to see who's to have the spare seat in the Douglas. This week is to be a series of nights' out. We are having a huge dinner at Tatt's Hotel which is expected to be a beaut. The C.O.s and all the Officers and N.C.O.s with whom we've come in contact are invited. And the Rotary Club and other organisations are giving us Smoke Concerts*. Wow! I'm afraid, Darling, that I'm going to be very "broke" during my few days in Brisbane, but that won't matter, so long as I can see you. *[Smoke, concerts, usually male-only affairs, consisted of a meal, speeches, and many long, drawn-out toasts. Between toasts, entertainment was provided.]

This morning I had various photographs taken with my flying kit on. If they're any good I'll give them to you.

I had a spring-cleaning this morning. It's funny the rubbish that accumulates. My port is only half as full as it was, which is a good thing. I was wondering how I was going to transport my luggage from here to Brisbane, and thence to Evans Head.

For a bit of exercise, last night Bert Tinkler and the chap who adores you decided to hike into town. We covered the distance in 55 minutes which is some hoofing.

Tomorrow I don't think I have any flying to do, so the day should be one of heavenly leisure, made bright with the anticipation of hearing you say you love me at night, so, with all this in front of me, your voice tomorrow, the parties, and flying during the week, and then seeing you next week, I feel more fortunate and happy than I have any right to be. But, darling, can I lap this up! I have missed a lot of happiness during the last six months, especially the joy of being near you, and the thrill of your kiss, since I heard you tell me for the first time that you love me, all this I have to make up for, and when I see you, I will.

This having no study to do is hard to take. I'm lost with no worries on my mind, and, strangely enough, I'm always tired, these days.

Well, darling, I'll say "so long" until tomorrow night. Please remember me to Margo, Nev and Laurie and the others. I love you so much, my darling, please keep loving me, and including me in your prayers. You are the loveliest girl in the world.

Ed xxxxx

P.S. Love me?

Ed x

August 5, 1941

My Darling,

Well, this letter finds me in a much different mood from the one I was in when I commenced the last. Then I was as happy as a man can be, revelling in the anticipation of seeing you next week – now I am down in the dumps, though I suppose I shouldn't be, because, after all it only means a postponement of a few days. I don't know how I'd feel if I'd been told that we weren't getting any leave at all. The latest rumour is that we can't leave here until the Saturday, but I think it's wrong. I can't see why they'd want to keep us here for ½ a day extra. You can forget my advice in the last letter about not writing again to here, darling. My best plan will be to give you a ring the night before I leave.

All our proposed dinners and Smoko's have been postponed to next week, now. Alas! Alas!

I have just got back from a Seven-hour trip in the "Doug," over 1200 miles. It was very bumpy, with heavy layers of cloud up to 8000 feet. The old kite was kicking and bouncing like a buck-jumper, which was not conducive to good Morse. I managed to pass the Exercise, although Static etc. made things a bit tough.

Yesterday I had a flip in the Moth. The bouncing of the Douglas today was nothing to compare with yesterday's trip. Once I was nearly chucked right out of the plane, only my safety belt saved me. It would have been a good test for my parachute.

I think, out of all the times I've rung you since I've been here, last night was the best. I could hear you so plainly as if I'd been standing alongside you. It was great, Darling.

Your letter arrived yesterday, dear. His friend's death must have been an awful shock to your Dad.

I was glad to hear that Kev had got his "call-up". I hope I can see him while I'm in Brisbane. As they are keeping all trainees at Sandgate for two months (instead of one like I was) now, he'll probably be there while I'm on pre-em leave. It would be good to run into him there. Please give Laurie my best wishes and congrats, Darling. I hope I can make Brisbane before his wedding comes off. Like you, I can't imagine Laurie married – but hell, I'm jealous of him. As I said before, darling, I expect to be kept for some months in Australian Squadrons, before I go overseas. We may be able to work out something, then. But we'll talk about that when we're together.

Today may have been our last flight in the Douglas, dear. I'll be sorry if it is. I've been looking on old A30-13 as my own property, almost since my first trip in her. Notice we're not superstitious in the R.A.A.F. The No. is 13. And there are always 13 in the crew.

I hope your hand is better, now, darling. My skulll, which you appear to be concerned about, is undented. You should have known, darling, that the only thing that deserved any concern, was the X-mitter. My head is too hard to be affected by a little thing like that.

My word, flying makes you tired – and – hungry. Lord! how hungry! I never seem to get enough to eat these days, no matter how I gormandise.

Maybe Laurie misses the good influence of my saintly company, darling. Personally I think he's a bit of a worried man. I think he's been talked into this step by his bride-to-be. She seems to have been determined to "get her man" since the first time she laid eyes on him. Laurie is not the type to appreciate anyone who chucks herself at his head. Frankly, Darling, I feel sorry for him and, although I'm usually optimistic in these matters, I'm worried about how his marriage will turn out; mixed marriages are never much good, at any time, and this one, in particular, has me very concerned. Because I like old Laurie a lot, darling. But for heaven's sake don't tell him anything, dear. I'd hate him to think I wasn't as pleased as Punch. After all, I suppose he knows his own mind best.

I'm a selfish blighter; I was so full of my own woeful news last night that I forgot to ask you if you had a good weekend.

Graham Campbell, or Campbell Graham (Darn it! I can never remember which it is) – anyway Isobel's brother and the others got their luggage back O.K. He's doing well.

I had a letter from Mat, yesterday and one from Joan today. Mat is well, and expects to be in Brisbane in August or September. I hope he's there while I'm in Brisbane. He's the same old Mat. I wish I hadn't remembered those letters. I'll have to answer them while I'm in the mood.

Please give my regards to all the Burstie crowd, especially Margo, Nev, Mrs. B., Butch, and Kev Coleman, and give my love to your Mother and Dad and Alice and the boys when you write.

I love you with all my heart, Darling. Please pray for me, and think of me now and then, dear, and love me a lot.

Ed xxxxxx   *P.S. Love me? Ed x*

August 7, 1941

Darling,

I was just hopping into the Doug. this afternoon when one of the boys came running up with your letter. I read it about 8000 feet above Forbes, while we were sailing along over a sea of glittering clouds. I bet our literary efforts have never reached such heights, dear.

I'm sorry I caused you so much disappointment, but, in a way, I'm glad you were disappointed, because it means you love me. Thank Margo for my clearance papers, Molly, but tell her that, as a forger, she's about as good as she is a sleuth. She'd better have some good information for me while I'm on leave, or she won't collect the promised stipend, let alone get the raise she wants.

I went to Katoomba* this morning. The trip was lovely, but the wireless conditions were very difficult – too much static, and I was flat out from the word go. I have no idea where we went this afternoon – after we passed Forbes the clouds got so thick that we never glimpsed the ground again until we dived down through them to land. It's an eerie feeling travelling through clouds so thick that the wing tips are invisible, – not knowing what lies on the other side. *[Katoomba is 103 km west of Sydney in the Blue Mountains, famous for its World Heritage Listed Jamison Rainforest, and a Scenic Railway that is considered the steepest railway incline in the world.]

I'm glad you had such a good time at Shorncliffe, darling. It must have been a grand change for you. I was sorry to read that you have a cold. They're hard to shake off these days, aren't they? Strangely enough, considering the coldness of this place, I've been freer from those darned nuisances of things this winter than ever before. It must be because we are pretty high above sea level here.

Speaking of cold, it's still as bad here as ever. In the mornings they sponge down the wings of the planes to wipe off the ice that coats them. Brr!

I got a letter from Joan yesterday and she had me puzzled, too. Wanted to know how I liked Evans Head. It appears that she knows a friend of a chap who was in 10 course here. They left for Evans Head last month. Our course – 11 – is just a month behind them; I suppose that's what has been the reason for her misapprehension.

It's about time Pat dropped me a line. I've been practically deserted by the "Mulls" – since I got back from leave. One letter, from Len is all I received. Whinger, aren't I?

I'm enclosing a photo of my ugly self. Don't look at it too hard, dear, or you'll begin to wonder why you love me. Ain't I 'orrible?

The photos you saw in Pix* were taken here, and were photos of the concert party who gave us the night I was so thrilled about. They did entertain the boys pretty well, apart from the concert. I, unfortunately (???) was not one of those entertained. Girls, apart from the one I love, have no attraction for me, now. That is a lie. They all attract me, and how! But they don't worry me. *[Pix was one of Australia's most popular magazines during the 50s, 60s and 70s, famous for its cover girls.]

A funny thing happened on Saturday night. After Bert and I had walked into town, Bert met the "object of his affections," and the three of us strolled up town, arm in arm. I told the young lady, I forget her name, that she had the honour to be the only member of the female sex to walk arm in arm with me in Parkes – and it was the truth. Sometimes I wonder if I have done the right thing, steering clear of all the very attractive girls that Parkes boasts. I'll be awfully dull and out of practice when I see you again. You'll look upon me as a country yokel.

I thought that last Monday night would have been my last ring to you from this joint, and could weep with disappointment now that I know it wasn't. I hope the line is as clear on Sunday as it was then. One thing – I do know pretty definitely that it will be our last weekly call. I'll try to ring you, or send you a telegram when I'm actually leaving here to let you know when I'll reach Brisbane.

Please give my love to your Mother and Dad and the others, and my regards to Margo, Nev, Butch and the crowd.

I love you with all my heart, darling, please keep loving me.

Ed   xxxxxx

P.S. Love me? Ed x

PSS. Hope you like the snap. I adore you. Ed x

August 10, 1941

My Darling,

    Days slip by and here it is Sunday afternoon again, and here I am waiting for a quarter past nine until I can hear your voice. I hope the line is as good as it was last Monday night. I thought, last week, that I'd be seeing you by now, and have enjoyed the thrill of meeting you, and hugging the life out of you, but things are beginning to look blacker than ever. There are rumours floating around that we may not be leaving here before next Monday at the earliest. I refuse to believe in any other day than this Friday, though, darling; if the Monday is correct it means that I'll have to wait until next Wednesday before we can meet, and it also means that we will have to be content with only two or three nights together. That is too horrible to believe, so we just won't consider it. I suppose I'm a grouse, moaning when we might quite easily have been granted no leave at all, but I can't help it. After all, we are only supposed to do 35 hours flying at the most here, and I have over 40 up now, so I can't see why the – they keep us here. We have to fly right up to Thursday or Friday, and that's what makes me so worried about getting away Friday night. If we finish on Friday the staff will have to do an almost impossible job to get our papers ready for us to leave on the same night.

    I just started a discussion with some of the boys and they won't hear of any but Friday night. I hope that tonight is our last 1000-miles-apart telephone conversation. They have been nice, our talks, haven't they dear? Are you glad I kept them up? I must remember to tell you not to write any more after tomorrow night's letter, because, if you post a letter any later than Tuesday night (12th) it will arrive here on Saturday, and I'll be gone by then, on my way to you, please God.

    I went to Sydney again on Friday morning and we took in the Hawkesbury River on the way back. It was a glorious trip. I'm getting a bit bored with the Douglases, though, sitting doing nothing but listen and send "dits and dahs" and gaze at the scenery becomes very monotonous after a couple of hours. The Moth is much more interesting. The other day I finished my Exercise in a few minutes, the Reception was so good. When I told my pilot, a friend of mine – Sergeant Dangerfield from Broken Hill – he said, "Good! We can have some fun." It may have been fun for him but I spent the worst half hour of my life while he turned the plane inside out, and frightened flocks of sheep by diving on them. While he was in the middle of a spin once the ground station called me up and I had to receive and send a message with the plane doing Catherine wheels. I heaped curses on his head but all I could get out of him was a laugh. When I went crook after we landed and pointed out the dangers of spilled acid, etc., he explained that he'd been to a ball the night before

135

and wanted to clear his head. Luckily none of the acid from my batteries had spilled (they have special non-spillable vents) or I'd have had a job of work cleaning it up. While we were up, a cobber of mine, Reg Collins*, was up in another Moth. Owing to the cloudy weather his pilot got lost. They landed in some farmer's backyard, and strolled up to the house to enquire their way. The farmer pointed in a general direction and said "About 12 miles over there." They took off again and had only risen about 100 feet when they saw the 'drome. It must have been a break in the monotony of the farmer's life. *[See story about Reg Collins in August 18, 1942, Diary entry.]

Last night Bert Tinkler and I again walked into town. It was a beautiful night, though as cold as billyo.

This is the second last letter I'll be writing you from Parkes, darling. It seems too wonderful to be true, doesn't it? In exactly one week, if things go right, I'll have you near me, to tell me you love me, and I'll be the happiest man in the world. Please give my regards to Margo and the others and my love to your Mother and Dad and the family. I adore you, darling, please keep loving me and praying for me.

Ed. xxxxxxx

P.S. Love me? Ed x

P.S.S. You'll meet me at the station, won't you darling? Please. Ed x

August 12, 1941

Dearest,

Well, here goes for my last letter to you from this miserable spot, so I'll try to make it a good 'un. I'm afraid, though, that it won't be much of a success, because my brain is so full of the thought that I'll be seeing you in five days that there is not much room for anything else.

I don't know yet whether we're leaving on Saturday or Friday, but things are swinging more and more toward the former. The latest development is that No. 14 Flight go on their mid-term leave on Friday and the Railway Dept. is kicking up a fuss about carrying so many men on the one train. Of course, poor old eleven Flight are the bunnies, as usual. No one would think of keeping 14 Flight another day. If you got a wire from me yesterday, darling, you'll know I'll be arriving tomorrow (Sunday) – this letter should arrive on Saturday, so when I speak of "yesterday" I mean Friday. If I'm not leaving here until Saturday night, which means I'll arrive on Monday afternoon, I'll send the wire from here on Saturday morning, and it will arrive about the same time as this letter.

If I have to wait until Monday before I get to Brisbane, dear, you won't be able to meet me at the station. In that case I'll call in to see you at work, or, if the train gets in too late for me to do that, I'll ring you, and arrange either to meet you after work or call out to Bursties for you. I hope I arrive on Sunday, sweetheart, we'll have to grab every minute we can together, now.

I had only one trip yesterday – an hour in the Moth. When I got up I found my Receiver had gone phut, so I had an enjoyable hour's joy-ride. All the rest of the day I slept or twiddled my fingers. I'm getting terribly lazy these days. You'll have to reform me when I get up. I doubt, though, that you'll be able. When I get to Brisbane, all I'll want to do will be sit and look at you.

I'm a selfish blighter; I go on talking about my little troubles, etc., and never mention yours. I've been worried about that darned cold that's been sticking to you for so long, darling. If it's not better by the time I arrive, watch out! Off I'm packing you to bed and I'm going to drown you in hot lemon drinks, etc. How will I go as a nurse? I'll be the best in the world (in my own opinion). Tell Margo that I don't think she's looking after you well enough, and that I relieve her of the responsibilities connected with the office of sleuth, and delegate her as nurse, until I arrive.

The "Smoko" last night was very tame. A fly wouldn't have got its feet wet in the minute quantity of beer that was provided. "Just as well," you say. O.K. old spoil-sport. I had to make a speech. Imagine my predicament when I was inoffensively chewing a sandwich, and the C.O. called on me to reply to some darned toast or other. I struggled through, and scored a very minor triumph. Everyone laughed, when I cracked feeble jokes. Perhaps it was the beer, or, more likely, pity.

The dinner, tomorrow night, should be a much better affair. I sincerely hope so. Last night very nearly approached the ranking of a pain in the neck.

Today I did nothing all day, except send a message or two from an Aldis Lamp. Loafing, as I said before, is becoming a major passion of mine.

This afternoon we suffered a fierce gale, and all the plains were a sea of drifting dust, and very heavy clouds hid the mountains. It became very dangerous and some planes, especially the Moths, nearly crashed on landing – so all the crates were "grounded." Just as well, I was due for a flip and didn't like the looks of things one little bit.

I don't get my stripes (if I ever get 'em) until I pass out at Evans Head, Darling, unfortunately. We get a rise in screw, though, as soon as we start there, which is more important than the stripes. I'll be getting twice as much there as here.

I hope I can get off on Friday night, darling. Every day I'm away from you seems to be a lifetime, now that my long period of waiting and longing is nearly at an end.

Dear Darling, it will be glorious, seeing you, and being able to hug you to my heart's content. Sometimes I'm afraid that it's all a dream, because I have so often dreamed that you were near, and have awoken, to lie in rotten disappointment until the morning. I'm afraid I won't really believe it until I have kissed you. In my dreams I always wake up before that happens.

Please give my love to Margo and the others, and especially to your Mother and Dad and Alice and the rest of your (can I say "our") family. I love you more than I'll ever be able to tell you, darling, much more than I'll ever be able to prove, though I'll try hard to. Pray for me please, dear, and keep loving me, that's all I ask of this world.

Ed. xxxxxxx

P.S. Love me? Ed x

Bombing and Gunnery School
Evans Head, N.S.W.

Hut 40, Instructional Section, No. 1 B. & G. SCHOOL, R.A.A.F.,
Evans Head, NSW

August 20, 1941

My Darling,

Gosh! I miss you, dear. I may sound like a bit of a Glug, but when I saw you for the last time (for a month) among the crowd on the platform, I felt like doing a weep. I love you more and more every day, and it's not because I miss you that I love you so much, either. I found that out when I was with you.

You made the six days in Brisbane a wonderful leave for me, darling. Sometimes I wish you had not been so nice to me, because leaving you is so darned hard.

We had a very uneventful trip as far as Casino; I sat in a corner and dozed, watched a game of poker and, most of all, thought of you.

Dinner was waiting for us at Casino, likewise three huge Buses, and into these we were packed like sardines. There were about 70 Observers and another 30 W.A.G.S, as well as we thirty from Brisbane. The bus runs for about 40 miles along the Richmond River and the scenery is not bad.

The camp is a huge one, and is situated so close to the Beach that, as I write, I can hear the breakers beating on the Heads. As it was dusk when we arrived here (we were delayed through a blow-out), and we have been flying about, getting bedding, tea, and undergoing Medical Inspections, I haven't been able to form an opinion on the Camp, but I think I'll like it. In contrast to Parkes, I'm wearing shorts and shirt as I write, which is a good thing! Our hut, too, is wooden, not galvanised iron, and it's lined. Only one half is sleeping quarters, and we have huge lockers. The other half has chairs and tables, and is ideal for reading and writing.

Hot and cold water is laid on – the water is much cleaner than Parkes and I'm feeling very refreshed after a beautiful shower. I'm looking forward to a swim tomorrow but I'm afraid we've got to work.

Mass is on at 7am and I've met the Padre already. I'm pretty sure he can get me off next weekend to go into Lismore to see Uncle Ed. Here's hoping anyhow.

I'll be able to make our calls longer in future. It only costs about 9^d to ring Brisbane from here – and, speaking of calls, there's only one thing I'm waiting for now and that's 9.30 tomorrow night when I'll be able to hear your voice.

I've no idea when this will reach you, darling. The mails are not cleared very regularly, here, from what I've been told.

Some of my old pals from my Sandgate days are here with me. Chaps who went away to be Observers at the same time as I went to Parkes. It's been good to run into some of them tonight. There's one special pal I had, Jack Sadd, who used to work with Pat in the Taxation; if you see her, tell her that he was asking after her.

Well, darling, the poorness of my hand writing tells me that I'm very tired – so I'll finish this now and roll off to bed. Please keep loving me, and please wait for me, dear. I'll make it up to you, when I have the right, and this stupid war is over. I adore you, my darling.

Ed xxxxxxx

P.S. Love me?

Ed x.

Undated (Possibly August 24, 1941)

My Darling,

Well, contrary to my first expectation, I found that this station is the best I've struck. I'm enjoying myself immensely, except that I miss you terribly. Our talk on Sunday night was much better even than any at Parkes, as far as interference, etc. were concerned, wasn't it?

For the first two days we were here we did absolutely nothing except lie on the beach and ride around the various Ranges in utes. I've got a good tan already, and if this keeps up, you'll find yourself getting afraid that your future husband will be a nigger.

Everything about this place is much better than anything in Parkes. We are never troubled by Officers and N.C.O's, in fact the only time we see one is during our lectures. The meals make me think I'm staying at the "Carlton" or some such luxurious hotel, and, to cap this, we are having a free dinner tonight in honour of the School's first anniversary.

So far I've been to the pictures two night's running, and on Sunday night, before I called you, I saw "The Strange Case of Dr. Meade" and last night "Thanks a Million." The pictures are free.

Our lectures today were very interesting; we were handling machine guns – taking them to pieces and putting them together all day. I like this kind of work much better than dry Morse or Procedure. They have those special gadgets here that you may have seen in the pictures. Model planes buzz around and we have to line all sights on them and press a trigger that takes photographs instead of firing bullets. I haven't got the results of my first "shoot" yet. If they are any good I'll tell you about them. (Skite, aren't I, Darling?) Tomorrow we go down to the butts and practice with real ammunition.

I'm going to try to get to Lismore to see Uncle Ed on Saturday. Some of the boys who have been there say it is a lovely town and the townspeople are wonderful, so I think I'll enjoy it. That is if I can really enjoy any place without you, dear.

Jack Jackson is sitting opposite me at the table, writing to his folks. I'm trying to persuade him to come with me but I'm afraid I won't have any luck as he thinks that he'll be flying on Saturday. I may be flying myself.

Since I wrote that last paragraph, I've managed to persuade Jack to go on Sunday. As the bus does not return 'till late Sunday night, sweetheart, I'll postpone our call till Monday night. If you are going home on the week-end, this may suit you better, too, but if you are going anywhere on Monday night, don't worry, because I can ring Tuesday, if you're not at home.

I wish I could have managed a week-end at your place while I was on leave; I'd have loved to have seen your Mother and Alice and the "kids" again. Give them my love when you get there, won't you darling?

I wonder what the dinner will be like tonight. As I have not had tea, yet, I hope it is good. The "smoko" afterwards should be alright.

On Sunday night before I went to the pictures, I strolled into "town." It's only a small place, but it looks very pretty, at night, doesn't it? I wish your holidays were on now, and you were visiting Evans Head. I get leave every night and we could have a marvellous time. I wish I wouldn't think of these things; they make me so darn miserable when I come to earth and realise they can't come true. Gee! I love you, Sweetheart! Do you love me?

I start my flying on Friday, and it will be much more thrilling than sitting punching a key. We use much faster planes and dive down on targets banging away with a machine gun. I hope I don't get the "wind-up." Another exercise: we chase a plane towing a target, like Robert Taylor in "Flight Command", only, I hope, we don't get tangled up in the darn thing. I'm so cockeyed that I'll probably hit the plane that is doing the towing instead of the target and will be very unpopular. Don't forget to say a prayer for me, my darling. I'll need your prayers more than ever, from now on.

Ken arrives here next month, so I'm told, then goes to Parkes for another month. I'll just miss him.

Please give my retards to Margo, Nev, and the others, and don't forget to give my love to your Mother, and please keep loving me, my sweetheart, because I love you more than life.

Ed XXXXXXX

P.S. Love me? Ed x

August 28, 1941

My Darling,

I was very disappointed when I didn't get a letter from you, today, dear, but knowing the terrible system of mail sorting they have here, I was not surprised. I spent half an hour searching through the mail, but couldn't find one. I think I'll ring you tonight, on the off-chance of catching you at home, because I want to hear from you before we begin our flying tomorrow. I love you darling. I've just booked the call, and I hope you're home, darling, because it's always a wonderful thrill to hear your voice, and also because I want to find out if there are any relations of Uncle Jack's I can look up in Lismore over the week-end.

I've a bit of a headache tonight, because I've been down at the range all day, banging away at a target with a machine gun.

It's pretty hard to keep on the mark, because the gun jumps about like a jack-in-the-box and the din is terrific. I didn't do too bad, but was not exceptional. We got the results of Tuesday's efforts with the Camera Gun today. I hit the target fair in the centre each time. (I pinched one of the films to prove it to you. Don't think because the plane is not exactly in the centre, but is a little above it, that I'm out. The plane, as you can see, is diving and we had to make allowance for its speed and direction. Aren't I a darn skite*? But I have to show off to you somehow.) *[Aussie slang meaning *boast* or *brag*.]

I'm looking forward to tomorrow. It will be fun diving at about 350 M.P.H. on to a target, banging away, even though I'll probably miss it by miles, and it will be even more fun chasing the drogue around the coast.

The work here is still ridiculously easy. As a matter of fact I'm beginning to be worried. If I don't settle down and do some myself, I'll be missing in the exams – I think that as soon as I finish this letter I'll get stuck into a bit. Yesterday we spent the whole of the afternoon down on the beach and I tried my hand at catching worms – with no success. Please don't tell Nev, as he once spent hours at Bribie, teaching me the

art. It was too cold here yesterday to have a dip, worse luck.

I'm trying, without doing any study, to learn the parts and mechanism of Gun, Gas operated, Vickers Mark* I but I'm afraid the struggle is too tough for your boy friend. You'll have to start your praying for me again, darling, otherwise I'm sunk. *[The Vickers K gun

143

was a rapid-fire machine-gun developed and manufactured for use in aircraft by Vickers-Armstrongs.]

By the time you get this, dear, you'll be back in the big city after your week-end at home. I know you had a swell time, and I wish I had been with you. I think the week-end we had there was one of the nicest we ever had. I hope your Mother and Al and the others were all well.

Last night, drat it, we had to do an hour's Morse practice. We needed it, though, because you go off at that game very easily.

How is work going, darling? I can imagine you at work, and I think of how easy it was last week to ring you, and how darn difficult it is now, and I wish I'd rung you ten times a day while I had the chance. I adore you, dear.

The dinner last night was "on the nostrils." It's rotten, listening to a lot of the dry speeches, with no fortification beyond a bottle of lemonade. I was fed up – in the psychological (Whew! Don't check up in Webster's!) sense, though not in the physical one, half way through the proceedings.

I'm looking forward to the trip to Lismore as I've heard it's a great place. I have to go this week-end, because it's the only week-end I get off. We fly during the remaining two week-ends. I wish you were coming with me, and Uncle Jack were there.

I'd better do that study I told you about, so please give my love to Margo, Nev, I Norman, and the others. Tell I Norman that her button is still a fixture.

I love you more than I'll ever be able to tell you, darling, so please keep loving me.

Ed xxxxxx

P.S. Love me?

Ed x.

You're the loveliest girl in the world. Ed x

August 29, 1941

My Darling,

It seems I did our Post Office system an injustice, because the letter you posted last night was handed to me this afternoon. Pretty slick, what? It was great to get back after being bounced around in a Fairy to find your letter waiting, dear – and it was better still to read that you love me so much.

It was a wonderful thrill flying today, though I admit I was more scared at times than I've ever been in all my career. In the first place you have to stand in an open cockpit and brace yourself against the wind, then the pilot turns the plane like a Catherine wheel and every now and then your target flashes past your sights at over 200 m.p.h. I've never travelled at that speed before, and you feel as if you were going to have your head blown off. I did very well, getting 10 shots into the centre of the target. I made sure I did because, if I hadn't I'd have had to fly again on Sunday and so missed my trip to Lismore. This is how the targets look from the air.

I was on "IX", so had a fairly easy shot, as the plane was fairly level by the time it got to mine. The arrows show the direction of the plane, though it never really was so straight a course as I've shown. The targets look not much bigger than I've shown them, though they are actually fairly big. The worst part is that you can't get a straight shot at them. If you aim directly at your target you're more likely to hit the next one.

Most of the boys were sick, as the sensation is much the same as being swung round in a bucket and the fumes from the gun and engine are sickly. I was lucky, having a cast-iron tummy, but even so I felt a bit squirmy at times. I suppose I was too scared to be airsick.

I was hauled up before the C.O. today on a charge of wearing my flying boots on Parade. As all the rest of the boys were hauled up too; this does not make me a criminal. Things looked a bit serious as far as losing my week-end leave was concerned, so, when the boss said "Have you anything to say before sentence is passed?" I ups like a shot and talked to such good purpose, and so long, that he grew dulled and tired and was pleased to say "Case Dismissed."

This will have to be very short as I have to do my washing and have a bath before lights out. So please forgive me, darling. It was lovely to hear your voice last night. Thanks for giving me your cousin's address to call on. I hope she's in. I'm glad you like the Grail* love, but don't like it too much and go and enter the Convent or something. *[The Grail is a Catholic women's spiritual, cultural and social movement, started in 1921 by a Dutch Jesuit.] *Remember I love you more than anything I could love. I think you are the only girl in the world – as far as I am concerned you always have been and always will be all I ever want.*

I'm pleased to hear the news about Geoff. Give him my congrats, please, darling. I must give old Ken the news, though, theoretically, he owes me an epistle.

I collected my win, but as it was made out to the G.P.O. Brisbane, it's no use to me here and I've sent it to Uncle Jim to collect for me. Don't forget to look after your eyes, darling, I'm worried about your eyes and the headaches they give you.

Please give my love to Margo and regards to Nev and Kev and the others, and please keep loving me, darling, because I love you with all my heart,

Ed. xxxxx

P.S. Love me? Ed x.

September 2, 1941

Dearest,

I had a marvellous week-end at Lismore; only one thing marred it – you weren't there. I'm in love with the city, and, if I had my way, I'd choose it to live in, the rest of my life – providing, again, that you were there. I rang Mrs. Magnay, and was disappointed to find that Nell was at Austinville. I called on Mrs. Magnay and Vic, and had quite a good old yarn. She wanted to drive me out to meet Nell on Sunday afternoon, but, as I had to catch a bus back to camp at 8 p.m. I wasn't able to take advantage of her offer – but I'll try to get there next Sunday. Mrs. Magnay, whose voice reminded me strangely of yours over the phone, sends you her love. She says Pat, her sister, is in Brisbane again.

Did you have a good week-end at home, darling? How was your Mother, Alice and the boys? And when does Leo join the ranks of the slaves of the G.P.O.? This paragraph sounds like a quiz, doesn't it, but I'm very interested in the doings of your family – after all, they'll be <u>my</u> family, someday not far away.

I met Uncle Ed after 7 o'clock Mass at the Cathedral in Lismore and we had a great old yarn over a huge breakfast supplied by the Mother Superior of the Convent. I was surprised to find the Sisters so interested in the War, and the R.A.A.F. They made quite a fuss over me, being Uncle Ed's namesake and favourite nephew, and I'm afraid broke a lot of their Retreat Silence, telling me about brothers and Relations they have in the Air Force, etc. The Mother Superior gave me a huge bag of chocolates and lollies. The Bishop of Lismore had given them to the Sisters; I didn't know much what to do with them so Uncle Ed gave them to some children we met outside. The poor kids; they were invalids, most of them in a mental way, thought we were Father Christmases.

Uncle Ed was very interested in the Rosary beads you gave me. He's very interested in you, too.

How goes my Lady of the Grail? Do you like the Society and the crowd that belongs to it, darling? The girls I've met who are members have been very nice.

I'm very tired tonight. I did a bit of drogue chasing this afternoon and had lined the target in my sights beautifully, but, after I'd fired only 11 bullets, the darn gun jammed. I took it to pieces, but found the internal works in a horrible mess of broken extractor springs and seized return springs. It was impossible to fix it without spare parts, so I told my pilot, F.O. Gray, to make for home. Instead of doing this he edged his plane over and commenced tapping his wing against that of the plane

147

towing the drogue. I know this takes some believing, but it's true. He's a marvellous pilot. After frightening the life out of me by this manoeuvre, the blighter put the plane into a series of spins, loops and stall-turns. He was surprised when I refused to get even a twinge of air-sickness, but I bet he'd be even more surprised if he knew I was too darned scared to be sick. Down below I could see a school of sharks cruising up the coast, and I thought all the while of my chances of beating them to the beach if we came down "in the drink." They supply us with a special inflated life belt called a "Mae West," for obvious reasons, when we do this "drogue chasing" because we go miles out to sea to avoid possibility of bullets hitting inoffensive surfers, etc.

I've just done my week's ironing, and this and my thrills of the afternoon have made me very weary, so I'll finish off now, darling. I'll ring you on Thursday night, but, if you have made any plans, or are going anywhere, don't worry, because, if you're out, I'll be ringing on Sunday night as usual. All my hut mates are crying at me to "put out the lights," so I guess I'd better.

Please give my love to Margo and my regards to Nev, I B. and the others. I love you more than I ever thought it possible to love anyone, darling. Please keep loving me, and praying for me. I adore you.

Ed xxxxxxx

P.S. Love me?   Ed x

Undated (Possibly September 5, 1941)

My darling,

It was wonderful to hear your voice last night. It always is.

Things have been going fairly well down here. The days simply fly. I worked for three hours this morning, then took a couple of books down to the beach and tried to study there. I think I read three lines. You've no idea how lazy I've become since I came down here; you'll have to drive me to work when this darn old war is over, love. This afternoon I've been sprawling in the sun on the beach for three hours, acquiring a lovely shade of pink.

I booked two calls last night five minutes apart; one to Uncle Jim to thank him for a bit of work he'd done on my behalf in connection with my Casket prize, and the other to you. In the usual slip-shod manner of the Post Office (since I left) they put the two calls through nearly simultaneously, so that was the cause of the delay. The service was good though; it seemed as if you were right alongside me. Everything here is much better than it was at Parkes.

What I was trying to explain about leave is this: If I am to go overseas, which is now only a 50/50 chance, I start my pre-em leave as soon as I finish here. This gives me six days in Townsville and travelling time. Then I come back to Sandgate and remain there until a convoy is ready. While I'm waiting I'll be on leave nearly all the time, which means I'll be in heaven – or in other words, with you. If however I'm posted to an Australian Squadron, I go straight to that squadron from here, which means I'll have to wait until my leave comes due, before I can see you.

This puts me in a funny position. I'd like to become attached to an Aussie Squadron, but, then, I've been looking forward to seeing you in a fortnight that I'll go mad if I don't. So I don't know what to pray for. I'm weighing the choice of seeing you soon, only for a short time, against that of being able to see you regularly, every month or so. Of course, if I'm posted to Archerfield or Amberley, that would be wonderful. I could see you every night or every week. So pray for that, please, darling.

The flying has been very interesting. I've never seen so many sharks in my life as I have from the air along the beaches here. Whales are a common sight, too – on their way back to the cooler waters down south.

I didn't strap myself in on Wednesday, and but for the fact that my harness caught in a projecting piece of the gun mounting, I'd have been chucked out of the plane. I stood on the seat to get a higher elevation of the rear sight of my gun on the drogue that was being towed almost directly below my plane. The wind caught me and at the same time my plane "hit a bump". I was, for a second, swinging in mid air, grabbing everything I could see and missing the lot. Luckily, as I said, my parachute harness caught in the gun mounting; otherwise I'd have had a long 5000 foot fall. My parachute would have been no good, because I'd taken it off the clips on the harness and stowed it away in the locker. Gee! Did I get a fright! I still shake whenever I think of it. Now, I always see that my straps are securely fastened.

I was glad to hear that your Mother and Leo were coming down for the week-end. I wish I were there to meet them. Tell Leo I hope he likes the Post Office. I wish I were still there, I know most of the crowd in the Telegraph Branch and could introduce him to them. Perhaps, with my reputation, it's just as well I'm not there.

Well, darling, I'd better make up for the loaf I had today, otherwise I'll know nothing about these dash guns. Please give my love to your Mother and Margo and regards to Leo, Nev and the others.

I adore you darling, please keep loving me, and please pray for me.

Ed xxxxxx

P.S. Love me? Ed x

Flight 13, the Devil's Squadron

1941 F/Sgt Eddy B Gallagher WAG Sunderland Squadron 10 and 461 3rd from right front Row

September 7, 1941

My Darling,

I have just returned to the hut after talking to you, and, as you can guess, I feel as though I were on air. I've forgotten even the sick feeling my sunstroke left me with. You must be happy to have your mother and Leo with you, love. I wish I were there too, darn it! It's great to be able to hear your voice, but it would be much better to be with you.

The photo I enclose is of the ugliest flight at Evans Head. We go under the vainglorious name of the "Devils Squadron" because our number is 13. What we lack in looks we make up in efficiency – or so we claim. Yesterday afternoon, my cobber and I (the cobber is the chap second from left in back row, Len Greme) shot our "drogue" to pieces. We got on the mark so well that the towing plane fired red Verey* lights at us to tell us to cease fire, and it just got the drogue to the towing post and dropped it as it fell in halves. *[The most common type of flare gun is a Very (often misspelled Verey).]*

I rang Mrs. Magnay last night and was lucky to find Nell at home. We had a long yarn, and, as I told you tonight, she sends you her love. She seems a nice person. I was sorry I had to fly this morning or I'd have gone in to Lismore. She said she had hoped to be able to get you down for the week-end, and I wish her hope had materialised.

Now that I have time to consider, I remember she said something about going up to Innisfail shortly.

Apart from an hour's flip, I spent today on the beach. I took some books down to study, but I'm dashed if I could pluck up the energy to open one. All I did was have two dips and acquire the sunburn I'm a martyr to now.

Regarding the dips, I didn't go in far; I saw a huge school of sharks this morning, just a few yards out from where we bathe. They were attacking a whale and it was a marvellous sight. I've never seen sharks in so many numbers before. The water was a mass of foam where the whale was lashing about with its tail. It was terrifying. My pilot dived on them and from only a few feet up I peppered them with a few bursts, but I don't think I did much good.

Like Brisbane it's been hot as billyo here over the last two days. We had a raging bush fire here last night. A lot of the boys were hauled out to fight it, and they got it under control in an hour or two. It was threatening the Wireless Station, which is about ½ a mile from the camp.

When does Nev go into camp? It is strange, Tommy wanting to join the R.A.A.F. I was wondering what his mother's reply to his request for permission was.

Has Len come out of Camp yet? Sheila was at Uncle Jim's when I rang the other night, and we had a yarn. She asked me if I had any message for you, and laughed when I told her I'd be speaking to you in a minute or two.

I wish I was waiting for our call instead of looking back on it. I wish there weren't so many dills hanging round the Telephone; I could tell you how much I love you, or rather, try to tell you. I don't think it's possible to tell you how much I do. It seems a long wait until Thursday until I can hear you again.

Have you heard anything regarding your holidays, yet, darling? It would be wonderful if I could be in Sandgate when you're on leave. We could do so many things, and go to so many places. I'm nearly mad with the longing to see you again. I know it's wrong, but I sometimes curse having to go to Townsville; I'd like to spend that leave with you, love. Isn't it a darn nuisance that my family aren't still in Brisbane?

In a letter I got yesterday, Dad says he and Mother and Mollie may be coming back to Brisbane on the train with me. I hope they do. I must arrange that you and Mother meet before I go away. I want so much to "show you off" to each other.

152

Well, it's "Light's Out," so I'd better toddle. Please keep loving me, darling, I love you more than life, or anything else I hold dear put together. You're the most wonderful girl in the world.

Ed xxxxxxx

P.S. Love me?

Ed x

September 10, 1941

Dear Darling,

I'm on night study tonight and am snatching an opportunity while the instructor is out of the room to write this letter. Yours arrived this afternoon, and of course it has already been devoured. I suppose Leo is by now an old hand at the telegraph and boarding game. Like you, I'm worried about your Mother*. She hasn't been the best for some time, now, has she? I don't think the worry about your dad's, Leo's, and your being away from home is too good for her. *[Molly's mother, Kate Thomson, lived in good health to the age of 94.]*

How is Leo liking Burstows? I bet he thinks he's been placed in a rat house for the first few weeks, but, after then, he'll like the place so much that it will be hard to leave.

We had our biggest exam yesterday, and I think I did fairly well. It wasn't too hard, or shouldn't have been if I'd done any study. This afternoon I had my oral exam on the guns. I think I did everything correctly, and answered all the questions. Don't forget to say a prayer for me, darling.

The Sergeant just poked his nose in the door and there was a hasty scramble to appear busy. He's gone again so I can continue.

One of the boys had a crash yesterday, through a flat tyre, but no-one was injured, though the plane was slightly bent.

I had two flips yesterday. On the first I had a stoppage in my gun, so only had to sit and enjoy the trip. My pilot, Sergeant Flack, who is considered the best pilot on the 'drome, put on a special show for my benefit. He zoomed all round the drogue, missing it by only a foot or so. Finally he did a loop right round it. It was thrilling. I was sorry when our hour was up. He and the pilot of the drogue plane had a "dog-fight," careering around trying to get on each other's tail. Of course we won, or so we say.

I'm glad to hear you like the Grail so much, darling. It fills in the time well, belonging to a Society such as the Grail, when you have a few friends with you. I sometimes worry that you may get tired of me, because I'm not there to take you out as I should. It is a poor sort of Romance (as Nev would say) I'm offering you. You must love me a lot to stick to me. Please keep on doing just that, dear; I'll try to make it up to you when this darn war is over. I'll have a lot of lonely hours of worry to make up to you, darling.

The boys are laughing and talking and it's hard to write with all the

154

noise going on. I'm expecting the C.O. to hear them and come barging in any moment. One of them killed a snake last night on the beach and the boys are chucking off because when he first told the story it was about four feet long, and now it has grown to about ten.

This is a terribly sandy spot. There's been a strong wind blowing all day and sand is everywhere. I've got it in my hair, eyes, ears, and between my teeth. Every time I bite it sets my nerves on edge.

How are the Kildare crowd doing these days? I haven't heard from them since I arrived, beyond a letter from Uncle Jim. They're a funny crowd. I was wondering if Len was out of camp yet, and how his wedding arrangements are going. I don't suppose that, like Nev, he's been called up for the duration.

There's a kit inspection on tomorrow night, curse it! I'll have to mark all my things tonight – when I can pluck up the energy. It will be the first one we've ever had, and I'm afraid that it means that our time in Australia is limited, now. Wish I could get something definite on the position, so I could ease your worries, darling. Sometimes, no, often, I wish I hadn't joined up this show. When I joined, I thought I'd never done much good in this life, and never would, and that I had nothing much to live for. Now I have everything to live for, and I don't want to lose that everything, darling. But I feel that I won't. I love you too much to allow anything to spoil your happiness. It is this that makes me sure I'll come back to you, all right. Please pray that I do, darling.

Please Give my love to Margo and Leo and the others. I'll wish Nev "Many Happy Returns" tomorrow.

I adore you darling; please keep loving me and praying for our happiness.

Ed xxxx

P.S. Love me? Ed x

September 15, 1941

My Darling,

I have sadly neglected my letter to you the last few nights, but they've been whopping the flying into us so much lately that all I want to do after tea is sleep. On Sunday night I was lucky. Jack Jackson has the bed next to mine. I was trying to concentrate on a Bolton-Paul Turret when I dozed off and Jack woke me just in time to dash up and get our call. It's great being able to ring you a couple of times a week, dear.

Speaking of Jack, your photo is on the ledge just over my bed, and, for a lark, he keeps shifting it to over his bed and telling everyone you are his sweetheart. I think the boys don't know whether to believe him or me.

As I told you last night, I had my medical exam on Friday. It's practically the same one we have to undergo to get into the service, and I was a bit worried whether I'd get through or not. I passed all the tests easily until I came to blowing up the mercury. The doc told me I am out of condition, which isn't surprising as the only exercise we've done in seven months has been a little elbow-bending.

I wish I had been at the party on Thursday night. Nev sounded as if he were in a good mood, and seemed worried about my attempt to dive into the Pacific from 5000 feet.

I'm almost certain to be arriving on Friday afternoon, Love. As a matter of fact I can say I am certain. Even if I'm posted to an Australian Squadron, I'll have the Friday off, and in that case I'll be coming up to Brisbane to see you, even if it is only for a night.

Today has been the easiest day I've had for some time. We didn't fly today, and spent the time trying to study. I fear I'm not doing too well at this game, although I suppose the same might be said for everyone.

I'm in charge of our Squad for the week, starting from yesterday, and it's a rotten job. I have to chase round like a hen all day rounding up the boys for this lecture and that, and on flying day, when they're scattered all over the place, my job is hell. I don't know why I was so unlucky as to be grabbed for the job – and I'm wondering if it's because I've been fairly lazy and they've caught up with me at last.

Yesterday I nearly went up on another charge. Soon I'll be branded an habitual criminal. My first flight was scheduled at two o'clock. At a quarter past eleven I was informed that the schedule had been altered and that I should have been flying at 11 o'clock. For missing my detail I was hauled up before officers and warrant officers and had to talk like billy-o to convince them that it was no fault of mine. This place gives me the willies. I'll be glad when Friday comes.

Gee! I'm looking forward to seeing you again, darling, and it's heaven to know that you're longing for Friday too and that you love me and miss me so much. I wish we could be married before I go away. I want you so much.

I rang up home on Friday night, and Dad and Mother and the girls are well, and appear wildly excited at the prospect of seeing me on Sunday morning. Not half as excited as I am.

The three weeks seem to have flown by, darling girl. Looking ahead they seem to be crawling, but, looking backward it seems no time since I was in Brisbane.

I won't be able to ring you on Thursday night, dear, because we have some darn Passing-Out ceremony and dinner on that night. I wish I could get out of it, because I never enjoy these dinners with all the speech-making, etc. I'll ring you on Wednesday night, but don't worry if you have to go out, because I'll send you a wire on Thursday at the office.

I'll go and do a spot of ironing now. It doesn't seem possible that this will be my last letter from Evans Head to you, dear. The time when I really have to leave you is drawing very near; sometimes I wish I were back at Parkes and still had our week together to look forward to. Please give my love to Margo, Leo and the others, and remember, darling that I love you more than I'll ever be able to say or prove, and that I always will.

Please keep loving me dear, and praying for me and all my intentions.

Ed xxxxxx

P.S. Love me?

I adore you. Ed.

7 Perkins Street, Townsville

September 25, 1941

My Own Darling,

We're having a night at home tonight, dear; Allan and Peg and young Noel are here for tea, and, oh! Darling! How I wish you were here too! Everything would be perfect, then. I thought I loved you before I came to Brisbane to come up here, but, Molly, I never knew <u>how</u> much I really did love you until I was on the train coming up here. You'd have thought that the prospect of seeing Mother and Dad and Rita and Mollie would have been enough to make anyone happy! – and it did make me feel that way in a way – but, every darn beat of the engine and every rattle of the wheels only seemed to say that I was being taken further away from you! So that my meeting with the folks, although I put on a fairly good show for their sake, was not nearly so happy as it might have been. Oh! Darling! I love you so!

But I'd better cut out this sort of nonsense or before long you, who are so sensible, will be wondering if your future husband (I am, aren't I dear?) is worth loving or not.

I went along to nine o'clock Mass on Sunday, and was introduced by Dad to a young Priest here who used to be one of my best cobbers at Gregory Terrace. [Ed was a student at St. Joseph's College, Gregory Terrace, a school for boys run by the Christian Brothers in Brisbane.] *Dad is one of the leading lights in the Holy Name Society and the St. Vincent de Paul here, so I had to be on my best behaviour. It was nice meeting old Mick again, though it was a strain calling him "Father Donlan."*

Except for going to Mass, I spent all day on Sunday sleeping, trying to recover from my 36-hour trip. There's no need to tell you, darling, that most of the day was spent in thinking of you. And, Darling! There's no better way to spend a day than to think of you.

After dinner Alan and Peg arrived with their offspring. They are so happy, dear, and Mother and Dad are so happy in their happiness that it makes me mad. If only it could be you and I, with someone like young Noel to be so proud and happy about! He's a wonderful youngster. I think Dad was right when he said that he's the nicest baby he's ever seen. He smiles and laughs all day. He's only cried once, and that was when I put him down. He must be a victim to my magic personality!

Yesterday was Dad's 55ᵗʰ Birthday. I was glad I was able to strike my pre-em leave at that time, so that coincided with his birthday. We had a great time together. He began seven weeks holiday on Monday and so we are spending the week together. He and Mother are just dying to meet you. Peg just interrupted me to give me a chocolate. She and Alan send you their love, and Peg says to tell you that there's a place at their home here for you if you ever come here on a holiday. I told her that there's more room at our place, here... Gee! They're a great couple, she and Alan. But! Darling! Do they make me jealous! Oh! I love you!

Dad and Mother and Mollie are coming back with me on Friday night, which means we arrive on Sunday morning. I wish you could meet us then, but I know how shy you are, and Sunday morning is an awkward morning. Joan has managed to get a flat for them. She says it's a lovely flat. I'll try to ring you tonight, dear, but if I can't I'll ring you tomorrow night, and I suppose you'd rather I called you and brought you over some time on Sunday. I've cursed myself up hill and down for leaving your photo behind in my overcoat on Friday night, I wanted so much to show it to Mother. Anyway, you're so much nicer than your photograph. I know she'll like you so much more when she sees you than she would the photo. The only trouble is, is that she'll wonder however I managed to get someone like you to fall in love with me. But I'll not let her worry too much about that.

Peg and Alan are on their way home now, love, and I think I'll stroll with them and ring you from town, if I can. Please, keep loving me darling, because you're all I ever could want for in this world, and I think in the next. I think Heaven would be a pretty empty place if you weren't there. I adore you. Please give my love to your Mother, Dad, Leo and the others. I'm looking forward to seeing Leo on Sunday. Also tell Margo I'm looking forward to seeing her.

You're the loveliest person in the world, darling!

Ed xxxxxx

P.S. Love me? I adore you! Ed x

Letter #1

2.E.D. Sydney. One penny stamp, and "Opened by Censor. Passed by Censor 1198" stamped on front.

Miss M. Thomson,
137 Moray Street,
New Farm, N.1. Brisbane, Qld. Australia

14 October, 1941

My Dearest,

I'm sorry that I won't be able to ring you tonight as I said I would last night. You will be disappointed, I bet, but they have us here like a crowd of prisoners. We may not post a letter or use the phone, as they have armed guards standing over the phone boxes. I tried to send you a wire to let you know about tonight, but found it was no go.

We have not been told where we're going or by what ship, so I can give you no information at all, just now. Tell Mother that I'm sorry I can't get in touch with her before I go, and give her my love, please Darling.

Dearest, I'm going to miss you terribly. I can only pray that this darn war will end quickly so that I can get back to you, because I love you so much.

There is a very slight chance that I may be able to wire you today, by some means or other, but the chance of doing this is very remote. I hope I can, because I know it will be very worrying for you, not hearing from me for so long. I know it's going to be a large slice of hell for me, not knowing how you are, or what you are doing. I feel like cursing and raving against this darned war, and against Hitler, and his fellow thugs especially. My quarrel with them is now not because of patriotic reasons, but because they are the cause of our being separated.

Pray for me, dear, whenever you can, for I need your prayers, now, more than ever before. You know how good your prayers were at getting me through exams, in the old days. I know they'll bring me safely home to you.

And, Oh! Darling! How happy I'll be that day, when I do come home. You will have been in my mind all the time, and, if it is possible, I will have gone on loving you more and more each day I've been away. Please keep loving me, dear, no matter what may happen. Your love is the only thing I want in this world, – if I should ever lose it, I'll have lost everything.

Tell Dad he was right in his guess about that boat that Alan was going to sell. I saw him in Sydney yesterday and he says that with the Petrol restrictions it's hard to find a buyer. I think anyone would be a dill to buy a Chris Craft that eats up the juice like Alan's does. Young Noel and Peg are very confident, though, that they'll be able to sell it before Alan goes overseas. I hope they can, because they'll need whatever money they can scrape together before he goes.

I went over to Manly last night before I rang to see I O'Flaherty. Cath, Jo's sister, played the piano, and I made horrible noises, supposed to be singing. Cath is being married on Saturday. I was invited to the Wedding and the reception, and said I'd be along. I was an optimist, but I never thought this would happen. The worst part about this place is that it's a "dry" camp, and we can't even get a drop of ale to tide us over our unhappiness.

I'm sorry that Mat is not going with us. I may be able to strike him over the other side.

We have a wonderful trip ahead of us. I'm going to see all the places I've ever wanted to see, but, still, it has no attraction. I'd rather stay in Brisbane with you, darling.

Don't worry too much about me, Darling, – we'll be well protected wherever we go, and I'll be especially protected by your prayers. I'll pray for you and for us every night, and, Darling, I'll keep loving you, always. I'll make sure that I keep myself always only for you; all my life I'll spend all my time loving you, and trying to make myself worthy of being your husband, which no man would ever really be.

Someday we may take this trip on which I'm going, together, and we'll be able to laugh at this journey of mine. I adore you, darling, I always will.

Ed   xxxxx

P.S. Love me? Ed x

Crossing the Pacific

Letter #2

Passed by Censor #23. Postmarked 20 Oct 1941, Auckland NZ. Written aboard ship between Sydney and Auckland.

Undated.

My Sweetheart,

I miss you terribly. You know, darling, I can hardly believe yet that we are so far apart, and that it will be so long before I see you again, or even hear from you. My brain can't grasp the fact, yet.

It's strange that I'm not enjoying this trip, because we are the luckiest troops ever to leave Australia, or for that matter, any country in the world. We Sergeants are travelling as first class passengers on one of the most luxurious liners* in the world. The crew and stewards threat us just like any of the other passengers and we are allowed the whole run of the ship. I have a bathroom in my own cabin. The passengers don't seem to be able to do enough for us, although most of them are not British subjects. *[The unnamed vessel was the *SS Mariposa*, a luxury ocean liner designed for service in the Pacific which was launched in 1931. After the attack on Pearl Harbor (December 7, 1941), she operated under the War Shipping Administration, although she was not officially a War Transport.]

When we were paid our final pay in Sydney, they gave us the currency used on this ship and we have some fun trying to work it out. It's strange to be able to buy the dearest cigarettes at about ¼ of their price in Australia.

I've never seen anything so beautiful as the appointments on the boat. Everything is like we have seen in films. Even the lounges and the dance floor and the bar make me think I'm taking part in some picture. I expect to see Lana Turner or Clarke Gable rubbing shoulders with me every time I buy a drink.

There is a picture show on board and they have a different show each night. I saw "Great American Broadcast" [a 1941 musical comedy starring Alice Faye, John Payne, Jack Oakie and Caesar Romero] *last night. Remember we were going to see it in Brisbane? I never expected to see it hundreds of miles out at sea. The dresses and jewels and make-up of the women passengers are fascinating. I had a couple of dances with some of them last night, after two whiskeys had given me the courage to ask them. They were very nice.*

I bought a ticket in the Caulfield Cup Sweep being run today. First prize is 300 dollars, so I hope I win. There's always some gamble or other on, but as a "quarter" is like a sixpence to the passengers, and like 1/7 [one shilling and seven pence] *to me, I lay off.*

So far, the boat has hardly rocked, and I have had no trace of sea sickness, though some of the boys have "fed the fishes." We've had bright sunshine all the way.

You need have no fear for me, darling, the Royal Navy is keeping eagle eyes on us.

Please keep writing to me, dear, and, after a while your letters will catch up with me. I'm sorry that they won't let us give you any address, but, when I left 2 E.D. I gave them, on their request, stamped envelopes addressed to you, Mother and Joan, and when they think we are far enough away for it to be safe they'll send you my address. In the meantime, address letters to: Care 2 E.D. R.A.A.F. Bradfield Park, Sydney (NOW ABROAD) *and they will get to me. I love you more even than I thought I did, dear. Dear God! I hope I come back to you, darling. That's all I want in this world now. I wish the darn war would end.*

I'll post this letter "Air Mail" from the first port we touch. I hope it gets safely to you, darling. – I'll keep numbering my letters, (this is 2, by the way) so you'll know if any go astray. Tell Joan I'll write to her tonight and post one to her too.

This trip would be marvellous if only I wasn't leaving you behind. I'll see all the places I've ever dreamed of seeing, and all for nothing. Even if I'd been paying I'd have travelled second class.

We are not allowed to tip the Stewards. The Company treat us as honoured guests, and have games of every kind, even swimming pools rigged for us. It's strange to be so far from land. As far as the eye can see is a broad expanse of blue. At night it is especially beautiful. You may think I'm mad, but I wander off to the quiet part of the deck each night and sing a few of the old songs I used to sing to you, remember. I hope you hear them darling. Silly, aren't I?

Don't forget six o'clock, darling. It's easy for me to remember, because our dinner bell goes at six every night.

There's no end of entertainment on board. All around me people are playing some game or other. We must be a good advertisement for Australia's financial position to them. They probably think Aussie is peopled by millionaires if they can afford to send their men to war in such style.

I hope your Mother, Dad, Leo and the others at home are all well, dear. Please give them my love. I'm sorry, dear, that I couldn't get in touch with you before I was shunted off. I was as mad as a hatter. I'll be disappointed now, till I see you again. All the time I'll be thinking, "If only I could have heard your voice once more." I suppose I would have thought that, even if I had.

Please keep loving me, darling. I'll be thinking of you every moment of the day. Pray for me please, dear, and we'll both pray that this war will soon end, and we'll be together again.

I adore you, Darling.

> *Ed*

P.S. Love me? Ed.

Letter #3

Postmarked Honolulu Hawaii, October 29, 1941 at 8p.m. Written in NZ or Tahiti. Passed by Censor #37.

Undated.

My Sweetheart,

You would make this trip a wonderful adventure for me, darling, if you were here with me, but without you it is a hell of loneliness. My cobbers, or most of them, are having the times of their lives, and it's no use denying that I have been thrilled by the new places and peoples I have seen, but I wish that you were here, or that the boat was going back to Australia, instead of away from it.

The population of the first place we stopped at gave us a hearty welcome. They drove us round the countryside in their cars and put dances and shows on for us, even though it was a Sunday night. The scenery and the strange boiling springs and geysers was interesting. I sent you a Cable and a letter from this place (They won't let me write the name). [This would be New Zealand.] *I hope you got them, dear. Ocean travel becomes very monotonous when you're out of sight of land for so long, and we were glad to see land again – the last British Port we will strike for some time. We marched through the city amid the plaudits of whites, half-castes, and full-blooded islanders. And the town was ours for the day. The niggers were peddling all sorts of articles in the town, from beads to coconuts. I saw a brooch I thought you might like and sent it to you. I registered it, so it should arrive all right. Did you like it, Darling?*

Rod Mac. And I had dinner at some hotel, and did they sting us! It'd cost a fortune to live long at that place.

I've never seen such beautiful silken dressing-gowns as were for sale in this town. I was going to buy you one until I learned that you'd have to pay nearly its value in duty on arrival in Australia. I found that duty is only payable at your end.

We sailed thence amid the plaudits of the populace, and I knew I was going farther away from you.

We had a curious experience this week. We went to bed on Thursday night and woke up on Thursday morning. There were two Thursdays in this week. Just as well it wasn't two Fridays or I'd have been sick of fish.

Last night I saw a good show – Alice Faye and Don Ameche in "Down in Rio"* or something. [*That Night in Rio* featured the singing and dancing of Brazilian, Carmen Miranda, "the lady in the tutti-frutti hat", of Chicka Chicka Boom Chick fame.] *The singing and the colouring were beautiful. Today we visited a real South Sea Island. Owing to some galoot contracting Measles we were not allowed to land, but the native populace entertained us on the wharf. The girls did hula-hulas for us and the men and women sang. We all enjoyed it immensely. I've never seen a more beautiful spot.*

I wish I could write and tell you the names and give you fuller descriptions of the places we have visited and are going to visit, but if I do write 'em, the "powers that be" will object. I hope, when I return to Aussie, and we are married, that we win a bit in the Casket and are able to do this trip together. You'd rave over it, darling.

I'm dying for your first letter to arrive. I always knew I loved you, but I never really knew how much until this separation occurred. The times before when I had to leave you hurt me so much that I sometimes thought I couldn't bear it, but then I knew it would only be a matter of weeks, or perhaps months before I'd see you again. But now it hurts more than I ever imagined before. Do you miss me badly, Darling? I hope so, but don't worry too much about me, dear. I've too much to live for, now, to let old Jerry hurt me, and your prayers and Mothers' and the others' will keep me pretty safe.

One loses track of days, and even weeks on a ship. Everyone has to work out what day of the week it is. It's very confusing. We are now right in the tropics and I've never known such heat. I'm tired all day and wake up even more so in the morning. I can sympathise with Beachcombers now.

The glamorous tales of the beautiful maiden of the South Sea Isles are, in the main, a lot of bunk, though there are undoubtedly some pretty girls among them. I've never seen such ugly specimens as the Maoris, but the Island girls have good figures, and carry themselves well.

The beer they supply is mainly Australian beer, gone pretty flat, so I've been on the water wagon on my shore leave.

I'll write you again, Darling before we reach the next port and may have some more news to tell you.

I've seen turtles and flying-fish by the score, and huge sharks, not to mention schools of whales.

Please give my love to Margo and the intended, and to all the crowd. I wish I were back with them again.

I miss you more every day, darling, and, if it is possible, love you more. Don't ever stop loving me, dear, and pray for me when you can. I adore you, Darling.

Ed

P.S. Love me? Ed. XXXX

Letter #4

Postmarked Honolulu, Hawaii, October 29, 1941 at 8p.m. Same date as letter #3. Opened and Passed by Censor 37. Stamp cut out. Unclear Frank mark: "Buy Defense.... Bonds and ... ."

Undated.

My Darling Molly,

This sea travel is a terribly monotonous business. I suppose I'd have a very different opinion if you were with me, but, as it is, it's getting on my nerves. We haven't seen land now for several days, something like "water, water, all around" – the unbelievably blue water of the Pacific. I never knew that such a shade of blue existed. Strange to say, we haven't had a drop of rain since we started – hardly a cloud in the sky.

The last few days have been as hot as billyo. It became so unbearable that we haven't had the energy to do anything but lie on deck-chairs, trying to imagine a cool breeze was blowing and sipping iced cocktails. It became especially bad when we were crossing the Equator. It seemed to get hotter and hotter when we were approaching the line, and now it's getting cooler. Many of the boys are sleeping on the deck at night. If it's no cooler tonight I'll join them.

I wonder how I'm going to keep from going "nuts" if I'm a long time away from you, darling. Every day I seem to miss you more. I haven't quite realised yet that I won't be seeing you for a long while and I don't let myself think too hard about it – it hurts too much. Please keep loving me, dear, and wait for me. I'll try to make up to you all this horrible worry I'm causing you as soon as this darn war is over. How I wish it would end today.

There is a strange collection of passengers on board the ship now. Most of them are Yanks, and their talk is funny until you get used to it. There are Chinese girls, and Free French Generals – one of whose wives walks about with a handbag with "Vive de Gaulle" on it. There are two Yankee Test Pilots on a world tour, and a few deportees. Also some titled people. I had Lady something or other as my partner at Deck Quoits – Dad would be able to write a good mystery yarn about them.

I'll post this and the other letter at our next port of call. I'll be able to give you more news when the trip is over.

Tomorrow we call at another place for a few hours' leave. It's a place I've always wanted to see, but never expected I should. I'll tell you all about it when I've seen it.

When we leave this place we have only one more trip by ocean, then, thank heavens, we strike a bit of land travel. I don't know how long it will be before we take to the water again. We are to be shown over some of the big Movie Studios soon. The Purser has arranged a tour of Los Angeles, Hollywood, Beverley Hills and other places of interest for us. It should be interesting. If I see Spencer Tracy, I'll give him your love, Darling.

I'm dying for your letter to arrive, dear. You have no idea just how much your letters will mean to me from now on, or how eagerly I'll look forward to each one. Don't forget to drop Mother a line now and then, love, and don't worry if Mollie answers them and not mother. She never writes letters. I think I've had one from her in all my life. She always gets one of us to write for her. I think she's afraid that she doesn't write well enough or something.

Don't forget to give my love to your Mother and Dad, Leo and Alice, Darling. I wish we could have seen them all before I went away. What a reunion we'll have when I come back. We'll have to decide on a place to get married, won't we? And I suppose you're the one that has the say about that.

Gee! I'll be a proud and happy man that day, Dear. I'm sorry at times we weren't married before I left, but, it would have been a hurried wedding, and I know leaving you would have been twice as hard. Now I have something wonderful to look forward to.

It's lovely, here, out on the top deck, with the stars shining both overhead and in the water. The sea is as calm as a mill-pond and the furrow from the bow is flecked with luminous green and white lights. I wish you were here with me, and we were on our honeymoon.

I started writing this during a lecture before dinner, but I couldn't write properly, so I chucked it up.

It's funny to hear oneself spoken of as an "alien". I've always looked upon "aliens" as rather strange people, mainly "dago" in origin, now I am an alien. To go on shore tomorrow I have to carry a special pass, and to the people I meet, I will be a foreigner, even though I speak the same language.

Well, Darling, I have a couple of other letters to write to catch the post tomorrow so I'd better end now for a while. Please keep loving me and praying for me; you know I'll always love you – I always have.

Ed

170

P.S. Give my regards to Margo and all at Burstows.

Love me?   Ed.

Chat Air Vice-Marshal J. S. Goble, RAAF, Australian representative in Empire Air Scheme, met airmen at dock, accompanied them to Warners. He is shown chatting with Jane Wyman, star of "You're in the Army Now." Flight Lieutenant D. K. Braddick was in charge of airmen.

Letter #5

Postmarked Burbank, California, Nov 3, 1941, 5p.m. Letter posted by actress Jane Wyman. Stamp torn off. Passed by Censor #36.

October 29, 1941

<u>At Sea</u>

My Sweetheart,

I have at last, some interesting news to give you. I've surfed at Waikiki, watched a hula-hula at Kailua, drunk beer at the Royal Hawaiian Hotel and worn ropes of flowers, like a sissy, round my neck for about 8 hours. I had a wonderful day. Never let me hear anyone running American's down again. They're the finest race of people in the world outside Aussie. [Molly has pencilled in "see letter of 21.3.43"]

Let me tell you how I spent my day in Honolulu. As soon as we got off the boat, Bert Tinkler and I walked down the wharf and were wondering what we would do with ourselves, when suddenly we were surrounded by a bevy of beautiful girls, all dressed in smart blue uniforms who wound string after string of the most beautiful flowers I've ever seen round our necks, and begged us to hop in one of the many lovely cars lined up. We were dragged into one, half dubious about it all – I didn't know if we had to pay or not – and then the girls explained that they were members of the Honolulu women's 172ecognize, and had prepared this surprise with gusto for us. I never knew how popular Australians were overseas before; the American fleet must have talked about the times they had in Brisbane and Sydney.

It was a long time before we got used to driving on the right hand side of the road, and to the steering wheel being on the left side of the car.

We rode along through the busy town, which mostly exists on its sugar and pineapple industries, feeling self conscious in our necklaces of flowers. The scent of these was exquisite. The girl who was driving took us to her Mother's home, which was the loveliest mansion I've ever seen.

We were ushered in by the butler, introduced to the Mother, and asked if we'd like a spot.

Our rather half-hearted refusal was taken for "yes," so in a second appeared a Jap with iced whiskeys and soda; it seemed as if we'd been brought to a large and exclusive hotel instead of a home. Then we set out on our drive again and went up a steep cliff with scores of waterfalls to a place where once the whole of the island's warriors were forced to leap to their deaths by a conquering king from Hawaii. (Honolulu is not on Hawaii, as I've always thought, but on Oahu, a smaller island nearby.)

Then we drove down through huge canyons, the tops of which were hidden in mist to a place which looked to me like a castle. Here we were introduced to more people, and given more "leis" (as these necklaces are called) and made a fuss of again. Thence we drove for miles along the coast, through indescribably beautiful country, which all seemed like one huge park, filled with new and exotic flowers. I can never hope to describe its beauty.

Although it is alleged that Americans skite [Aussie slang for "brag"] *about their country, they couldn't possibly exaggerate the loveliness of Honolulu, and we stopped at a wonderful little spot, called, I think, Kailua, where all the other cars were drawn up. We had a huge picnic there, of hamburgers, hot dogs, pineapple juice, bananas, coconuts, lollies, cigarettes, in fact everything you could wish for – all given to us, with the most friendly spirit in the world. I'm usually self-conscious about taking anything for nothing, but this never entered my head. We felt, and were made to feel, as if everything was ours. The ladies were all drawn off the beach, and those of the boys who had not brought their togs were able to swim in their birthday suits.*

They had a band there and some hula-girls, who were very pretty.

Our party left early, because Tink and I wanted to swim at Waikiki, – just for the fun of saying we'd swum there. The girls said it was not as

Royal Hawaiian Hotel

good a surf as usual, but I thought it was good. You can go out for miles, and there's no undertow. I enjoyed watching the antics of some of the lads on their surf-boards. After the swim we had a beer at the Royal Hawaiian, the grounds of which run down to Waikiki beach, and then we had to hurry to see the places we missed.

We saw the famous "blow-hole" and numbers of other scenic spots, too numerous to remember. Then we visited the Aquarium, and on my way back through the town I posted two letters to you and to Mother.

Then we tore out to see the famous Butler Museum.

The girls were interested in our accent; the one who was driving has been to Europe and says our accent is much pleasanter than the English. She drove us to the pineapple canning factory, and her husband, who is manager or something there, took us over the huge works. Tink and I were very interested.

Then we had to hoot to catch the boat and just got on board in time. Youngsters swam round the boat as it pulled out into the harbour, diving for coins thrown from the boat. One of them dived from the top deck into the water, with a mouthful of coins subscribed by the boys.

As we pulled away from the wharf, we, in accordance with time-honoured custom, flung our leis into the sea, the girls having explained that it signified that someday we'd return. I hope I shall.

Everyone of the boys was spell-bound by the reception we had been given. It is impossible to imagine anything better. Oh Darling we must go there, some day!

It's a wonder some of the boys didn't jump the ship, so beautiful is Oahu. I think it's the loveliest place I've ever seen, or ever will see. I wish you had been here to see it with me.

Even this wonderful time, though, Darling, wasn't able to pull me out of my protracted fit of the blues. Everything like it now only arouses the question of "why aren't you with me?" in my mind. I suppose, after a while I'll be able to control it, and settle down, but it will always be there. I seem to miss you more when I'm enjoying myself than when I'm doing nothing. Do you miss me terribly, too, dear? I hope so, and I hope you always will, until I come back again. Please, do, Darling, and please keep loving me and praying for me. I'll always love you, more than all the world.

Ed.

P.S. I adore you, – Love me? Ed.

Letter #6

Knights of Columbus War Services envelope postmarked Montreal, P.Q.
November 11, 1941, 12:30p.m. Royal Canadian Air Force insignia.
Franked with: "Remembrance Day Canada – VETCRAFT POPPIES
Jour du Souvenir Legion Canada COQUELICOTS VETCRAFT"

November 9, 1941

My Darling,

You can see, from my seat in this train, miles of whiteness, stretching as far as the horizon. My eyes are sore from its glitter. Every time the train stops we hop out and have a battle-royal. The train is centrally-heated, thank the Lord; outside the temperature is as low as 20° below freezing!

I had better give you a resume of what has taken place since I last wrote. We had a wonderful day in Los Angeles.

We saw all over Warner Bros. Studio. Jack and I went without lunch and wandered off by ourselves. We saw a scene of a new picture, in which Kay Francis is being starred, in the process of being filmed. That chap (I forget his name) and his famous mouth-organ band were in the scene. I met Kay Francis, who, by the way looks better off even than on the screen. Jack and I had a whale of a time! We were introduced to Bette Davis and Jane Wyman, both of whom, like Kay, are very charming and, I think, better looking off than on the screen.

I had nine letters in my pocket to post – four of my own and five for a couple of chaps who had been bad boys and were not allowed on shore. I asked Miss Wyman if there were a Post Office handy or someplace I could buy stamps. She offered to post them for me, and, when I tried to give her the money, laughed me to scorn. So you can say you've had a letter posted to you by a film-star. Number (5) it was.

I saw all over Hollywood and Beverley Hills. You have no idea how beautiful the homes are! Los Angeles, at first sight, is a maze of oil-derricks. They look like a large forest. It would take a fortune to live there, though! I saw the famous Brown Derby, Ciro's, the Chinese Theatre, with the foot-prints and hand-prints of the stars; I never saw Spencer Tracy or Clark Gable, though, so was unable to give them your regards.

San Francisco is a beautiful spot. We stole into its Golden Gate at dawn, and saw its wonderful bridges. Its famous prison, Alcatraz; and

Present Jean Fitzgerald, who will soon be seen in "The Male Animal," presents an Australian cadet with luncheon box. Some of the cadets will stay in Canada for further training, but most have already graduated from flying schools in Australia and New Zealand. These will go to Britain for immediate action.

APRIL 28, 1942.

PIX

Treasure Island, which was built for the World Fair.

From San Francisco, I travelled overland to Vancouver. It's a lovely drive, through California, and Oregon, then British Columbia. I sent you a Cable from Vancouver. Everyone in America had friendly smiles and we were cheered wherever we went.

I walked over as much of Vancouver as I could in the few hours we stayed there, and liked the place very much.

Canada has strange liquor laws. The Hotels are not allowed to serve anything but beer, and then, if you want to drink you must sit down at a table. If you want to drink a nip of rum, or a glass of whiskey, you must obtain a license (25 cents), then buy it by the bottle at a liquor store!

The trip across the Canadian Rockies is awe inspiring. Snow clad peaks, glaciers, racing torrents with leaping salmon are everywhere.

When the train stopped at Winnipeg, the populace greeted us with supper and a dance, although the train only stopped an hour or two. We had half an hour's walk around Edmonton and Jasper; and at Melville we put on a march through the township for the inhabitants; the march

176

developed into a snow fight.

These trains are very comfortable. I have my own bed to sleep in at night, with clean linen every night. I sleep like a top.

We are getting near the dangerous part of our trip, now, darling; but, strangely for me, I'm not worried – and please don't you worry, either, dear. I <u>know</u> I'll come back safely to you. My only worry is that you may have found someone else, much nicer than I, and will no longer want me for a husband. Please keep loving me Molly Darling – no matter how long this dreary waiting and separation may last. I'll make it up to you when it's over, and I'll go on loving you more and more each day. We'll be the happiest married couple ever.

Pray for me, darling – and remember that I'm thinking of you all the time.

I adore you,   Ed xxxxx

P.S. Love me? – Don't forget to give my love to your Mother, Dad and the kids – or to tell them how much I love you.

Ed xxxxx

Melville, Saskatchewan

Postcard: Envelope posted 4.15 pm 26 NOV 1941 at Bournemouth, Poole. 2½ penny stamp with image of King George VI.

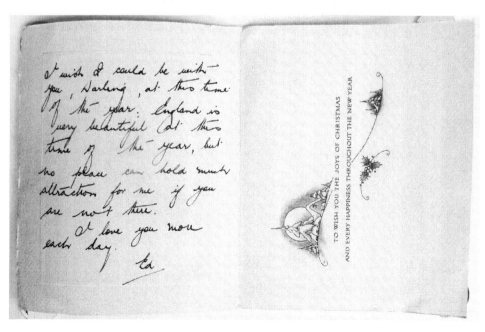

I wish I could be with you, Darling, at this time of the year. England is very beautiful at this time of the year, but no place can hold much attraction for me if you are not there. I love you more each day.

Ed

TO WISH YOU THE JOYS OF CHRISTMAS
AND EVERY HAPPINESS THROUGHOUT THE NEW YEAR

Diary, 1941
England

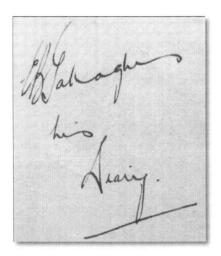

Oft times, I'd like to be able to pour my past, as I've seen kids do with castor-oil, down the drain, and thus rid myself of it without a qualm, but then, when I remember some of the happy times spent, and the grand people I've met – (one in particular comes to mind) – I'm not so sure. Anyhow, this Diary, if I keep it up, should show what would be a wise course.

E.B.G. 1/1/42

179

The year of Grace – 1941 – has been the most interesting of my life. No other has seen so many changes, or been so full of incident. At the end of January, I resigned my job – temporarily – in the G.P.O., Brisbane and donned the uniform of the R.A.A.F. at Amberley, near Ipswich. After a month I went to Parkes in N.S.W. where for six months, which included a fortnight's leave at the end of three, I tried to master the intricacies of various radios and was driven insane by the monotony of the Morse Code. I passed out among the highest in the course, and a month later topped the Gunnery course at Evans Head, near Lismore, and was presented with three stripes and a wing. Thence to Townsville on "pre-em" leave and I recall a great celebration and a headache I shared with Dad, who returned with Mother to see me off in Brisbane. Here I was stationed at Sandgate, and saw much of Molly, but not enough. The best happening of the year was her agreeing to marry me on my return. Went to Bradfield Park in Sydney where I embarked on the S.S. Mariposa for parts unstated. Saw many and wonderful places. Auckland, where the N.Z.'s were hospitality itself. Suva – a lovely spot; Pango Pango, where the natives entertained us on the wharf; spent a day in Honolulu. Honolulu the most beautiful part of this earth! Gee! I loved it and its people! Went to Los Angeles and visited world-famous Hollywood, but, like Victoria, was not amused – or impressed – a Jerry-built place. Then on to San Francisco and by train thence to Vancouver, which is slightly reminiscent of Brisbane, though dirtier and smellier and with crook beer and peculiar liquor laws. Went across Canada and was entranced by the glory of the Rockies. Joined a convoy at foggy Halifax and a fast uneventful trip across the Atlantic found us in Scotland. Trained it to Bournemouth, a pretty town by the sea. Got leave there and hied me to London where I sated myself on the old places that Jerry had missed and other things of interest. Spent Christmas in Bath, the oldest city in England, with a farmer and his wife and son. Indulged my never-flagging interest in things Historical again to my heart's content – spending hours wandering around "Beau Nash's town" on my own. Was posted to the famous 10 Squadron, and this New Year's Day, 1942 finds me at Pembroke Dock, wishing like hell I were back home with Molly!

Letter #7

Envelope stamped: Bournemouth Poole, 24 Nov, 1941. Passed by Censor #28. Stamps: brown one-shilling and purple threepence, both with images of King George VI.

405206, Sgt. Gallagher, E.B.

November 14, 1941

My Sweetheart,

My heavens! It's cold! I never knew what cold could be like. Even at Parkes we had a bit of sunshine during the day to make life worth living, but here, somewhere in the Atlantic Ocean, there's only gray skies overhead all day, and, as I write, snow is falling, covering the decks with a thin layer, and making the other ships of the convoy, and the escorting battle-wagons, indistinct blurs in the distance. If you go on deck you have to keep moving to prevent your feet from freezing.

I'm going to get one of my wishes – Christmas in England. How often I've read about the old Christmases they used to enjoy in days before Hitler spoiled everything. The Carol singers, the snow, the Church bells, the quaint old Christmas trees, the general air of gaiety and good-will, the holly and mistletoe and the feasting. Now, I suppose, nothing remains but the snow, and the good-will.

I wonder where you will be for Xmas? I suppose you'll go home for the holidays, and Yandina will welcome you with open arms. I remember last Xmas, when you went home and I went to Bribie with the lifesavers, and I remember how I missed you. I think it was then that I first knew how much I loved you, and I had my first taste of being away from you. And it was then, I think, that I first realized how much I wanted you, and I was both sad and glad that I'd joined up the R.A.A.F. Sad because I knew I'd have to leave you for a while, and glad because your happiness and freedom were worth fighting for; although, when I joined up, it was only for the fun and excitement, and I had almost come to regret the step before I met you, I was very pleased I had, afterwards. Eric told me the same thing happened to him. Tell Joan I hope I run into him.

Travelling in a convoy brings a strange feeling of unreality, almost as if one were acting in a film. You have to carry your life-preserver everywhere, and a subtle strain is apparent in everyone.

Everyone is gay and cheerful, and even feeble jokes raise laughter, and it only needs one of the boys to break into song for the lot to chorus out. None of the old filthy jokes are cracked, and I was surprised yesterday to hear a couple of the roughest mouthed chaps in our lot "shushing" and telling off another for blasphemy.

There's not much danger around, but it doesn't take much to bring a chap closer to God. I have a sneaking feeling that a few of the boys who have never prayed in their lives offer up a few home-made ones of their own of a night now.

The tucker is not the best these days – as a matter of fact it's "on the schnoz," but you can't expect too much on a troop ship, and, up to now, we've been living like millionaires, which has probably spoiled us.

News is pretty scarce, or rather, for some time I can't tell you much, because to tell you, I'd have to mention the places I've seen by name, and "snip" would go the censor's scissors.

We were not given any leave at our port of embarkation – just marched off the train on to the boat, then off we sailed. I wanted to send you a cable to let you know I was O.K., but had no chance. I hope you got the one I sent from Vancouver. In my next letter I'll probably be able to give you my correct address. It's about time they told us.

I hope your Mother and Dad and Leo and Alice are in the pink. Give them my love, please, Darling.

Have you heard from my family, lately? It's rotten, here, not hearing a word from anyone at home, wondering how those you love are, and hoping they are well – but not knowing.

I miss you awfully, dear, more and more it seems, every day. I wish I could work a miracle and be back with you, even if it were only for an hour. Please keep loving me, darling, and pray for me, when you can. I'll always love you – there's no power on earth could make me stop doing that.

Ed xxxxxx

P.S. Love me? Ed xxxxx

Letter #8

Posted "Bournemouth Poole" 12 Dec 1941, 10.15a.m. Three-penny postage stamp with image of King George VI.

R.A.A.F., c/o R.A.F. Records Office, Gloucester, England.

November 30, 1941

My Darling,

At last we've reached Journey's End! The worry, and ceaseless scanning of the horizon for specks denoting Enemy planes and subs is over at last and we're safe. We came straight to this lovely spot in the south end; when I call it lovely, I'm understating it. You know, darling girl, my idea of English weather is sadly out. I thought Christmas was a time of rain and snow – of Holly, mistletoe, and Yule logs. It's only on very rare occasions that they have snow here, and, just now, it's as warm as Brisbane is in March or April.

Our first sight of the British Isles was a barren and bleak coastline; but this soon gave way to a lovely Loch, with the "Ordered Woods and Gardens" on each side. I love these "ordered woods and gardens," as Dorothea Mackellar* called them. *[Dorothea Mackellar (1885-1968), wrote Australia's most well-known poem "My Country" on a trip to Europe in 1904. The poem begins: "The love of field and coppice, Of green and shaded lanes, Of ordered woods and gardens, Is running in your veins."]

This town, which is one of England's most popular watering places, is as pretty as a flower. The quaint, neat looking houses, the absolute cleanliness of its winding streets and the green loveliness of its woods and gardens, with streams meandering through them and the beach (marred now by barbed wire entanglements) take my breath away. The woods seem to be constructed especially to hide fairies, elves and pixies. I wouldn't be surprised to see one pop out at me anytime. Everything, even the populace, is quiet and well ordered. I like the English people very much – and realise that the Pommies we get out in Aussie are generally the lower class of Englishman. Even their speech is the same as ours, especially that of the better classes.

Our uniforms stand out well against the drab grey of the Canadians, New Zealanders and R.A.F. men, and people seem to like making a fuss of us wherever we go. The Black-out does not stop the night life here – there are dances on every night and plays and picture shows. The town is full of A.T.S. girls and W.A.A.F.s* and they are always arranging dances or something. [Auxiliary Territorial Service and Women's Auxiliary Air Force.]

Good news has just arrived. Jack just blew in to inform me that we have been granted leave for seven days! Whacko! Look out London! Here we come!

Some of the lads are going to the country as guests of different monied people, but my urge for history is going to take me to London. Jack is keen to go there, too. Piccadilly, Leicester Square, Soho, St. Paul's, The Tower, London Bridge, Waterloo Bridge – all the places I've read so much about that they seem part of me will be mine to walk about and stare at to my heart's content! Oh! Darling! How I wish you were here to share this with me! Dad and Joan would go mad with delight, too, if they were here.

Up to now, Jack and I have done nothing, except be recommended for Commissions, and sample the hundreds of different makes of ale on sale here. The hotels here open from 10 to 3 and again from 6 to 10.30. Rather a good idea. They open Sundays and all. I've never seen a drunk yet, in England.

I haven't heard from you or anyone in Aussie, yet. It's rotten to have no news. I hear that Air Mail takes at least 6 weeks to get home from here! I've sent you a wire and one to Mother and Dad. I'll send you a Cable every week to let you know I'm well, but don't worry if one does not arrive, even the Post Office can err and I may forget (though this latter contingency is unlikely!) Do you still remember our promise re six o'clock? It's just six now.

There's no sign of war here. As a matter of fact Jerry rarely pays England a visit, now. He's met more than his match in these Spitfires and Hurricanes that are always roaring overhead.

Jack Hulbert and Cicely Courtneidge are appearing at one of the shows. I saw their show, and they are a great combination. Claude Hulbert completes the family ensemble – Jack & Cicely are husband and wife. [The show was probably *Under Your Hat.* Cicely Courtneidge (1893-1980) was an Australian-born star of stage and screen who was married to Jack Hulbert for 62 years.] *The pictures showing are mainly revivals, owing to the difficulty of obtaining new ones from America.*

I forgot to tell you of the scene of our arrival at our point of disembarkation. The townspeople had a band waiting for us. As we dropped anchor, one of the escorting destroyers slid alongside and the crew gave us three cheers, to which we responded, with gusto. Our first experience of German exaggeration on the radio was listening to a German station broadcasting the "fact" of our having been sunk in the Atlantic. I hope the "news" was not publicised at home, or you'd have been worried.

184

We are only waiting now to be posted to a station for further training and brushing up in Morse. Then we go to Operational training. We have nothing to do, and all day to do it in.

Please let Joan know how I am when you get a wire or a letter from me, Darling.

Well! I'll have to pack now for our trip to London. Jack is telling me if I don't make a move soon, we'll miss the train and have to wait till morning for the next.

Dearest, I wish I were back in Brisbane with you. Dear God! I hope this war ends soon, so that I can hurry back to you. I love you so much, and miss you so much that it hurts. I'll never feel really happy again until I'm back there with you. Please give my love to your family, and to all the folks at Bursties, and, of course, to Joan.

Pray for me when you can, please, sweetheart – I will for you, and for us, and please keep loving me, because you are all my world.

Ed.

P.S. Love me?   Ed.

P.S.S. My address is as shown on page 1.

P.S.S.S. I'm enclosing some snaps Bert Gall gave me.   Ed.

Letter #10

Envelope stamped Bournemouth Poole, 17 Dec 1941, 2½-penny stamp franked "POST FOR CHRISTMAS". Letter written on YMCA paper ("WITH HIS MAJESTY'S FORCES" insignia). Patron: His Excellency the Right Honourable The Earl of Athlone, K.G., Governor General of Canada. "At this Christmastime our thoughts turn to what the New Year may bring. May it bring peace and good will to all men." Athlone.

No. 405206 Rank SGT. Name GALLAGHER E.B., Address: R.A.A.F. c/o R.A.F. RECORDS OFFICE, GLOUCESTER, ENGLAND

December 9, 1941

Darling Molly,

Every day I seem to miss you more. I thought, once, that I could never love you any more than I did, but the old saying "Absence makes the heart grow fonder" is much truer than I expected, and I find myself loving you and wanting you more each day.

You must forgive me darling, for not writing for over a week but Jack and I were granted leave unexpectedly, and we raced up to London, and Girl! What a week we had there! Oh! Darling, I will never be contented until I have taken you there. If you only think that twice the population of the whole of Australia lives within the confines of this city, you will grasp what a city this is! I'll start off by telling you what trouble Jack and I had in moving 500 years. We were lost before we started – and we stayed lost the whole week. Only the unbelievable courtesy of the policemen got us anywhere. It was better even than I expected. Despite the war, London is a city of Fun. It must be beautiful at night, when all the billions of signs, now darkened on account of the blackout, are ablaze. Locals told us night was like day, then. If we got lost in the day, you can imagine, darling, how we got lost at night. We staggered hither and yon, apologising to people and lamp-posts we collided with, tripping over gutters and generally having a hectic time. Finally we found a pub and had a pot or two.

On the Monday we saw St. Paul's – one of Wren's masterpieces. You have no idea how awe-inspiring it is to walk through this building, where countless feet of the famous and infamous of centuries have trod. To gaze on the tombs of Nelson, Wellington and Florence Nightingale and Scores of others.

We walked up Fleet Street where all the famous newspaper offices are, along the Strand, past old "Gaiety" Theatre, now condemned as unsafe due to building faults, and the Law Courts, to Trafalgar Square.

Feeling fit, we trudged through the "Mall", under Admiralty Arch and past St. James Palace, which was built by Henry VIII on the site of a Leper Hospital in 1532, to Buckingham Palace, where a friendly policeman prevented our going along to meet the King.

Buckingham Palace was built by the famous Duke of Buckingham in 1703.

Now, staggering a bit, we went up Constitution Hill in low gear, and, at Hyde Park corner we got a bus to Victoria Station. Going we knew not where, we caught a "tube" to Piccadilly Circus where are most of the theatres. We had tea in some famous restaurant, the Corner House, then saw a stage show, "Black Vanities" in which Flanagan and Allen were appearing. They are better on the stage than the Radio. Jack and Tom and I enjoyed them immensely. How we got home in the black-out is one of those modern miracles.

Next day we saw over Westminster Abbey, which goes back to the sixth century. A lot of it is now considered unsafe and is being rebuilt, but Jack and I went through doors formidably marked "Keep Out" and in one dim old cloister came upon the inscription "Dunstan" but could not read the date. St. Dunstan was one of the early bishops of Westminster. An old clergyman we met there showed us how the coronations are ceremonised there. It was all very interesting. Nearby is No. 10 Downing Street, where the Prime Minister's house is situated.

Past the Houses of Parliament we trudged, and through Waterloo via Westminster Bridge, to Waterloo Bridge.

Remember the night we saw that picture, dear? I wanted, most of all in London, to walk across that Bridge because it brought back memories of you so vividly. I had it all planned out to walk it on some night alone – sentimental idiot, aren't I. But to my disappointment it has been pulled down since 1924 and a new one is being constructed. Only a temporary one remains. Westminster Bridge, though, bears a marked likeness to the one in the picture.

We made our way by devious means to the Tower of London, but could not get in, as only arranged parties are allowed. A Beefeater, in all his finery, repulsed us with dignity, as his ancestors did Wat Tyler, (after he'd tricked them.) [Wat Tyler was the leader of the English Peasants' Revolt of 1381.] *Not being as wily as Wat, we did not get in. Back to the excitement of Piccadilly and Leicester Square, and the nightingales of Berkeley Square, and thence to bed.*

On Wednesday we spent hours seeing over Madame Tussauds. It was a marvellous show. We saw all the heroes and villains of the past *and present, even Bradman* and Crawford and Kingsford Smith* looking more than lifelike in wax.* [Sir Donald George Bradman (The Don) is widely acknowledged as Australia's greatest cricketer; Sir Charles Kingsford Smith (Smithy) earned global fame when he made the first trans-Pacific flight from the US to Australia.]

The "chamber of horrors" is all its name implies – although Jack and I would have liked to have taken on the bet that no-one has spent a night there alone.

Thursday found us trying to enter the British Museum, but it has been closed for the duration, so we staggered around Oxford Street and Oxford Circus, near which are many world-famous shows, including the "Hippodrome," and "Grosvenor Square,"; made our way through "Lincoln's Inn Fields" along Kingsway, near which is the famous "Old Curiosity Shoppe" and back through "Covent Gardens" to Trafalgar Square.

We went to Piccadilly, where we saw a show at the famous Windmill Theatre. It was great!

A few pots, then to bed. Friday found us included in a party going over the Tower of London. It is an awe-inspiring feeling to tread the same walks as Queen Elizabeth did, as Raleigh, Sydney, Drake, Lady Jane Grey, Anne Seymour, and thousands of others through the centuries, for parts of the Tower visible today go back to Roman times.

We saw the famous "Bloody Tower" where the two Princes were murdered. Traced Colonel Blood's path when he swiped the Crown Jewels, saw St. John's Chapel, and the block where Jane Grey, Anne Seymour, Anne Boleyn, Sir Walter Raleigh, Essex and hundreds of others parted company with their heads, and saw the little chapel where they were buried, called by Lord Macaulay "The Saddest Spot on Earth." He was right. Nearly everyone there met his or her death at the hands of an executioner, mostly unjustly, because the real place of execution is a spot outside the tower walls, Tower Hill. This is now a sort of "Domain" where free speech is allowed. Only popular people, who might have been rescued by the mob, like Lady Jane Grey, or Mary, Queen of Scots, were executed inside the Tower.

I wondered at the thoughts and fancies that must have passed through the minds and memories of these people on their last walk. I have read of their unflinching bravery, but I wondered if what I'd read had been eyewash or not. One of them, a relation to Jane Grey, refused to "bow her head to the axe" and the headsman had to chase her round the place, making random swipes, until she was "cut to pieces." Nice thought!

188

On Saturday we just wandered round at random. We saw over St. Paul's again, and saw much we had missed before.

Trafalgar Square, Leicester Square and Piccadilly hold a strange attraction and our footsteps generally led there. Jack and I had decided to have a drink at the "Ritz", so we wandered in, bold as brass and had a couple. They were expensive, but the experience was worth it.

Now we are back here, our one wish is to see London again. It would take a lifetime, and then some to really see all the places I wanted to see, and a century to do all I wanted to do.

No sooner were we back than we were told we may be given a week's leave again at Christmas. If we can get to London, that's where we're going.

It's rotten, darling, not having heard from you for so long. I have no knowledge of how you are, and can only pray that you are well. I don't even know if you've got my telegrams or not, or if those dolts at 2 E.D. have forwarded you an address to which to write. I hope I hear from you and the others at home before Christmas.

Please give my love to your Mother and Dad and Alice and the boys and to the crowd at Burstows. Don't forget, if you ever shift, to leave a "change of address" at the Post Office, because I won't get to know of it for months. I love you more than ever, Darling, and I miss you terribly. Please wait for me, and pray that we will be together again soon. – I adore you, darling.

Ed xxxxxx

To M.G.* on her 21st Birthday
Landsdowne Grange 27.12.41

The years have gone, – and dear, – each fleeting day

An Angel must have spent in ceaseless toil,

To form the charm that Age can never spoil,

The Beauty that is yours – To make the gay

Shy sweetness of your smile, your dear brown hair.

The tenderness that lingers in the blue –

Deep heaven of your eyes, – in ceaseless care,

To make the sweet perfection that is you.

And, Dear, – the fleeting years will but adorn

The grace and beauty that is yours today,

And, when in other ages yet unborn,

Back through Life's rose-strewn paths our Mem'ries stray,

We'll find that Life and Love had just begun

In those dear days when you were twenty one.

E.B.G. 27.12.41

[M.G. is probably Mollie Gallagher who was Ed's younger sister. At that time, his Molly (Thomson) would have been M.T.]

Letter #12

Mailed December 30, 1941. Bournemouth. Received April 21, 1942

December 29, 1941

My Darling,

I'll never be able to tell you how thrilled I was yesterday night when I returned from my week's leave at Bath and found three telegrams – one from you and one from your family and one from the "Mulls" waiting for me. It was the first time I've heard from anyone in Australia since I rang you that Monday night, and so you can see, darling, it was a little piece of heaven. And, then, this morning, there was a letter from you.

I suppose you will have forgotten writing it now, dear, – it was the one you wrote on the 23rd of October, and posted just after receiving my first cable. – Gosh! I love you, sweetheart! I hope you have been receiving my cables; I've sent one about every week since I arrived here, and one from about every port we touched. I've lost the slip of paper I used to tick off the number of the letter on, and I forget whether this is 12 or 13, so I'll call it 12 to be on the safe side.

I had a lovely Xmas at Bath. I stayed at an old farm-house as a guest of the farmer and his wife, and they couldn't have been kinder if I'd been their own son. There was a Lieutenant Commander of the Navy there too and he and I had a great time. The farmhouse dates back to the year dot, and is complete with ghost (which we never met) and all.

Bath is one of the oldest cities in England and we partook of the same mineral waters as did the Romans in 54BC. The water comes from a hot spring and was always considered of great mineral value and a cure for all sorts of diseases as far back as that time. They built magnificent baths which are in a good state of preservation today. That's how the town gets its name.

I saw there many places of interest, such as Sheridan, the famous actor's house, Beau Nash's house, Governor Phillips' (our first Governor) house, the theatre where I Siddons* first appeared, the Assembly Room, made famous by Dickens, and the famous "Crescent" and the Circus mentioned by Dickens in the Pickwick Papers. Pickwick is still a well-known family in Bath. *[Sarah Siddons 1755-1831, was a British actress most famous for her portrayal of the Shakespearean character, Lady Macbeth.]*

I learned a strange thing about the Crescent. The centre houses of this block were leased by Sir Percy Blakeney, who was a great friend of the king at the time of the French Revolution. You may remember that

191

"The Scarlet Pimpernel" was Sir Percy Blakeney. This was the man about whom the Baroness Orizy wove her talks, and he was known to have saved many people from the clutches of the Robespierre gang and their Guillotine. One such was the poet Wordsworth who got mixed up in some trouble, as a young man at the time, with the Revolutionaries and was only rescued by Blakeney's intervention. I always thought that the "Scarlet Pimpernel" was a fictitious character.* *[Baroness Emma Magdolna Rozália Mária Jozefa Borbála "Emmuska" Orczy de Orczi (1865-1947) was a British novelist, playwright and artist of Hungarian noble origin.]

We had a marvellous Xmas dinner, with Turkey and Ham, wine and whiskey. I hope you had a nice Xmas, dear, and all your family enjoyed themselves. I got their Cable, and thought it was lovely of them to remember me. I won't say I hope you didn't miss me too much for that would be a lie, because I want you to miss me, dear, but I hope you weren't worrying about me, because I'm as safe as houses here. This Jap. Business* is getting me down, dear. All of us here are trying to get back to Aussie. When I left I had not the slightest idea that you might ever be in danger. If I had I'd never have gone. That's all I pray for now, that you are safe. *[On 19 December, 1941 the Japanese attacked the island of Timor. Australian and Dutch troops resisted the invasion but on the 23rd of February more than 1,000 men were forced to surrender. By the end of March 1942, the Japanese had conquered Malaya, the Netherlands East Indies, most of the islands to the north and east of Papua New Guinea, and occupied the main coastal centres of Lae and Madang on the New Guinea mainland.]

I haven't heard from the family at all, and I wonder if they received the "slip of paper" (as you call it) I left to be forwarded to them. The reason that queer epistle arrived was that they refused to tell us our address and all we could do was leave a stamped and addressed envelope for them to forward you the address after we were safely on our way. I'm glad you got my Cable from New Zealand.

Gee! Darling! If only you could have seen my face when I got your letter, this morning, you would have got a small idea as to how much I love you. Please keep loving me, dear, and, though it is hard, wait for me. I'll spend the rest of my life trying to make up to you for all this worry I must be causing you. Please give my love to your Mother, Dad and the family, and to Margo and the Burstow crowd. Don't forget to keep in touch with Mother and Mollie, and to pray for me when you can. – I adore you. Ed xxxxx

P.S. Owing to my stopping, every now and then to re-read your letter, this one is very disjointed, please forgive me, darling, because I love you.

Ed x.

Darling, I nearly forgot to include this effort. I wrote it in Bath on Xmas afternoon, just after listening to the Broadcast of conversations between men of the services and their folk at home. How I envied the fortunate blighters. I know it's not nearly so good as my usual, but you'll forgive me, dear, when you realise that I wasn't in the mood for writing good poetry – I was missing you more than I have ever done before.   Please like it. Ed.

SONNET No 203 To M. Xmas '41.

Oh! That I could but hear one whispered word,
From your dear lips, – this Christmas afternoon!
– It need not be of love, – the blue-cloaked moon,
– Of Starlight in the stream, where softly stirred
These shadowy trees, that mask the rose filled park
We knew so well: – Nor need it be of nights,
Or memories of days, that linger like the lights
That live within a gem when all is dark. –

Sestette.

Yet it be but one word! – Today our own,
And foreign Tongues, held converse to and fro,
While love laughed at the seas; and in the torie,
That trembled from their Throats, I felt their inward glow.
– One whisper, – breathed, in the silence, like a zephyr spent –
Is all I ask, – and Darling, – I will be content. –

25. 12. 41.

1942

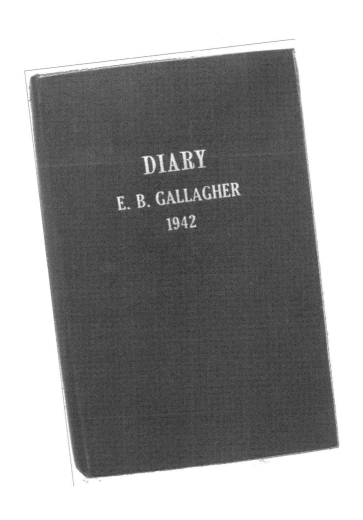

Thursday, January 1, 1942

So this is Pembroke Dock! – A bleak place enough! Walked into the village this afternoon and found myself whispering to Jacko as if I were in Church: It's Goldsmith's "Deserted Village" come to life (A funny metaphor now I think of it!). Here are the evidences of a few visits from Jerry in bye-gone days but not very much damage is visible. My first impression of Taffy [slang for a Welshman] is decidedly unfavourable. 10 Squadron is busy packing up to shift to Mt. Batten. We arrived here on the stroke of midnight last night and found no one expected us! What a start for the New Year – cocoa and bread in the Airmen's Mess!

ROBOT KILLS Q'LD. AIRMEN

LONDON, July 7 (Special-A.A.P.).—Flight Sergeant Oswald Ferguson, B.E.M., of Proserpine (Qld.), who was killed by a flying bomb in London, was buried yesterday.

Flt. Sgt. Ferguson was one of the key maintenance men of Australia's oldest Sunderland Squadron—No. 10—of which he was an original member. In addition to being awarded the British Empire Medal, he was mentioned in dispatches.

Other Australians who have lost their lives by flying bombs include Flying Officer Dick Smith, of Brighton (Vic.), who was a wireless operator and air gunner with the R.A.F., and Squadron Leader Gordon Wood, of Beverley Hills (N.S.W.), a Methodist padre, who was killed at a service in a chapel with many others.

Friday January 2

We gave the boys a hand with the packing up today and I found why the boys so hate the "Pongos," which is another word for "Pommies." A Flight Sergeant caught us tugging a set of wheels towards the trucks, accused us of pinching it, and with a great show of the real Pommy whom a bit of authority has given a bad case of swelled head – threatened to put us all on charges and tried to have one of the* boys arrested. Ossie Ferguson hove in sight; a few quiet, well chosen words, and the wheels went on the truck and the F/S toddled off with his tail dragging. *[Flight Sergeant Oswald 'Ossie' Ferguson was 196ecognized with a British Empire Medal for working "night and day under very bad conditions". He was killed in 1944 (while on sick leave in London) by a German flying bomb ('doodle-bug') in the vicinity of Australia House.]

Saturday January 3

More loading and another example of a "Pongo." The driver of a truck almost succeeded in killing Ossie, myself, Bill and Jacko. Ossie abused him unto the fourth generation. If I'd been called any one of the things this Pongo was likened to, I'd have crowned Ossie with a bar of iron, or the spare wheel, yet he took it all with the dumb meekness of a moron.

Sunday January 4

Wandered around the camp generally trying to dodge some work, unsuccessfully. I haven't worked so damned hard since – come to think of it I've never toiled like this before in my mis-spent life. All the kites have gone except "K" which is being repaired after sustaining damage in a successful attack on a tanker. I don't like the look of the holes in her – makes me think!

January 5

Loafed all day. The boys of 10 squadron seem to be a bit crooked on us having three stripes. It appears that they do not come under the E.A.T.S. and their crews consist of A.C.1's and L.A.C.'s [Aircraftman first class and Leading Aircraftman (one rank above AC1)], etc. – it's not our darned fault, but I can see their point.

January 6

Wandered sadly into the Village tonight and had a few jugs at the "Bush" which had been recommended to me. I met there "Mary of the Bush", who is certainly as lovely as the boys claim, but methinks a flirt. Got a bit merry, and then toddled back to camp, where I'm writing this. The day was bleak and very cold, and bed is very inviting.

January 7

Bit of a party in the Mess to celebrate our leaving this God-forsaken place. The new camp promises to be more full of life than this one. Let's hope so. Found out tonight why the S.P.'s here are so polite to Aussies, and hard on the Pongos. It appears they were not so polite when the squadron first moved here from Mt. Batten, (where we're going tomorrow) but after being beaten up a few times adopted quite a different attitude and everybody was happy

January 8

By train from P.D. to Plymouth. I like the look of this new place, already. The train trip was a hell of a journey, but as we had a special, was not so long as the trip we 11 course blokes did from Bournemouth to P.D., nor did we have heavy kit bags to lug about.

January 9

Yes, I do like this joint. – We were interviewed by the C.O. this morning and he seems a very decent bloke. Find though that it is a fair way to go to get into town and the last train comes back at 10.15 p.m. The camp is beautifully laid out and our bunks are not bad at all. The meals in the mess are good and everything looks rosy.

January 10

One of the old wireless men of the squadron introduced me today into the mysteries of the wireless equipment used in Sunderlands! Ah! Me! I fear there is much work ahead for poor little Ed. Don't know how I'm going to get the hang of this stuff. However it appears that for a while we are going to fly as third operators until we get the hang of things.

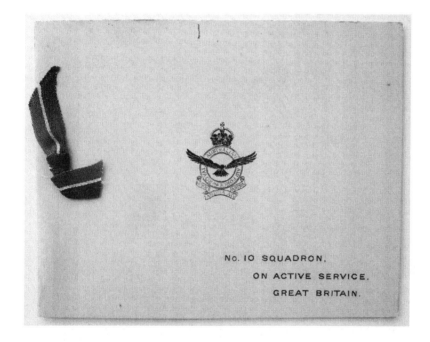

Letter # 13

Undated letter postmarked January 10, 1942; received April 21, 1942. Sent from Plymouth Devon at 6.00 p.m. Letter written on Royal Air Force paper.

Aus. 405206 Sgt. Gallagher E.B.

10 Squadron, R.A.A.F. c/o RAF Records Office Gloucester, England.

Dearest Molly,

Much has happened since I wrote last week. As you can see, by the address, I have been posted to 10 Squadron, and consider myself one of the luckiest airmen in the world. 10 Squadron is Australia's most famous. You often read about us in the papers, as we are the only wholly Australian Squadron in England. We fly those enormous Sunderland Flying Boats and are always sinking "U" Boats, and escorting convoys, etc. You can imagine how proud I feel when I tell you that Jack Jackson and myself and a few others are the first Empire Air Scheme trainees to be posted to 10 Squadron, and they consider us good enough to take up work straight away without going through a course or doing Operational Training as the rest of those who came over with us have to do. Your prayers must be pretty powerful. This is a much safer squadron to be in than any other, as our planes are so huge and well armed. Although it has been operating since the first days of the war, no plane of our Squadron has ever been shot down by an enemy. This should make you happy, darling.

Our mail is very slow. So far the only words I've heard from home were the three cables at Xmas and your letter. I've heard nothing from Mother, Dad or the girls. You don't know how heart-breaking it is to hear nothing – especially from you.

I hope you got my last letter and the "Sonnet" I enclosed.

It's great fun being in a Squadron at last – especially in one where everybody is an Aussie from the C.O. (who is a marvellous chap) to the lowest "A.C. plonk." Everyone calls one another by their Christian names, and there are no "Pongos" (as they call the Pommies here) to worry you.

Everyone is trying to make us feel at home, and to help us in our work, most of which is a bit strange to us.

There is another thing about the squadron that makes it attractive – we do tremendous "flips" – often as far as Cairo. Someday we may even make Aussie, because we belong exclusively to Australia and not to England. That is why we are the first of the Empire Air Scheme trainees to go to this squadron. All sorts of business had to be gone through before we could be posted. I hope we don't let the Squadron down.

I have been feeling so "down in the dumps" lately, dear, through missing you and not hearing from anyone at home – that I needed a break like this to cheer me up, and it has cheered me up considerably.

At night I lie awake for hours thinking about you and home, and wishing for all sorts of miracles to happen so that I could be with you again – and when I go to sleep I dream they have happened and wake up disappointed.

I have your photo on the shelf over my bed and, so far, every Sergeant in the Squadron has asked me about you. They all think you are lovely, and so different from me – I know it!

You have no idea how comfortable our planes are; they have beds and a kitchen on board, and even ash-trays attached to each table so that you can smoke in comfort! It's a long walk from the nose turret to the tail.

I wish I were with you now in Yandina and your Mother and Dad and the kids were around, and we were having as nice a week-end as I had that other time. I think it would be even nicer, now, because we love each other so much more.

I must write to Joan tonight; it's weeks since I sent her a letter.

Please pray for me, darling, and keep loving me. You are all I want to live for in this world, and I love you more than life.

Ed xxxxxxx

P.S. Love me? Ed xxxxx

January 11

Visited the local rubbedy-dub – the "Boringdon" Arms – tonight and found it a pleasant spot for a quiet bit of imbibing. Joyce, the Landlord's daughter, is fair to behold and pleasant to behold, although only sweet sixteen. Lord! Can she swear!

Mount Batten with Sunderlands at anchor.

January 12

Was given a test at receiving and sending by Keith today and surprised him by doing 25's – also myself. Thought I'd forgotten all I ever knew about Morse, but apparently it's like riding a bike – once you can, you can. Also did a bit of Lamp reading – fairly well.

January 13

Went into Plymouth* this arvo. A sad sight. Jerry, without doing any military damage at all, has plastered this lovely old city and it makes your heart bleed to look on it. Hardly a stone on a stone in some parts. Even here you can raise a smile. I did, when I saw the battered remnants of what was once a fine edifice, on the one standing wall of which was "Permanent Building Society" proudly lettered. [In early 1941, five bombing raids on Plymouth reduced much of the city to rubble. Attacks continued as late as May 1944. During the 59 bombing attacks, 1,172 civilians were killed and 4,448 were injured.]

Letter #14.

January 13, 1942

My Darling,

I'm writing this to you in the galley of a Sunderland, and the rocking of the boat makes writing a bit difficult. This is my first night on board a flying boat and I've just had a feed of steak and chips – cooked beautifully by the first fitter – who has a flair for cooking, which, unfortunately for him, lands him the job every time. It's these nights on board that make me think more of you than at any other time – for they contrast so much with those gloriously happy nights I used to know – when you were near.

I wonder what you are doing now? It's about 8 o'clock on Wednesday morning in Aussie; I suppose you are bustling about, running to catch the tram for work. Gee! Darling I wish I were with you!

I suppose Nev and the other boys are all in camp now, with the threat of Japan so very close. That is another thing that worries me terribly. The thought that you may be in danger while I am so far away and safe as houses in this huge plane, unable to do anything to protect you. I haven't got any letters from you yet, darling, except the one I got at Christmas, and it and your cables are the only bit of news I've got from Aussie since I left. All the other boys are in the same boat, some of them have got nothing at all, and yesterday Bill Isles got a Cable that was sent from Aussie on the 4th December. They must have a pretty horrible system at Gloucester.

I suppose Brisbane is blacked-out now. It must be rotten, groping your way about there in the darkness. Be very careful, dear – it's dangerous here, during black-outs, and every precaution is taken by people who are used to them, after two years. It will be three times as bad in Brisbane with its open drains and motorists who are not used to driving in darkness.

Jack Jackson is with me on the plane. It's great to have him still with me, in the same Squadron.

It's a bit eerie here, lying at anchor, with the waves lapping against the floats, and black-out screens over the windows making it impossible to see what is going on outside. I just heard the air-raid sirens on the shore. Jerry must be aloft somewhere, the blighter. Hope he gets his. I have my Mae West handy in case it's a case of swim for it.

It's very cold now, and I'd hate to have a dip tonight. There's ice lying about all day and the wind is bitterly freezing. Every time I change my position I shiver. I tried writing with gloves on at first but found it was too awkward.

There's a dance on at the station tonight, but dancing holds no thrill for me now. I wish you were here with me; they tell me that the station dances are very good. There are about 400 W.A.A.F.S. on the place and some of the boys have found "Romance" as Nevvy would call it. How is his "Romance" progressing, by the way?

Do you see much of Len and Sheila these days? I often wonder how his married life is treating him, and suspect that he will get as fat as a house. Who was his best man? Laddie or Lou or who? I wish I could have been. We always said that whoever was married first would have the other as his best man. I suppose the wedding was a grand turn-out.

Do you hear much from Townsville these days? I hope you do, because I want you and the family to be the closest of friends. You'll be one of it, as soon as we can end this darned war, anyhow. I sent you a Cable last night to let you know that I was well and happy, and I started a Bank Account here which I hope will be of considerable size by the time I get home.

How are your Mother and Dad these days? I hope they are well, and that things are going as they should be in Yandina. Don't forget to give them my love. I'll write to Alice tonight. Is Leo still at the Markets P.O.? I hope he's getting along all right at his job.

It's written in the book of unwritten laws of Sunderlands that batteries must not be run down so I'd better get that letter to Al done soon so I can switch off the light.

I wish a letter from you would arrive tomorrow. Every day I wait hopefully while the mail is being handed out and I feel more down in the dumps each day when there is none for me. I suppose you feel the same way about me, and my greatest fear is that you may think that I have not sent you anything. You know better than that though, Darling, because you must know how much I adore you. I'd give half my life to be with you for only a few minutes just now. Perhaps, if I wish hard enough, that dream will come true, but, Lord knows, I've wished it till it hurt.

Please keep loving me, dear, no matter what happens, though nothing can – because your love is my hope of Heaven. – I adore you,

Ed xxxxxxxxx

P.S. Please give my love to all at Bursties. I wish I were home there, now, instead of lounging on my bunk here in this galley with a Primus to keep me warm.   Ed   xxxxx

January 14

Heard details as to leave today. You are attached to a crew, and when the crew is due for leave, which is twelve days every three months, you all go off together. Spent the day delving into the tuning procedure of a Marconi transmitter. These are beautiful jobs. All the boys are very anxious to get a flip. Paul and Roy got a go today and say the Sunderlands are grand to fly in.

January 15

More swotting up the old Radio. This afternoon I sneaked off into town and saw a show at a theatre in town – the Odeon. It wasn't bad, but I've seen better. It's twenty minutes walk from here to the railway station and I very nearly got lost in the blackout. Found a crowd gathered round some poor blighter of a Pongo who had fallen over and cut his head. He was bleeding all over the place. I got him on the train, and found a friend of his who took over. I think he was full, but he'd given himself a nasty knock, which may have dazed him.

January 16

Nothing much to relate in today's chronicle. Did a bit of Morse, on the key and by lamp, and a bit of work on the set. 'Twas a cold bleak day, real English weather. Practised a bit of mooring up, etc. on one of the kites that was at anchor. There's a lot more in these aircraft than meets the eye. Raj. Bendixon, who comes from Molly's home town, or near it, asked me to do duty hand for him and I've agreed.

January 17

Laurie Benham and I did duty hand last night. This consists of sleeping on board a kite and remaining out on the drink until relieved, which is after 24 hours. You collect rations and can cook quite a good meal on the primus stove. There are two primuses in a small oven, and Laurie gave me a great dish of steak and egg and chips for tea last night, and bacon for breakfast. Two of the boys came out about ten and we had several games of Five Hundred. Good fellows these. I wish I were on this crew. "Jerky Joe" and Geo. Dunlop came in just now and told me they were taking me to P.D. tomorrow. Whacko!

January 18

We set off this morning on W3994 – R.B.X. for P.D., bringing down the crew of R.B.K., whose repairs are reputed to be completed. Joe sat me at the desk and said "O.K. you're the operator. I'm going downstairs to sleep." I had the wind up I'd make a mess of things but did all right.

Jacko sat in the mid-turret on the way down. Coming back we swapped places. It's a marvellous sensation sitting in the turret, apparently quite removed from the kite and you get a marvellous view of the scenery. Luckily, perhaps, we saw no Jerries, although I caused a laugh by reporting one of the balloons* at Plymouth as an aircraft. They're impossible to distinguish at ten miles. *[Balloon barrages were a passive form of defence designed to force the enemy to fly higher, and therefore bomb much less accurately.]

January 19

Nothing of note took place today. Had a bit of a sing-song down at the Mess tonight and consumed a few beers. Am feeling a bit melancholic; been thinking too much of home, I think. It's no good dwelling on the subject. I wish that I could see Molly and Mother and the folks again just for a minute.

January 20

Told to stand by today as third operator on first available ship. This standing by is a nuisance. You can't nip out of camp, nor can you wander about the Station. You've got to keep in touch with Flight Office all the time and at night you're liable to be yanked out of the land of dreams unceremoniously and told to dress in a hurry and make for the ship with all speed. I expect to be woken about 3 a.m. tomorrow morning.

January 21

Well, I've done my first patrol, and found it more tiring than exciting. At 12.30 a.m. I was rudely dragged out of bed by Jack Forbes and told to dress. I had everything ready to hop into and two minutes saw me on my way. Laurie Benham was the W.E.M. [Wireless Electrical Mechanic] and while he was being "briefed" I went with the second op to collect the pigeons*. We were on board by 1 a.m. and then waited around like gloms. Took off at about 3 a.m. – sneaked through the night down to the Spanish coast. Saw Cape Finisterre. This is the first time I've flown at night and the sensation is eerie. You seem all alone in endless space, especially away in the rear turret. I enjoyed the trip immensely, though. I was tired enough to be glad when we arrived home here just before nightfall. *[Each plane carried two homing pigeons in a container; an SOS message could be attached to their legs. During WW2, the UK used about 250,000 pigeons. The Dickin Medal, the highest possible decoration for valor given to non-human animals, was awarded to 32 pigeons in the 1940s for "conspicuous gallantry and devotion to duty".]

January 22

I felt like a washed out rag this morning when I awoke, but the tiredness has worn off now. I find I'm duty hand tonight again. Laurie (gee! I like that chap) is getting the rations and we're going out to relieve the two who stayed on last night. I must get stuck into some letters tonight. It's over a week since I wrote to Molly.

January 23

Spent the day on board. Laurie has introduced me to the mysteries of doing a Daily Inspection. This has to be done each day and the Operator must see that every bit of his equipment, which includes all the electrical gear on the kite, is in good working order. I had no idea that there were so many gadgets. It's strange how dirty one looks and feels after 24 hours on the kite. I think the Paraffin Stoves are the cause.

January 24

Took off soon after dawn on a Navigation Exercise. We touched the South west coast of Eire and so I got my first glimpse of the Emerald Isle. Mother or Molly would envy me if they knew of this trip. Ireland was aptly named the "Emerald Isle." It looked like a green jewel. I'd love to wander round some of the valleys and tramp the hills I saw.

January 25

Took off with the crack of dawn and went on a submarine hunt somewhere down in the Bay of Biscay. Lord knows where exactly. After leaving England we saw nothing but layers of clouds so thick that sometimes we could hardly see our wing tips. This weather was right down on the deck. Landed by flare-path about nine o'clock tonight. Absolutely a waste of time I reckon. I'm improving at the handling of the Radio. Had no trouble whatever.

Letter #16

Postmarked Plymouth Devon, 27 January, 1942. Franked with: "Post early in the Day". Knights of Columbus War Services envelope, 2½ penny stamp with image of King George VI.

25.1.42.

Darling Molly,

Yesterday was a red-letter day for me, three letters arrived – one from Joan, one from Rita, and yours dated the 3rd of November. You can imagine how avidly I read it. It was the second letter I've got from you, dear – the first arrived about New Year's Day.

I was glad to read that you enjoy your Grail work so much; Sheila's party must have been fun – I wish I could have seen the act and seen Sheila's face when she was presented with a ready-made family including twins. It made me feel very homesick when I read that you were going home for the week-end, and would be seeing your Dad who had arrived back. I hope he was well, and still is. Don't forget to give the family my love every time you see them.

You had hard luck in the Cup*. I never knew it was on, until a few days after it was run. We were at Sea and you lose touch with days and dates on the water. "Yours Truly" was rather a poor horse to draw – has it come in, yet? I know Skipton won, but haven't heard any of the other places. ["Yours Truly" came in 7th out of 22 in the 1941 Melbourne Cup, Australia's major thoroughbred horse race, which is run on the first Tuesday of November. Skipton, a three-year-old, was at the tail end of the field, a mile from home, but passed horse after horse to win by two and a half lengths. The Melbourne Cup is marketed as "The Race that Stops a Nation".

It makes me very happy to know that I mean so much to you, darling. In Joan's letter she enclosed the snaps we took that Saturday, and they were much better than I expected. I nearly cried like a baby when I saw you looking so lovely and standing with my arm around your shoulder. Memories of those last few happy days we had together before I was dragged away seemed to rise in my throat and choke me; I want to yell in futile rage when I think that you, whom I love much more than life or anything worthwhile, are exposed to danger from those little yellow hounds, and I am over here, supposedly fighting for Aussie, yet apparently doing nothing. I feel like a coward who has run away when his country is in need of him. I hope these "Pongos" hurry up and give Mr. Curtin* the help he is asking in planes. *[John Curtin was Australia's 14th Prime Minister; he died in office on July 5, 1945.]

I suppose that Mother and Dad are worried now that the war clouds are looming so close to Townsville. It's about time that the Yanks did something. From what I hear these days the only people doing anything effective in the air are the Dutch.

I'm glad that you like your namesake so well, dear. She's not a bad kid. If you get a letter from her, it will be an interesting one; she writes the best letters I've ever read.

Like you, I find it rotten, writing, and not knowing when, and even if, you'll get the letter, but with sea traffic so uncertain, you just have to put up with it.

Thanks for your prayers, my darling. You know how effective they have been in the past whenever I needed to pass exams, etc. They must be more so than ever, because I had such a safe and interesting trip, and have been posted to this Squadron, which has always been a dream, since I entered the R.A.A.F.

It's awfully difficult trying to write to you, dear and give you news. I'd love to be able to tell you of some of the exciting, and near-exciting times I've had on patrol – the pots we've had at Subs and surface vessels, but I'm not allowed to do that. Most flying, though, is very interesting, and consists mainly of seeing the sea, searching until the eyes ache, for the tell-tale "feather" from a periscope, until every "white-cap" becomes a submarine, and scanning the skies in case a Heinkel or Dornier or Junker is sneaking up on your tail. It gets very monotonous, and at the end of a trip you're fed up with flying and anything connected with it.

I seem to miss you most of all, darling, on patrol; especially if I'm doing a lonely watch in a mid-turret, with only my thoughts for company. It's not so bad if I'm on the wireless, because then I'm kept fairly busy. The longing for you gets so intense at times that I feel like yelling out your name aloud. No one would hear me if I did, as long as I had my microphone switched off, but I suspect that if I forgot to do that, the Captain would think he had a madman on his hands if he heard one of his crew singing out "Molly."

I've a stiff neck at the moment, which is probably due to my sitting in a draught or something as silly. It's a bit grim, walking around with my head on one side and it hurts like billy-o every time I try to turn my head. Must be a punishment for one of my many sins.

I've got to sleep on board tonight, and will seize the opportunity of writing some letters to people I promised to write. I've got so many letters to write these days that I need a secretary or two. I've "bit" one of the boys for some ink – funny how a pen won't write unless you fill it occasionally.

Rita is very anxious to meet you. It seems that she hears wonderful reports of you from the family, who are all "mad about you." So they should be – you're the most wonderful girl in the world. I hope you are able to get up there for your holidays as she says you may do. Gee! Darling! If only I were back there and we could take our holidays together! It would be the thrill of my life.

I saw a lot of mail arriving today; hope some of it is for me – and from you.

I love you more, darling, than I ever realised it was possible to love anybody. Please keep loving me or the bottom will drop right out of my life – and life won't be worth living. You mean more than anything to me, dear. Keep up your prayers for me, darling and I'll be safe. I pray for you every night and often during the day, but my prayers are greedy ones – when I pray for you, I really am praying for myself. I adore you, dearest,

Ed xxxxx

P.S. Love me? Ed xxx

January 26

Went to a show in Plymouth and nearly broke my neck in the fog and black-out. Got back in time for a jug or two at the Boringdon where I met some of the boys. Had a few and finished up at the Mess, slightly pickled.

January 27

Did a test flip today. The kite had been gone over and checked. Afterwards all the crew got down on hands and knees and scrubbed the kite from stem to stern. It looks like a new pin. Laurie and I did the Bridge and are proud of the result of our efforts. Are first available again tonight.

January 28

Had some fun today. We were airborne about 2 a.m. and dawn found us out in the Bay. Stooged around for some time in and out of clouds. Got the fright of my life when the alarm buzzer sounded while I was lying on the bunk. Found two J.U. 88's on our starboard beam. Before they could close we ran into a lovely bank of clouds and lost the B's. Then, on the way home, about 150 miles from the coast of England, we sighted an F.W. 200 (Kurier or Condor) but it made no attempt to attack us. Thankful to be in bed safe and sound tonight! The J.U.'s are lovely looking kites, and as deadly as sin.

January 29

Had a "do" in the Mess tonight. Was excited to get some letters from home. Feel tired tonight so am turning in early, if the blokes who are still at the aforesaid "do" let me. They talk for hours here before going to sleep.

January 30

Took off at dawn on a different sort of job today. We escorted a large convoy somewhere or other. Darned if I know how our navigator can find such a small dot in the ~~Pacific~~ Atlantic. It's a better job than submarine hunting – somehow you seem to be in touch with someone and it's a good feeling knowing so much depends on you – and a grand sight to see the huge collection of ships of all sizes steaming steadily on their course. We saw no subs or aircraft. We left for home as night fell after obtaining and giving information by Aldis Lamp. On reading this over I find I've overstated the range and speed of a Sunderland. Fancy convoying a collection of ships in the Pacific from England!! Atlantic, mug!

January 31

Did a navigation exercise today in the Irish Sea. It was nearly my last trip! Coming through a break in the clouds we came right on top of a British Ship which booped off at us with great gusto! They have trigger minds these A.A. gunners. Luckily their shooting was a bit wild, but did we skedaddle! Find I have over the century of hours up now, counting my flying in Aussie.

February 1, 1942

Been in this war about a year now. I wonder when the damned thing will end? I wish I were back home with the boys, getting the beer for a party at Bursties tonight. Wonder what Molly is doing just now?

February 2

Did the rounds of a few pubs in Plymouth tonight. Found a good spot – "The Woodman's Arms." Met Wally and some of the crowd and had a real good time. I'm going to P.D. for some night landings tomorrow. Brownie is going to try to get his Captaincy. He should.

February 3

Did some local flying at Mt. Batten this morning and took off for P.D. after dinner. Landed at Angle Bay and Tommy Egerton put Brownie through his paces there until dark. Brownie then went solo with myself and the fitter and rigger and made some beautiful landings by flare path. He qualified all right. It would have been too bad for us if he hadn't!

February 4

Down at P.D. things are as dull as ever. Renewed my acquaintance with some of the pubs, including, of course, the "Bush". The people were surprised to see us and hoped it meant that 10 Squadron was back (bringing with it a boom in business which has slumped since we left). Mary is as beautiful as ever.

February 5

Duty hand tonight and Brownie is to get in some more night landings when night falls. Here he is now – if I continue this Diary it will mean I'm still alive. Still alive! Brownie handles the kite as well as Tommy, I think. We're going back tomorrow.

February 6

Home at Mt. Batten again and find we're first available again which is a bad thing. Had an uneventful trip from P.D.

Nothing much happened while we were away. Pay day – Good Friday today. I went into town and bought a brooch for Molly's birthday. I'd intended getting it earlier in the year so that it would be home before March 3rd, but, darn me, Diary, I've forgot! Fancy forgetting that, but nowadays we don't even know the day of the week. – Never live for anything except the moment.

February 7

Did a trip down the bay in search of Subs but saw nothing but usual French fishing boats on the 100 fathom line and bags of clouds. "I.C." [integrated circuit] packed up and had a busy time fixing it. Then "R.T." [Radio Transmitter] went for a row and we had a hell of a time getting flare-path shifted at Batten. The dills had laid it in a crook position. Dave Vernon was the skipper and he was mad as hell.

February 8

Took off this morning in glorious sunshine for a trip to the Scillies. These small islands – there are over forty of them, I'm told – are a glory to see in good weather. They are like gleaming emeralds on a background of scintillating blue. I'll never forget the sight I saw today. Wish we had landed there; they invite exploration. They are making a film to be called "Coastal Command"* and Nicko tells me that our kite will be used. Nicko is first and I am second operator now. Laurie has retired from the game. *[Coastal Command is a 1942 British film, directed by Jack Holmes, and made by the Crown Film Unit for the Ministry of Information. See "The Diane Watt Connection" in the *Appendix* for the family coincidence regarding this film.]

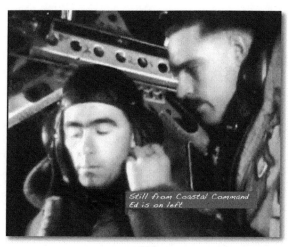

*Still from Coastal Command
Ed is on left*

Letter #18

Envelope dated **12 Feb 1942** Plymouth Devon. 2½ penny stamp.

Aus/ 405206 SGT. GALLAGHER, E.B.,10 SQUADRON, R.A.A.F. c/o
R.A.A.F. HEADQUARTERS, KODAK BLDG. LONDON ENGLAND.

February 8, 1942

My Darling,

*I miss you terribly. Every day seems to be a year while I'm away
from you; already it seems a lifetime since I saw you last on South
Brisbane Station. I wish this darn war would end, or some miracle could
happen and I could be back with you again. This Japanese business is
driving me crazy with worry that Australia might be attacked, and you be
in danger while I'm so far away.*

*I'm writing this on the boat at the moment while he is riding at
anchor in between flights, and only the lapping of the water against the
hull is keeping me company. I suppose in a way I'm terribly lonely, but
yet, I doubt if I can ever be lonely any more, except if you cease to love
me. Even when we're on a long trip and I'm doing a watch in a gun
turret, I'm never really lonely, because you are with me, all the time.
Gee! I love you, dear.*

*So far, only two of your letters have reached me, although, strange
to say, I've had a lot from Joan in the last week. She told me all about
Len's wedding, and it seems to have been a swell affair. I wish I had
been there to see.*

*It's awfully cold just now – well below freezing. I have all my flying
togs on, including my wool-lined boots, but I'm still shivering. I wonder
what a swim would be like? Wow! I'd hate to fall "in the drink,"
tonight; there'd be no question of swimming; three minutes in the water
and I'd be a block of ice. In the morning I'll have to warm up the water-
tin before the tap will run.*

*Jack Jackson got some "Courier Mails" today and it was good to
read the old rag again. They date from the 6th to 15th November and it
made me more homesick than ever to see all the old places mentioned,
and to know that you had probably read the same paper. Remember how
we used to split up the "Sunday Mail" at Bursties in the "good old
days?" I wish it were Sunday again, and I were in Moray St., just coming
back from Mass with you after listening to Father. I can remember the
first Sunday morning I was at Bursties and you dragged me out of bed. I
wonder, often, when it was I first fell in love with you? You know,
darling, when I think of my "flirting" days and of the girls (hundreds of*

213

'em) I thought I fell in love with, I can always place the day and time I "fell" but, with you, it's different. The only explanation I can think of is that I have been in love with you, since I first reached the age of reason, and, perhaps, was in love with you for a million years before that – or Since Time began. Perhaps the fact that you are the answer to all my dreams, even my hope of Heaven, is the reason why I'll never be able to know the day I fell in love with you. All I know is that I will always adore you – that it would be impossible now for me ever to stop loving you, even for an instant – you're part of me.

I bet you're saying "Heavens I've fallen in love with a sickly sentimentalist!" But, Darling, I _am_ feeling sentimental tonight! I feel like kicking a hole in the side of this crate to let off some steam. I want you to be near me, so much.

It's just over a year since Jacko and the boys and I donned the uniform; we had intended to celebrate in right royal fashion, but we propose and the exigencies of war dispose, and, up to now, we haven't had a chance.

Maybe it's just as well; we'd all have headaches next morning, and do dough for nothing.

I hope your Mother and Dad and the rest of the family are well, dear. Don't forget to give them my love; I think they're the nicest family in the world, and my only hope is that they think I'm good enough to one day be a member.

It will be your birthday next month. If I cable you tomorrow, the cable may arrive in time. I have an idea for a present for you, and I'm getting it next Friday – if I can without coupons. Lord knows when, or if, it will arrive. I hope you like it, dear.

I was advised on Saturday not to send any more air mail for a – judging by the time it has taken for your letters and Joan's to arrive, it's not worthwhile – so I'll send them in future by ordinary mail. I'll send this one by air, though – just in case.

My feet are like two blocks of ice, and I think I'll crawl into my sleeping-bag and go to sleep. I pity the poor Russians, fighting in -50° of frost!

For tea tonight I cooked myself some bacon and eggs with fried bread and chips. An order has just come out that all flying crews had to have eggs, and I, who hasn't even heard a hen cackle for months, hopped into my egg-ration with gusto. Never knew they tasted so nice. When you marry me, you'll have a treasure, dear. It's not every husband can wash, *sew, and cook like I can, since I joined the R.A.A.F. When I think of the old poster "It's a Man's job!" I gurgle with laughter.*

I went to a show yesterday afternoon with Jacko. He and I are on the same crew, and when there's nothing doing we generally manage to wangle an hour or two off. We saw "Private Nurse" and "Unfinished Business", both of which, though old, were good shows. It's funny how Jack and I have kept together, ever since we were at Amberley. I have been made First, and Jack, Second wireless operator on the same kite. We fight like old Harry, until someone picks on either of us, then we stick like glue.

Have you kept in touch with the family, darling? I hope you have, because it means so much to me. I want them to love you as much – no – that's not possible – as I do.

My fingers are getting stiff with the cold, so off to bed. – Goodnight, Darling girl, – I'll say a prayer for you before old Morpheus gathers me in. Please keep loving me, and say a prayer for me when you can.

All my love. Ed xxxxx

P.S. Love me?

P.S.S. I don't think I've ever told you before, but remember our agreement re six o'clock? As the times have kept changing since I left Aussie, I've had to alter my time to make it agree with your six o'clock. Now that our time is nine hours later than yours (B.S.T. is one hour ahead of G.M.T.) I have to keep my part of the bargain at 9 o'clock in the morning – when my watch shows 9 a.m. it's 6 p.m. in Aussie. I know you haven't forgotten, sweetheart.

Ed xxxxxxxx

February 9

Duty hand on board tonight, and think I'll sneak ashore for tea. I'm too tired to attempt to cook the horrible rations they gave me.

Tea on shore was crook. I'm putting on the kettle now to make some tea and toast. Have a tin of tomatoes which should be good on toast. Been playing patience – am bored to death with my own company. Lay a while thinking of Molly and home.

February 10

A still from "Coastal Command"

The film mob came on board today with miles of wire and tons of stuff they use. We flew about making landings so that they could capture the swish of water that is caused when the boat makes contact. Then we rehearsed a few scenes. In one I'm supposed to get a message and take it up to the skipper who "looks startled." – Nicko and I both rehearsed but I fear Nick must be better at this acting game than I am, because when they shot the scene, they took him a few times, but poor old me only once. Surely the famous actor of "Professor Tim"* (shades of Holy Cross) would be good enough to appear on the silver screen. *[Refers to a role he played in amateur theatre at Holy Cross Catholic Church in Lutwyche, Brisbane.]

February 11

Went to a show at the Odeon tonight. It wasn't bad, but I've seen better. Returned to bed via the Boringdon and the Mess. Am in a fairly happy frame of mind. John Mac came to the show with me. In some weak moment I promised to take young Joyce of the B'don to a show tomorrow if I'm free. Hope I'm down the Bay!

February 12

Joyce missed out, thank heavens!

Took off this morning in good weather for a sub hunt. The Bay was lovely until a damned J.U. 88* hove in sight with obvious designs on our persons. [Junkers JU 88 was a German Luftwaffe twin-engine, multi-role aircraft. From 1936 to 1945 more than 16,000 were built.] Was in tail turret.

Let him come into five hundred yards before opening with a short hosing burst. He broke away and tried a port quarter attack. Boofed off at us, but missed by a mile. Got in a long burst into him and he seemed to falter, then drop like a stone. He recovered after dropping about 500 feet then side slipped again into some low clouds. Never saw him again and I think I must have got him. No credit given, though Woodsie [Flight Lieutenant S. R. C. Wood] (who was skipper), was rooting for me.

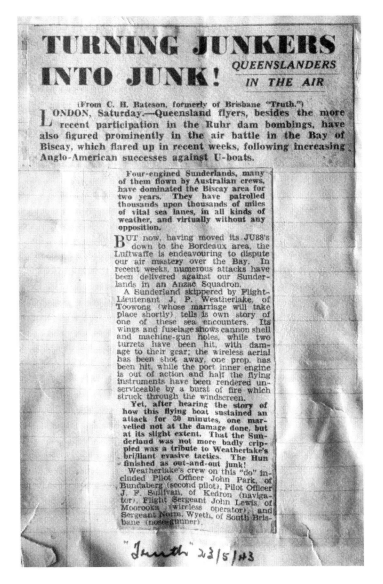

TURNING JUNKERS INTO JUNK!

QUEENSLANDERS IN THE AIR

(From C. H. Bateson, formerly of Brisbane "Truth.")

LONDON, Saturday.—Queensland flyers, besides the more recent participation in the Ruhr dam bombings, have also figured prominently in the air battle in the Bay of Biscay, which flared up in recent weeks, following increasing Anglo-American successes against U-boats.

Four-engined Sunderlands, many of them flown by Australian crews, have dominated the Biscay area for two years. They have patrolled thousands upon thousands of miles of vital sea lanes, in all kinds of weather, and virtually without any opposition.

BUT now, having moved its JU88's down to the Bordeaux area, the Luftwaffe is endeavouring to dispute our air mastery over the Bay. In recent weeks, numerous attacks have been delivered against our Sunderlands in an Anzac Squadron.

A Sunderland skippered by Flight-Lieutenant J. P. Weatherlake, of Toowong (whose marriage will take place shortly), tells is own story of one of these sea encounters. Its wings and fuselage shows cannon shell and machine-gun holes, while two turrets have been hit, with damage to their gear; the wireless aerial has been shot away, one prop. has been hit, while the port inner engine is out of action and half the flying instruments have been rendered unserviceable by a burst of fire which struck through the windscreen.

Yet, after hearing the story of how this flying boat sustained an attack for 30 minutes, one marvelled not at the damage done, but at its slight extent. That the Sunderland was not more badly crippled was a tribute to Weatherlake's brilliant evasive tactics. The Hun finished as out-and-out junk!

Weatherlake's crew on this "do" included Pilot Officer John Park, of Bundaberg (second pilot), Pilot Officer J. F. Sullivan, of Kedron (navigator), Flight Sergeant John Lewis, of Moorooka (wireless operator), and Sergeant Norm. Wyeth, of South Brisbane (nose-gunner).

"Truth" 23/5/43

217

February 13

Got out of bed about 10 a.m.; had a look at the weather then got back in again. Wish today had been pay-day.

Too tired to bother about you tonight, Diary old thing.

February 14

Did another round the Bay trip; almost know it like the back of my hand by now. Saw naught that was suspicious nor did I want to see anything. I don't like being fired at by perfect strangers. I enjoy this lazy floating along on the wings of the wind, with only the sky above and the sea below.

Struck a beautiful cloud formation through which we plunged like a fish through water. Looking back at times from the tail turret, I could see the perfect shape of the kite formed as a hole in one of the clouds.

February 15

Sing-song and beer-up in the mess in honour of something or other – nothing I think. A good time was had by all, including your handsome author, Diary. Feel good-o tonight; wish Len and Les and the boys were here with me. Whacko!

February 16

Did another uneventful patrol today. I never seem to see a sub. Must be a jinx or something. Clouds were thick and low down the bay – almost 10/10ths in fact – and spoiled our chances a lot. Just got home before weather closed in properly, and were circling Batten preparatory to landing when I got the laconic message over the R.T. – "Balloons are still at 1500 feet!" I've never been so scared in all my life. When we landed, by the luck of the devil never hitting a cable or a balloon*, Woodsie was white and shaking and it takes a hell of a lot to rattle him! He tore the mob up in ops to shreds, then jumped on 'em. *[During WW2 in the UK, about 310 friendly aircraft hit balloon cables, causing 91 crashes and 38 forced landings.]

February 17

Saw a show at the "Gaumont"* in town today and then had tea at a Dago's in the main street. It was a good feed – steak and tomatoes. I met some chap – don't know his name – on the way home in a tiny three-wheeler car. We stopped at a nice little inn and had a few jugs on the way. Never seen it before. [The 1931-built Gaumont Palace Picture House in Plymouth later became the Millennium Complex.]

February 18

Don't think I've introduced Jacques Hazard* to you before Diary. He used to fly a seaplane from the huge French sub that was in dock at P. when the French chucked in the towel. He became so popular with the lads of 10 Squadron that they kidnapped him when they went to P.D. from here, and have refused to let him go. I went for a flip with him testing a kite this arvo, and he can sure handle a Sunderland. One of the nicest chaps and best personalities I've met. [Jacques Hazard joined 10 Squadron in July 1941. On June 21, 1942 he disappeared with his crew during a search for a downed plane; it was his 59th Coastal Command mission – he had completed almost 700 flying hours.]

February 19

We went off after a German Convoy down the French Coast this morning. The weather was awful. Sometimes it was too rough to let "George" fly and it was an effort to walk up to the tail turret. Wing-tip visibility made the finding of the convoy almost an impossibility, and we didn't see a thing. I've never felt so much like being sick before in an aircraft, unless it was in a Fairy Battle doing air to ground gunnery at Evans Head. I'm a wreck tonight.

Ordnance Survey Dartmoor Special District (Relief) Map, 1936 showing the Mount Batten Seaplane Breakwater, bottom middle.

Letter # 19

Dated Feb 21, 1942. Received May 15, 1942. Sent from Plymouth, Devon at 10.15 a.m. with a 2½-penny stamp.

February 20, 1942

My Darling,

I have been frightfully busy lately, and I feel as tired as I've ever been in my life; my brain is too weary to rest. I'm paying in full for my numerous sins, these days, for I thought I'd be able to get a good night's slumber tonight, but the fitter on my kite has just popped in to inform me that I have to hold myself in readiness in case there's a job on tonight – Lord! How I hope there's none.

I got a pleasant surprise on Saturday, when a parcel arrived from the Commonwealth Public Service. We enjoyed a great old party of peaches, pineapple and cream and cakes and biscuits. It was the goods.

It was great to get all the details of Len's wedding. I'm darned crooked that I missed all the festivities, and I bet that Len missed me.

I scored my first century of flying hours the other day, and so I now consider myself a veteran. The hours mount up quickly on these long patrols, and I suppose that it won't be long before I've got a thousand hours to my credit. You've no idea how tiring it is to fly for more than a dozen hours through the night, or how longingly one watches for the dawn. The hours drag by like snails, and one's whole being revolts from the shuddering and roaring of the machine and the icy coldness.

During these times I think of you a lot dear; I try to concentrate on you, and to remember every little detail of your appearance, especially your smile. It's a wonder that you don't feel my thoughts, so intensely do I focus my thoughts on you. In the short periods of rest, in between watches, I lie on my bunk and shut my eyes, and, sometimes when I half-doze, it seems that I have only to open my eyes to find you beside me, and I curse the chap who breaks the spell by asking me to take over. Please keep loving me, darling, you know how my world would collapse if ever you ceased to care.

My career as a film actor has come to a sad end, owing to the call of duty. The director was heart-broken at losing the services of one who had all the qualities of Ronald Colman, Paul Muni, Spencer Tracy, and Clark Gable rolled into one. It was fun while it lasted. If ever a film comes to Aussie, called "Coastal Command," see it, because I am in it. My acting in the scene where I have to receive an important message and dash with it to the Captain has never been surpassed. It was a pity that I spoiled the scene where the Captain is talking to me by bursting into laughter, but how would you like to keep a straight face if someone, especially a tried and trusted Squadron Leader, were to say to you, "Glub. Blurb. Horseradishes, Cauliflowers, Blah. Blah. Lollies and Peanuts" etc. They take the scene first, without sound, so it doesn't matter what you say. It should be worth seeing.

I wish I could tell you of some of the lovely places I've seen on patrol, but you'll have to wait until after the war to hear all about them. I never dreamed that I'd see all that I have seen, especially under such circumstances.

Some of the boys are going to Ireland for their leave. I'd love to go there, and probably will. Have you any friends or relatives either in England or Ireland I could call on. It's crook knowing no one in this land. I like meeting new friends.

How are all the family doing? I hope they are all well and happy. It's nice of them to take such an interest in my doings and I hope I'm worth that interest. Don't forget to give them my love, Darling.

Spring is nearing us now, but it's colder than ever before. If you put your nose outside the door it will be frozen off. It's funny that only a few weeks ago it was pitch dark about five o'clock, and now it's bright daylight up to half-past seven. They say that it is still bright at eleven o'clock in the middle of summer. It must be hard to know when to go to bed.

One of the boys got a letter addressed to all of us from a steward off the Mariposa. It was decent of him to remember us, and he gave us some quite interesting news on the state of things in America since the Japs declared war.

Speaking of the Japs, I see that the rotten little yellow —'s have bombed Darwin*. Excuse the swearing, dear, but I burn up whenever I think of them, and that they may be endangering you. I wish you were living in Cunnamulla or somewhere comparatively safe. Look after yourself, dear. *[The Japanese bombing raids on Darwin on 19 February 1942, the first of almost 100 in 1942-43, were the largest attacks ever mounted by a foreign power against Australia.]

It's almost impossible to go to Mass on a Sunday. We have to travel miles to the nearest Church, and generally it is impossible to secure leave. So please pray hard for me dear. I need your prayers terribly.

One of the boys has just told me I'm mad, and should be sleeping while I can. I suppose he's right, but this is the first chance I've had to write to you for some days, and so sleep will have to take second place.

I fell over in the Black-out on the station the other night and had the luckiest escape from killing myself I've ever had. However, a skinned face and hurt feelings was the extent of my damage. In future I'll be more careful. I haven't had a chance to get you your birthday present yet, and Lord knows when I will get the opportunity. I haven't even been able to go into town to get a hair-cut, lately, and soon I'll look like the "Old man of the forest."

Do you see much of Joan these days? I owe her a letter and must seize the next opportunity to write to her. She's a great kid, Molly, one of the best.

I often wonder how the old Bribie Island Club is faring these days. Gee! I envy you people, living in a nice warm country. The cold – I've always hated it – gives me the willies, and I'll never get over having to undergo two winters in a row. Strangely enough, I haven't the least sign of a sniffle.

Do you hear regularly from the folks in Townsville? Mollie is about the only good correspondent in the house up there.

I wish I could ring you up like I used to from Parkes and Evans Head; it would be Heaven, just to hear your voice, darling, like it was in those days. I wonder when all this madness will end, and I'll be able to see you, and better – kiss you again? I'd give years of my life to make it next week. Oh! Darling I need you.

Please keep praying for me, dear, and remember that I love you more than I can ever tell you, and always will.

Ed xxxxxx

P.S. Love me? Ed xxxx

February 20

Flew to some point about 200 miles off the Scillies on a Nav. Exercise for some new chaps. One of them landed the kite on our return – or thought he did – but his perfect landing was about 50 feet up in the air! We bashed into the water and I, who was standing up, changing over from W.T. to R.T. was thrown against the back of the 2nd pilot's seat, and knocked out cold. All the boys were badly shaken, but I came off worst. Woke up in hospital and have been kept there for five days (I'm filling this in on the 26th) for observation, because I had slight concussion.

Interior of Sunderland at the RAF Museum, Hendon, UK. The Museum Attendant and I read this part of Dad's Diary describing the accident near Plymouth when we were inside the plane. We tried to determine where he would have been thrown to from his Wireless Operator's position when the pilot performed his "perfect landing".

February 21

Have had hell of a headache all day. The M.O. says he thinks I'm O.K. – but wants me to lie up for a few days just in case.

February 22

Spent the day in hospital reading, and writing. Hoped the folks wouldn't get a scare and imagine all kinds of things when they read I was in bed.

February 23

Same as yesterday. Feel good today. Headache is gone, but bruise on my skull still painful.

I bet Mother would say – "Poor old Ed. He's always knocking his head on something."

February 24

Thought I'd be getting up by this but Doctor says to give it a couple more days. The pilot (I forget his name) who made the "lovely" landing last Friday came along and apologised to me. It wasn't bad of him but quite unnecessary.

February 25

Some of the lads paid me a visit and brought me some chocolates and cigarettes. Good of them. The old kite had a float damaged in Friday's crash, but it has been repaired. Dave Bell is flying in my place.

February 26

Was discharged from hospital today. My head must be pretty solid to stand all the bangs I've given it.

Went to Flight Office and had myself reinstalled on the crew of old "U."

Came back just in time to do duty hand, which is a bad thing! There's a Commando raid practice on and all the crew, including the 1st pilot, are on board. We are keeping the R.T. going and have to report anything suspicious we see on the water; also we are prepared to repel boarders. The boys have a pile of old spuds ready to use as missiles. I have a Shanghai* I made out of Flame Float* washers. *[A *Shanghai* is an Aussie slingshot. *Flame floats* were dropped from aircraft to mark a position in the sea.]

February 27

Went to the Scillies and back on a test flip today. The weather was pretty fair and I sat in the nose turret, admiring the scenery and occasionally shooting at gulls for practice.

Went to a show at the Royal this evening and stumbled through the blackout to Friary St. Station. Gee! This blackout business is a nuisance.

February 28

I was woken up about 2 a.m. and, after collecting my pigeons, we were soon off down the bay. We sighted a sub just as we were turning for home, but it saw us as soon as, or before, we saw it, for, by the time we arrived, it was gone. Dropped D.C.s on a swirl, but saw no oil or wreckage. I think we were too late. Anyhow I've seen a sub at last.

March 1, 1942

Went down to the "Boringdon" tonight with Jacko, Les, and George, and had a few rounds. Mr. Hogg offered me the use of his car, but I was forced to refuse. Think he thinks I'm keen on young Joyce. Good Lord! Finished up at the Mess, where by some miracle, we managed to talk John Mac into playing for us. He's pretty hot on the "goanna,"* but too darned shy. *[Aussie slang for a piano.]

Letter #20

Postmarked March 2, 1942   from Plymouth, Devon. Received in Brisbane May 8, 1942.

March 1, 1942

My Darling,

I'm as usual feeling very lonely, and am missing you terribly. It will be your birthday on Tuesday, and again, I'm fated to be away. Remember last year? You saw me off on my way to Parkes at South Brisbane Station, and I bet I wasn't half so miserable then as I am now. I think Joan gave you some flowers, and you had dinner together. I wonder when we'll be able to celebrate our two birthdays together, and be happy?

I've just come out of hospital, where I had been in residence for over a week. I had a bit of "hard-cheese"*, but I suppose I was lucky to get off so easily. Sorry I can't give you details, but I'm right as rain again, and if any job is forthcoming, will be flying again tonight. *[Slang for bad luck.]

I had a lovely rest, and, I think, read more books in a week than I've read in a year normally. Gee! I missed you, dear. Remember how you used to look after me, when I, like a big "glom" (another 10 Squadron favourite word), pretended to be much worse than I was, just for the joy of having you near me? I think, darling mine, that when we're married, you'll have to view any illness of mine with suspicion. It's so darn nice to be looked after by you that the temptation is sure to overcome me. I wish you'd been near last week.

Just had tea, which wasn't bad, though, again, it wasn't good, which means I'm still hungry and looking forward to supper. My sojourn in the Hospital didn't interfere with my appetite.

I feel I picked up a cold there, though; my nose is trying to out-do an artesian bore.

Haven't received any mail for over a fortnight. Gee! It's crook; every day you look forward to hearing from home, and there's nothing worse than "there's nothing for you." I asked the boys to bring my mail up to the ward, when they came to visit me, and I felt like chasing them away, when, every day they came up empty-handed. The Red Cross were good. Every night we got free cigarettes, chocolates and soft drinks and biscuits.

I wonder what the other chaps who passed through Parkes and

226

Evans Heads with me are doing these days? Sometimes we get a line from one of them, and it's strange to see the way they are scattered over the island. I'm very worried about Mat. I hope he got away from Singapore*, although that is apparently very doubtful. *[On February 15, 1942, General Edgar Percival, the British commander in Singapore, signed a surrender document. More than 100,000 Australian, British and Indian troops became prisoners of war, joining 50,000 taken by the Japanese in the Malayan campaign.]

Suppose Len, Les, Cec and the rest of the boys are all flat out preparing to resist the damn Japs. I wish I were with them, dear, and near you.

Just let my head go and had a much-needed shave. I was beginning to resemble, I'm told (if Darwin was correct) one of my ancestors, and I feel a lot (and look a lot) better.

I see the Japs have bombed Darwin and done some damage there. I hope the boys there gave them Hades.

The news of the fall of Singapore came as a dreadful shock to us boys. We have always looked upon the base as one of Aussie's main defences. Someone must have had an exaggerated opinion of its invulnerability.

Do you see much of Joan or the Mulls these days, dear? I hope they're looking after you well for me – not that you need looking after. I wish Mother and Dad and the girls were living in Brisbane, so that you could see each other often.

The Russian news is very heartening. They seem to be giving the Huns a bit of a hiding at the moment, and it was good to hear of our Paratroops attack* on the Radio-Location plant near Havre last night. A few more attacks of this kind from this "Island Fortress" would make pleasant living. *[Operation Biting, also known as the Bruneval Raid, was the codename given to a British Combined Operations raid on a German radar installation on February 27 in Bruneval, 12 miles north of Le Havre in northern France. The capture of the radar array revealed important information to scientists, and was a great morale booster. The raid was featured prominently in the British media; Churchill awarded nineteen medals.]

I think I'll go to the pictures tonight. They sometimes have a good show at the Gymnasium. The only drawback is the expectation of hearing your name bellowed out, and having to scuttle off to your kite, and in a few hours finding yourself somewhere out over the cold Atlantic or Spain or Scotland or Norway. The only thrill left now is the variety. You never know what strange place you'll be seeing before next dawn. The only thing you can say with a fair amount of surety is that you'll be seeing the sea.

I haven't told Mother anything about my enforced holiday in the Hospital. She worries too much already.

I hope all your family are well and happy, darling. Please give them my love; I wish I was up at Maroochydore these days.

How is Leo getting on at the Post Office? I bet he's indispensable to them now.

Please give my love to Margo, Marie and Mrs. B and my regards to all the boys. I bet Laurie feels good as the proud father. Give him my best wishes and congratulations.

Pray for me, now and then, my Darling. I love you more and more every day, and I miss you more every hour. You're all my world.

Ed xxxxx

P.S. Love me? Ed xxxxx

P.S.S. Just had a look at your photo. Gee! you're lovely ! Ed x

461 Squadron Insignia

March 2

Molly's birthday tomorrow. Hope she's got the brooch I sent her. I nearly didn't get a chance to celebrate it though! We were caught by bad weather out in the Bay and found a break at P.D.* just enough in size and duration to let us get in with hardly a gallon of juice. "Q" was not able to find the break so they tried to put down near a convoy in the Bristol Channel, wiped off a float, turned over, nearly drowned, then were picked up by a trawler. I saw them this arvo wandering around P.D. dressed in a peculiar assortment of garments. Roy Chinnery was on "Q" and he tells me he expects to get "Survivors" leave. *[Pembroke Dock in Pembrokeshire, south west Wales, is 98 miles (158 km) north of Plymouth.]

March 3

Bad weather didn't allow us to leave here today. We all went into the village on a tour of the local inns, or what is regularly called a pub crawl. Saw some of the old faces. Nicko introduced me to the owners of a little joint called the "Prospect Inn." I'd never found it before, which is a strange thing. I certainly celebrated Molly's birthday. Don't think she'd be pleased with my method of doing so, but Lord! I missed her! Wonder if she's thinking of me today – now?

March 4

Went from P.D. to Mt. B.* this morning and now I'm duty hand. Johnno is with me in spirit. He's a B. the way he always ducks out of hand. Hope he comes back soon because I think there's something on tonight and if he's not here when Woodsie comes on board there'll be hell to pay. *[Mount Batten. Between 1917 and 1945, with some gaps, it was a flying boat base for both the Royal Air Force and the Royal Navy. The RAF operated search and rescue launches from the base.]

March 5

Johnno came back last night and, as I thought, our slumbers were rudely shattered by that dratted cry of "Wakey! Wakey!" in the early hours of the morning. We set out and reached our position just after dawn and dropping through some clouds, lo and behold, there was a sub. Sitting on the surface waiting for us. He tried to crash dive immediately but we blew him back on top with D.C.s. Then he tried to man his deck guns but Snow and the boys withered the gun crews before they could get to their guns. Then the sub slowly lifted her tail right out of the water and dived out of sight, leaving some of her crew clinging to floats and others swimming about on the surface. Poor beggars

March 6

Slept in this morning but got up in time for pay. Went into the Barbican and put a few quid in the bank. I'll need some dough when, and if, I get leave.

Sunk an ale at the "Continental" where I ran into some of the lads, but tore myself away from them and am retiring early. I thought once that if I took part in the skittling of some other men, I'd be all shaky, but I've already forgotten those poor beggars yesterday. It's all so darned impersonal.

March 7

Am down at P.D. tonight and I hear we're taking off from here in the morning on a special job. All of us have to sleep on board tonight. Woodsie is a good skipper. He made the long trip out to us in the Dinghy to let us know that we could go ashore until midnight but none of the boys wanted to, so here we are.

Johnno is making supper and the rest of us, except Bill Vout, are playing cards in the ward-room.

March 8

Went out about four on a special Anti-sub patrol. Seems to'v'been a lot of others on the same job because we were sighting Lockheeds and Whitleys, etc. all day. Met up with a "Kurier" who had a crack at us from nearly a mile away and missed by almost as much. We never fired a shot at him and he refused to come any closer. We saw no subs or enemy vessels. We landed back at Mt. Batten.

March 9

No sooner did we land than we were off again on another Sub strike. All of us were tired as hell. We were sent out to finish off a sub that had been damaged yesterday, but some other blighter beat us to it. When we arrived on the scene all that was left was a huge oil patch. While we were taking photos of this, two Arados[*] which must have been lying in wait for us, tried to sneak in. Snow in the tail poured a lovely burst into one which dived straight into the drink, the other bloke went like hell. Boy! Did he go! These Arados are nasty little float planes, but no match for a Sunderland, especially R.B.U. (Har! Har!) *[The Arado Ar 240 was a German, twin-engine, multi-role heavy fighter aircraft developed for the Luftwaffe during World War II. There were several versions.]

March 10

Slept nearly all day. Didn't get up for breakfast or dinner, but hearing we had a day or two off I slipped down to Torquay this afternoon and am writing this in my sumptuous room in the Queens' Hotel. I've never been here before, but wish I had.

It's one of the loveliest spots in England. I wish I could describe it properly. Found some lovely pubs and other places of interest.

March 11

Wandered around Torquay, drinking in my fill of the scenery all day and was delighted with what I saw. Came back here on the six o'clock bus and found Batten much as I'd left it, though drabber than before, after the loveliness of Torquay. First available again tonight! Fed up with flying and everything connected with it, especially Sunderland Flying boats!

Sunderland at Hendon RAF Museum.

231

Letter #21

Dated March 13, 1942 Plymouth Received June 12

March 11, 1942

My Darling Molly,

The number of letters I have written to you since I left home has at last "come of age," and it seems as though twenty-one years have really passed since I last saw you. Sometimes – and they are bad times, dear, when everything about me appears as though looked at through smoked glasses – I wonder if Someone isn't having a grand old laugh at me, and if I'll ever see you and hold you in my arms again, or hear you call me "Darling." It's then I get the rotten feeling that it doesn't matter two hoots whether I come back from the next patrol or not. At such times my only recourse is to act on your suggestion and say three Hail Marys to Our Lady and my fit of despondency vanishes in no time. It's at such times, though, Darling, that I really know how much I love you, and I come to wonder how lofty ideas about duty and all that baloney (or is it) notwithstanding, I ever came so far away from you.

Nothing much has happened of interest lately, except that I received another parcel from the G.P.O. and was lucky as billy-o to get it. It seems a miracle, and you'll understand why I say that when I tell you the circumstances. Owing to bad weather at our home port occurring while we were out on patrol, we were diverted to a strange Station*. We landed safely and I went ashore and strolled up to the Sergeant's Mess for a noggin to celebrate. Idle curiosity made me read the notice-board, and you could have slain me with a badly frayed feather when I saw "Parcel for Sgt. Gallagher E.B.". Even then I thought there might conceivably be another of the same initials (unlucky one!) but thought I'd better make sure. It was for me, all right, from the old crowd at the G.P.O., and it even had my number. I'm still trying to figure out by what stroke of genius it got to that remote place, and also the thousand to one chance that brought me there to get it. I was lucky because if I had not turned up it would have gone to "any Digger abroad," being so marked. I wonder if I'd better make a tour of all the other Air Force Stations here, seeking mail and parcels.

On that same patrol an amusing incident occurred; we were proceeding on our stately way when out of the blue appeared a Condor one of friend Jerry's largest planes. It sneaked up cautiously until about a mile away, then, to our surprise and amusement, started popping away at us with his cannon. How the dickens he expected to hit us at that range is a mystery. Maybe he thought he was William Tell or Robin Hood. We treated him with profound "ignore," not even deigning to

232

alter course, and after a while I think he must have wakened up to himself, and, not being game to come any closer, scooted off about his business. I think that the powers that be in Germany have instructed their pilots to treat Sunderlands like poison, and I don't blame 'em. I suppose, though, that this particular chap went home and gave graphic descriptions of our "diving into the sea in flames."

One of our kites some time ago shot down two Heinkels that foolishly traded shots with it, and then continued on with its patrol as if nothing had happened.

Things are looking very grim in the Pacific, just now, and, Darling, I'm terribly worried. I pray the Japs will not try to touch Aussie. Dear Heaven, if they do – and if one hair of your head is harmed, or even if you are only frightened by air raids, I promise that while I live the only good Hun or Jap will be a dead one. When I read of the awful atrocities perpetrated by the yellow scum in Hong Kong and in China my blood boils and I feel like murdering everyone with slant eyes. I know that even wars should be fought without hate, if one is to live up to the true Christian ideal, but, Darling, I can't help hating the Japs. If I were home, now, I fear that it would be an awfully hard struggle to keep from shooting all Jap prisoners of war, after a little judicious torture. Why! The animals don't know how to live in peace decently, let alone fight a war decently. Even Jerry is a gentleman compared with them. Like you, I could hate some of the Aussies (if you could call 'em such) at home as much. Fancy striking or grumbling about having no Races when Australia is in such dire peril! I suppose Kelly will be in uniform by this though. Mr. Curtin is doing a good job, and it's amazing the popularity he has gained among Aussies over here; and, almost as wonderful, is the scorn in which his predecessor* is held; I know not why. *[Arthur Fadden (Country Party) was Prime Minister for one month before John Curtin (Labour Party) succeeded him on October 7, 1941.]

A letter from Mollie arrived today and she tells me that the photos I sent from Canada arrived safely. As I sent you some at the same time I expect yours arrived safely as well; also the letters.

I was glad to hear that Toni had visited you. It must have been a great re-union, and I bet that the old tongues wagged. On one of the few occasions I managed to get into town I saw "Sundown," and liked it very much. Please give Toni my love and Alan also. Mollie tells me that Peg Broadhurst has been staying with them for a while, but she neglects to mention why, and where Alan has gone. I was wondering if he were coming over here, or going to Singapore, and I hope it was the former. Mat went to Singapore, and I've been terribly worried about him – just another reason for my declaring a hate on the Japs. Gee! I wish I could swear.

233

Did I tell you that a chap who comes from Nambour, "Raj" Bendixon, who used to be in the Maroochy or Mooloolaba life saving club – I forget which – is here. He's very popular, and in the same game as myself – Wireless.

How is the "Grail" going? I was thinking the other day about Sheila and wondering who had taken over her job.

Well, Darling, that's about the end of the news – if it may be called so – and sleep is calling. Please keep loving me, and wait for me – I love you more than all the world. Pray for me, when you can, because I need your prayers and your love more than ever before.

Ed xxxxxxx

P.S. Love me? Ed x

Crew of Sunderland moor the "boat". RAF Museum, Hendon, UK.

March 12

Were dragged out sometime this morning to a convoy. Spent a pleasant day playing ring-a-roses with the ships which were a bit suspicious of us at first. They always are, these days, especially Polish destroyers which open up on everything. Woodsie always identifies himself well and truly before coming into range of any of our ships. A wise old bird is he.

We saw nothing but our ships and another Sundy-bomber which relieved us when our time was up.

March 13

Another Friday the 13th which I spent on the camp, and then did duty hand. I'm writing this in the ward-room, where all is quiet except for the lap of waves against the float and the occasional roar of a dinghy plying back and forth between the kites and the dock. Went up on the wing and gazed at the stars for a while; tried to compose a Sonnet for Molly, and have the makings of a good one, I think. Miss her a lot.

March 14

Celebrated that wonderful day – my birthday of course, Diary – somewhere down the Bay. We brought a Sub to the surface somewhere between the Scillies and Corunna and left her in a hopeless condition. The crew all took to their dinghies then waved white rags thinking no doubt that we were like they are and wouldn't hesitate to finish them off in their defenceless state. When I think of the women and children they've probably slaughtered in cold blood, I feel now that it might have been a good thing for the world if we had butchered them, but then we'd only be descending to their level! So we're glad we let 'em paddle away from their sinking tub.

March 15

They sent a Wimpy[*] out to finish off the Sub we got yesterday and I learned this arvo that he'd completed the job. There were no Jerries around it when he arrived. I suppose they were picked up by a BTV or a rescue launch, though the latter would probably have sunk the sub instead of leaving it, unless it was in a hurry. Maybe the crew had re-boarded the sub and were trying to repair it when the Wimpy blew it to hell. If so – they were dead unlucky – very dead! *[The Vickers Wellington, a British twin-engine, long-range, medium bomber, affectionately known as the "Wimpy," was armed with twin .330 machine guns in the nose and tail turrets.]

March 16

Went out on a quest for submarines this morning as soon as it was bright and struck an old Kurier somewhere off the Scillies. He tailed us for some time, hoping, I suppose, that we were on a convoy escort and would obligingly lead him to the ships. Woodsie let him stooge along, taking absolutely no notice when he, growing tired of the game, booped off at us with his cannon, missing by only twenty feet. He stayed too far out for accurate shooting so we didn't waste ammo and eventually we lost him in thick clouds.

March 17

They are giving the kite a thorough overhaul and I've seized the opportunity to duck down to Torquay for a day or two. Reached here tonight and put up at the Queen's.

The flowers are just starting to spring up after the passing of the real winter months and here it is beauty everywhere. I wish that Uncle Jim could see some of the gardens. I must come here next month when the flowers are really beginning to bloom. Had a few jugs tonight all alone.

March 18

Met Billy Vout and Glen Bulfield this morning and we wandered around the place together. A slight drizzle drove us to partake of some liquid refreshment.

In a music shop I saw a copy of "Sleepy Lagoon" and bought it. The girl on the Reception Desk at the "Queens" wrapped it up for me very nicely, and I sent it to Joan.

We met Alan today, resplendent in his cap with a white flash in it! Fancy going in for a Pilot's course after 1800 operational hours as a Wireless Op.

March 19

Was dragged back to camp today, Lord knows why for the kite is not ready. We generally seem to get treated like this according to Johnno, but his whinging is a by-word.

Spent the night in the mess with Wally and some of the boys. Had a few beers and now I'm off to bed.

March 20

Put the old kite down in the water this morning and gave her a test flip this afternoon. She was as sweet as a nut. There's a free party on in the Mess tonight. – Free beer I mean.

I stayed till 9.30, then left, as I'm off before dawn on some job or other.

Wish I were in Torquay. I love that joint.

March 21

Escorted a Convoy today, and saw absolutely nothing. Had some trouble finding it as it was well off the estimated position we'd been given before leaving Batten. Only about thirty ships in all but there were big-uns among them. I'm very tired tonight. Don't care if Jerry does come along tonight.

March 22

Flew for about an hour today testing "George" who went U/S last trip. He seems O.K. and fully recovered. Mae West and he will do duty hand with me until the morrow as Johnno has done one of his disappearing tricks. He hates doing duty hand for some reason or other. I've even known him to give a bloke five bob to do it for him. "Micky Mouse," "George," and "Mae" are unbribeable, but do the job for nix.

March 23

Got dragged out of my bunk in the early hours to do another Convoy job. Johnno came out with the boys, to my surprise, as I thought he'd ducked into town. Found the Convoy and while doing one of our sweeps ran into a strange merchantman. "What ho!" quoth we, "A Raider!" and prepared to blow hell out of her. We were mortified to discover her as a harmless "Panamanian." Bet we sent the crew into hysterics. I suppose they've all changed into another pair of pants and the ones they were wearing are drying on the line now.

March 24

Went into a show at the Odeon. On the way home bought a pile of fish and chips at the local chippery (Fosters') and ate them with a pint or two down at the Mess. Got a letter from Molly today. Gosh! She's lovely!

March 25

Were sent out on an abortive A/Sub patrol. 10/10 cloud all the time and we just got into P.D. The weather was well and truly closed down at Batten.

I bet we could have run into a sub today before we saw anything and we were well and truly pleased when Woodsie decided to chuck it up and make for home. Just as well he did or Lord knows what we would have done, for just after we landed here the weather closed in completely.

March 26

Weather lifted sufficiently today to let us get into Base from this dump. Woodsie frightened hell out of me by asking me to come up and fly the darn kite. After a while I got the feel of the thing – they're a hell of a lot different from Moths or Miles Falcons – and quite enjoyed the experience. I doubt if Snow in the tail did, though!

March 27

Took off on an A/Sub sweep and ran across an "E" boat. [To the Germans they were S-Boots or Schellboots (fast boats). To the Allies they were Enemy boats or E-boats.] Woodsie went in low and blew it to bits with a direct hit. One minute it was there, next it was not, sort of thing, and all that was left were a few heads on the surface. They were bloody awful shots. Never went within cooee of us with their A/A guns. Sometimes I wonder what sort of chaps they were – whether I might not, in happier days, have sunk a beer with them in Unter den Linden Street*, or what. When you go in to bomb a boat or sub you never think of the men on it, only of the boat, and treat it as you would a ferocious wild animal that was after your blood. *[The best known of Berlin's boulevards, in the central Mitte district. During WW2, Hitler ordered the linden trees to be chopped down so that the road could be widened. They were replanted in the fifties.]

March 28

Rested from my labours. Spent a lazy day reading and writing letters. You know diary, I never seem to get any letters, yet I'm always writing them. I'm getting tired of it. I'm even getting tired of you, damn you! The only one who writes me regularly is Molly. If the others don't brighten up I'll only write to her, and Mother.

Letter #23

Postmarked 31.3.42 from Plymouth, Devon. 6.35p.m. 2½-penny stamp. Received May 25, 1942.

March 28, 1942

My Darling Molly,

It's over a week since I last wrote to you, dear, but things have been so busy that my only spare time has been devoted to sleeping, and there hasn't been much of that. I have been doing very well here; so far, have done nothing to incur the displeasure of the "Powers that be." As a matter of fact the chaps who joined the Squadron with me have surprised the "Bosses" by the quality of our work. Parkes must have given us a good training.

I got a letter from you yesterday – the first for some time. It arrived in about the same time as the Air Mail letters took, so the advice you got was sound. I was glad to hear that you had such a happy X'mas. Oh! Darling! What I would have given to be with you and your Dad and Mother and the "Kids" and Uncle Dick and the rest. Tell Dick that I had a "pot with the flies" on Xmas day and toasted all the crowd at home. I've just got a photo that was taken while I was at "Bath" for Xmas. It's of me and the chap and his son at whose farm I stayed. Gee! I'm ugly.

I'm expecting to go on leave in about a fortnight's time and don't know where to go. I'd like to go to Ireland but know no-one there. As a matter of fact I don't know a soul in England except the chap who is with me in the photo. Maybe I'll go to London – the wicked city – but I think I'll try Edinburgh and Scotland. Wish I could go to "Gay Paree!" Wish I could go to see you! – that would be the greatest thrill I know of.

Did you hear the news the other night of my old ship's sinking an "E" boat? I'd just been shifted to another kite. My luck to miss all the fun!

I'm spending the night on the sea again – guarding the ship with my life! Gee! I don't mind how much we fly, but I hate this time spent on board when we're on the water. In the "Pongo" Squadrons, as soon as the boat lands, the crew walk off and a maintenance crew comes aboard and looks after it. In our Squadron we do our own looking after, which, I think, is unfair. I reckon we, who do the flying, which after all is the riskiest part of the job, should have all the time off we can get when we're not flying. Grouch Club!

I was at the Scilly Isles recently. It is a lovely spot, and if the water was only a little warmer, I'd have had a swim. I need a good old sun-tan and a bit of surf to buck me up. There were daffodils there, growing wild, and I can understand the Poet Wordsworth's going mad over them. – They are lovely.

By the way – the time is 8 p.m. and I've still no thought of putting up the black-outs on the boat and turning up the light!

The Huns have been very quiet here recently – you rarely hear the sirens go. But touch wood! I wish I could tell how the black-out is going in Brisbane. It must be pretty grim there!

I can see my old kite moored a few yards away from me, and someone with a sense of humour has painted a skull and cross-bones over the door and "dive-bomber". Imagine a Sunderland doing dive-bombing.

The Jerries never even scratched the hull with their "ack-ack". Some great glom is tearing past me causing a terrific wash and the ship is wallowing like a duck in convulsions. If this keeps up, I shall have convulsions! – of sea-sickness.

How goes the Main-Roads Comm.? You should be running the place, just about, by now.

I see by the papers that tea is being rationed very harshly in Aussie just now. I'm glad I'm not missing my half-a-dozen cups a day. (Drat that glom! He's playing ring-a-rosie – I've a mind to take a pot at him!)

It'll soon be April, and, remembering "Oh! To be in England, now that April's here," I'm looking forward to seeing something. I'm getting my leave at a good time.

I've had a motor running recharging my batteries, – must go up and shut it off.

Nearly fell off the main-plane through placing my great hoof in a patch of oil. Now am greatly upset. If the afore-mentioned glom does come back – off with his head! A turret with umpteen machine guns in it can sure salivate a bloke! Am getting hungry – must be at least an hour or two since I ate. Wish I had the energy to cook the junk of meat I've got. Wish you were here to cook it for me!

Had a bit of luck coming home from patrol the other night. Some glug had left a balloon where it should not have been and we missed it by feet. Never said so many aspirations and Hail Mary's in such a short time in my life! It was funny after it was over! I bet it never happens again – it's a wonder the glug wasn't lynched by the crew.

The weather is growing warmer every day, though out on patrol the nights are still very cold. Some of the old hands laugh at an English summer, saying if you should happen to sleep in one morning you might miss summer altogether, which, I think, is a bit of an exaggeration, – or at least, I hope!

I wish I could get a trip to Gib. Or Malta or Alexandria. I'd have a swim. Well, darling, I think I'll grab a bit of shut-eye – I'm nearly out of my pins. Please keep loving me, and praying for me, because I need you and your prayers more than life. - I adore you, - I always will - Give my love to your family and regards to all the crowd. You're the loveliest girl in the world!

Ed   xxxxxx

P.S. Love me?

Ed   xxxx

The Wartime Postal Institute Magazine, April 1942

Official organ of the Queensland Postal Institute.

Alma Affleck is off on three months' furlough, and we wish her a very happy time. News was recently received from Eddie Gallagher (Telephone Accounts), who is now in England in the R.A.A.F. attached to No. 10 Squadron, Sunderland Flying Boats. He is the first Australian trained under the Empire Air Scheme to be appointed to this squadron. Good luck, Ed! Olwen Wooster, Townsville, is now training as a wireless operator with the W.A.A.F.'s in Melbourne. Miss Corrie Campbell, Engineering Branch, is enjoying a combination of sea and mountain air - the South Coast and Lamington Plateau will be her address for the vacation.

March 29

Did a trip to the Scillies and landed there for the first time. However, we drew lots as to who would stay aboard and, as usual, muggins lost! However I had a great meal of steak, eggs and tomatoes and chips. The skipper brought some army big-wigs back with him unexpectedly and I gave them a thrill, I think, by giving them cocoa and toast. They were amazed at the Sunderland's size and comfort.

March 30

Had a round of Golf this arvo with Keith and Hughie. Didn't do too badly, hitting a 90. I liked the course very much. Jerry blew the club-house to blazes, but the course itself is in good order. Wrote some letters, including one to the crowd at the office. Had a jug or two at the Boringdon and the Mess.

Think I'll turn in, now.

March 31

Circuits and Bumps all morning. I haven't flown for over three days which is unusual. (Ops – I mean). I did a bus ride to Plympton this afternoon, had a walk round, then came back and saw a show. It wasn't bad. There were a few murders in the first, and the second was a song and dance show. Called in at the local fish shop and am munching chips as I write this.

April 1, 1942

Set out on an A/S sweep early this morning and landed about half-past five tonight. We had a running scrap with two Arados but they didn't hit us and I don't know how we got on with our guns. They never came in closer than 500 yards at any time. They seem to be scared of us since Sal Abadee's memorable feat, when he shot down two J.U.'s with 120 rounds (in all) from the tail of R.B.K. Sol should have got a gong for that, I reckon.

April 2

Saw a show at the Odeon this evening which was good. Had a jug or two at the Woodman's Arms over the road and then caught a train.

I wish I hadn't, for I ran into Wally and the gang and have just finished a session down at the Mess.

April 3

Had to get up early this morning, grab the pigeons and race out to the kite in a heck of a hurry. Took off by flare path and dawn found us down the old Bay. Saw nothing of interest except a huge school of killer whales. Trip was boring in the extreme, which is a good thing. No Jerries arrived to spoil our serenity. Landed this afternoon and I've just finished a sing song down in the Mess.

April 4

Johnny Lewis got some seeds today, and not having anywhere to plant them, he doughtily dug up some seeds from a bed that was newly planted and stuck his in their place. The old John is a scream. Bill Isle took my photo today. If it's any good, I'll send it home. Jacko Jackson is still the same as ever, and Tommy Holland, Paul Bird, Roy Chinnery, and John Macdonald, George Bentley and Les Wilson are the same good fellows. We stick like glue.

April 5

Did a Navigation exercise today, back and forth across the Irish Sea, and saw some beautiful scenery. In a part of the coast of Ireland that we approached I saw some old ruins that look to have been there since the beginning of time.

I went into town with Jacko and we went to Benediction. Had a few beers together and then went to the Mess where we joined in a party. One of the usual Mess parties that go at the least excuse. Sometimes, I think, to celebrate being still alive. I know that's one of the main reasons why I imbibe so much!

April 6

Did a Convoy escort, from which we were recalled by T.29 on account of bad weather. Just made P.D. before it closed in properly. Hope we don't have to stay here long! Visited the usual pubs with the boys, not forgetting the Bush, where Mary is as charming as ever. The old "Black B" got fairly full and had to be restrained at one time from whistling at all the girls he saw.

April 7

Slept the night in the Mess. Old Thomason and the crowd are still there.

Today the weather was still too bad to allow us to get back to Batten and we spent the dreary time wandering around the camp making faces at ourselves. Had a few drinks with the mob in the Mess tonight.

April 8

Got back to Batten today, thank heavens. I went into town and did a show this afternoon and arrived back in time to do my duty hand. Got good rations, including eggs.

Jerry is about at the moment so I have good old Mae handy in case I have to swim for it.

April 9

Had a little excitement today. We went on an A/S patrol, somewhere off the coast of Spain, and on the way home, off Ushant, we ran into a couple of damned J.U.88's. There was plenty of cloud cover, and we made good use of this and got away before things became too hot. Snowy Couldrey got in some good bursts, and as he is fairly deadly, I think he did some damage.

April 10

We were sent to P.D. today. They were calibrating the loop of a new D.F. Station and we flew from P.D. all over the place, sending signals on M.F.D.F.* frequency. It was quite an interesting job and I had some good Radio practice. We are staying here for some time. Woodsie has gone back to Mt. B. in 'X' and Tommy Egerton and Brownie are staying with us to get in some Bombing and gunnery practice. Alan Petherick, who has passed his Gunnery Leader's course and is waiting for his commission, is with us as Gunnery Leader. *[Medium Frequency Direction Finder]

April 11

Saw over Carew Cheriton* today, and "Lucky" nearly had a fight with a Pongo. Were given instructions as to our course, and had an A/C identification test. I've rigged a spare reflector sight in the Astro Dome for Alan, so that he can use it to estimate range. *[A Coastal Command airfield, which attracted the attention of the Luftwaffe with a number of air raids between July 1940 and April 1941.]

Did the rounds with the boys tonight.

Mr. Jensen has passed on to Nicko and I the congratulations of the chaps in charge of all the Group D.F. work for doing what he calls "the best job of its kind yesterday," on the calibration trip.

Letter #24

Mailed April, '42 (unclear) from Pembroke Dock at 10.45 a.m. on letterhead which reads: "A.C.F. Australian Comforts Fund (Victorian Division) With which is affiliated the R.S.L. War Service Fund, Y.M.C.A. and Salvation Army"

Undated

Darling Molly

This letter finds the chap who loves you in a distinctly sour frame of mind – I expected by this to be in London, on my way to Ireland on leave. Yes, I've decided to go there – aren't you jealous? At the last moment our leave was cancelled and we were posted on detachment to this out of the way spot – about 100% deader than the proverbial doornail. Maybe we'll get leave in about a fortnight and then I'll be off like a shot. I intend spending a few days in London, and am looking forward to renewing my acquaintance with Piccadilly, Leicester Square and the rest.

I was lying on my bunk on my old kite (known to the WAAFs who work us on the R.T. as "U" for "Useless") the other day, listening to the rain rattling on the duralumin*, and I had only to close my eyes to imagine myself back home with the rattle of the rain on the iron roofs. – Gee! It made me homesick, – so much so that I could have wept! I felt like kicking a hole in the side to vent my anger. I wanted to see you and be near you more than I have ever done before! And then, after a while, I dropped off to sleep and had a dream so vivid about you that I woke and thought it real for a while. It took me some time to realise it was only a dream and that you were thousands of miles away. *[Duralumin or Dural is the trade name of an aluminium alloy used on rigid airship frames.]

Supper is on and I'm being dragged away by Alan and Bill drat 'em!

Well, Darling, Supper is over – three hours ago – I'm afraid my unusually weak will has deteriorated to a minus quantity; I was inveigled into a game of darts and a few jugs of ale, and time flew.

Tomorrow I will have to undergo a sort of test on aircraft recognition – just to make sure I won't open fire on a Spitfire instead of an M.E.109* one of these days. Luckily the test doesn't matter a bit whether I fail or not, or I'd be hounded out of the R.A.A.F. Even that – providing I was sent home – would be a good thing. *[The Messerschmitt ME109 was the backbone of the Luftwaffe force.]

I have a slight touch of the 'flu at the moment which is causing me some annoyance, but the source of the annoyance seems to be passing

245

fairly rapidly – I hope. Alan just said he feared he had an appendix, and was unsympathetically informed that he'd be a freak without one, and has hidden his head 'neath the blankets after pointedly hinting that the lights might be extinguished. Bill reproved him, saying that he was interfering with the course of true love, and asked him if he were writing to you – pointing out your photograph – would he like to be interrupted in a letter by some drunk with an appendix. I seconded the remarks and told Alan to boil his head, and if that wasn't enough to add his appendix.

Some of these Pongos annoy me. Most of them have been sitting, eating their great fat heads off so long that they – to use one of their expressions that I find particularly obnoxious – are completely "browned off." This results in their wanting – after they have considerably added to their courage with alcohol – to fight anyone who is doing a bit towards the war effort – and who is smaller than themselves.

Anyone who is in the Air Force (and the Air Force are the only ones, excluding the Commandos, who are fighting) becomes the object of their spleen. Alan and I were walking down town yesterday evening, at peace with the world, when we were suddenly attacked. Luckily the attackers were small in number and very "full". I think I must have breathed heavily on my opponent because I'm certain I never hit him, for the last I saw of him was a crumpled mass in the gutter. The three who were concentrating on Alan – he had already disposed of one – seeing that the odds were now only three to two in their favour, backed off, yelling for aid. We walked on, and no aid being forthcoming, they began tending their injured comrades, gallantly forgetting selves in their solicitation for their wounded – and we finished our stroll without further molestation. The English womenfolk fill me with admiration for their courage; frankly there's never been finer displays of bravery in the face of whistling bombs and incendiaries, but I have little time for their men folk. In air raids on this particular station it was the Aussies and the W.A.A.F.s who fought the fires, the men (ground crews) fought the horrors of the Air Raid Shelters. I think though, to do them justice, they are fine soldiers, when confronted with something they can hit back at; they proved it in Libya and Greece and at Dunkirk. Maybe the ones I've come in contact with are the worst type; I hope so, anyway.

I had a letter from Dad the other day, and a birthday parcel from Mother. They love you, Darling. Dad seems to be filled with wonderment that I had the sense to ask to be my future wife the most wonderful girl in the world, and threatens dire penalties if ("if" I say) I should change my mind. Little does he know the impossibility of that. There's as much chance of my changing my Religion and my Faith. Not even Death could alter them, or my feelings towards you. You're as much a part of me as my heart is – more so – because, after all, my heart is only a part of my

246

body, and you are part of my soul. I love you – there's nothing more to say than that. I might just as well say "I breathe air" – both statements are facts, and facts are unchangeable.

It is wonderful, dear, to be receiving your letters, and the sight of your handwriting on an envelope quickens the beat of my heart. Sometimes I become a little scared that maybe this letter may tell me that you have ceased to care – all my life I'll have that fear – even when we have been married for years, because I know how unworthy I am; and then I turn to the last page and see your postscript, and life once more resumes its distinctly rosy hue! It's better, by far, than winning a casket.

Dad's letter made me envious to read of the weddings of Charlie Goggins and Jack O'Shea. Why the heck did I have to be the mug and leave Aussie? If I hadn't, maybe by this we'd have been married, or at least well on the way to wedded life! I curse myself for a fool, and only the consolation of knowing that you think I did the right thing keeps me from getting really down in the dumps.

Well, sweetheart, it's now 12.30 or, rather 2430, so I'd better turn in. I have to be up early in the morning. Please give my love to your Mother and Dad and Al and the kids. Tell Al, I hope she got my letter. Also give my regards to all at 137 Moray St.

Pray for me, please, sweet, – I need your Prayers, almost as much as I need you and your love,

I adore you

Ed xxxxx

P.S. Love me? Ed x

April 12

There has been a hitch in proceedings and we can't start our bombing and gunnery for some time.

So today we did a trip up the English and Scottish coast and down the Irish coast with Brownie and Tommy doing all the navigation. They can't have been too bad, for we're home safely at P.D. I like this non-operational flying!

April 13

We have to fill all the mags and belts we'll be using on the Gunnery Exercises and load all the practice bombs. So today we spent getting things ready for tomorrow. We have to paint some of the bullets as some of us will be firing at the same drogue. I'm duty hand tonight and am tired as hell, so will shut you up, drat you, Diary!

April 14

Had great fun this morning, firing at a drogue. I fired with the port and stbd. Free guns and used red bullets. They'll tell us our scores tomorrow. Helped Glen Bulfield to reload the racks for the bombing this afternoon. They dropped 60 bombs, so I'm tired tonight. Glen tells an amusing story about an armourer who was prone to airsickness. He got so crook he couldn't reload the racks and stood on the bunk with a bomb in his hands, watching the racks. As the release trigger tripped, he dropped a bomb. Lord knows how the Pilot's bombing records were – probably better than usual, I bet!

April 15

Only did gunnery today. Our take off for the bombing was delayed through engine trouble and we arrived on the Range too late. I topped the gunnery yesterday with 30% which is good considering I was shooting against Snow.

Spent the night in the Mess.

Couldn't get into the pictures. You have to book days in advance to get a seat.

April 16

Did bombing in the morning and gunnery in the afternoon. Snow topped yesterday's score. I find I'm not so hot in a turret as with a free gun. Did duty hand tonight again. Bill Vout is writing a letter opposite me on the ward-room table and I have a good yarn I want to get stuck into.

April 17

Only Gunnery today. I didn't fly on the bombing trip this afternoon. Too much like hard work. Bill Vout and I walked around the village instead and left Nico, Johnno, Glen, Snow and the pilots to do the work.

Tonight we had a party in town. Cooke, Egerton, Brown, and Jensen came along.

I don't think the Pongos understand how we Aussies mix together. The idea of an officer drinking with anyone who has no commission is beyond them.

April 18

Did a record trip from P.D. to Mt. B. I think this is the longest it has ever taken to do that trip by air. Usually it is just under the hour, but we took seven. We came home via Scotland and Ireland and the Scillies. Brownie and Egerton wanted to do a Nav. Exercise.

I've enjoyed this practice and feel it has improved me considerably, both in gunnery and Wireless. We've had plenty of practice at the latter as no wireless silence was in force.

April 19

Did an A/S sweep but had no occasion to bring into use any of the knowledge we've acquired over the last few days either in gunnery or bombing, for Jerry kites and subs were conspicuous by their absence. Saw many fishing boats, the occupants of which gave us the usual waves and "V" signs. I often wonder if Jerry is using these beggars to spy on us. Anyhow I think they give us the "V" because they are scared – not patriotic. Don't like the French – and I don't think I'll ever trust them. Duty hand again tonight, curse it!

April 20

Finished duty hand about nine, when Snow took over. The kite is having an inspection which means a day or two off. I had a round of golf in a slight drizzle, and am going to Torquay first thing tomorrow morning.

Had a few in the mess tonight.

April 21

Spent the day in Torquay. I like this place more every time I come here. I wish we were stationed here.

249

Have to return to Batten first thing in the morning as we may have a job on. Am at the Queen's, as usual.

Returned to many of the haunts I'd found last time I was here, and met a lot of old friends, who remembered me. Must be my handsome face!

April 22

Arrived back at camp just in time to miss being A.W.L. Lucky, too, because we went to Gib. I liked the "Rock" very much. Everything except beer is cheap there. Whisky is 9/- per bottle and cigs. About 2/6 a hundred. Needless to say I smuggled some of both back with me, both for myself and the boys back in camp. Didn't have time to see much of the Rock as we only spent a night there. All civvies (Spanish) are allowed on the rock after a certain hour in the morning (if they have a pass) but must be out before night. Some Gibraltese policemen made us very welcome last night. I had a drink of some stuff that has a kick like a mule's.

April 23

Left for Mt. B. about mid-day, laden with contraband.

Had an uneventful trip except for a fight with an Arado, just after clearing North Spain. Snow shot it down from the tail turret.

Gee! He can shoot, can Snow. I'd back him against anyone in the Force with four brownings at a moving target.

April 24

The crew that is on leave comes back tonight and we go on leave tomorrow. Thanks to my Gib trip I have plenty of smokes. I bought a lighter on the Rock for 2/6 and it's not a bad 'un at all!

Spent the day packing and getting leave pay, etc. Should have plenty of dough as I have about a tenner in the bank as well.

Letter #25

April 24, 1942

Dearest,

Man proposes, but the god of War disposes – so it seems. Once more my projected visit to Ireland has been postponed and I will have to be satisfied with a day or two in London, a few in Oxford and one or two in Torquay. That is – perhaps. One never knows what is going to happen these days; it's like sitting in an Air Raid Shelter with Jerry hovering overhead; you don't know whether the next bomb is going to bounce on your head or not, and, after an hour or two you don't care, much.

It is funny, even though it is so darn serious, crouching in a Shelter with a crowd of the boys. I think wit reaches into greatest heights under these circumstances. Everyone laughs uproariously at each sally, and everyone kids himself it is the cold that causes his laugh to tremble when that "whee-e-e" sounds above the noise of the laughter. Actually, except for a direct hit, one is as safe as houses in a Shelter (a poor simile) – and the possibilities of a direct hit are less than those of being knocked over in the street by a car, but a car doesn't make such a hell of a noise!

Your cake arrived yesterday, dear, and it has already been eaten – the boys fought over the last scraps, and, contrary to what you said you feared in the note enclosed, no ill effects were observed. Does it give you a thrill to know that your cake was eaten thousands of feet in the air, somewhere over the Atlantic?

I had another two days in Torquay this week, and enjoyed myself even more than the last time. Gee! It's a swell place, Darling, you'd love it!

I wish I had some of the old crowd here with me, dear, especially Len, Mat and Bro. We could have such a wonderful time in this place, in the same Squadron. When I think of the gay, good old times we had in the times that seem so far away, I get horribly sad. I wish this darned war would end, so that we could recapture those times, and their spirit before it is too late.

I haven't received any mail for some time, now, except a letter from Joan. I sent Joan a song *[sheet music]* from Torquay, one we couldn't buy in Australia. It was Eric Coates' "By a Sleepy Lagoon," – you know it.

Speaking of Songs. It was a thrill to read in your last letter the mention you made of Donald Noris' Singing "Diane." I still think it is

251

the best. Gee! I love you, dear!

How are your Mother, Dad, Alice, the boys and the good Uncles? I think I'm the luckiest fellow in the world to be going to marry into that family. (I <u>am,</u> aren't I, dear?)

Tell them I wish I were with them, and ask them to pray that I will be soon.

I was sorry to read that you are having more trouble with your teeth; you've had some bad luck with them, dear. I've been fairly lucky with mine (touch wood.)

I have a rotten cold at the moment, the worst for years, and I feel as miserable as a centipede with corns. I would catch one just as I am about to get a bit of leave. Must be a punishment for one of my major crimes. Speaking of crimes. I must try to get to Mass as often as I can during my leave. I get very few opportunities here, and I'm beginning to feel like a heathen.

It was great to hear of the Yank's attack on Tokio. That will give 'em a bit to think about. One of the papers showed a cartoon of a blitzed sign which, after the explosion, looked something like this:

A few more "O.K.'s" to them like that would be very acceptable!

Well, dear, tempus fugit, or rather ten past eleven, so I think I'll enter the land of Nod, and have a ride on the barque of the "fishermen three". [From Eugene Field's poem: "So cried the stars to the fishermen three: Wynken, Blynken, And Nod."]

I love you, dear, more than ever, and I miss you terribly. I think that being so far away from you is the greatest trial I ever have had, or will have to face in the world. Pray for me please, sweet, - I pray for you.

Ed xxxxx

P.S. Love me? Ed x

April 25

Left for London today. I intended staying at the Victoria League Club, but couldn't get in tonight so have a room in the U.J.C. [Union Jack Club] I'm going to shift to the V.L.C. tomorrow when a room will be vacant.

This is the first real leave I've had in four months and I'm revelling in the freedom.

I find I have forgotten much that I gleaned about London on my last visit.

Found the whereabouts of the nearest R.C. Church so that I can toddle off to Mass tomorrow. It'll be a change. I haven't had the opportunity of hearing Mass for months.

April 26

Shifted to the V.L.C. before dinner. Had dinner at Lyons' Corner House in the Strand and then went to Aussie House. This place has been vastly altered. It is now the most beautifully laid out club in London. It has a good snack bar in ultra modern style and a nice dining room downstairs. The chairs are upholstered in leather and plush, and the whole club is done up in marvellous manner.

I enquired if any of the lads were in town, but could find no-one I knew.

I went to the Sussex to see if there was anyone about, but was told that nowadays all the lads go to the "Cogers Club" in Fleet Street. I'll look it up tomorrow.

April 27

Went to Aussie House and thence to the "Cogers," which happens to be in Salisbury Square, off Fleet Street. Met an uncle of Norm Tritton's, also a fellow worker of Joan's named Dulhunty. It's a small world.

The "Cogers" is a lovely pub. It's a little bit of Australia in London. Evie, whose mother owns the place, got me to sign an autograph book in which appear many Aussie names. It is only for Australians. I saw Keith Truscott's and many others. The only "foreigner" whose name appears is Paddy Finucane.

Caught a train for Oxford this afternoon and am at the "Mitre." [The Mitre stands at the corner of Turl and High Streets where it has stood serving ales since 1261.] Can only get room anywhere for one night so am off back to London first thing in the morning.

April 28

Had a "Bo peep" at St. Paul's. Spent some time wandering round the Crypt, seeping myself in History.

I found Bill Vout is staying at the V.L.C. too, and he told me he had free tickets for a show tonight and asked me to come.

I'm glad I went. It was the Operetta "Tales of Hoffman" by Offenbach and was inexpressibly lovely. I wish Joan could have seen this. She'd have been in raptures.

Saw very little of Oxford as I only stayed last night. Got the 8.40 train back here this morning. What I saw though looked very lovely, and I'll be back there again some time.

April 29

I wandered around Piccadilly today. Had a drink at the brasserie near "Auberge de France," and afterwards went to the Windmill*, which was really good. *[The Windmill opened on 22 June 1931 as a playhouse. The owner, Laura Henderson, hired a theatre manager (Vivian Van Damm) who developed the idea of a *Revudeville*, featuring glamorous nude women. As long as they did not move, it was OK by the Censor ("If you move, it's rude!"). It's famous motto "We never closed", in reference to the Blitz era, was humorously altered to "We never clothed".]

Billy Vout was with me. He started his leave before I did and has to go back to Camp tomorrow. I think he'll be going back to Australia soon. This V.L.C. is a nice place to stay at. My room is clean, and the breakfasts of a morning have been good.

April 30

Cy Richardson arrived in town today. He's doing a course at some factory or other. Together we walked into town this morning from the V.L.C. This afternoon we saw one of George Black's productions – "Black Vanities," which was rather good.

Tonight we spent in having a few jugs at the "Cogers," where we ran into some of the boys. Billy Vout left for Camp this afternoon. He wasn't so sorry as I'll be when I have to go.

Q'landers At "Codgers" In London

(From C. H. Bateson, formerly of "Truth's" Brisbane Office.)

LONDON, Saturday.—Two brothers who have been together since joining up as Empire birdmen are Pilot-Officer Jack Gordon and Sergt.-Pilot Horrie Gordon, of Auchenflower. They arrived in Britain recently. Pilot-Officer John Evans, of Dalby, who has been with them throughout, also arrived.

They are all three pilots, and at present they await posting to a squadron. They will join the Coastal Command, going on Liberators or Wimpeys.

Other new arrivals include: Sergt.-Pilot Jack Turnbull, of Innisfail; Pilot-Officer Observer John Stickley, of Rockhampton. They came over direct from Australia, putting in a month in the United States, where Stickley managed to see New York and Boston.

TURNBULL will go on single-engined aircraft, while Stickley is destined for the Bomber Command after completing training.

Sgt.-Pilots Fred Lippiatt, of Moggill; Dave McNeil, of Auchenflower; and Sgt. Air-Gunner Ian Holmes, of Brisbane, came with them.

At present on embarkation leave is Flight-Sgt. Pilot Eric Ball, of Townsville, who recently completed training. Along with Flight-Sgt. Pilot A. N. Clark, of Mackay, they will go on Spitfires or Hurricanes with an operational squadron shortly.

Sub-Lieutenant Hugh Cassidy, D.S.M., of Bardon, who is on motor launches with the Royal Navy's coastal forces, is at present on embarkation leave. Pilot-Officer Jim Cassidy, Hugh's brother, was on leave in London at the same time.

Flying-Officer Air-Gunner Ian Whitson, of Ayr, who flies with Wing Commander Bob Holmes, of Western Australia, Commander of the Australian Coastal Command squadron, has been doing great work on the Norwegian coast.

Flight-Sergeant Air-Gunner John Stevens, of Kingaroy, is another Coastal Command boy, who has had

a few encounters with enemy fighters. He has been serving with an Australian Sunderland squadron, having originally been in the crew of Flying-Officer C. W. Steley, of Ayr. Stevens has already got 500 operational hours to his credit.

Sergeant Air Gunner Darcy Paul, of Mitchell, is at present on seven days' leave in London. He came over to Britain in September, 1941, later joining the Bomber Command; but owing to injuries received when his kite crash-landed he has been off flying for many months. He is now looking much fitter.

Among Queenslanders who have recently signed the visitors' book at "The Codgers," one of the most popular rendezvous for Australians in London, are:—Pilot Officers B. M. McLoughlin, of Ashgrove; J. Kennedy, of Auchenflower; Sergeant Radio Air Gunners J. D. Bailey, of Mount Isa, and G. W. Duncan, of Ipswich, who before joining the R.A.A.F. served for three years in the Australian Army Medical Corps.

Others who have recently signed the book include:—Noel Cook, of Rathdowney; Phil Danahar, of Brisbane; C. Fussell, of Brisbane; L. J. Jeffries, of Brisbane.

Over 3000 Australians and New Zealanders have already signed these books at "The Codgers," revealing the extent of this favorite "down-under" meeting place.

"Truth" 9/5/43.

May 1, 1942

Went with Cy to see Mme. Tussaud's today. It is certainly worth seeing. The wax work figures of historical and contemporary figures are very life-like. It is in Baker Street or rather, near the station of that name. This afternoon we walked round Hyde Park in drizzling rain and saw the famous Serpentine. From Hyde Park we walked to Buckingham Palace and down Constitution Hill to The Mall, and through the latter to Trafalgar Square. Walked down the Strand, Fleet Street and up Ludgate Hill, past St. Paul's, along Cannon St. past the monument to London Bridge. Here we caught a bus back to Strakers near Aussie House where we had a good tea. Had arranged to meet Keith Oates and the boys from Kodak House at the Cecil, and we had a few drinks with 'em there. Are my feet sore!

May 2

Walked into town along Edgeware Road, Oxford Street (past Marble Arch), Regent Street, to Piccadilly. Spent part of the morning walking round the Circus and then went through Haymarket to the Square. Had dinner at Lyons in the Strand. After lunch I wandered along the Strand and turned up into Covent Gardens. From Leicester Square, where I had a few jugs, I strolled along Charing Cross Road peering into the second hand bookshops. Caught a tube at Tottenham Court Road, and thence made for Temple. I had tea at some little I in Fleet Street, and then went to the Aldwych Theatre to see Diana Wynyard in "Watch on the Rhine" – a marvellous show.

May 3

Cy and I went to Mass at a lovely Church near the V.L.C. and found it was the anniversary of the foundation of Poland or something. I found the place full of uniforms and the sermon was preached in both English and Polish – which made it rather a long business. After Mass, some middle-aged Polish lady gave me a small medal of St. Christopher which I thought was very nice of her. We did a show at the Gaumont in Haymarket this afternoon and spent this evening between the Cogers and the Cecil.

Funniest saying for some time:– Cy to a news vendor who was making himself a nuisance endeavouring to sell us his wares:– "What? Lord, we don't read the news. We make it." Surely an entry for the "Line book!"

May 4

Had a haircut this morning at a shop in Edgeware Road. Then I caught a 15 bus into Trafalgar Square and set off along Charing X Road. Had a jug or two at the Sussex, then cut across to the Museum, but it was closed for the duration, unfortunately, so I toddled along Oxford St. to Oxford Circus and then down Regent Street peering in shop windows until I came to the Circus (Piccadilly). Had a drink at the Irish Bar (Mooneys or Wards, I forget whose it is) and some counter lunch, then went to the Odeon near Leicester Square, where I saw a fair show. Met Keith and W.O. Thomas and some of the lads when they finished work and had quite a party.

May 5

Only a couple of days left, drat it.

Today was fairly drizzly, and I wandered about in it all day. Went to see the Tower of London this afternoon. I'm glad I did. A Beef-eater showed me over it, and I always get a feeling of awe when I see old places such as this. It was first built by William the Conqueror, and is a wonderful example of mediaeval architecture. Didn't see the Crown Jewels, but saw where Ann Boleyn, Lady Jane Grey and others lost their heads. Others, who were not so popular that it was feared they might be rescued by the people from the executioners, were deprived of their heads outside the castle on Tower Hill. Saw the White Tower and the place where Richard had the two boys murdered and many other things of interest, not the least of which was the Chapel.

May 6

Drew last few quid out of the bank today, so will soon have to be going back to camp.

Went to have a look at Lords today. Am not very enthusiastic about it as a cricket ground. I called in at the "Cogers" about dinner and had a drink or two with Evie. Then I made for Aussie House and had a good meal there.

Looked over Westminster Abbey, which was slightly bomb damaged, but very interesting. I then had a look at and said a few prayers in Westminster Cathedral, which is not a very beautiful piece of work.

Went to see Bernard Shaw's "The Doctor's Dilemma" – with Vivian Leigh*. She is very beautiful and acted magnificently. The play was good. *[Leigh's co-star in *The Doctor's Dilemma* was Cyril Cusack, and later Sir John Gielgud. In all, she performed the play 474 times. Its success had a lot to do with audiences wanting to see 'Scarlett' in person after seeing her in the hugely successful movie, *Gone With The Wind.*]

May 7

Am back at Batten tonight, and have to start work tomorrow. I've picked up the deuce of a cold and think I'll see the M.O. tomorrow.

Had a few jugs with Evie before catching my train and she gave me a huge parcel of sandwiches to eat on the trip. I thought it was very nice of her.

The train trip was as monotonous as ever.

May 8

Saw the M.O. and, after he had taken my temperature, he packed me off to bed. Feel pretty crook tonight. I've a hell of a cough.

A few days in the bed should just get me over the effects of the leave.

I hear I'm being posted as sort of foundation member – instructor to a new Aussie Sunder-bomber squadron. Hope it's not true. I was not down for posting originally, but all the others refused, and I think they took advantage of my being away on leave.

May 9

Spent the day in bed; Doctor says I'm better today and should be up and doing soon.

Read some magazines and am in the middle of a good detective yarn at the moment.

Some of the lads called in to see me a few minutes ago and brought me some smokes (which are forbidden me) and chocolate from the Mess.

They send a W.A.A.F down to the Sergeants' Mess to bring me my meals, which are good.

May 10

Still in bed, curse it, but my cough has got a lot easier and I feel much better. Wrote some letters today, and read a lot. It's hard to get to sleep at night here. I suppose it's because I'm lying down all day.

May 11

Another dreary day has passed. I'm going out tomorrow, thank Heavens! Was allowed out of bed this morning, and I feel quite O.K. again.

May 12

Left the hospital this morning, and went to Flight Office to make sure I was put back on my kite. I shall soon be going to the new Squadron. Some of the officers – Squadron Leader Burrage, and Bullsie and others have already gone but 10 Squadron still wants us.

I spent a quiet night letter writing tonight. The days are very long now.

Flight Lieut. Graham Pockley (shown here with his wife) was nick-named the "U-boat Magnet", by his mates when he was flying with the Australian Sunderland Squadron in England. In two years he sank two U-boats and damaged three others. He also damaged several Nazi supply ships. He is now back in Australia.

barrier mail: 29/3/43.

May 13

Set out on an Anti-Sub strike last night, or rather, early this morning, and attacked a sub on the surface, down Pockley's Corner* way but we were chased off by Jerry fighters before we could see, let alone photograph, results. Had a few holes shot in us, and found two unexploded cannon shells in the main port tank on our return to base. Oh Lordy! – if they'd have gone off!

However, all is for the best, and it means a couple of day's rest, while they're patching her up. *[Area in the Bay of Biscay named for H. G. (Graham) Pockley DFC and Bar, who established a reputation within 10 Squadron and Coastal Command for his ability to find U-boats there. Squadron Leader Pockley and crew went missing in Borneo in March 1945. He was 32 years old.]

May 14

Went into town this morning and played golf this afternoon with Hughie and Keith. There was an E.N.S.A.* show on at the Gym this evening which was particularly good. *[The Entertainments National Service Association was set up in 1939 to provide entertainment for armed forces personnel. The popular translation of the acronym was "Every Night Something Awful".

May 15

Spent the day lounging around and had a game of fives this afternoon, after tea. The boat is down in the drink again and I've just finished a flight test on her.

I suppose we'll be on the job tomorrow, with the weather as good as it is.

Tonight I'm sleeping aboard as duty hand.

May 16

Was rudely awakened about three by the usual "Wakey! Wakey!" and banging on the hull, and we set off to find a reported German Convoy. This we came up with down in the Bay somewhere, and dropped our eggs. We missed them, unfortunately, and cursed over the I.C., but went close enough to a tanker to start a few leaks, I bet, and frighten hell out of them. They were a bit closer to us and wounded our navigator, P.O. Winstanley in the hand, and the First Pilot, Oscar Wientholm, where he sits down. I was sitting at the set next to the Nav. And a big junk of shrapnel just missed me.

We're laid up again for a few days.

May 17

Spent the day sailing in a boat out on the sound. It was good fun and I'd like more of it. Had some anxious moments once when we nearly fouled a Sunder-bomber in Jennycliffe*, but luckily missed it. I'm going into the flicks now. *[About a mile south of the Boringdon Arms at Turnchapel.]

Later. Saw a show at the Odeon and had a few jugs at the mess when I got back to camp. Some of the boys were celebrating someone's birthday and I got mixed up with the party somehow or other.

May 18

Played some records on the Radiogram* this evening and Paddy Druhan, who has joined us now, played the piano. Reminded me of days gone by, at the Roadhouse in Parkes, N.S.W. We had some grand fun. *[A piece of furniture that combined a radio with an amplified gramophone.]

Blue Eva came with Paddy. They don't know whether they're in 10 Squadron or the new one, which is to be 461 Squadron.

May 19

The boat was put down the slipway this afternoon and we gave her a test flip. She seems in fine fettle. I'm duty hand again tonight, blast it! I never seem to miss out. Whenever the boat is on the deck, I'm not duty hand. (If I were, it would mean that I would be lucky and not have to do it.)

I suppose my sleep will be disturbed as usual by that damned "Wakey! Wakey!"

May 20

As I thought! We took off about midnight to escort a Convoy somewhere in the Atlantic, and boy! Did we have fun!

Six J.U.'s also found the ships, and of course, we had to try to keep them off. They were too many for us, altogether, but the convoy put up a marvellous barrage. They never hit a ship, but one of the destroyers shot one of the kites down and damaged another. This was the most exciting trip I've ever been on.

May 21

Did some local flying at Mt. B. today. Some new coot was doing some training. He wasn't bad either.

There's talk of a special job tomorrow. I hope it's not true. Spent the night at the Boringdon. I'm very popular with the proprietor, his wife and daughter. I don't know if I've mentioned it before to you Diary, but they rejoice in the unromantic name of Hogg!

The B. is getting more crowded every time I go there. It seems to be full of W.A.A.F.S., Pongos and Aussies. Don't like WAAFS. Hope Joan never carried out her intention of joining them.

May 22

Went out on an A/Sub sweep today and very nearly blew a British sub to blazes! He was exactly where he was supposed not to be.

Apart from that bit of excitement the trip was uneventful. We saw only the usual fishing boats, etc. Too tired tonight for anything but bed.

May 23

Played a round of golf today. I'm a bit crooked. I have been using a chap's clubs who is going back to Aussie, with the understanding that I could buy them when he was leaving, but now he has rescinded his offer. They are a lovely set of clubs, too.

I did an 82 this afternoon, which is about my best, over here.

Went to the "Boringdon" and to Harry's with Geo and Les and some of the lads after tea. We finished up with chish and fips at the Mess. Circs and Bumps all morning.

May 24

Did another Convoy job today. This was not so eventful as the last. All we saw was a couple of old "Flying pencils,"* which were also on the job. On the way home we sighted a J.U. 88 in the distance, but either he didn't see us or was scared, for he made no move to attack.

Bed early tonight, on the kite; it's my duty hand. Jerry is about so out go the lights. *[The Dornier Do 17, named because of its narrow fuselage.]

May 25

Spent the day on board the kite, cleaning up, etc. The place looks like a new pin now. Hope it keeps like that – but it won't! Am going over to the new Squadron soon. See they have a couple of kites now. I already spent some of my time taxiing them when necessary, but haven't done a flip yet. Went to town before tea and saw a show at the Gaumont. Finished up at the mess.

End Of Nazi Supply Ship

THE end of a German submarine supply ship at Pockley's Corner in the Bay of Biscay. The ship was tending a U-boat when Flight-Lieut. Pockley, of the R.A.A.F., sighted it. He pretended to be deceived by the British ensign it was flying and the R.A.F. markings on its hatches and waggled his wings in recognition. He then dived suddenly to almost mast height and scored two heavy hits, bombs exploding under the vessel's bows. The picture shows water, thrown up by a bomb burst, pouring over the forecastle. The U-boat crash-dived on being damaged by Pockley.—Department of Air photo.

'Courier Mail' 29/3/43

Letter #26

Postmarked Plymouth Devon, May 26, 1942, 6.30 p.m.

Received August 3, 1942

May 25, 1942

Darling Molly,

Well, it was a glorious leave! You've no idea how hard it was to drag myself back to the darned war; I had almost completely forgotten that one was going on.

I'm glad now that I changed my mind about going to Ireland. I don't think I'd have enjoyed myself half so much. Cy Richardson and myself arrived in London about 6 a.m. then had to tour around the place to find a bed. We finished up at the "Victoria League Club", a grand place to stay at, then made for "Australia House." Cy was quite determined to remain in London but I was equally fixed on seeing Oxford. Days went by without the place getting any nearer, and we indulged in an orgy of Show-Seeing. I think the Opera-Ballet – "The Tales of Hoffman" by Offenbach (You know – the one in which "The Barcarolle" is sung) was the best of them all. The Ballet was exquisitely beautiful and the singing was glorious.

Cy is another Mat, and you'll be surprised and pleased to know that we went to Mass nearly every morning. I met a Polish lady at Mass one morning and she gave me a Holy medal to wear. I thought it very nice of her. On the Sunday I was there it was the anniversary of the forming of the constitution (or some darn thing) of Poland. There were Poles everywhere, from the President down. High Mass was celebrated and it was a most impressive sight. Cy and I were the only Aussies in uniform (except for one Squadron Leader) and we were awed to be rubbing shoulders with a General. The Sermon was preached in both Polish and English, and, as you can imagine, lasted a heck of a time!

At last I made up my mind and hopped on a train for Oxford. When I got there I rang hotel after hotel from the Station and had almost given up in despair when I struck one with a bed. It was "Ye Olde Mitre," an Inn that has been open for hundreds of years. Oxford is a lovely old town. The river, filled with punts and row boats, is the essence of quietness and peace. I enjoyed my visit immensely. But the lure of London proved too strong and it wasn't long before I was on an overloaded train bound for that city.

I saw all the old places again and liked them even more than before. Cy laughed to see me back so soon and was prone to adopt an "I told

263

you so" attitude.

This new Squadron is pretty hard work. I have umpteen fellows to train in the arts and guile of Operational Flying, and I was never intended to be a teacher. Things are going very well, though, and I have become the apple of the eyes of the "powers that be." As the chief Signals Officer of 10 Squadron told me – promotion should be rapid. I was given the choice of whether I went or not, and though I am sorry to part with all my old cobbers of 10 Squadron, I'm glad to know that Jack Jackson and a few of the others will soon be joining me.

Mail has been an annoying problem lately. I haven't received a letter from you or the folks since time immemorial. You've no idea how rotten it is to expect a letter day after day, and find none. That was a silly statement! I suppose you are having the same trouble with my mail, and it is just as worrying for you as it is for me.

I miss you terribly, darling. Sometimes I curse myself for a fool for not urging you more and more to marry me before I left home. It would be wonderful to head my letters to you "My Darling Wife" instead of "Molly". Would you have agreed if I had been insistent enough, dear?

I often think of your Mother and Dad and Alice and the "kids" and the wonderful week-end I spent at your place that time. Gee! Darling, I wish I could see them all again. I hope they are all well and happy, and not too worried about this darned war. I wish the blooming thing were over! I'm about fed up with it. I'll be fed up with just about everything until I see you again! And then, seeing you will make me forget everything. Dear God! I'm looking forward to that day, and praying that it will not be too far off. I know you are praying for the same thing, dear, so the combination of our prayers should make some impression. One thing I know, – when I see you again, I'll never leave you for a day, no matter what the reason! I've had enough of this being parted from you. The months at Parkes were too long, without this time in England!

I think I'll finish off, now, Darling. Please give my love to your family, and regards to all at "Bursties." Pray for me, dear, as often as you can. I need your prayers very badly – almost as much as I need you!

All my love, Ed xxxxx

P.S. Love me? Ed x

May 26

Did one of the "Round the Bay for a Bob" trips. We saw no subs. Or aircraft, only fishing vessels, which waved to us as we swept overhead. We flew almost over Corunna. It is strange to see a town not blacked out, with all the lights blazing.

May 27

Did some test flying at Mt. B. and had a bit of a thrill when stbd. Inner cut. However Woodsie put her down without any fuss.

Had a round at Turnchapel and did 87. My golf has improved on my Australian standard. I think, though, that the courses here are easier. The soft grassy fairways suit my spoon shots.

May 28

Took off before dawn on an Anti-sub patrol but it was uneventful. I should be going over finally to the new Sqdn. Tomorrow. This was my last trip with 10 Sqdn.

The boys all say they are sorry to lose me. Had a few jugs with Ossy, Bruce and the lads down at the Mess. Snowy and Nicko and I got fairly full and we had a great old sing song. I wonder what the new mob will be like?

May 29

Did a training trip from Mt. B. to P.D. on "A" of the new Sqdn. I was fitter, rigger, Operator and what-not.

We came back almost immediately and I'm glad we didn't have to spend a night in that place.

Sqdn. Ldr. Lovelock flew the kite. He is Stationmaster of the new Squadron and seems to be a very nice chap. Went down the Boringdon and to Harry's tonight and had a few jugs.

May 30

Got my wish at last and went ashore at the Scillies. Poor old Terry Brown of 10 landed "B" of that Sqdn. Here a few days ago and a gale sprung up. The buoy broke and "B" finished up on the beach. Halliday, [Wing Commander Neville Anthony Roy Halliday] the C.O. of this Sqdn. Flew down today to conduct a "Court of Inquiry" and we got ashore while this was going on. I bought a knife for Laurie Benham to add to his collection, and posted some photographs to Molly and Mother.

The Scillies are very beautiful. I had a great time wandering around.

Got home at dusk – about 10 p.m.

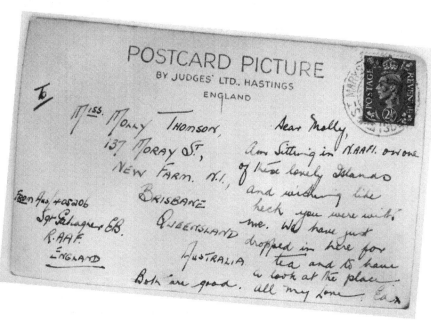

May 31

Did a navigation exercise with P.O. Buls, late of 10 Sqdn. As skipper. I never knew he could handle a kite so well. He'll do me for a captain if he passes his night captaincy test.

Spent the night in the Mess, playing the Radiogram and swigging a few beers.

June 1, 1942

Had a quiet rest all day. The spring is certainly all the poets crack it up to be. Perhaps it's the contrast to the long gloomy winter with its rain and fog and general dreariness. I'm certainly not looking forward to October.

Had a walk round the station and sat for an hour or two on the rocks at Jennycliffe.

June 2

Showed some new coots the ins and outs of a Sunderland. Was taxiing out in the Bay on the outers when the starboard seized. Had a very unpleasant five minutes until a large dingy arrived and took us in tow.

Played golf with Hughie and Keith this afternoon after tea and did the course in 86 which was fairly good for me.

June 3

Did some work with the new-comers. Showed about a dozen how to moor up. It's strange that I, who am a wireless operator, should be showing fitters and riggers their jobs. Some of the so called flight engineers don't even know how to dope up an engine!

Had a few jugs in at town tonight with Bullsie and some of the boys.

June 4

I wish Mother* had been with me on this trip. We flew along the south coast of Eire somewhere near Cork. Ireland looks very beautiful from the air. I must spend my next leave there. I wish I could get some civvy clothes so that I could get across the border between Eire and Ulster. I'd love to see Killarney and those places.

June 5

Bullsie and some of the Pilots have to get in some night training, so F.O. Gillies (one of the best chaps in 10 Sqdn.) flew us down to P.D. about 12 o'clock. About 11 o'clock we began our night training and flew till dawn.

Crawling into bed as soon as I've written this.

Alan fell in the drink mooring up today and Mr. Gillies lent him his coat to wear while his togs were drying. He walked up town in Ron's coat, returning salutes from all and sundry.

June 6

I slept all day today and got up about four o'clock when Mr. Walker came on board to do some circuits and bumps. We've been flying again all night and I'm dead tired.

Alan and Jeff went for a row in the dinghy today and it blew up and they had to swim for it.

The Rations here are as lousy as ever.

June 7

Slept all day again until almost tea time. Went into town after tea. P.D. is just as dead as ever. Had a jug at some of the old pubs and met some old acquaintances.

About midnight, Mr. Gillies put Dick Miedeke through his paces and we flew until dawn. Turning in now for a few hours.

June 8

Left P.D. at eleven o'clock. The place was full of rumours that our squadron was to be stationed there when properly formed. Lord preserve us from that!

Had another game of golf this afternoon but did a 93. Not too good!

Nearly killed a Pongo, who was wandering about the course, with a lovely drive from the fifth tee.

June 9

Spent the day dodging work and writing letters. Hear we have to go back to P.D. tomorrow. Good Lord!

Wonder if old Thomason will be there? No doubt he will be, swamping beer at the Mess.

Everyone seems to dislike him, and no wonder.

June 10

Bullsie and Lovelock flew us down to P.D. today about 6 p.m. and as soon as it was dark we began those damned night landings again. We flew until about two or three a.m.

I dislike this night training. It tires you too much.

June 11

Thank heavens the weather is too bad tonight to fly. It means a decent night's sleep for a change. Spent the evening in the Mess, downing a jug or three with the boys.

I wish we'd get started on operational flying.

June 12

Did a test flip to test the engines at P.D. about three this afternoon and about five began to do circuits and bumps until the weather closed in.

Am sleeping on board.

June 13

Had a shooting match down at the range today with rifles. Missed one point out of the possible and so was beaten by Brad who got the possible.

Some of the boys displayed a distressing lack of accuracy; I hope, for my sake, they are better with machine guns!

Near midnight began circs and bumps and flew till morning.

June 14

Weather was too bad today for flying so all the boys had a good day's rest.

Everyone, including the officers, repaired to the "Castle" tonight and we had a good party to celebrate Bullsie passing out as a night captain.

Sleeping in the Mess tonight.

June 15

Did a flip out to sea today and had some good practice firing at flame floats.

Stayed in tonight. I rang and tried to get a seat at the one Theatre this village boasts, but it was full. Had a few with Bullsie and the boys at the Mess.

June 16

Did an engine test and had some gunnery practice this afternoon and then flew all night doing circuits and bumps.

We're going back to Batten tomorrow. Are we glad!

June 17

Flew from Angle Bay, where we moored up last night, to P.D. and, after being briefed, returned to Mt. B. The place is much the same – heaven after P.D. Going to bed early tonight, after I write to Molly, to make up for the sleep I lost at P.D.

June 18

Had a day in Torquay and, as it was raining, didn't see much except the bar of the "Angler's Arms." I wanted to take a stroll round the parks and see the flowers, which I'm told are beautiful, this time of the year, but was forestalled by the weather.

Returned to camp early and finished the day with a sing song at the Mess.

June 19

Went into town after dinner for a much needed hair cut. Was beginning to look like the wild man from Borneo. Afterwards I met Mac and went to the "Odeon" and saw "The Road to Zanzibar" with Bing Crosby, Bob Hope and Dorothy Lamour. It was quite a good show and we enjoyed it thoroughly.

The days are very long now. It's strange to come home from the pictures and go to bed in broad daylight.

June 20 (A Squadron)

Jerry kept us down in the shelters for some time last night, damn him, but he did no damage to the Station.

W.C. Halliday flew us down to P.D. today. They have picked a permanent crew for "A" – Bullsie is Capt., Ross Baird First Pilot, Gippsie second, Graham White is navigator, Winkie Youl first engineer, Bob Stewart Second, Brad is mechanic, I am first operator, Harry is second, Jeff is rigger and Alan Mayne is tail Air Gunner.

June 21

Spent the day at Carew Cheriton, being instructed as to the bombing and gunnery course we are to do for the next few days. It seems quite a good course, and I'm looking forward to it very much. I love firing off my old guns. Arranged a programme with the Signals officer here to do some key bashing, so that Harry can get in some good practice. Bullied old Thomason re his R.T. station here, which is terrible.

There was a dance in the Mess tonight. Mary of the "Bush" was there. She had a few drinks with me to celebrate old times. Took her and her Mother home after the do.

June 22

Spent the morning dropping practice bombs on a target in the bay here, and the afternoon firing at drogues towed by a Lizzy*. Haven't got the results of the Gunnery yet, but we should get them in the morning. Did the rounds of the locals tonight with Jeff and Harry. Harry has achieved a romantic attachment with the daughter of the prop. Of the "Prospect Inn." However he was a bit glum when I informed him she is only sweet sixteen. *[The Westland Lysander, was used for artillery spotting, drogue training, reconnaissance and close support training.]

June 23

Winkie Youl won the shoot yesterday with me second. We did some more drogue shooting this morning. I got in some lovely bursts from the tail at about three hundred yards. This afternoon we did bombing practice. As the load consists of about sixty practice bombs, the racks have to be replenished several times which is hard work in a bucking kite. Yesterday we carried two ground armourers to do the work but they got too sick so we left them behind today and Winkie and I did the job.

Duty hand tonight, drat it. Rations lousy, as usual here.

June 24

Won the competition yesterday. Winkie and I were armourers again this morning. Gee! It's hard yakker. Gippsie got four direct hits out of five. Some WAAF's we took up for a trip were very sick.

Chased the old Lizzy up and down again this afternoon. Jeff nearly shot down the plane instead of the drogue in his excitement. Don't know how I went.

Spent the evening in the Village with Harry, who was anxious to revisit his love at the Prospect Inn. Was mortified to learn she was back at boarding school! Lord! How I laughed.

June 25

Alan and Harry and I went to Carew Cheriton after breakfast and were tested in Aircraft Recco. I made a wild guess at the first, a difficult one, and was right, so he only concentrated on poor Harry and Alan, who, I'm sure, are better at it than I'll ever be! Came first in the gunnery yesterday afternoon so Bullsie didn't give me a shot today so the others could get more practice. After all, I did this course before, last February with Tommy Egerton and Brownie of Ten Sqdn.

Winkie and I were armourers again this afternoon. These eleven and a half pound practice bombs seem to weigh a ton about the end of the day!

June 26

Funny thing happened today while we were bombing. The rack tripped all right but one of the bombs hung by a whisker, while we were over the water, but as we were coming over the land, fell off. It just missed a Pongo Soldier by a dozen feet. Lord, was he lucky*.

Gunnery practice on a drogue this afternoon, and I had a shot from the front turret.

Going home tomorrow.

*N.B. See the reference re above on October 1st.   EBG 1.10.42

June 27

Came back to Mt. B. today, and are glad to get away from P.D. There's a Mess dance there tomorrow and even that didn't make us sorry to be leaving.

Good news awaited us on our return. We are to go to Ireland tomorrow by plane to pick up a new kite. So I'm to get to old Ireland at last! Whacko!

June 28

Left Mt. B. by train tonight for London. Staying tonight at the Union Jack Club. Am meeting the rest of the boys at Euston tomorrow, where we are going to entrain for Stranraer. We were originally supposed to go by plane, but this was cancelled. Thinking the whole trip was off, Harry Muller and Alan Mayne ducked into town this afternoon and so have missed out. The C.O. asked me to pick two other chaps and I got Blue Eva and Paddy Druhan. They are as pleased as Punch.

June 29

Am writing this in the train. I never could write so well as this in our trains back at home! We left Euston at 4.30 and have been going ever since. We expect to arrive in Stranraer about 5 a.m. Bullsie has got us a sleeper each! Sheets, blankets and everything.

June 30

Arrived in Stranraer about 5 but were allowed to sleep until seven. Then we boarded a boat for Larne, in north Ireland. We had a magnificent breakfast on the boat, which Paddy Kirke, who managed to get himself included in this trip with us because his home is in Belfast, worked with his brother-in-law, the Steward.

We trained from Larne to Belfast, and put up at the best pub here, the "Queens." It's a corker place. Jeff and I are sharing a double room. Found the boat is all ready for us to take away tomorrow.

Belfast is blacked out, just like England, at night.

July 1

Walked all over the town today. Had three good meals at the Hotel and all at the expense of the taxpayer. The weather report was too bad for us to take off today. The beer is frightfully dear here – 9^d a glass, but the stout is cheap and what lovely stout it is. There is no conscription of women here, and it is pleasant to see all the girls in dresses of many colours instead of them all being drab grey.

July 2

Weather still too bad. Sent some photos home to Molly and the folks. I love what I've seen of Ireland! Went for a long bus ride in the country this afternoon and saw some of the most beautiful scenery I've ever set eyes on. There's an old castle nearby which is simply glorious. The people are very friendly, too, and the girls have it all over their English cousins in looks and vivacity.

July 3

Couldn't get off again today and Bullsie is tearing his hair. The funds are dwindling rapidly and if we don't get away tomorrow we'll have to take up a collection in the streets. Eked out the dough they'd advanced back at Batten for the trip by putting all the dough we have on us together.

Some old bloke gave us free tickets for a dance today and we all traipsed along to it. Had the time of our lives. I got a bit merry and danced with

273

everyone there. It was like I'd always imagined an Irish dance would be. Everybody had the time of his or her life. I was dead sorry when it was over.

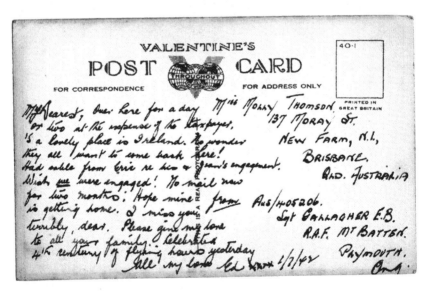

Letter #30

Postmarked Belfast 9.15 a.m. 4 July, 1942. 2½ penny stamp, blue with image of the King. Letter written on "Queen's Hotel, Victoria Street, Belfast" letterhead. Telegrams: "Queen's Hotel, Belfast." Managing Director: A. Cambell. Telephone: 211281

Aus/405206 Sgt. Gallagher EB, R.A.F. Mt. Batten, Plymouth.

July 3, 1942

My Darling,

I was expecting some leave at the beginning of this week, and had intended coming here. Fate works in strange ways – my leave was cancelled and I was sent here for a day or two to do a job. I don't mind – all expenses are being paid. No mail has reached me from home for over two months, now. I hope mine is getting through.

Belfast is a lovely town. It's good to be in a place where there is a ton of life and laughter and where Jerry has done very little damage. The Irish face is unmistakable. Walking down the street, every second face you see, every expression, is familiar. I see hundreds of Patty Mulligans, Mat Donovans, Aunty Marys and the others. To be in Belfast is to be in Brisbane.

I was given a wonderful time at a dance last night. These Irish love dancing and get more enjoyment out of one dance than the English get out of a night. No one seems to mind whether you are dancing correctly or not. The only thing that matters is that you are enjoying yourself. I have been invited out to more homes here in two days than I have been in England – all the time I've been there.

I don't like the Yank's I've met. Hope the type in Australia is better, or I can see the boys there getting very annoyed with them!

Only news from Aussie lately has been a telegram from Eric telling me of his and Joan's engagement. Lord, I'm pleased, dear! Eric was my best cobber and I think he's one of the best chaps in the world. Just the bloke I'd have picked for Joan. Wish I could get home, too. Maybe we could arrange a double wedding.

I wish I could get some news from home, darling. You've no idea how rotten it is to know of all the activity that must be going on there, and yet to know nothing of how the ones you love are.

Don't forget to give my love to your Mother and Dad and Alice and the rest. I wish I were back there with you.

275

I have just completed my 400 hours flying and am growing fairly sick of the sight of a Sunderland. Think I'll ask for my long service leave.

The new Squadron is going along fine. I really believe it will be a better one than was 10 Squadron. Everyone, from the C.O. down, is dead keen, and the old Hun is due for the shock of his life.

Here's the skipper looking for me, so I'd better finish. Keep loving me, dear, and praying for me. I miss you terribly, and love you more than all the world.

Ed xxxxx

P.S. Love me? Ed x

July 4

Fog still thick today. In desperation we visited the local R.A.F. station today, explained our pecuniary difficulties and, to our surprise, they advanced us three quid each! This made everything O.K. and now everyone is happy. Nearly had a fight with a yank tonight. Gee! I dislike the ones I've met here. I wonder if the ones in Aussie are the same nasty types? They love themselves; think they are much better than any other person. I nearly donged that little B. tonight! Lord! Why didn't I?

Had dinner today at a factory which we were being shown over, and it was some feed! Even had pineapple! Tinned, of course, but the first I've tasted in this country

July 5

Weather cleared sufficiently to enable us to get away this arvo. We ran on a sandbank taxiing in the harbour and had some anxious moments for a while. Things were a bit primitive. I had to make up my own call-sign and choose my own frequency and everything, but the Wireless was first class.

Landed at P.D. where we are stuck for the night. Lord! I hate this joint!

July 6

Handed over kite we bought from Belfast. Had some anxious moments getting her up the slipway in a heavy gale, but managed it O.K. Gippsie was taxiing and he did a fine job. It's the hardest thing in the world to taxi Sunderlands, as I know well. Then we took over another kite to bring to Mt. Batten. There's a lot to do in checking the inventory of one of these kites. There seem to be thousands of things on the list.

July 7

We did a test flip at P.D. this morning, and then took off almost immediately for Batten where we arrived in time for dinner, which, after P.D. fare, was not bad, in fact, bosker.

Alan and Harry got out of the trouble they had landed themselves in by missing the trip, but were disgusted with themselves for doing so.

I find that we are going to be refunded all the dough we spent in Belfast, which is a good thing!

July 8

Find we are heroes tonight. We set off at dawn this morning and about midday sighted a smoke puff on the water. Descending to have a look we found six chaps in a rubber dinghy. Went down lower to land and the sea was terrifying. Halliday set her down beautifully and we soon dragged 'em in through the rear hatch. Found that they were off a Whitley whose cooling system had given up the ghost. I sent a message in code to base: "Patrol Completed. Returning with six passengers, one slightly injured." Found doctors and ambulance waiting for us. The whole camp is excited. Afraid we'll all have swelled heads, over this. Halliday flew the kite. We used "E", the new one we'd just brought from P.D. Bullsie was a bit crooked on H's using his crew and leaving him behind.

Ed is fifth from the right, at back, looking down

July 9

We were paraded before the A.O.C. this morning who shook us all by the hand and congratulated us on "a fine show." I'd rather have brought off a job like this one than have sunk a dozen subs. I've found it is much more gratifying to save life than to destroy it.

We flew from Mt. B. to P.D. this afternoon in Steeley's bus for a new kite. P.D. gave us the same nasty sort of welcome. I hate this place. Invisible notices of "Strangers are not welcome" seem to hang everywhere.

July 10

We spent the day checking over the new kite, swinging the compass. Got her down into the water late this afternoon and I'm doing duty hand on it tonight. P.D.'s rations are, as usual, lousy.

Daily Sketch, Wednesday, July 29, 1942

DINGHY AND SUNDERLAND — THEY'RE LIFE-BOATS TO AIRMEN

Here's another instance of the value of the little rubber dinghy and the giant flying boat in saving airmen's lives. This Whitley bomber crew were kept afloat a night and a morning until a Sunderland flying boat landed on the sea to rescue them.

Perilously perched on a wing, two of the Sunderland's crew – one stripped for any emergency – haul the dinghy alongside. Only one of the rescued airmen had been slightly hurt when their plane was forced down by engine trouble.

"Illustrated" Photo essay of rescue at sea. 1/8/42

"Illustrated's up-to-the-minute War Pictures Exhibition contains enlargements of our cover and the big picture above."

"Far out over the grey waters doing just one of the routine jobs of their command, a Whitley of Coastal Command developed engine trouble while on submarine patrol.

A distress signal was sent out. The Whitley lost height. At last it hit the waves. The dinghy was inflated and the crew clambered in to overburden the tiny craft.

There were six men in that floating cockleshell – and one of them was injured. There was no land in sight, but the crew took it in turns to paddle.

But another Whitley on patrol had sighted smoke on the horizon – the funeral pyre of her sister plane. After investigating, the pilot reported the dinghy's position.

All night and next morning those six airmen drifted, hoping against hope that rescue would come their way.

At last a Sunderland flying boat landed near them. They were picked up, given dry clothes, fed, rested. They were saved. They'll be out after those submarines again.

HOPES OF RESCUE ARE REALIZED. AT LAST THE INFLATED DINGHY COMES ALONGSIDE THE RESCUING SUNDERLAND

A SUNDERLAND TO THE RESCUE

Illustrated's up-to-the-minute War Pictures Exhibition contains enlargements of our cover and the big picture above

Far out over the grey waters doing just one of the routine jobs of their command, a Whitley of Coastal Command developed engine trouble while on submarine patrol.

A distress signal was sent out. The Whitley lost height. At last it hit the waters. The dinghy was inflated and the crew abandoned in no overhanging aircraft. There were six men in that floating cockleshell—and not a man was injured.

There was no land in sight, but the crew took it in turns to paddle.

But another Whitley on patrol had sighted smoke in the horizon, the funeral pyre of her sister plane. After investigating, the pilot reported the dinghy's position.

All night and well into that day the airmen drifted, keeping against hope that rescue would come their way.

At last a Sunderland flying boat landed near them. They were picked up, given dry clothes, fed, rested.

They were saved. They'll be out after those U-boats again

LIFEBELTED RESCUER MAKES FAST THE DINGHY

HELPING RESCUED CREW INTO SUNDERLAND

"FOOD CAN WAIT," SAY RESCUED AIRMEN. A SMOKE FIRST
    "AFTER FOOD COMES SLEEP." RESCUED CREW IS EXHAUSTED

CAPTAIN OF RESCUING PLANE, WING COMMANDER HALLIDAY
    JOURNEY'S END. RESCUED CREW CLAMBERS INTO LAUNCH

HOME AT LAST. THE TWO CREWS COME ASHORE TOGETHER
    THEY ARE CONGRATULATED BY AIR VICE-MARSHAL BROMET

TO A LOST LOVE

Long have I searched, – not knowing what I sought,

And in my quest played many a sorry scene

With Love the curtain's fall; – yet found there naught.

But shadowy dreams, wherein grim faces, – lean –

Mocked at my wasted hours: – then have I fought

Long nights with dull despair, and losing seen

Life's tangled thread more mazed, – and vainly thought

To drown in drink the voice of Might-have-Been!

Little I knew! Since I have found Love, Dear,

(Yet may not make you mine) – though oft a tear

Unbidden dew mine eye, So am I filled

With joy of knowing you, – that voice is stilled!

And when Death comes, and my last breath is spent,

If I but dream of you, I'll be content!

E.B.G. Pembroke Dock 9.7.42

Letter #31

Postmarked 13 July 1942. One orange 2-penny stamp, and one green ½-penny stamp. Airforce paper Per Ardua Ad Astra.

Aus/405206 Sgt. Gallagher, E.B. 461 Sqdn. R.A.A.F. England

July 10, 1942

My Darling,

Two marvellous things happened the day before yesterday. The first was this: We were cruising along at peace with the world about 300 miles out in the Atlantic when we sighted a tiny speck on the ocean. We tore over to investigate and were astounded to see a tiny rubber dingy with six men in it. Despite the heavy sea the old "Winder" landed and we picked them up. Darling, you should have seen their faces! I think I've done the best deed that I'll ever do in this war. For 36 hours they'd sat in a space where there was hardly enough room for one or two men to stretch out. All their grub was eaten and they fired their last "Verey" cartridge on seeing us. We were just about to sit down to a lovely feed of steak and sausages when we saw them and you should have seen the way they tucked into it. We went without dinner but no one grumbled. After the feed I made up our bunks for them and they were asleep in ten seconds.

I sent a message out after we got off again (and were we lucky to get off in that sea!) and all I sent was "Patrol finished, returning with six passengers."

You can imagine the pleasure and excitement that was felt back at base. The Intelligence Officer sent wires out of his own pocket to the families of all the boys, and you must imagine how happy their families must have been to hear that they were safe and sound after being given up for lost.

The Navigator took a lot of snaps and in one of them I'm all in the limelight, helping them through the rear hatch. When they're developed I'll send them home. You can realise how happy and proud I feel to have assisted in an action such as this.

The A.O.C. came along yesterday and shook us all by the hand and congratulated us on a "very good show." I shouldn't be surprised if the "Winder" got a D.F.C. out of it. Gosh! I feel good, though, Dear.

The second grand happening was almost as pleasurable. When we landed I found a letter from you waiting for me – the first that's reached me from Aussie for months. It is wonderful to read that you are well, and still love me as much as ever. Please keep on loving me, darling. All I live for now-a-days is to see your face smiling at me when I get back to Brisbane. Oh! Darling, I love you! You are all I ever want in this world. I only hope that I am good enough for you.

Things have been going very well for me lately, what with tripping around the place and seeing the countryside at the War Office's expense and picking up crashed airmen. Hope they keep as good.

My week in Belfast was a grand time. Old Ireland will do me! I think, when I get leave, I'll go back there.

I'm glad to hear that the Grail is still going along O.K. The best news I've heard is that Mat is safe and sound! Gee, that was a bolt out of the blue! I very nearly executed a tap dance round the room when I read that! Give the old blighter my best regards, dear, and tell him to have one at Johnno's for me, and to remind Johnno he owes me an epistle.

I've been recommended for my crown – not before time with 400 hours up, "dicing with death," as we call it. Ho! Ho! (Actually living on the fat of the land.)

Have you heard from the folks in Townsville lately. Please keep in touch with them, dear. After all, you'll be one of them one day soon, please God. I'm glad to hear your family are all well; don't forget to give them my love. (Also remind Alice she owes me a letter, the blighter.)

Well, dear, night begins to fall – it's about 12 o'clock, – so I'll roll into my bunk. Hope old Jerry stays away tonight, blast him!

Pray for me, dear, and please keep on loving me, and waiting for me. I love you with all my heart, – I always will,

Ed xxxxx

P.S. Love me? Ed x

July 11

Jerry dropped a lot of stuff around last night while I was trying to sleep. I kept a Mae West handy.

This morning we did a test flip and found that everything was O.K. but when we left for Mt. B. this afternoon had only gone half an hour when all of a sudden the Stbd. Inner began to roar like a motor bike revving up. Just made P.D. before other engine packed up. When Winkie and Stewart checked up they found all the plugs had not been tightened and had worked loose! Bullsie is tearing huge strips off the ground staff here.

Courier Mail, Brisbane

New R.A.A.F. Squadron C.-M. Special and A.A.P.

London, July 12. The Coastal Command Sunderland flying boat squadron, which ultimately will be composed of Empire-trained Australians, began operations in Britain on July 1. The foundation personnel transferred from the original R.A.A.F. Sunderland squadron – which has been operating in Britain since the war began – include Pilot-Officer Bruce Buls (N.S.W.) Sergeant wireless-Operators or Air Gunners Edward Gallagher (Brisbane), John Lewis (Brisbane), and Leslie Wilson (N.S.W.).

So far the squadron has carried out four uneventful shipping escorts and anti-submarine patrols, involving a flight of 1500 miles.

July 12

Got off this morning and made Mt. B. O.K. Had no engine trouble this time.

This afternoon we found that they had completed the repairs to our own kite and so we took it for a test flip. It went as sweet as a bird. My wireless works extra special.

July 13

Some excitement today when two J.U.'s went for us down "Pockley's Corner" way. Alan and I reckon we got one each – I saw one of them dive straight into the drink.

On the way home we ran into an old Kurier who exchanged bullets with us for about an hour. Some of his cannon shells burst uncomfortably close. He must have tired of this sport, for he began to flash a lamp at us. From the mid turret I read – "So Long"!!!! Russ Baird sent him a ruder retort. So chivalry isn't dead in the German Air Force!

July 14

The boys laughed back at camp over our experience with the Kurier, yesterday. The Captain must have had a sense of humour and a fair knowledge of English idiom. I suppose he must have spent some time over here before the war.

Had a swim down at Jennycliffe this arvo and the water was very pleasant. I had to darn quite a few holes in my old trunks which are rapidly falling to pieces.

July 15

Had a pleasant trip down the bay and saw a sub which must have seen or heard us first as it was gone before we could get into position. We found lots of fishing boats, around the 100 fathom line.

Saw a couple of what we thought were J.U.'s but which turned out to be Beaus. They look very similar from a few miles.

July 16

Did a test flip at Mt. B. this afternoon. Bullsie threw the old kite around as if it were a spit fire. He can handle these Sunderlands better than anyone I've flown with. A couple of W.A.A.F's and A.T.C. kids regretted their request to be taken for a ride, judging by the mess in the bomb room. This afternoon Russ Baird, Graham White and myself were sent to Davenport where we boarded an armed trawler. I'm writing this down in the Coxswain's cabin. It's 5 a.m. We've been watching aircraft practising attacks on a Submarine which we are guarding. It was very interesting. The Coxswain plied me with rum at intervals, which kept me in good spirits.

July 17

Played a game of "Fives" with Jacko Lewis this afternoon. It is a game very much like a handball, but you use a racquet instead of your hands.

Jerry came over very high and the A.A. missed him by a mile. Am back from the trawler. The practice attacks continued all morning until dinner, when we re-entered the sound and were back in camp by 3.30. I enjoyed the experience very much, but am sorry to confess that the worst attack was delivered by one of our kites. The crew of the Sub (on which we'd thought we had to go, at first) must have been kept busy, crash diving every half hour. I've arranged to meet some of the crew of the trawler in Plymouth next week.

Letter #33

[Postmarked Plymouth Devon 18 July, 1942. 2½-penny blue stamp with King's image. Letter written on Australian Comforts Fund (Victorian Division) paper.]

Received 22.10.42

July 17, 1942

My Darling,

It was grand to get three letters from you, all in the one day, on Wednesday, and I very nearly performed handsprings to the edification of my room-mates. One from Joan arrived as well; it's just as well that you and she write to me so often, dear, for I haven't heard from anyone else for donkey's years.

I was worried to hear of your bad turn at Benediction "last night," (which was the 3rd of May) – I suppose you'll have forgotten all about it by this. Remember, darling, the scare you gave me that Sunday, at Mass? Gee! You frightened ten years off my life. I bet I was whiter than you were. Thank Joe for being so kind – and tell him I'm damned jealous of him, or, for that matter, of anyone else who is near you to be of help to you. I wish it had been me to act as doctor.

Sorry to hear of the demise of Bonzer, much as I detested the little tike. I bet Mother and Dad are glad to have Len in Townsville, and the rest of the gang. I can imagine the time they had when Len and Nev got together.

Of course I don't mind your going to dances, darling. I only wish I were there to take you. I would be all kinds of a glom if I had any objections. Hope you enjoy yourself at them, sweetheart. Where are they holding the C.B.O.B.F.C.* dances these times, in Finneys* or in the "Leader?" [Christian Brothers Old Boys Football Club or *Brothers.*] [Finney Isles & Co., a Brisbane department store since the 1860s, was taken over by David Jones Ltd. In the 1960s.]

I was glad to hear of your promotion. I know you'll be able to hold the job down O.K. – but I said the prayer for you, as you asked. It must be fun having Alice down with you, but I bet your Mother misses you both – or rather three, for I suppose Leo is still keeping the G.P.O going in Brisbane. How is the old son of a gun, anyhow. You never tell me.

Joan tells me in her letter that she was writing to you. I'm glad that you two are keeping in touch. Have you met her Eric, yet? He's the best guy in the world (after me, of course.)

Had more press reps – (Australian ones this time) interviewing our crew today about our "heroic" rescue effort. Maybe I'll get a write-up in the Courier. (And, again, I may not.) Anyhow they took our names.

There's free beer on at the Mess tonight but, unfortunately, (or fortunately) I can't have any as my kite is first available. Alas! Poor Ed!

There's no rest for the wicked, – I've been working like heck lately, but I'd rather be that way than kicking my heels. After all we came over here to give Jerry a headache, and we can't do that by loafing.

I saw the photos of the rescue yesterday and have ordered several copies. I'll send them to you. They're not bad.

I found another photo of the Scilly Isles in my box and am enclosing it. Did you get the one I sent you from there?

Well, dear, I'll crawl into bed and try for some shut-eye. It's darn hard to go to sleep in broad daylight, even though the clock says 9 p.m.

Say a prayer for me, dear, and please keep loving me, – I love you more than all the world, – I always will.

Ed   xxxxx

P.S. Love me? Ed

July 18

Did an uneventful A/S patrol down the old Bay this afternoon and morning. It was a lovely day and we saw a lot of French and Spanish fishing vessels, from which we received the usual waves and "V" signs. Very pro-British when they see one of us. I suppose they give the Nazi salute when a J.U. or a Kurier hoves in sight. I'm off to Torquay first thing in the morning.

July 19

Spent the day in Torquay and saw the place was lovely beyond description. Just outside Paignton there is a park full of flowers, the delicacy of whose petals and the glory of colouring took my breath away. I'll never forget the beauty of that scene. I wish Uncle Jim were here to admire it.

Re-met some old acquaintances at the "Queens" and on the beach.

July 20

Spent the day out in the Atlantic guarding a Convoy. It was quite an interesting trip but we had no excitement. The days are very long now. It is quite bright at ten o'clock at night.

No subs or Jerry kites arrived to break the monotony of the trip today.

July 21

Spent the day reading over my collection of letters and writing a few. I wonder if these letters are getting through? They have a long and hazardous trip now that Japan is in the game. I only get one now and then from home, these days.

July 22

Set out on an A/S patrol last night and sneaked down the French coast in bad weather, then along northern Spain. We expected to strike some Jerry fighters and did so. Some 109's attacked us near Bordeaux and we had quite a merry time for a while. They had no idea of tactics – must have been trainees for they never hit us. I was belting out on the Radio so never got a shot at them. Alan, Jeff and Jock say they got one or two of them. They should have. Some of them came so close you could have poked a hole in them with your finger.

July 23

Test flying passed most of the morning. I had some fun showing my Radio to a few A.T.C. kids who are very enthusiastic over everything. I went into town this evening and saw a show at the Gaumont, some mystery thing or other which wasn't bad. Had a jug or two in the Mess when I got back to camp.

Brisbane Telegraph, 22/7/42

NEW RAAF SUNDERLAND UNIT IN BRITAIN

"Telegraph" Special London, July 21

Australia has a new RAAF coastal command squadron operating in Britain. One-third of the squadron's personnel already is Australian, and the proportion is increasing weekly.

The enthusiastic Empire air trainees, all of whom are of a particularly fine stamp, and a stiffening of older hands from No. 10 RAAF squadron are anxious to make the new squadron's work felt in the Battle of the Atlantic.

So far they have carried out over 15 sorties. Most of these have been offensive sweeps. Others were escort duty. The latter means close protection for convoys of ships against U-boats and enemy aircraft, such as Fockewulf, Kondors, Kuriers, and JU88's, while the offensive sweeps are a positive contribution to the RAF Coastal Command's important role in the battle of the Atlantic.

Wing Commander N.R.L Halliday, of the RAAF, commands the squadron, and other members of the RAAF include Flight-Lieutenant – Medical Officer G.C. Wilson, from Hawthorn, Victoria, five flying officers, 23 pilot officers, and one flight sergeant. Flying Officer-Observer, F.B. Gascoigne from East Malvern, so far has participated in most of the squadron's excitement, which has ranged from picking up survivors from a crashed plane who were in a dinghy in the Bay of Biscay, to an inconclusive close quarter battle for 45 minutes with a JU 88.

Duel Between Planes

The enemy plane, which had not recognised the Sunderland, asked for recognition signals. It got machine gun bullets instead. The enemy turned and fought, but its shooting was the poorest. In five attacks, two of which brought the aircraft within 150 yards of each other, not one bullet hit the Sunderland, while the Sunderland shot scores of bullets into the Junkers, but did not bring it down.

The new squadron is most keen to meet up with a U-boat. They have not had much luck so far. A whale which the crew prepared to attack before they identified it has not been counted, but they are improving their tactics and navigation daily. It is a job lacking in spectacle and glamour. Most of it might be termed dull routine, but it demands the highest standards of character, training, and stamina. It combines the lore of airman and sailor. Numbers of Australians are now mariners of the air and the new squadron promises to uphold their fine record.

A Proud Record

No. 10 flying boat squadron, which holds almost every worthwhile record in the RAF Coastal Command, broke its own and the Coastal Command's record in May for the greatest monthly tally of operational hours.

Its pilots flew 851 operational hours. Its previous record was 785. Their total operational hours since the establishment of the squadron has exceeded 12,000 at June 20, equivalent to about 1,200 sorties, aggregating 1½ million miles. Their total flying hours are now 143,000. Five pilots and five observers at least have individually exceeded a thousand hours' operations, varying from normal Atlantic convoy patrols to bombing U-boats in the Bay of Biscay.

Some of the squadron's original members had similar figures. Personnel who have left the squadron mostly for Australia include observers, gunners and airmen. Original members still on the strength comprise seven officers and 27 airmen.

Ground Staff Efficiency

No. 10's high record rests on one major factor – the efficiency, skill and initiative of the Australian ground staff which is acknowledged to be the best in Britain. Australian artisans in the RAAF squadrons already have proved superior to all others and No. 10's records contain numerous official tributes to them.

Flight Lieutenant Eric. B. Martin of Parkside, South Australia, said: "Our main job is hunting the U-boats which must come up to the surface to recharge the batteries. Our job is to find them when they surface. It is a cat and mouse game. The men might fly 500 hours and not see a U-boat, and then suddenly sight one, and our job is to get over it as quickly as possible and drop bombs. The whole action usually lasts not longer than a minute.

No. 10 with its high operational record has a low casualty rate. It is the lowest of any squadron in Britain.

July 23, 1942

My own Darling,

Here I am, living on the fat of the land, watching over the well-being of my beloved "Sunder-bomber," and, incidentally, missing you terribly. Darling, it is hard to believe it is only 10 months since I saw you last – it seems a life-time.

Mail is arriving very irregularly – in fact not at all for some time, – I hope mine are reaching you. The photos of my thrilling (to quote the rags) rescue of those six chaps in the rubber dinghy while out on patrol have not been finished yet, but I'll send them on as soon as they are. I'm enclosing a snap that Bill Isle took of me. I think, except for too much exposure, it's a better one than the professional took in P. that you have.

I still am waiting for the never-forthcoming leave. I haven't made up my mind what I'll do when it does arrive. Snatched a night in Torquay on Sunday. Gee! I love that place. It's lovely to get to a spot untouched by the damned Germans, and relax. I swam during the afternoon and the water, though a trifle cold first off, was grand. There was hardly a cloud in the sky, and the flowers seemed even more beautiful than ever. Cherries are abundant just now, – likewise strawberries and gooseberries and I'm wiring into as many as I can. When I get a day off I'll get a few of the boys together and we'll go picking wild blackberries.

Had a rifle-shooting match last week and came second with just one point under the possible, which wasn't bad for a mug like me.

How are the Brothers' Dances going, dear? Again, I wish I were home so that I could go along with you. Have you seen anything of Les, Cec, and Mat these days?

Thought there was an air-raid on, but it was only the boys on the batteries shooting at a Drogue towed by an old "Fairey Battle." Wish they wouldn't frighten me so.

Went up to the "quack" this morning with a bit of a cold in the head which has broken out into a slight inflammation of the gums. He said I am a bit "run down" and need some leave. Hope he does something about it. I'm about fed up. The only real leave I've had since I got here was 12 days, last April, which I spent in riotous living in London. Next time I'll go somewhere quiet and have a good rest. I have only to lie down anywhere these days and I go off to sleep. But my sleep is uneasy.

Went along to see the Adj. the other day to enquire into the delay in the appearance of my Flight-Sergeant's crown. He promised to hasten things up.

How are the Family? Don't forget to give them my love when you write, and tell Alice and Leo I wish I were, like they are, near you.

Things have been looking slightly better lately on the Russian and Middle Eastern fronts. I think we'll beat old Jerry this year or early next. Wish he'd hurry up and chuck in the towel; I'm fed up to the back teeth of this War and all it entails, especially keeping us apart.

Oh! Darling! I love you! I miss you more than I ever dreamed I would, and I think I'll remember with a shudder, all my life, these rotten days away from you. Please keep loving me, and praying for me, for you are all my hope of happiness in this life.

I adore you.

Ed xxxxx

P.S. Love me? Ed x

To S., 23/7/42 — also revised as Sonnet No. 174

To Friends at Oxford, England, 12/1/43

Octave

I will remember, Friend, in years unborn,

When Age has dulled my mem'ry with the glass

Of sweet forgetfulness, – long shadows on the grass,

At Eventide in summer; – golden corn

Contrasting with the green of meadow land

And mossy bank; Cathedrals steeped in Time,

Quaint rose-grown cottages; – the scent of thyme

Breathed in a quiet dell, for fairy revels planned.

Sestette

I will forget these shuddering nights of fear,

When Heaven rains hell, – and only will I hear

The song birds in the dawn, – and only know as now,

The soft cool kiss of real rain on my brow:

And, in the end, should Death's shade steal these few

– Loved memories, – Dear friend, – I will remember you!

July 24

We took off about seven on an all-night patrol but after three hours were forced to return with a faulty 24V generator. Brad and I tried to fix it but found that a winding was burned out, so had to tell Bullsie to turn back.

We found a heavy mist at Batten on our return and Bullsie did a magnificent job in putting her down safely without a flare-path or very good visibility.

July 25

Slept in till midday today and then only got up because I was hungry. Went into town with George and Don, and they took me to a lovely little inn I've never seen before – the "Blue Peter" at Turnchapel. George and Don are great company on an expedition such as this. A chap I haven't met before came along too, a New Zealander named Norm Aldridge, who seems a very nice chap.

July 26

Lord! Am I glad to be writing you up, Diary! I never thought I'd be seeing you again. I went out on the most shaky do I've ever been on today, when we attacked a Jerry convoy in the Bay. We did over 300 M.P.H. in a dive at one stage. The Huns put up a frightful barrage – there seemed to be flack everywhere. They shot hell out of our Stbd. Wing and blew a hole in the floor of the bridge just where I had been sitting repairing a fault in the set five minutes before! Funny how close I feel to Molly when we're in a patch like this. It must be her prayers and Mother's that get us out every time. First run over, the bombs refused to drop, and then, when we did get a go, three hung up! We damaged a large tanker then went like hell for the clouds.

July 27

Had to run the kite up on the slip straight away for repairs. She should be O.K. in a few days. In the meantime I'm off to Torquay for a day or two. Have booked in at the "Queen's." I wish I could have all the old crowd down here with me! What a time we'd have! I think this must be the loveliest part of the world! Met a beautiful blonde at tea who, though I see she is married, seems to entertain romantic notions. Shall take her for a stroll tomorrow as she says she has never been here before.

July 28

Met the blonde at breakfast and strolled down the esplanade and through the parks. The flowers are a riot of colour. We sipped cocktails in the lounge before dinner this evening and I'm taking her to a dance tonight.

She has the honour of being the only girl I've ever taken out dancing in England. I feel a bit untrue to Molly. I wish she were here.

Later: Enjoyed the dance no end. Ann is good company and I was surprised to find that she is an R.C. Her husband is in the Navy, and she seems to be very keen on him.

It's 1.30 a.m. and bed is calling.

July 29

Got up about ten and breakfasted heartily on sausages and bacon. This is a good place to stay. Met the blonde Ann at lunch and went hiking this afternoon with her around the countryside.

Had a few drinks this evening together with Stewie and a few of the boys who have come down for the night. They brought the bad news that I have to return to camp first thing in the morning.

Said goodbye to Ann tonight 'neath the stars, very unromantically, with a handshake. Gee! Molly and I could have had a grand time these last couple of days!

July 30

Arrived back here at Mt. B. this morning and found that the repairs to the old boat were completed. Bullsie took her up on a test flip this afternoon and she went like a song.

We're off tomorrow on a patrol, I think. This place gives me the willies after Torquay.

Letter #34.

July 30, 1942

My Darling,

'Tis almost the end of July, and summer is passing fast – too fast for me. I'm lying on the grass outside my billet and enjoying a sunbake, even though it is eight o'clock in the "night."

With this letter I'm enclosing some of the snaps of our "heroic" sea rescue, also some newspaper cuttings. I'm sending some to Mother too, so you can exchange yours with her, if you like. I only appear in one – when we were being congratulated by the A.O.C., but one of the "Illustrated" magazines gives a lovely picture of my back as I helped the boys aboard. I'm sending you the magazine under separate cover, – also one to Mother, so you needn't worry about passing it on.

I have been having quite a bit of excitement lately, but unfortunately, I can't tell you about any of it or I'd be up before the Censor. I'll have some marvellous experiences to tell you of when this darned old war is over.

A huge batch of Aussie mail arrived yesterday and today, but none for poor old me. Maybe tomorrow I'll have better luck.

I saw a show yesterday – the first for months and months. It was "The Missing Million" and "Lady for a Night," both of which were not bad. Have you been seeing many shows lately, Dear?

We're having a Squadron Dance next Thursday night which should be good-oh! Wish you were here so that I could take you; you'd enjoy the dances over here. Some chap is singing some sentimental ditty over the way and he's horrible. Hope I don't sound as bad when I warble. For about a quarter of an hour he's been singing the same tune over and over. "The Anniversary Waltz" is the name of it.

Please excuse writing, love – I never could write leaning on one elbow. My arm keeps going to sleep.

I hope you are well and happy, dearest, and don't worry too much over your Ed. When I think it over, sweet, I've been a dead loss to you as a sweetheart – caused you nothing but worry right from the start, but, please God, I'll make up to you for it all when we are married. I'll try to, anyhow, as hard as I can.

Are your family all well, love? Give them my best regards and ask

299

them to say a prayer for me now and then. Give your Mother a big hug for me when you see her.

Have you heard from Joan or the others regularly? Please keep in touch with them, dear. They love you, you know, and Mother had never ceased wondering where I got the sense to pick on someone like you for my future wife.

Please keep on loving me, darling and don't forget me in your prayers. I will always adore you,

Ed xxxxxx

P.S. Love me? Ed x

An Airman's Prayer
By
Sergeant Observer H.R.Brodie
R.A.A.F.

Almighty and all-present Power,
Short is the prayer I make to
                    Thee,
I do not ask in battle hour
For any shield to cover me.

The vast unalterable way
From which the stars do not
                    depart
May not be turned aside to
                    stay
The bullet flying to my
                    heart.

I ask no help to strike my
                    foe,
I seek no petty victory here,
The enemy I hate, I know to
          Thee is also dear,

But this I pray, be at my side
When death is drawing through
               the sky,
Almighty God, who also died,
Teach me the way that I should
                    die.

July 31

We came clean out of the clouds on top of a sub, just about dinner time. They had no time to dive and elected to fight it out. I was in the nose turret and hosed the deck with great gusto. I never knew I could be so cold blooded, but I've found that you never think till afterward of what you're doing. I watched a group of men around a gun just wither away like chaff before a cutter. I feel a bit crook tonight thinking back on it, but I suppose it was them or us. I wonder how many helpless women and children they have killed? Bullsie, with nothing to fear from the guns, made a steady run over it and blew it to bits, almost, with D.C.s and S.A.P.s

A good day's work.

August 1

Spent the day reading and writing. I like a lazy day such as this. I wish there were more of them. I reckon it's about time I had some leave, feeling a bit seedy lately.

I'm duty hand again tonight, so will continue the good work with the letters when I go out.

Later – I'm out on the kite, waiting for my supper to cook. Have some steak and tomatoes frying. Smell good!

Did a few circuits and bumps early this morning.

August 2

Johnny Lewis called over in a dinghy and invited me to have lunch with him. He was on his own in "D". I took a risk and left the kite at the mercy of "George," "Mae," and "Mickey" and found that Johnny had prepared a sumptuous feast. Steak, sausages, tomatoes, chips, rice pudding and custard, some lollies he'd got from home, washed down with tea. 'Twas some feed!

We expect to be off in the morning.

Met John Sutherland (the coxswain of the trawler I was on some time ago) and some of his friends in town tonight and had a jug or two with them.

August 3

Took off on an Anti Sub patrol and ran into a couple of Arados about 150 miles out on our first leg. They were gamer than they usually are and made the going tough for a while. I pounded out a call for help, and they were so busy attacking us that they didn't see a couple of Beaus* until it was almost too late. Then they went like hell for some clouds with the Beaus after them in full cry. Don't know how the fight finished. Apart from this the patrol was uneventful. *[The Bristol Beaufighter became a national hero during her service in the Battle of Britain and beyond.]

August 4

Feel tired all the time these days. I need some rest badly. Some of the boys were given some leave recently but were recalled straight away.

It appears as if we are going to be lucky to get a leave in this Squadron. The C.O called a hate session today, but we didn't get much satisfaction.

August 5

I was duty hand with Harry Miller today and just before dark the C.O. called alongside in a dinghy and asked me to go for a flip with him and test his turrets. The Pongos are useless. I had to fix and load all the guns, as well as test them. When I got back to "A" I was done to a frazzle.

I lay down for a few minutes and was woken by Harry who said he thought I was in a fit. He says I'm a mug not to put in for some leave. I feel rotten. Think I'll see the M.O. tomorrow.

August 6, 7, 8,

Got no chance to see M.O. for we took off early on what was to prove to be the best job I've ever been on. Off Ushant, we sighted a dinghy with six R.A.F. chaps in it. Just as we were about to go down for them, two Arados and a J.U. hopped on to us out of the sun. We had the devil of a fight for about an hour. Said many a prayer and thought we'd had it many a time. I was quite resigned when two more Arados popped up; the thing that hurt most, Diary, was the thought that I'd never see Molly again. Funny how clearly you can think in times like these. My guns went U/S at one time and I had a hell of a time. Had shot down one Arado when, suddenly, out of the Sun, dived three Beau fighters. We had been supposed to meet them earlier, but they were late. I suppose they picked up our calls for help.

What fun there was then! We stooged steadily along while all around us dived twisting, turning, and flame belching aircraft. You could hear the cannon above the roar of the engines. Another Arado went spinning down with sparks and smoke pouring from it and hit the water with a splash.

Suddenly the Jerries decided they'd had enough, and turned tail for a cloud front that was about ten miles away. Gleefully the Beaus tore after them. Before they reached the clouds I think another Arado hit the dust and then the sky was empty except for ourselves, and we were able to breathe again. Bullsie had handled the kite so magnificently that they never hit us once! I thought Graham would be hopelessly lost after all this twisting and turning but he brought us back right over the dinghy and they never even had to fire a Verey cartridge for us to spot them. We landed and picked them up. They had seen the scrap and knew the Jerries were using them as a decoy but could do nothing at all to warn us, and had given us and themselves up for lost. While we were on the water we got a scare when a kite appeared on the horizon, but either he didn't see us or he was a Beau keeping a watchful eye on us, for he didn't come near us. Find ourselves the heroes of the hour. Hope nothing exciting happens tomorrow or the next day for I've used up all the space.

August 9

Had a rest yesterday and the day before. Saw the M.O. yesterday and he saw the C.O. and insisted I get some leave. Bullsie is for me, too; told me to go ahead and make arrangements. I'd better wait to get confirmation from the M.O. first. Had some excitement today. Did an A/S patrol off Cape Finisterre. On the way home after an uneventful patrol, we ran into two more of those damned Arados. Alan shot one up so badly that it flew off with smoke pouring from the starboard wing but the other was game. He stuck to us until a Beau fighter popped up out of nowhere and blew him to hell with a beautiful cannon burst. I think the blokes who are running this business have woken up to themselves and are giving us long range fighter protection in the shape of these Beaus.

August 10

Spent a couple of hours doing circuits and bumps. Some of these new pilots are more dangerous than any Jerry could be. They'll break their silly necks and ours too, one of these days. One chap today, in attempting a landing bounced her about fifty feet into the air first go. I think the fifth bounce was a good landing, for it was the last.

Went into town and had a few jugs tonight and returned home and finished off in the mess. Am turning in slightly pickled, but not so pickled as to forget you, Diary, old thing. How I hate you, you silly red faced excrescence!

August 11

Received confirmation of my leave. It appears I'm to have ten days starting from next Monday. I've put my laundry in today with the promise that it will be ready by Monday afternoon for sure. Did a patrol this afternoon and evening down Corunna way but, for a change, saw absolutely nothing. Hardly even a fisherman. Wrote a letter to Lady Frances Ryder* tonight asking her to try to find some quiet place for me to stay at. Hope I get a reply before Monday. Think I'd better ring her about Friday. *[Lady Frances Ryder ran the *Isles Dominion Hospitality Scheme*, which put servicemen in touch with British families who were willing to give them a taste of home life during weekends and leave periods.]

August 12

Was too tired to do anything except doze all day. Have a rotten headache; am doing duty hand with young Drury. He's a pretty good kid and I think he'll be flying instead of me while I'm on leave. He's welcome to the job. Hope we don't fly tomorrow. Am fed up with everything, particularly Sunderlands.

August 13

Did an A/Sub patrol down the Bay but saw slightly less than nothing. A very monotonous trip. Steeley's mob attacked a "U" boat according to a message I intercepted, but from what I could make of the position given, it was in a prohibited area. Hope the silly B's – it's their first Op's trip – didn't sink one of ours. George Bentley and the crew of "B" went out to pick up some blokes from a rubber dinghy, and are long overdue. Last message received was that they were going in to land, having sighted the dinghy. Jacko who was on a 10 Squadron kite on the same job, says it was too rough to land. Hope that mad "B" Halliday hasn't skittled the boys. Our crew volunteered to go out and look for 'em, but permission was refused. [On August 12, 1942, Wing Commander N.A.R. Halliday of the RAF, who was the first Commanding Officer of 461 Squadron, along with ten crew, in attempting to rescue the crew of a downed Leigh light Wellington aircraft, crashed his Sunderland (UT-B) in rough seas. All managed to escape into the dinghy, which, overloaded, quickly collapsed. One man, the Navigator, Flying Officer John Watson, offered to swim (he had been a lifesaver) for an empty dinghy they had seen before landing. He miraculously found the floating dinghy, and after five days in it without food, miraculously (again!) found the crew of the downed Wellington. The next day they were rescued by a launch, but not without more drama, as the skies were filled with German 190s, Junkers, and Arados. The story is much better told in Ivan Southall's "They Shall Not Pass Unseen" Halstead Press, Sydney, 1956, that tells some of the exciting "exploits of a community of airmen who flew Sunderland flying-boats in the Battle of the Atlantic." Unfortunately, the book is out of print. Norman Ashworth, in "The Anzac Squadron" Hesperian Press, 1994, also has a vivid description of Halliday's crash into the sea, and the subsequent rescue of the Wellington crew and the one survivor of Halliday's Sunderland crew.]

August 14

Did circuits and bumps at Mt. B. No news yet tonight of "B". Good old George will come out all right, I bet. Damn that coot Halliday! Geo. Was one of my best cobbers. Met his girlfriend this morning while on the way to the mess. She was as happy as Larry and I got a hell of a jolt when I knew I'd have to break the news to her! She hadn't heard! I did it as gently as I could and was almost in tears myself when she looked at me in that funny questioning way – "Surely you're joking! – But then surely you wouldn't joke like that!" She didn't say anything – just looked at me, kind of dazed, then thank heavens! the tears came. I told her Geo. was sure to be O.K. Must be a prisoner of war by now. God make me right, please!

August 15

Rang Lady Ryder tonight and she tells me that she has arranged with a I Aikman in Bucks. To put me up for about ten days. I'll see the M.O. tomorrow and get away on Monday. Don't feel at all well. Bullsie and Harry and the boys tell me to forget all about flying and Sunderlands. I'll take their advice. I'm going to turn in early tonight.

Postmarked Paddington W.2A, 9.15a.m. 18 August, 1942.
Received 14.10.42. Opened by Censor, Passed by Censor.
Aus/405206 Sgt Gallagher E.B. 461 Sqdn. R.A.A.F. Abroad

August 14, 1942

My Darling,

This rescuing people from the sea appears to be becoming a habit with me. Last Thursday we put down in the "Drink" and picked up another six chaps who seemed destined for a watery grave. I had to send another surprise message back to base informing them that we were coming home with six passengers, and when we arrived we found ourselves the heroes of the hour.

Next day we were dragged out and questioned by all the mighty and congratulated on our exploit. We made a record for the B.B.C which will be heard at home. I hope that you hear it, darling girl. I only say a few words, – Sgt. Bradley, the other Wireless Op. and myself tell of our experiences balancing on a wing and dropping a rope on to the men in the dinghy as they passed beneath. I have some more photos which I will send you.

Good news yesterday. Someone has at last woken up that I am due for a spot of leave, and, unless I am again unlucky, I'm to start in a day or two. I'm going to some quiet place where I can have a good rest. I'm just about brassed off.

No news from home for many a long day, and I'm feeling as lonely as heck.

I have lost the list of the number of letters I have written you and I think this is 35. Anyhow I'll start off from that number again.

Many of my old Parkes mates are arriving these days and it's a pleasure to see the old familiar faces again. I wish all the Wireless Ops. In the squadron were my old Aussie cobbers.

I miss you terribly, dear. My only prayer now is that I may see you again, and soon. The other day, out on patrol, we had a rotten moment of anxiety and I thought it was all up with us. I said a short prayer and then thought of you, and, dear, you've no idea how rotten was the thought that I wouldn't see you again. Luckily we came out on top, but I don't ever want to experience that horrible feeling of regret again. I love you more than I can say.

I hope that Joan and Mollie have been writing to you regularly.

306

How is the job going these days? I bet you're busy and wish I were with you so that we could have a good old moan about too much work together. Is Alice finding things to her liking at the G.P.O.? I had a letter from Bill Moffat the other day and he gave me all the news regarding my old office in the Telephone a/cs. I think I'd be a stranger if I went back there now; so many changes have taken place.

Have you heard from many of the boys lately? I miss the old days and the golf and fishing we used to enjoy so much, and the parties at Bursties. I suppose Sergeant Nev. Is a busy man these days.

Well, dear, I must finish off now as I have a job of work to do. Please give my love to your family, and my regards to all the crowd. I love you more than all the world,

Ed xxxxx

P.S. Love me?

Ed x.

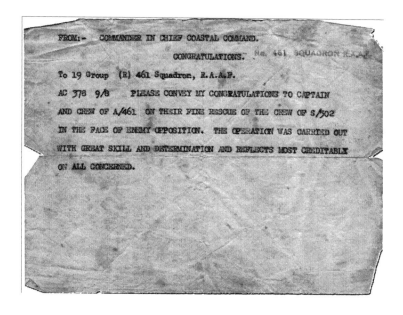

August 16

Spent a busy day arranging leave passes, etc. It's strange the amount of mucking that's necessary to get away for a few days. Had a few jugs in the mess with some of the boys and enjoyed myself no end. – No news of George and the boys.

August 17

Squadron farewell dance was held in the Continental tonight. I waited for it and left about ten o'clock for London. Had a good time at the dance and as my laundry was ready for me when I called for it everything looks O.K. for the holiday. Am staying at the Union Jack Club for the night. I hate this place, but I suppose I'm lucky to be able to get in here so late at night. Bed calls so, Diary, go and boil your great fat head.

August 18

Rang Mrs. Aikman this morning, and she sounds extra nice over the phone. I arranged to come down this afternoon, but whom should I run into at Aussie House but Reg Collins, my old Parkes and Amberley cobber. I thought I was seeing a ghost, because I knew he'd been shot down in the 1,000 bombers raid on Cologne.* Reports of his death were exaggerated for he tells an exciting story of escaping through Belgium to Holland and back, France, Spain and from Spain to Gib. He took me out to meet some friends.

I rang Mrs. Aikman again (I think I was very rude), explained the position, and asked her if she'd mind my postponing my visit for one day. She said it was quite all right, so I stayed with Reg and we had a grand time. *[The first "Thousand Plane Raid" by the RAF was codenamed *Operation Millennium*; Cologne was chosen as the target and the raid took place on the night of May 30, 1942. Reg Collins, the only survivor of his downed Wellington bomber, landed via parachute near Acchen on the Belgian border. After three days walking without food or water (other than what he found in muddy puddles), he collapsed; he was miraculously delivered into the hands of supportive locals who smuggled him to France. There, while moving from safe house to safe house, he spent a night hiding in the attic of the Nazi SS headquarters. He then travelled through the rugged Pyrenees and on to the British Consulate in Madrid, arriving ten weeks after his plane was shot down. He attributes his life to a woman known as "The Little Cyclone — Countess Andree "Dedee" de Jongh, who had set up a system of safe houses and contacts (the Comet Line) between Brussels and Paris. Dedee, her father and all of her friends involved in the Comet Line were "sold out" in January 1943. Her father was shot and she was sent to a concentration camp. After the invasion of Germany she was released and spent the next thirty years in Africa helping lepers. Source: Darren Lovell, *The Sunday Mail*, Brisbane, June 9, 1996.]

308

August 19

Here I am at "Darney Dene"* in Flackwell Heath in the County of Buckinghamshire. I arrived this afternoon and Mr. Aikman [Arthur James Colville Aikman, B.Sc.] and his son Robin – aged 10 – met me at the Station. They were the kindest people I've ever met. I Aikman seemed as pleased to see me as Mother would have been. I have a lovely room and have been made to feel really at home. Their house is beautiful, with a huge garden full of fruit trees and with lovely lawns. Mr. Aikman and I ducked off for a quiet noggin at the local inn and then home, and now I'm off to bed. [When I visited Flackwell Heath in 1998, I noticed that the name on an old post in front of the house on Chapel Road actually reads "Darley Dene" and not "Darney Dene".]

August 20

I rose fairly early and had bacon and – wow! eggs for breakfast. I'd nearly forgotten what hen-fruit looked like! Hilary and Robin took me for a long walk this morning. Hilary is nearly four and the loveliest little kiddy you'd imagine, Diary. Gee! I like this family. The afternoon I spent in walking round the neighbouring district. It's a lovely part of the country. Tonight Mr. Aikman took me to visit a friend of his, Mr. Baker, or rather, Captain. We stopped for a beer and bought a couple of bottles. Mr. and Mrs. Baker are charming people, very well bred, and witty in their conversation. I enjoyed the visit.

August 21

Took a bus ride to High Wycombe, a neighbouring town. This is a fairly large place, and very clean for an English town. I enjoyed myself, as usual, walking all over the place. Ran into an Aussie sailor and had a jug with him and a long chat. He knew a chap I used to know in Sydney. Was home in time for fried steak and tomatoes for lunch. Mr. A. comes home for lunch every day. He cycles there and back to his work, which seems to be in connection with the printing of photographic paper.* He's a chemist – quite a young man. *[After World War I, Glory Mill, in Wooburn Green, made photographic paper and small amounts of other speciality papers.]

August 22

I went to Bourne End to carry out a promise I'd made to a chap in Aussie House last Tuesday. The chap he asked me to call on was out but his wife made me very welcome. The man, I find, is a Congregational Minister.

This afternoon or rather, Evening, so long are the days, Mr. A. and I cycled to a nearby village to see a very old inn. The first time I've ridden a bike since I was a kid. The inn was very interesting and on the way back Mr. A. showed me the grave* of an old friend of Dad's and mine – Edgar Wallace. It's very simple – just a plain marble slab with two dates and the name "Edgar Wallace." *[In Fern Lane Cemetery, Little Marlow, Buckinghamshire.]

August 23

Took a run into Maidenhead today. This is one of the loveliest places in England. People were boating on the Thames in punts and electric canoes. It was a beautiful sight, with the sunlight filtering through the trees on to the water and the gay crowds.

I had a jug or two at "Skindles"*, a pub I've read about back at home. It's where society goes for the week-end – generally with another man's wife or another wife's husband, says Mr. A. *[Skindles was the famous riverside hotel in Maidenhead known as Soho on Thames.]

August 24

I took young Robin with me for a run into Windsor today. We strolled around the town, tried to get into the castle but failed, then saw Eton college, and wandered along the bank of the Thames. I found a nice little "Air-gunners" brooch which I bought and I'll give to I A. tomorrow morning. I have to meet Reg in London tomorrow. I've liked my stay here very much. It's been the quiet rest that I needed so much.

August 25

I left Loudwater this morning and arrived in London about eleven. Reg met me and we had a great old yarn over a few beers. At night we went out to his friends' place then repaired to the local inn where we had a dance. We both stayed with his friends and they were very kind to put us up. I shan't relish going back to Batten tomorrow. Good night, Diary, old thing.

August 26

Back in camp, again. Shouted myself a cab from North Road Station in Plymouth to Batten. The trip up wasn't too bad, though monotonous. Am too tired to worry about you, drat you, tonight, Diary.

August 27

We're doing a trip somewhere tonight; I think it's an A/Sub patrol. I'm curling into bed as I don't expect I'll enjoy a long rest. They weren't long in getting me back into harness, although Bullsie said I was mad not to ring him up, because he could have got me a few more days.

Spent the day wandering around the station. Saw Doc. Wilson who seems pleased with my improved condition.

I think George Bentley has gone for a row*. The navigator of his kite has been picked up and he says all the others were drowned. I'll miss George. He has a young wife back in Aussie too. Geo. Was one of the best. It's a shame he should have been thrown away in such a mad attempt. *[Slang for "deceased".]

August 28

Took off before dawn tonight and flew nearly all day and saw nothing at all. Bad weather forced us to land at P.D. where tonight finds me doing duty hand.

Was interrupted in the writing of this by the arrival on board by Bullsie and the boys. We're back at Batten now and there is great activity going on. The weather lifted, and I've just finished refuelling the kite – (on my own!) for a trip to Gib. In the early hours tomorrow. I'm greasy from the oil and some petrol has got into my watch and it's refusing to raise a tick.

Good night and blast everything!

August 29

Reached Gib about three p.m. and I've just returned from a tour of the "Rock". I've bought some smokes and a couple of bottles of "Black and White" (at 9/6 per bottle!). Some of our passengers were very seedy on the trip down. One in particular made a hell of a mess in the Ward room. It was a lovely trip; the coast of Spain was glorious in the brilliant sunshine. We saw no aircraft whatever. I wonder what the Spaniards are doing and thinking these days? Spanish women are either beautiful beyond words or as ugly as sin; there are no in-betweens.

August 30

Slept on board kite last night – we all did. They never have any room for us on the "Rock" – thank the Lord. Very early we were roused from sleep and have just got back to Gib. After doing a bit of a sweep of the Med. Saw only some French kites, and have heard a few minutes ago that they shot a "Cat"* up badly. I suppose when they saw us they immediately reported it to their German masters. Lord! I hate the French as a nation! Bullsie says that if any of them get too close to us and look like attacking us we'll blow 'em to Hades. I won't wait to be told if I'm in the turret. *[The Consolidated PBY Catalina was an American flying boat of the 1930s and 1940s; no other flying boat was produced in greater numbers.]

August 31

Back at Mt. Batten again tonight. Ran into a flock of FW 190s* on the way home but Bullsie's wonderful handling of the 'plane and Alan's good shooting from the tail prevented their getting in a good shot at us. I thought our numbers were up and made a quiet act of contrition, but they ran short of juice I think, for suddenly they all buzzed off. *[The Focke-Wulf Fw 190 Würger was a German single-seat, single-radial engine fighter aircraft, which, when it was first introduced in 1941, was quickly proven to be superior in all but turn radius to the Royal Air Force's main front-line fighter, the Spitfire Mk. V. This captured FW190A, circa 1942-43, has replicated Luftwaffe insignia.]

They've flown the legs off us lately. I'm sick of the sight of the boat, the roar of the engines and the smell of petrol. I've become pretty fair at handling these kites now. Bullsie always lets me fly from Scillies to Mt. Batten.

September 1, 1942

Took off at dawn loaded with S.A.P.s [Semi-Armour-Piercing bombs] after a Dago ship that was reported sneaking up the coast of Spain. "R" and "U" of 10 were on the same job and we ran into them down "Pockley's Corner" way, dropping bombs on two subs they had found. "R" had found them first and they elected to stay on top and fight it out with Pockley and his merry lads. They must have been Italian subs. Great must have been their chagrin when Woodsie arrived in "U", then a few minutes later, us. I had a great time in the nose, spraying the decks at two hundred yards. Wish we'd had D.C.'s. We could have blown them to bits. However we found on our return here that we'd killed nearly all the crews of both and they had been run aground in Spain.

September 2

Bad day today. They sent "F" out with D.C.'s to finish off the subs we crippled yesterday – not knowing at the time that they had been run ashore, but "F" must have run into the fighter protection the subs had asked for, because all they've heard from her was that she was engaged in a running fight with J.U.'s and a faint "S.O.S". Blue Eva and Roy Chinnery were aboard. I think it would have been Roy's last trip as he was awaiting a medical board which would have grounded him, probably. Three of our original ten have gone, now. Billy Isle, George, and now Roy.

September 3

Went out on a dawn Bay patrol and had a pleasant uneventful cruise, strange to say. The old Bay is getting as busy and crowded as Queen Street these days. It seems to be full of subs, ships, Wellingtons, Sunderlands, Whitleys, Lancasters, Beaufighters, J.U.'s, Arados, Kuriers, etc. Life is getting very uncertain these times.

September 4

Went down Town this arvo and had a feed. Steak, Tomatoes, Chips, etc. – Then ran into bad company in the shape of some of the boys and made the rounds of the pubs. Came back on the last ferry and finished up eating fish and chips in the mess. What a night!

September 4, 1942

My Darling,

Well, the unexpected bit of leave was very pleasant. I went to a lovely spot on the Thames Valley, in Buckinghamshire, called Loudwater, and I think that this is the prettiest spot in England. The people I stayed with were kindness itself – a wonderful family. The husband is the boss of a big concern and has apparently pots of cash, and he gave me a marvellous time. There were three youngsters from six months to 10 years and they treated me as an uncle. One little girl aged four is a bosker kiddy – wish she were ours.

I visited all the neighbouring towns, including Windsor, where I wandered along the banks of the Thames, watching the punts and canoes plying merrily up and down. War seemed far away.

Maidenhead is about ten miles from Loudwater and is beautiful beyond words. I'd love to take you into the lounges of some of the hotels there and dance with you with the happy crowds there. Some of them are world famous – Skindels, the Riviera, etc. I saw Edgar Wallace's grave at Flackwell Heath, – a very simple one – no more outstanding than any other in the tiny graveyard.

I had a day in London on the way home and enjoyed myself as usual in that metropolis. Gee! Darling! I wish you were with me so that I could show you these places. I hope I may, some day.

You can imagine how much I enjoyed coming back to camp after my marvellous time. However, my disappointment was somewhat alleviated by my finding that we had only three trips to make before becoming due for another lot of leave – this time without being ordered by the M.O.

Those three trips are things of the past now, and here I am about to go on more leave. I think I'll go back to Loudwater – I have a standing invitation there, to treat "Darney Dene" as my home away from home.

How are things at home, dear? I'm worried night and day whether you are safe or not – Take care of yourself, darling, for if anything were to happen to you, I think I would die.

I received a cable from Joan saying that she and Eric are being married on the nineteenth. Give them my love, sweet. Aren't they the luckiest people in the world?

How are Pat and the rest of the Mulls? I haven't heard from them

314

for ages. Wish someone of my old mob would write to me regularly! I think you must be the only one that really cares for me, dear. Your letters seem to arrive.

Despite the prospect of leave, and more of Loudwater, I'm feeling a bit low tonight. I'm Duty N.C.O (which means I'm in charge of all the crews in the Squadron, and have to see they're all nicely tucked in, and drag them out of bed if they're wanted to fly) and I've an office all to myself and I'm missing you a hell of a lot! Excuse language dear, but that's how I feel. When I see Eric and Joan and Len and Sheila happily married, or rather about to be, I feel like cursing and swearing at myself for being such a fool as to leave you. I need you so much! Pray God this darned war will soon end, so that we can be together again, always.

I had a smack at a sub the other day, he tried to retaliate but missed us by yards. They're mug shots these huns.

Jacko Jackson is on leave at the moment. I wish I could have gone with him. We always have a good time together. He asks me, whenever I write, to give you his love. He's still the same old Jack, though a lot older. I think we are all a lot older, we chaps who have been here a year. You may not love me so much as you did before I left when you see me again.

I have now spent 450 hours over the old hunting grounds for Subs, apart from my other flying, and the many brushes with Jerry have added a few years to my age. I suppose though that when this war is over, I'll be so relieved and happy that I'll forget all about it, and treat these years as some fantastic nightmare that only existed as part of a dream.

Well, darling mine, I've bored you enough for this time. I'll cable you while I'm on leave. Please keep loving me and praying for me – you are all my life. I adore you,

Ed xxxxxx

P.S. Love me? Ed x

September 5

Took off before dawn on a shipping strike. There was 10/10 cloud all the time so we saw our inner motors and very little else. It was a nice safe trip, and I had plenty of time to think. Gee! I miss Molly and the folks, especially on long uneventful trips such as this one. We are going to our new base tomorrow. I hear that it is a very pleasant spot.

September 6

We left Mt. Batten for good today and flew over to our new base at P. [Poole] We had some difficulty in landing owing to the numerous sandbanks and anti-invasion devices.

Our mess is a large hotel in the middle of the town and is the tops! I think I'm going to like this place a lot. My room is on the top floor and has huge bay windows opening over the street. The beer in the mess is the best I've tasted in this country.

Tomorrow we are going by train to Stranraer to pick up a new kite – "L".

September 7

Arrived in London tonight and I stayed with Reg's friends out at Clapham North. It was very good of them to put me up.

I took the two daughters and son up to the "Plough" where we had a few jugs.

September 8

Had a few beers this morning and met the crowd at Euston Station where we found we would have been mugs to get any but the 4.30 train, so Graham White and I went to the Cogers and yarned over a few jugs until 3 p.m. when the rest of the crew arrived and we caught the train. It was a terrible journey and when we got to Stranraer in the early hours this morning found a transport waiting for us. Slept in a bed in some ramshackle joint and was dragged out by Bullsie at 10 a.m.

September 9

Bullsie had us taken to the slipway at Wig Bay, where, as we expected we found the kite was not ready. We swung the compass and did a few jobs then put her down into the drink. The wireless is in a hell of a mess, and I see myself working like hell tomorrow. This place is on the Schnoz! We have to walk about three miles from our billets to the mess, where, by the way, we get nothing to eat, and another three miles thence to the slipway! The C.O. of the station, is, I'm told, the biggest B. in the world. So bad are conditions that two blokes have committed suicide here already.

September 10

Got away from that damned Wig Bay today, thank heavens! We were in such a hell of a hurry to get away that I kicked the two so-called Wireless mechanics off the kite, told Bullsie to take off, and got the set working after fifteen minutes.

On the test flip we did, the other Pongos couldn't get a peep out of the damned thing, though I found the trouble to be only stiffness in the generator.

Hope I never see that blasted place again.

September 11

We are due for our leave, but have to do another trip first. I think we'll be going off on the morrow, and I hope we do. I'm duty hand tonight and for once I won't be glad of a good night's rest. I hope they wake me up before midnight and get this last trip over.

I brought a fishing line on board with me but the fish refused to be cajoled. I had visions of a nice plaice for supper.

September 12

My wish of yesterday was granted. I remember now that "B" was lost on its last trip before leave and this was nearly my last trip in many ways.

We took off before the sun was up, and had half completed a square search for a ship, when two Arados hove in sight. We had a long scrap with them and it was only when one made a mistake and Alan, in the tail, and I, in the mid-upper, nearly cut him in half, that we won. Seeing the fate of his mate, the other turned away. As he turned, Alan got in a lovely burst and he hit the sea, bounced off the swell and disappeared into low clouds. I think he was a goner.

September 13

Hanging around the station all day getting leave passes, pay and warrants fixed up.

They haven't enough money in the pay section to pay us, so we have to wait until tomorrow when the banks open.

I think I'll wait until Thursday before going on leave. I like the look of this place. I've written to Mr. Aikman accepting his invitation to stay with him, and I'll ring him when I get up to London.

There was High Mass this morning and the choir was about as good as the old Holy Cross Choir. Should I have written "as bad"?

September 14

Were paid today, and I stuck mine in the bank in case I should be tempted to squander it before Thursday. Went round the town tonight and made the acquaintance of several of the local Innkeepers.

I sent a cable to Joan wishing her and Eric the best. I hope it arrives before the wedding. I wish I could get home for it!

September 15

Went to a dance at the Continental with Tubby Sullivan. Had a good time; there are so many girls in this place that they come up to you and ask you for a dance! This is the first dance I've been to for months, and there seem to have been many new styles of dancing evolved since my last appearance on the floor.

Luckily I was slightly merry, so I was not so shy and awkward as usual.

September 16

Guest night at the mess and we had a bit of a dance and a do. Many bright young things arrived and a good time was had by all. The boys think there must be something wrong with me since I don't fall for any of the fair sex. I imbibed a few noggins of ale and made a good job of changing the records for the dancers.

September 17

Went up to the bank today and received a jolt when I was informed that deposits must be left four full days before being withdrawn. Despite this I went to London, where the branch of the bank near Aussie House was much more accommodating than that back in camp. I met a few of the boys there and went to a show. I'm staying at the Union Jack Club. John Mac and Alec Walters are in town and are the same as ever.

September 18

Walked around all the old places today. Waterloo Bridge is just about completed and is a magnificent piece of work. [The "new" Waterloo Bridge was partially opened in 1942 and completed in 1945.] Saw a show tonight at the Palladium – one of George Black's – and enjoyed it immensely. Evie was surprised to see me back so early and said I'm lucky to get so much leave! I had a jug or two with her and on looking at her autograph book was surprised at the number of names in it now – well over the thousand mark.

September 19

Met Reg this morning and we took Lily and Nora to dinner. Spent the afternoon at Lily's place and then went to the "Plough" to listen to the music and imbibe a few ales. Reg and Lily are engaged, which is, I think, a good thing.

Joan and Eric are married by now I expect. I wish I were home for the ceremony. I bet there will be a huge party. Gosh! I wish this damned war had never been! Had a quiet drink, on my own, at the Plough, having slipped away from the others, and toasted Joan's and Eric's happiness. They're grand kids!

September 20

Went to Mass this morning at the Cathedral, and afterwards walked down to the Embankment and strolled along the river.

Visited the Cogers and then strolled down Fleet Street to St. Paul's. Found there was a service on so didn't go in and walked down to the Tower Bridge. There were several "spruikers' [Australian Slang for a long-winded speaker] as usual on Tower Hill. I wonder how many people have been dragged over those cobbled stones to their death at the hands of the headsman. I bet the scene was different there four hundred years ago!

September 21

Rang I Aikman today and told her I'll be up tomorrow. She said they were all looking forward to my visit. I went to a show at the Windmill and found it was not nearly so good as previously. Went to the Mapleton and found the bar shut. It used to be a happy hunting ground of mine in the old days.

Piccadilly is just as lively as ever, the bars and restaurants are crowded and the demimondaines still ply their trade. I walked to the Haymarket and finished up in Nerone's in the Square. Nerone's has changed hands and the three beautiful daughters of the proprietess are in the Services.

September 22

Arrived in Loudwater this afternoon and was made at home right away. The Aikman's are grand people. Mr. A. is learning Morse code, which will be of some use to him in his spare time job, which is "Special

Constable," so tonight I trained him and the Village Policeman in the gentle art. They are not bad at all and, since they could take my horrible sending at about 12 words per minute should not be long in becoming proficient.

Gave Mr. A. the record I'd bought him and he was awfully pleased, but said I was silly to spend my dough on him! I see I A. was wearing my brooch tonight, which I thought was a very nice gesture.

September 23

Went into Maidenhead today. It is just as lovely as ever, though the crowds that were there when I was there last (it was on a Sunday or holiday) were missing. Visited Skindles and the other places of interest. One lovely hotel has its bar overhanging the river. I missed the last bus back to Loudwater and had to scoot to get the last train.

September 24

Spent the day sleeping and reading and went with Mr. A. to the Bakers after tea. Mr. B. is very ill and he was no end glad to see us. He asked me to call up and see him some day, and I think I'll go along on Saturday. I feel very tired and run down tonight, although I've been resting all day. I A. had left a lovely supper laid out for us and I was almost too lazy to eat it.

September 25

Shades of the angels! What the hell is wrong with me, Diary? I went to sleep last night and awoke to find a strange face bending over me. He explained that he was a Doctor, he had been called in by Mr. A. – It appears that I had thrown some sort of a Mickey and Mr. A. had heard me. I've never been in the habit of throwing fits! He told me that I'll have to consider giving up flying, as I've been doing too much, and that he is going to send a letter to Doc. Wilson! Good Lord!

I've had a hell of a headache all day, and took a ride into High Wycombe this afternoon by bus.

September 26

The Doc. called to see me today and gave me the letter he mentioned yesterday. He has advised me to take things very easy.

This afternoon I went to see Capt. Baker and had a good old chat with him. He is being allowed up tomorrow and says he's going to take a much needed holiday shortly.

I was in bed early. My headache has almost disappeared now, but I feel tired as hell, so Diary, ta ta!

September 27

Went for a run into Maidenhead again. The usual Sunday crowd was there and enjoying itself immensely.

After Tea Mr. A. took me to his club at the factory and we played a few games of billiards, which he won.

I have to go back to camp tomorrow as my leave finishes at 2359.

September 28

Arrived back at camp tonight. I left Loudwater by the first train in the morning and spent some hours in London before catching my train from Waterloo. Said goodbye to Evie and the mob over a few jugs.

Poor old Graham White broke his ankle, I hear, on the third day of his leave! He's been in hospital ever since.

September 29

Saw Doc. Wilson today and gave him the letter from the chap in Loudwater. He says he's going to arrange for me to see a specialist in Bournemouth. Also, strange to say, he appears to think that my flying days are over. Don't know whether to weep or throw my hat in the air.

September 30

It's strange, having nothing to do. This is the first time I've been in this position since February last year when I donned this old uniform. I think I'll go off my rocker if this enforced idleness lasts too long.

October 1

Went to a show at the local today and had a few jugs in the mess tonight. The new Radiogram doesn't sound too hot.

A strange thing happened today. I ran into a chap from P.D. and mentioned to him (he was an army fellow) about nearly killing a swaddy [a private soldier] with a practice bomb last June. To my surprise he said. "So you were the blokes! That chap spent four weeks in hospital with shock, and has been discharged from the army, medically unfit. He still stutters badly when he speaks."

October 2

There was a Mess dance tonight and a great time was had by all. Everyone was a bit pickled from the G.C. down. Paul Bird and I had an argument, quite friendly, about the identity of the aircraft that was shot at today, and Ginger Howells, who never before has shown any marked affection for me, knocked Paul down, and burst into tears. When Paul, slightly dazed, and myself a bit angry asked Ginge the reason for the haymaker, he explained that Paul should not have been arguing with me. It's the first time I've ever achieved the distinction of omniscience!

Very funny scene – An inebriated female, leaning on Johnny Lewis's shoulder saying to our most famous misogynist: "Kiss me – Kiss me just once!"

October 3

Watched a very poor soccer match this afternoon between very poor teams.

Read a yarn about prison life by some bloke who spent ten years inside one, so he should know his subject!

Points for days' funniest saying I award to myself – (Wipe that sneer off you, – blast you, Diary). – Describing a dill [Australian slang for *idiot*] of a Pongo Flight Sergeant, I said: "He's so wet, you could land a Sunderland on him!"

Loud laughs, a few cheers, and sundry minor "boos" ensued.

October 4

Got a few letters from home which, as usual I've read about a dozen times already! Especially one from Molly – Whacko! She still loves me!

I have to see the specialist tomorrow.

Sundays are no different from any other day here. Once or twice I've missed Mass through not knowing what day it was! The work goes on the same – mail is handed out (a good point), the pubs are open, picture shows still go on, kites still take off and land – it's a strange world and sometimes I wonder if it's real.

October 5

Saw the specialist after waiting for hours today. He gave me a pretty gruelling questionnaire, tested my reflexes, etc. and confirmed Doc. Wilson's opinion. He says I may never have another attack like I had at

Flackwell Heath, yet there is the possibility that I might, and it would be dangerous if one should happen in the middle of a fight with J.U.'s, both for myself and the rest of the crew. I suppose he's right.

October 6

Played Tubby chess tonight. Found that Eric Fuller has a set. Tubby plays a grand game! I won two out of five and was lucky to do as well.

October 7

Harry Miller and Bullsie have been sent on a refresher course to Brighton. I suppose if I hadn't been a "sick man" I'd have gone too. I hear that it's a real "B" of a course, so I'm not sorry.

October 8

Nothing of note to relate. The days pass very slowly. Walked into Poole from camp for exercise. It's a good long walk and I felt much better for it.

October 9

It's strange to sit back and watch the other boys taking off and landing – the work going on just the same. Gives me a proper sense of my indispensability, if I ever had a wrong idea on that subject.

Yet I feel terribly "out of things." I wish I were home!

October 10

I wonder if they'll reduce me now that I'm of no further use to them as a member of an aircrew? They don't worry about you a lot when you've served your usefulness.

Squadron Leader Lovelock has recommended me for my crown again, also Les Wilson and a lot of the others. I think he should have recommended Les and I separately seeing the number of hours we've got up, and the fact that we trained most of these new blokes.

October 11

Went to Mass this morning at the little Church round the corner. I like the old Priest there. I think Bill would like to meet him. I tackled him again this morning about his conversion, but he is off to P.D. today for some time. I must ask Molly to pray for it. She's been pretty hot, as far as I've been concerned, in the number of prayers answered.

October 12

Was made Duty N.C.O. today and could have refused the job, but took it on for something to do. There's not much in the job except seeing the crews on board in time, inspecting the aircraft, etc.

Had a few beers in the Mess tonight and played Tubby our usual chess battle.

October 13

Jerry comes over every day but so far has not hit anything near here. He got a bit close this afternoon and I made good speed for the shelter.

He's a damned nuisance, especially now that I'm a non-combatant!

October 14

Got caught in a fog tonight while I was out in a dinghy inspecting the kites, and had a hell of a job getting back. To make matters worse it was raining fairly heavily, and as cold as Charity. Guest night at the mess and all, too.

October 15

Saw a show in at Bournemouth tonight – Costello and Abbot in some funny picture. I had a good laugh. Getting fed up with doing no flying. I walked over one of the kites that was up on the slip today and sat at the old familiar bench. Gosh! I wish I were back in the game!

Letter #43

Postmarked Bournemouth Poole 15 Oct. 1942. 2½ penny blue stamp with image of King George. Received 11 January, 1943. Opened by Examiner 2664.

October 15, 1942

My Darling,

It's now nearly a fortnight since I wrote a letter, and I'm feeling darned ashamed of myself. But things have happened so quickly since I came back from leave that I haven't known whether I've been on my head or my heels.

I haven't told you before, but for some time now I haven't been feeling too good, and, so, as soon as I got back I went up to see our grand M.O., Doc Wilson. He said I was to come off flying immediately and sent me to a specialist. The specialist said I had done too much flying and refused to let me fly again. It appears that although I've been able to put my fingers to my nose at Jerry in all my hundreds of hours of flying here, still old Mother Nature has been a bit too good for me. I feel terribly down in the dumps, but the C.O. and the rest of the Squadron, most of whom are new chaps whom I've had to initiate into the ways of Sunderlands, tell me I've done more than my share in this damned war, which is some sop to my pride.

The Specialist, who was very sympathetic, and who seemed sorry to have to ground me, is trying to arrange a course for me, so that I can go back to Aussie and train the new blood there. Won't you like that?

In any case I should be home within the next few months of your receiving this! Oh! Darling! I'll be happy! God has been good to me; I think it has been your prayers that have brought me safely through all the danger up to now, and I'm sure now that they will keep me safe until we're together again.

If I can't get this instructor's course, Darling, I'll re-muster to an armourer, or some job on the ground. It may mean giving up my stripes, and everything, but that won't worry me so long as I am doing something to give Adolf a smack in the eye. I owe him a hell of a lot. So many of my old friends – the best chaps in the world – have gone, all because of his insanity! The Doctor said I could apply for my discharge if I wanted, but I'd feel lost if I wasn't in the Air Force these days. Anyhow I can look back to a lot of good times, and excitement, and to an unsurpassed number of flying hours – in this squadron at any rate – so that I think no one can accuse me of not having done my bit. I was mad as a hatter when the Specialist grounded me, but, deep down, dear, I'm glad – I've felt terribly tired now for months, and my nerves have been jittery. I think I could have kept going for another few months then I'd have had an almighty crack-up. Doc Wilson said that he was glad I'd come to him, as he'd got me just in time. All I need is about six months rest to put me right, (as a matter of fact – since I've been away from the strain of flying I've begun to pick up amazingly) – but more of these long days and nights in the air might affect my whole future health – so no more.

Anyhow, sweetheart, the knowledge that I'll soon be seeing you again has acted like a tonic, and outweighs all the glumness. Dear Darling, – we'll be married soon after I get home, won't we? I shan't be able to wait much longer than I have. You fill all my waking hours and a lot of my sleeping ones, too.

It's strange not to be flying, love, – to walk over the old familiar kite, to sit in front of the old wireless bench, and to know that never again, unless a miracle happens, will I pound that old key. When I look back and remember the messages I've sent, and when I see the old guns in my turret and think of the times they've saved my life, I feel a terrible longing to be back in it all again, which even the knowledge that I may soon be with you again can't altogether assuage. I can't explain the feeling quite. These old kites get in your blood. The other day I got two copies of a letter – or rather a copy of two letters from the A.O.C. congratulating myself and the rest of the crew on our picking up those two Whitley crews from a watery grave, which I'll treasure all my life. I'm more proud of those two episodes than I have been of any attacks on submarines or ships.

I will cable you dear, when I think it is inadvisable for you to write any more to me. I got a letter from you yesterday, and devoured it as usual. Also a pair of socks for which thanks a lot, sweet. They'll come in very handy. You mention on the note enclosed with them that my famous (?) name had figured in the "Courier Mail." What crime have I committed now?

I went to a new church for Mass on Sunday and a dear old Priest celebrated. I think I'll go there always from now on. I have a great chance at the moment of getting an engineer in the Squadron to become a Catholic. His wife and children in Aussie are, and he's very keen. Say a prayer for this intention, please, dear.

Well I suppose that's enough for one letter. Don't worry or anything about me, dear because of this business – I'm well and happy – in fact the happiest man in the world, because I know that soon I'll be with you again, and very soon, we'll be married. Pray for me please, dearest, I love you with all my heart, – I always will,

326

Ed xxxxx

P.S. Love me? Ed x

P.S.S. You're wonderful. Ed x

October 16

Walked back and forth between Hamworthy and Poole today, just for the exercise. I'm well and truly fed up with this inaction. I wish they'd either send me home or put me back again into a crew! Had the usual few beers in the mess. Wrote the usual letters. Seem to do nothing but write letters lately. Hope they get home safely.

Graham White got out of hospital the other day, went to bed in his mess last night, walked in his sleep and fell from a second story window! He's in a very bad way with an injured spine and has various things wrong with his internal organs. I hear Graham and I are in the same boat. I doubt if he'll ever fly again. I find it's exactly a year today since I left Aussie.

October 17

Went into Bournemouth this afternoon and strolled around some of the old places. In the Norfolk, some bloke who had been in the county for three weeks asked me if I'd just arrived in the last batch from Aussie. Lord preserve us! He was very apologetic when I put him wise.

The place hasn't changed very much. I had enough by 9 p.m. and caught a bus home. Can't get interested in anything these days!

October 18

Mass today at 11 o'clock as I slept in. The Choir hasn't improved any during the last few weeks. Thought of offering my services, but better nature prevailed. The English have suffered enough from Jerry without my adding to their tortures!

We boys, Johnny Lewis, myself, Paul Bird, Les Wilson, Paddy Druhan, were all at the Mess party tonight. I can hardly believe it's over a year since we left Aussie. We had a sort of private little party and drank to II course. Wish Jacko, Tom and John Mac were with us. Drank to them and to Geo., Roy, and Billy Isle, and to the other II course boys who've gone.

October 19

Had a busy day as duty N.C.O. today; nearly had to slam some bloke on a charge. I suppose this inactivity has made me a bit touchy, but these Pongo's give me the willies. I don't know why some of them ever took on aircrew jobs.

Letter # 44

Postmarked Bournemouth, Poole, 20 Oct, 1942. Received 28 Feb 43. Passed by censor 77. 2½ penny stamp.

Aus/405206, Sgt. Gallagher, E.B., R.A.A.F. England

October 20, 1942

Dearest,

Things are still very quiet here as far as your future husband is concerned. Frankly it's getting on my nerves, for I haven't had so much leisure since I joined the Air Force. I wish they'd make up their minds as to what they are going to do with me. I haven't heard a thing since I saw the Specialist last Monday fortnight.

I got a letter from Ralph Moores and a parcel from Mother and Dad last week, and, best of all, a letter from you. You are by far my best correspondent, Molly Darling; I can usually bank on something from you at least once a week. Maybe you are lucky at dodging the Japs.

I made a very interesting trip to a certain place lately, and sent you a couple of postcards per one of my pals who managed to sneak off enough time. Hope they arrive safely. This was my last effort before being grounded; probably the last one I'll ever make.

The days are drawing in now and winter will soon be on us again, drat it. Fogs and dark long nights and all the inconveniences it means will soon be the order. I hate the grey English Winter – the cold and the snow.

The Squadron is continuing with the good work. Its record so far has been fully as good as old 10's, and the crews are a grand lot on the whole. Most of them are only happy when they are flying. The gunners are pretty hot, as Jerry has found to his cost. A J.U.88 that attacked one of our kites the other day by diving out of a cloud was just about blasted out of the air by the tail and mid gunners.

Our Captains and Navigators are a grand lot, and I think they are just as good as our old 10 Squadron lot. My ex-skipper Bruce Bulls, now a Flight Lieutenant, can throw a Sunderland about like a Tiger Moth, and I'm told that some of the others are even better than he is.

Half the success and efficiency of a kite depend on the good feeling and confidence that exists between individual members of the crew, and if all the crews are like mine was (and I think they are) then the various kites must come out on top of Jerry every time. For instance, I always felt safe at the desk when I knew Alan Mayne was in the tail, and "Winkie" Youl, Jock Stewart, Jeff, Harry Miller, Bullsie, Graham White and Russ Baird were in their positions. I knew nothing could sneak up on us, and that if anything did attack us he'd get the shock of his life – as a few did.

One thrill I'll miss all my life – the controlled excitement and wild delight on sighting a submarine, and the glorious satisfaction of seeing oil and wreckage after dropping our depth charges. The impersonal feeling is strange. You never think of the poor devils that are skittled; all your thoughts are on the submarine itself, as if it were some wild beast that had to be destroyed.

Did you hear the broadcast I made while I was in London? I hope you didn't mind my mentioning your name. It was great to be able to get an opportunity of saying something to you, yet, funnily enough the B.B.C gave us £1 and 50 cigarettes for expenses! John Macdonald and another chap and myself spoke. I think it was rebroadcast on Monday night – 28th September, in Aussie.

I hope, Darling, that your Mother has now fully recovered, and is her old self again. It must be very worrying for you, to have her ill. I know how I would feel if Mother should become sick. I wish I were home so that I could try to comfort you, instead of being so far away and only adding to your worries.

Well, sweetheart mine, I think I'll finish off now, and try to catch a bit of shut-eye. Please give my love to all your family, and my regards to all at Bursties. Tell Alice she owes me a couple of letters – in fact, I haven't even got one from her since I left Australia.

Pray for me, please, sweet, and remember always that I love you with all my heart.

Ed xxxxx

P.S. Love me? Ed x

October 20

Saw a show at the local flea circus tonight which was pretty good.

Feel as tired as hell tonight, for some reason or other.

October 21

Did the rounds of the various pubs with Jeff and the others and finished up at a party. Sang around the piano and some people were so full as to imagine I can sing!

October 22

This Duty N.C.O is getting on my nerves. It's no good getting dragged out of bed at all hours of the night. I think I'll chuck it up. Doc. Wilson would have a fit if he knew I was doing the job.

Played Tubby chess and was soundly trounced.

October 23

Mess dance tonight and every one had a good time. I think all the pretty girls in town come to our dances. The bar took forty odd quid last dance. The women in this county, no doubt because of the dangerous times, drink and smoke more than the men. Young girls of eighteen may be seen in any pub, lining up to the bar with the men. I think this war, if it does nothing else, will succeed in cheapening the status of womanhood, and I, for one, don't like it!

October 24

Had a few beers in the mess tonight, and in a fit of cholera, rang up Raban, told him I shouldn't be doing the job of Duty N.C.O., and told him to get someone else. He apologised to me, told me he didn't realise the circumstances and asked me to suggest someone else. I took the opportunity to get square with my particular bête-noir, the laziest B. in the Squadron, and dobbed him in.

October 25

After early Mass, I went out to the station and spent the day at Flight Office reading and writing letters. I'm glad to be rid of the job of Duty N.C.O. Have offered P.O. Beale, the Engineering officer, to give him a hand, and he's said I'd be very helpful. Anything for something to do to pass the time!

Posted the solution to a chess problem to one of the papers this afternoon; hope I win the prize offered.

October 26

Have been pestering Doc. Wilson to hasten up my business, but he says he can do nothing. Have given up the grog. I wonder how long the resolution I made last Saturday will last?

Drank lemonade tonight to the surprise and amusement of the boys.

October 27

Saw a film tonight entitled "Texas Ranger" or "Lone Star Ranger" or something. Anyhow it was damned awful. Despite the various temptations of the mess, I remained firm and stuck to the lemonade.

October 28

Guest night at the mess and the girls were surprised to learn of my reformation. I found that I can get just as tight and have just as good a time on Ginger Beer as I could when on the beer. Think I'll stick to it. It's much cheaper and better for you. Tubby played the piano and I sang. Don also sang and he surprised everybody by the quality of his voice which, if trained properly, would make him famous.

Letter #46.

R.A.A.F. London postmark. Nov 2, 1942. Received Jan 13, 1943. "On Active Service Royal Australian Air Force Concession Postal Rate". Passed by Censor #95. No stamp.

October 28, 1942

My own Darling,

Your letter dated 30th August arrived today and, as usual, made me very happy. It's strange, but every time I find one from you in the rack, my heart gives the same old jump it gave the first time I got a letter from you. Yet it's not strange – because you mean all the world to me. And every day when I go along to the rack and find it empty I get the same old feeling of disappointment.

Gee! I'm reforming. I just shocked Harry Miller, who was passing, by asking him to get me a pint of ginger beer from the bar. I've signed the pledge for a week! Don't laugh, Darling, I mean it!

Please excuse this writing. Jerry is overhead and Ack Ack is bursting overhead like thunder gone mad. I've got the wind up well and truly. No need to be ashamed of being frightened, as you say you were, when you heard your first alert, love. The first time I heard an alert I nearly threw a sixer! I still do. Must dash out to have a look. I must explain that I had started this letter last night, and had got up to the second paragraph when Harry returned with the ginger-beer and the news that the bathroom was empty, so I made a quick dash. After the bath I felt so cold that I decided to go to bed. It's very cold here just now. I'm writing this in the crew-room.

Well I've had my look. Saw a few kites overhead – little specks, thousands of feet in the sky, and black puffs of A.A. bursting around them. Away in the distance I saw a Spitty* climbing like heck to get above a couple of kites. Then he dived. Heavens! It was a lovely sight, darling. He came swooping down like a swallow, and just at the crucial moment the three disappeared into the clouds and haze. *[Because of the wing shape, the *Spitfire* had a distinctive silhouette, which helped it to achieve legendary status during the Battle of Britain.]

About 15 minutes later, right into the middle of everything came an old Wimpy, stooging along calmly and sedately as if it hadn't a care in the world, apparently utterly oblivious of the scrapping and the A.A. She sailed across from horizon to horizon and disappeared also in the haze.

Just afterwards back came the Spitty, flying as though it were

333

licking its lips, with almost a cocky air. Then, so high that almost only vapour trail could be seen came a flight of Spittys – also flying as if they'd just made a kill and were looking for more prey. There goes the "All Clear."

I'm still hanging around, waiting for something to turn up, doing absolutely nothing; as per the Doc's orders – taking things easy. Getting terribly fed up with it. It's so long since I was allowed to fly that I'm feeling as much an extinct bird as the Dodo; – perhaps more so.

As you said, I felt terribly "out of things," not being at Joan's wedding. Tell her she'll have to have another one, when I get home. No! Darn it! We'll have one of our own. It was funny, you running into her at the Shingle Inn.

"Shingle Inn."* Gee! That brought back memories, sweetheart. I thought of old Brisbane again when I read the words. You know, I'd nearly forgotten what the old place looks like. You'll have to show me around when I get home. *[A 1938-built café at the corner of Queen & George Streets in Brisbane].

The Squadron has instituted a system of mail of its own, now. We haven't to pay postage, and I'm told by the boys who have been using it that it is faster than the ordinary mail. I'll send this by it to test it out.

Hope you enjoyed the batching effort with Joan and Aileen.

I'm sorry to have to say that it was old Berty Gall who is missing. Dear old Bert. He and I have been together right up to the time I was posted to 10 Squadron. I remember our Christmas together. Did you get the photo of me he took? He was one of the very best of the best. Did you ever meet him? You know, Bert never drank, smoked, nor did I ever hear him swear, yet he was one of the most popular chaps in Eleven Course. I never heard him say a bad word about anybody.

It was certainly bad luck about the Duke of Kent*. He and his wife were a very popular couple over here. *[The Duke of Kent (1902-1942) was the fourth son of George V. He died when the Sunderland in which he was a passenger crashed on August 25 into a hillside in Northern Scotland, while en route to Iceland and Newfoundland. Questions involving assassination and sabotage remain about this mission and the role of Winston Churchill in his death. It was believed the Duke was in favour of peace with Germany.]

Thank your lady friend very much for her kind thought. I hope the cigarettes arrive safely. They should, because Dad sent me some lately and they were O.K. cigarettes – especially good ones are hard to get here, (as I hear they are at home) and so I'll appreciate them very much.

334

I wish I could see Len's baby! Gosh! I bet he's proud as punch! I hope Sheila and it are well and happy. Please give them my love.

Don't forget to pray for that special intention I asked you about, darling. You remember – that chap's conversion. You must be tops in Heaven. Look what your prayers have done for me.

I was reading through my flying log book the other day and, Lord, I've had a lot of fun since I've been over here! Got some more ink.

I'm going clay-pigeon shooting tomorrow. It's good fun, but I'm not too hot at the game.

What is Lad Deady doing these days, darling? I haven't heard of or from him since I left home. If he's about tell him to drop me a line one of these days, and wish him all the best from me.

How is your family, darling? I hope your Mother is well again, and the report she got in Brisbane was a good one.

There goes the "All Clear" again. I never heard the "Alert." Must have been thinking of you.

Well, I think I'll pack up now. I have to see the dentist to get my teeth scaled or something. Hope he doesn't make me yell.

Please pray for me, dear, and, no matter what happens, keep loving me. Your love for me is the most wonderful thing in my life. In fact, darling, it, and you, are all my life.

I adore you,

Ed   xxxxxxxxx

P.S. Love me?   Ed x

October 29

Maybe this Ginger Beer stunt is not so hot? I felt pretty crook today and if I'm not better tomorrow will see the Doc. Doc. Wilson is on leave. Am turning in early tonight.

October 30

Saw Doc. McGill this morning and he seemed a bit concerned about me. Asked me about my Medical History, if any of the family had kidney trouble, and, when I told him about my fit, gave me some dope and told me to report every day. Beer is forbidden me, and I told him about being on the wagon, which seems strange to me.

October 31

Feel better today and toddled along to see the quack. Doc. W. was back and laughed to scorn the idea of my having anything wrong with my kidneys. He sent me along to a big wig in town, Sir someone or other who tested a sample and said there was no trace of anything. I'm to go back to see him tomorrow.

November 1

Saw the Pathologist again this morning, bringing with me a sample in a bottle. Lord! Would I have been embarrassed if I'd dropped it on the way. He made further tests and confirmed his statement of yesterday. Found my last week's solution to the chess problem was correct, but that I was not lucky enough to be the first solution submitter to have his envelope opened.

Postmarked Southampton 6.15pm, 17 Nov., 1942. Received 27 January, 1943.

November 2, 1942

My own Darling,

Well, here I am still, doing nothing of importance, and feeling, as the Pongos say "thoroughly brassed off."

The M.O. is not too satisfied with me – Lord knows why, for I feel as good as gold, – and he says unless I'm better tomorrow he's going to bung me off to hospital somewhere near Southampton for a course of treatment. Now don't go worrying, sweet. There's nothing serious the matter. If there were I wouldn't disturb you by telling you anything about it. It will only be for a few days, and the only reason I'm going into sick bay is so they can keep their eyes on me and see I take my dope at the regular times, etc. I'll enjoy a lie up as a matter of fact. It's bitterly cold these days and the thought of spending them between nice warm blankets is very attractive. Maybe there'll be a pretty nurse. – Jealous? I wish you were here to mollycoddle me, as you used to do.

I'm sitting in the Flight Office here and just now the Senior Dental officer (Australian) walked in and set up a seat and pulled out a few wicked looking instruments. He's from H.Q. in London and he's touring round all the Squadrons examining the Aussies' teeth. Seems a good chap. I've been yarning to him and he's been giving me all the good oil about home. His home town is Warwick and he and I have discovered many mutual acquaintances.

My teeth, he tells me, are good-o. Which is a good thing. Alan Mayne is in the chair at the moment and has asked them not to swipe the large piece of gold in his front tooth. Alan is a wag. Used to be on my old crew. He married a girl from Bournemouth last month.

Have you had your leave yet? – You should insist on getting it, love; remember the old adage about "too much work," and also what it did to me. I'm never going to hoe in so hard or go so long without a spell again. A man's a nitwit to laugh at old Mother Nature.

I've just been shooting a horrible line to the Dental Officer. Gee! I'm a skite! Don't believe half the things I tell you about my heroic episodes when I get home. Harry Miller just walked in and helped me spin a few yarns.

Poor old Harry has just come back from a discipline course at "Prune's Purgatory" and he's very sour about it. He and Bullsie and Alan Mayne did the course. Harry used to be my second operator and has now graduated to first through my retirement.

Your letter containing the photo and the news of Joan's wedding arrived yesterday and I was glad to hear it was so lovely. It was bad luck about Eric's best man. I wish I had had the job, but then I suppose I'd have lost the ring or done something as silly!

It's time to catch the transport back to the Mess. I'm going to a show tonight with Harry – Judy Canova in "Sleepy Time Girl;" I hear that it is a swell picture.

10 p.m. – Just got back from the flicks. It was a good picture and my sides are sore from laughing. John Sullivan has challenged me to a game of chess. As he's drinking beer and I'm still on the Ginger Beer, he should be easy.

12.15 p.m. – He wasn't. – I only won one game out of three. "Tubby" is pretty hot at chess, full or sober. I think sometimes he's better when he's full.

November 5, 1942

I saw the Doc. Yesterday morning and he told me I'd have to go into sick bay, and so here I am, curled up in bed. There's no pretty nurse, as yet. All of them are well past their first youth, and so you have nothing to fear, darling.

I have to take some horrible dope every few hours and when I say horrible, I mean horrible. It's not bad to take, but it makes me feel pretty crook. It's supposed to be "building me up" and quieting my "war torn nerves," so I've got to put up with it. The Doc. Says I'll be a new man in a few weeks. Maybe I'll be able to fly again; I hope so, anyway. They must think I'm pretty valuable, anyhow, to take all this trouble with me.

The boys in the Squadron made a very nice gesture before I left. They clubbed together and gave me 300 cigarettes. It was good of them; and they also expressed the wish that I'd soon be back with them again. I hope they're right. Anyway, if this spell in the hospital does me no good, I won't mind, in a way, because it will mean that I'll soon be sailing home to you. And when I see you, if I don't make an instantaneous recovery, then I'll be the most surprised man in the world.

I feel terribly guilty, lying here and feeling as well as I have ever felt. However my conscience in these matters is remarkably elastic, so

338

I'm not worried over duly.

How is your Mother, Love, and the rest of your family? I hope they are all well and happy. Please give them my love.

I'm dying to see the table cover you've bought. It must be a lovely thing. Did you buy it for us?

Where is Joan going to live, now that she is a married woman? Does she intend keeping on with her job, or is she living with Eric? More to the point, what do you intend doing when I get home, sweetheart? Of course you know what I would like you to do when we are Mr. & I, but then you may have your own ideas on the subject.

Poor old Graham White (the chap who has always been my navigator in this Squadron) is somewhere in this hospital too, with a broken ankle and an injured back. I must get along to see him as soon as they let me up. Graham and I have always been the best of cobbers. It's strange that we should be laid up and should finish up in the same hospital. They tell me, that like me, Graham may be finished with the flying racket.

Well, Darling, I'd better get some shut-eye.

I'll write you very often while I'm laid up here. Pray for me, please, and remember that I love you with all my heart, – with every fibre of my being, – I always will, – you are so much a part of me, dear, that I think that I always have, from the beginning of time.

Ed xxxxx

P.S. Love me? Ed x

November 2

Doc. Wilson says that all that was wrong with me was a mild attack of epilepsy brought about by the strain of too much flying under war conditions. Dr. McGill is not so sure and wants me to go into hospital for some time where I can be kept under observation. As it's very cold these days, the thought of spending a few days in bed, between nice clean sheets under warm blankets, with pretty sisters flitting hither and yon, is very pleasant, and I've a good mind to agree.

November 3

Played Tubby our usual game of chess tonight and was in bed at one o'clock. Gee! The time flies when we get our heads down over a tussle.

November 4

Was admitted to hospital today. Doc. McGill thinks I may have some form of kidney complaint, though Doc. Wilson does not. However I agreed this morning to undergo a course of treatment. Was tucked in bed by a sister (not pretty, darn it – just my luck!) and am reading a book by Bailey – *Mr. Fortune's Trials* – not a bad yarn.

Had a pleasant trip by train and feel as good as gold!

November 5

Got some muck today at intervals of four hours. So far don't feel any better than before taking it. Some big-wig of an M.O. has interested (my word! He has all the pips etc. imaginable) himself in my poor self. Hope I'm not a guinea pig!

November 6

Even the sisters seem to look askance at me (or is it my guilty conscience?) and I look askance at myself. Why the hell am I lying here like some damned invalid, getting my temperature taken at intervals? Woe is me! I wish Molly were here to hold my hand instead of that old battle axe of a sister (not that she ever holds my hand, or ever will unless I get delirious, which Heaven forbid!)

November 7

Lo! The battle-axe has been replaced by a vision of beauty. The whole ward has assumed a brighter hue. This is a red letter day. The aforesaid vision brought me five letters this afternoon – one from Molly – three from Townsville and one from I Aikman which contained some snaps Mr. A. took while I was on leave. Alas! Though, the vision shows no

340

marked inclination to hold my hand or cool my fevered brow! I'm reading another of Bailey's *Mr. Fortune* yarns in solitary splendour.

Molly tells me she is worried about something and asks me to pray for a special intention. Gosh! I hope she is all right. I wish I were home with her!

November 8

Time drags. I asked to be allowed up today but my request was frowned upon. I wrote some letters and gave them to the battle-axe, who has returned, to post. – Oh! Lord! I wish I were back at Poole. Death! Where is thy sting?

I wish Molly had told me what was worrying her, in her letter yesterday – I've been thinking about it all day. I wonder if her Mother is ill?

November 9

Still here! The Padre called on me today and seems a cheery soul. – Like hell! I don't think I've ever disliked a Priest before, but this one is a poor specimen. He made me glad when he'd gone. I've had a busy time explaining to my ward mates, most of whom are non-Catholics, that he is the only one of his kind. Can't think why I disliked him so, unless it was his sarcastic manner in connection with a book he'd lent one of the chaps who couldn't find it tonight to return it.

November 10

The vision is back with us again. My temperature has risen considerably, because she held my wrist while taking my pulse. Had a long chat with her tonight re Aussie and the folks at home. She has never visited Aussie, but would like to. Should I have proposed? I showed her some of the exciting (?) parts of you, Diary, to make myself out a ruddy hero, and don't know how I went. She saw my reference to Molly on the 26th July – an oversight on my part, so I fear my cause has been damped.

November 11

Armistice Day eh? Bought a flag for a zack [Australian for sixpence] and so did my good deed for the day. The Colonel's wife sold them so I was just about forced into the sale. Read and read. May be allowed up tomorrow, says the vision. I asked her would she walk with me in the park to see I didn't come to any harm from the fresh air, but was rebuffed. It was a mistake letting her find out about Molly! Ah me! Such is life!

November 12

Tottered about the grounds today and crawled up a million stairs to see Graham White. He looks pretty crook, poor old chap. He always was thin, but now he's worse than a shadow! He was very pleased to see me. I'll have to trot along every day to cheer him up. Come to think of it, I'm not a very hot cheerer-upper, but I suppose it's good to see one of the old faces again. It's strange both of us to be laid up here after the hundreds of hours we've spent side by side over the old bay, and the excitement we've shared.

November 13

Black Friday. Wish I were home today so that I could buy a Casket Ticket. Thought I'd be out today or tomorrow, but the idea was laughed to scorn by the Battle-axe. "You don't seem to realise, Sergeant, (she always calls me 'sergeant', but the vision calls me 'Ed') that you are a sick man," says she!

Sick me foot!

November 14

Took a ticket in a football sweep today. Lord knows why! I know nothing about any English football team and care a hell of a lot less!

Read myself to sleep this afternoon. Wasn't allowed up all day.

November 15

Ran out of cigs. today but, just as I was getting desperate the battle-axe brought me a parcel from the Red Cross which contained some. Also a magazine. They do some pretty good work, the Red Cross, especially for prisoners of war. Johnny Lewis and Johnny Gamble dropped in on me tonight. See poor old Graham too, and he must have been pleased by their visit. I got up and Johnny L. took a time exposure of me in my hospital uniform. It'll be a scream if it turns out O.K.

November 16

Went walking in the park today. The trees are browning and dead leaves are scattered everywhere. Winter will soon be on us. A line or 2 from the "Belle Dame Sans Merci" kept ringing in my brain, – I think they are "The leaves are withered by the lake, And no birds sing." [John Keats' words are: Oh what can ail thee, knight-at-arms, Alone and palely loitering? The sedge has withered from the lake, And no birds sing.]

Saw a bit of activity on the water, – barges and warships, which reminds

342

me that the news in the papers, which I'm almost too tired to read these days, is very good.

November 17

You know, these Pongos make me mad. Not a line of the Jap attacks on T'ville* has ever appeared in any paper here, yet they print divorce cases, etc. The first news I ever received of the attacks arrived in Dad's letter the other day! Damn and blast the yellow B's! *[Townsville, which was an important military base in Queensland, was raided by Japanese flying boats on three nights in late July, 1942. On the night of July 29, a single flying boat attacked the town, dropping six bombs into the sea and a seventh which lightly damaged the town's racecourse.]

Saw Graham today. He's looking, I think, a bit better and tells me he may be allowed to get up for a while tomorrow.

November 18

Well Diary, I'm so fed up with this place, even though they are treating me well, that I think I'd run off – only they've pinched my clothes and all have is a pair of pyjamas and a horrible blue hospital uniform! I think I'll make faces at the battle-axe, who is knitting. Hell! Hope she didn't see me or they'll put me in the rat house!

Graham wasn't allowed up today as he expected and looks very sour on things in general.

November 19

The vision is sitting by my bed of pain, reading, much to the annoyance of the other boys. Wonder where she got those blue eyes? Looking at her closely, covertly when she's not looking, I decided she's not as pretty as Molly. Wish I hadn't forgotten Molly's photograph when I came here. I thought of asking Johnny L. to send it along but was too much a moral coward. John is a noted misogynist and am afraid he'd consider the request "sissy."

Alas! The vision has caught my glance, looked at her watch and cried "Lights Out, boys." Wonder if she's a mind reader, Diary? Anyhow, if her scheme is nefarious, I shall go under, fighting to maintain my honour.

November 20

The sun rises, or rather attempts to rise these days, I think. Don't know because I never see it. A thick blanket of fog – a real London pea souper – blankets everything. A Cockney would think he was at home again.

Plaintively asked when I would be allowed to go home but, receiving no definite answer, fear that with the Raven they should have squawked "Never More." [From Edgar Allen Poe's *The Raven*: "Quoth the raven, 'Nevermore'."]

Saw Graham who is still bewailing his fate at not being allowed to rise and caper around the countryside.

November 21

Found a chap in the ward who imagined he could play chess, today. His knowledge of the game would have shamed a two year old horse. Got disgusted after two or three games which I won easily and went back to bed to read. The library people must think I'm crazy. I've averaged two books a day. Besides this I've read a lot of books other patients have taken out. The vision says I'm overcrowding my brain, but when I offered to stop reading if she'd hold my hand, showed a deplorable lack of enthusiasm for her job, which is, after all, as I pointed out, not doing anything to make me well. She made some rude noise or remark, which sounded like "Pish" or Tish" or something.

November 22

Distressing laziness has prevented my shaving for some days and I am bearded like the pard. [From Shakespeare's "All the World's a Stage". Jacques: Then a soldier, Full of strange oaths and bearded like the pard.]

Old battle-axe threatened to get to work with a pair of tweezers unless I removed offending growth, so I complied. Looking at my face, which now resembles the nether portions of a baby, I fail to see why, for so long, I have concealed this thing of beauty from the world.

This I pointed out to the b.a. but she merely replied that she was going out to buy a false beard so that, once again, the gruesome sight might be concealed from mortal eyes.

November 23

Some of the boys – Johnny L. and Johnny G. again – dropped in to comfort me. Makes me feel such a glug to be laid up when I feel perfectly all right. They brought me some Aussie papers but no mail.

November 24

Spent a most interesting (like hell!) day. Read another two books; was not allowed out as it was raining. Books usual murder yarns.

Didn't see Graham but sent him a yarn I think he'll like.

344

November 25

Was discharged from my bed of misery this morning. I think they're satisfied there is nothing wrong with my kidneys. Think my trouble must be purely mental as Doc Wilson thought.

I've applied to be allowed to go home tomorrow morning and the request has been granted. Graham looked brighter when I saw him today. He'll miss me and my cheery countenance, he says.

The vision, who will not be on tomorrow, bade me good-bye, with a tear in her lovely blue eyes, but refused me a parting osculatory benediction. Said she'd kiss the b.a. for me.

November 26

Left hospital this morning and arrived back at camp before lunch. Had a snack down the road and needed it. Wonder how much weight I've lost? No letters at all waiting for me! I was so hopeful that there'd be some after all this time. Feel like weeping or biting the carpet like Adolf. [In *The Rise and Fall of the Third Reich – A History of Nazi Germany (1960)*, William L. Shirer intentionally mistranslated the German "carpet-chewing" idiom (similar to "climbing up the wall" in English), as if Hitler literally chewed carpets when he was anxious. But apparently, going by Ed's comment, the carpet-biting rumour already existed.]

Have the satisfaction of knowing my kidneys are perfect and that organically I'm as sound as a bell. Also that if I take things quietly I may never have another attack like the famous one at Flackwell Heath! So the senior M.O. told me before I left.

November 27

Saw Sqdn. Ldr. Magill this morning and he got me six days leave. I'm writing this in my room – and what a beauty it is! – in the "Strand Palace" about 100 yards from the old "Gaiety Theatre." Had some trouble getting a room anywhere in London. Place is full of yanks on leave – also Aussies recently arrived in this country. Rang and inquired after Reg. Lily was in and at risk of incurring his displeasure have invited her to lunch tomorrow. Lil asked me to stay at her home when I told her of my trouble in finding a room, but luckily I refused and have got in here. Lil tells me she and Reg. are being married early in New Year. They'll make a good pair, methinks. Train trip up here was fair. – It's raining outside, now.

November 28

Up with the crack of dawn – (10 a.m.). Showered and breakfasted then went to Aussie House and saw no-one I knew. Called on Evie at the "Cogers" Inn and drank a slow Shandy. Met Lily and took her to dinner at Strakers in the Strand. She brought me home where I met Nora and her sister and brother-in-law. Reg arrived at three and at five we went to a local show where we had to queue for an hour before seeing "Three Gay Sisters." Not a bad show – Barbara Stanwyck and George Brent. Was in bed by 10 p.m. Had a Shandy (to the surprise of the waiter) down in one of the lounges here a few minutes ago. Am lying in bed writing this and as sleep seems far away, think I'll try to do a crossword puzzle 'fore dowsing the lights.

November 29

Rang Lily at 1 p.m. and made some apology for not coming out. I saw "Holiday Inn" at the "Carlton" in Haymarket this arvo and it was good – Fred Astaire and Bing Crosby. Liked the songs – particularly "White Christmas" and "Be Careful, it's my Heart." Am turning in early tonight.

From the gay crowd downstairs in the Lounge you'd never guess there's a war on, and by the variety and colour of the uniforms I almost imagined I was taking part in a pre-war (1914 one) musical comedy. I love this gaiety and colour and music!

Went to Mass at a little church near the Strand this morning and made usual wishes. Hope they come true! It's called "Corpus Christi" and is beautiful inside.

November 30

Called at the Boomerang Club and got a free ticket for Sidney Howard's show at the St. James – "Night of the Garter." It was hilariously funny. Well presented. Joan Shannon is very pretty – even in a horse blanket. Play is about three married couples and the awkward situations that ensue through one of the husband's attempts to recover from the wife of another a garter (diamond studded) he'd given her before she was married!

Let my head go and had a glass of ale during the interval between First and Second acts.

December 1

Went to the Windmill this afternoon and to the Aldwych tonight. Windmill gone off to billy-o. Was very disappointed. But Novello's show "The Dancing Years" at the Aldwych (in the Strand) was the best stage show I've ever seen! Met Cookie there and he was just as enthusiastic as I am. Lovely songs and singing, beautiful costumes and settings, and the dancing was glorious! I'll never forget this show! Wish

Joan were here or Molly. They'd go mad over a stage presentation such as this one!

December 2

Saw "Venus comes to Town" – a somewhat undressed presentation – at a Matinee at the "Whitehall Theatre." Mildly rude and pretty crude, but withal not bad. A much better one was "Murder without Crime" at the "Comedy" – only four actors in the play, but I enjoyed it thoroughly. Leading man overacted a bit, but the villain of the piece was superb. Surprise ending finished off a very well done bit of work. I bought "The Nun's Chorus" from "Casanova" by Strauss at H.M.V's studio this morning and funnily enough, outside the Studio, ran into Cookie again. He repeated his praise of "The Dancing Years" and I agreed again.

December 3

Back at Poole again. Managed to get time in London, before I left, to see "Fantasia"* – which alone of all England (I think) I'd never seen. It was glorious. I had to drag myself away half way through the second time round to get my train. *[The revolutionary animated Walt Disney classic, combining classical music with imaginative visuals, presented with Leopold Stokowski and the Philadelphia Orchestra.]

Said farewell to Evie at the "Cogers", and caught the 4.35 from Waterloo. Arrived back here eightish. Not a bad trip. Read some dreadful yarn about a few murders. London was foggy and drizzly when I left – The makings of a real pea-souper. The boys have been busy here during my absence, so I'm told.

December 4

Saw Doc. Wilson this morning and he sent a wire to try to hurry them up about my going home. It's about time I heard something. Walked into town and had a feed at the local snack bar.

Saw a show tonight – "A Yank in Dutch." Franchot Tone and Joan Bennett. Rather good I thought. Lots of laughs. Found a Red Cross parcel awaiting me containing some milk chocolate and cigarettes. It had been sent to hospital and re-posted thence to me.

December 5

Did nothing all day. After tea tonight Tubby Sullivan played me a few games of chess and beat me every time. I'm improving, but he's getting better every game. He plays the best game of draughts I've ever seen, and his chess is just as good.

December 6

Mass this morning and then called on the mob in the Orderly room. Paddy Kirke has advised me to apply for a job as permanent Duty Pilot. If I'm accepted it will mean my accepting a commission which I don't care for. The job is only open to aircrew grounded through medical reasons. Saw two old shows tonight "Scarface" with Paul Muni and "Hell's Angels" – Ben Lyon and Jean Harlow. They were good shows in their day. Wrote a few letters this arvo.

December 7

Got up about 10 a.m. Alec and Ron were going on leave with Tubby Sullivan today. Alec and Tubby went, but poor Ron is crook and I think he'll spend his leave in hospital. Played some Chess with Tubby before dinner and was in very good form.

Ray Goode plays a grand game of chess, as I discovered tonight. We had a tussle that lasted an hour.

Going to bed early.

Posted letters to Molly and Mother this morning.

December 8

Had a very lazy day. Hardly left the Mess. Some of the boys wanted me to go along to the dance up at the Centenary but I knocked 'em back.

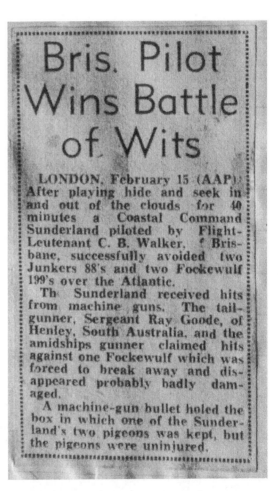

Bris. Pilot Wins Battle of Wits

LONDON, February 15 (AAP). After playing hide and seek in and out of the clouds for 40 minutes a Coastal Command Sunderland piloted by Flight-Leutenant C. B. Walker, f Brisbane, successfully avoided two Junkers 88's and two Fockewulf 199's over the Atlantic.

Th Sunderland received hits from machine guns. The tail-gunner, Sergeant Ray Goode, of Henley, South Australia, and the amidships gunner claimed hits against one Fockewulf which was forced to break away and disappeared probably badly damaged.

A machine-gun bullet holed the box in which one of the Sunderland's two pigeons was kept, but the pigeons were uninjured.

Played Ray chess and beat him easily one game, but got cleaned up in the second. Thought of going to a show in Bournemouth for a while – Abbot and Costello – but decided against it. I may go to one tomorrow.

See the Adj. wants to see me, according to the notice board. May be news.

Bill Mabe dropped in for a yarn just before I started getting ready for bed.

December 9

Intended going to a show tonight, but received so many bad reports about both theatres that I changed my mind. I played a few games of snooker with Alan Mayne this morning and draughts with Paddy Druhan, who was Duty N.C.O. this evening. The days are very short now. It's dark about 4.30 and the sun doesn't rise until after 8 a.m. No letters now for over six weeks, I think. Wonder what has happened to the folks and Molly. I suppose the Japs are to blame. Called on Orderly room, but found I was wanted for a very unimportant reason. Nothing to do with my being grounded at all!

December 10

Played Alan Snooker at the Institute this morning and afternoon and we went to a show at the Regent tonight. Saw "The Adventures of Martin Eden" and "Sabotage at Sea," both of which were fair. Re "Martin Eden" I'm betting Jack London would not have recognised his novel. Remembered I once lent a kid at Wooloowin State School Doyle's "Lost World" in exchange for that book, and never got it back.

December 11

Spent another day doing nothing. Played Alan snooker and draughts. Had a look over old "A," in the afternoon. Alan took me for a doubler on his old motor cycle and we nearly succeeded in breaking our necks.

Finished up a party with Bill, Ricky, Clarkie and Maurie in the mess at 2.30 a.m. – Drinking lemonade with a colouring of beer.

December 12

Slept in this morning. After dinner Alan and I went into B'mouth where we played snooker until 5.30. Then we tried to get into the Odeon, were frightened off by the size of the queue, and finished up at West's where we saw "Penny Serenade" and a Nick Carter show. Home on 10.30 train and had a couple of Shandies in the mess.

December 13

Had a game of snooker with Vis Alsop at the Institute, then went to 11 o'clock mass. It was a sung mass and the Choir was just as bad as ever.

Went out to Hamworthy after dinner, and had a look at old "A." Think I'll go for a test flip in her when she's ready.

Guest night in the mess tonight was as dull as ever. Save the little Redhead, who was at our first dance, with Brad. She was getting as full as ever. Should be heartily spanked and sent home to her Mother.

Note to Molly on back:

Darling, These chaps with me have often been mentioned in my letters. They are two of the best pals any man ever had, - Paddy Druhan and Tubby Sullivan (in the middle).
Lots of Love. Ed. / x

Ed is on the left.

Letter #50.

No envelope. Aus/ 405206 Sgt. Gallagher, E.B.
461 Sqdn. R.A.A.F., England,

December 13, 1942

My own Darling,

I feel pretty ashamed of myself, for it is nearly a fortnight since I last wrote to you. I have a bit of excuse, for the M.O. gave me six days sick leave as soon as I got out of hospital, and I've been in London.

I had a really great time, dear. About the best time I've had in this country, and strangely enough, I think it was because I never had a drop of beer.

I had a real orgy of show-seeing though, for I nearly averaged two a day. I was in fine fettle too, for I felt particularly well after my rest in bed, and it was rather an effort to drink Lemonade with the boys in such familiar haunts as the "Cogers," the "Cecil" and the "Sussex." Some of my 10 Sqdn. Flying acquaintances were in town on leave too, and they did their best to tempt me, but I was firm. I can almost see the halo round my head, already.

The shows I saw included "Watch on the Rhine," with Diana Wynyard, Shaw's "The Doctor's Dilemma" with Vivian Leigh, "Night of the Garter" with Sydney Howard, "Murder Without Crime" – Raymond Lowell, – The Windmill Revue de Ville, one of Geo. Black's productions at the Whitehall, and the best of all "The Dancing Years" – Ivor Novello. All these were Stage Shows. I have never seen anything so lovely as "The Dancing Years" – the music, singing and settings and the dancing were all perfect. I wish I could see it again.

In the Cinema line I saw "Holiday Inn," "Fantasia," "The Road to Morocco," and "Who done it?" I never had time to see a number of shows I wanted to see.

I have been worried about you darling, since I got your last letter. No mail has arrived for me since November 1st, now, and in your last letter you said you were very worried about something, and asked me to pray for a very special intention. I have been doing so, sweet, but I wish you had told me what was on your mind. I guessed there must be something with your Mother. I hope she is well and happy. You know, dear, – she'll be my mother, too, someday soon. I almost look upon her as such already. Got a cheek, haven't I?

I sent you a cable from London last week. I hope it arrived before

351

Christmas. I was going to send you some airgraph* letters, but the day when the last one was allowed to be sent found me still in hospital, so I had no luck. I could have got the Doc. Or one of the sisters to send them for me, I suppose, but I didn't want them to read what I wanted to say to you, anyhow. *[In 1941, microphotography was used by the Post Office to produce the Airgraph. Because each message was numbered and photographed, it was possible for any mail lost in transit to be reproduced from the original.]

How are Alice and Leo getting along? I got a letter from the G.P.O. while I was in hospital informing me that I had been appointed to a job in the Telephone a/cs in Melbourne, which entails a rise of about £50 a year – which is not bad, is it?

How does living in Melbourne appeal to you? If you are "agin" it, I can have it cancelled, or arrange a transfer or exchange, I suppose.

I went into Bournemouth yesterday with Alan Mayne, and saw a show – "Penny Serenade" with Irene Dunne and Cary Grant, and played snooker in the afternoon.

The night before I went to a local show and saw "The Adventures of Martin Eden," and liked it. I'd read the book years ago; it's by Jack London, but failed to find the slightest resemblance to it in the picture, which is usually the case.

I'm glad to hear you are so interested in the "Grail," dear, and that you are finding it so instructive! We'll have to have a competition when I get home to see who is the most useful around the house. I, with my Sunderland training, should win, I'm sure.

Had a letter from Uncle Jim while I was in bed, and he tells me how glad they are, whenever they see you, and only wish you would go out more. Pat and Ail are great kids, aren't they?

How goes Sheila and the offspring? I hope they and Len are well and as happy as can be expected, these days. Gee! Some people have all the luck, haven't they?

Poor old Alan, with whom I went into Bournemouth yesterday, had bad luck. About three weeks ago, his little daughter, who had been born three weeks previously, died. He hasn't got over it, yet. His wife is still pretty ill.

I've just been playing Ray Goode chess, and I thought I had him licked, but to my surprise, just as I made the winning (as I thought) move, I found myself checkmated! Such is life!

There's a party in the Mess tonight. I think I'll go to a show and

352

dodge it. It will only be a beer-up.

I got back from Bournemouth late last night and slept in this morning, with the result that I had to hurry to make last Mass. It was a "sung Mass," and the choir was awful!

Still nothing has been done about me by the R.A.A.F. I think I am the forgotten man. It's nearly two and a half months since I was recommended by the Specialist for a discharge, yet I'm still waiting to hear from the powers that be. Doc Wilson sent them another wire last week, but I fear his is a "voice crying in the wilderness" – like St. John's in today's Gospel.

I'm sending you two snaps Mr. Aikman took of me while I was on leave, last September. They're tiny, aren't they, but good things come in small parcels.

Some of the 10 Sqdn. boys I saw in London while on leave told me Jack Jackson is still well. Do you remember Jacko? I introduced him to you at the corner of Adelaide and Albert Streets one day.

I had a letter from Townsville when I was in Hospital. They are all well. Do you know, Darling, I hadn't even heard that the old home town had been bombed by the rotten Japs., until I got that letter. I was glad to hear they were so ineffectual, but it made me worry a bit.

Have you heard much from them? Gee! they love you. Mother says that you are the one girl she'd have picked for me, if she had had the chance. All she wonders is how I ever had the brains to fall in love with you. As if anyone could help doing that.

Well, dear, it's time for tea, and where my tummy is concerned I'm always there. Please keep loving me and waiting for me, and take care of yourself. You are always in my heart, I adore you,

Ed xxxxx

P.S. Love me? *Ed x*

P.S.S. Sorry, Darling, I've just about torn my room to pieces, yet I can't find those snaps I mentioned. They are only the size of postage stamps. Aren't I a mug? *Ed x*

December 14

Saw M.O. first thing this morning after C.O.'s parade – a large lump of B/S. No news yet for me.

To Orderley room where received same news – none. Went to a terrible show at the Regent with Steve – "Alibi" and "The Avenging Stranger." The latter was an old time cowboy film. Shades of Tom Mix!* Nearly got up and left. To bed after a few Ginger beers. – Jerry is overhead. Heard today the definition of a "W.I.F.F." – Officially it's a "W.A.A.F. with "B.O." *[Thomas Mix was Hollywood's first Western megastar.]

December 15

A Lazy Day – as usual. Got up about 10 a.m., and then mooched about until dinner. After lunch, Richie Hattam and Alan played Jeff and I four handed Snooker and we won fairly easily. Mess meeting at 1.30 and my proposal for a new Radiogram was passed.

After tea went for a stroll around the countryside with Steve. We were half drowned by a sudden shower and took shelter, much too late, at the "Shah of Persia," where we had a shandy each.

Home early to bed.

December 16

Wrote a few letters this morning. About 1245 Jerry came over – a Do 217* – and dropped a stick across. He did very little damage except scare hell out of me and the boys. I never even heard the sirens go. Mess meeting was continued, but very little of note came out. Seems we are to serve the Airmen's dinner at Xmas. *[The Dornier (Do) 217 was a Luftwaffe heavy bomber and reconnaissance aircraft which was the first in aviation combat history to deploy a precision, radio-guided, free-fall bomb.]

Last night I was going into Bournemouth or Parkestone to a show, but decided against it, or rather Alan did by not turning up – and had a good old yarn in the Mess with Johnnie Lewis, Lex Bateup and a few of the lads. Alan Barnum, the official R.A.A.F. Cartoonist, was there. Seems a decent sort of chap.

December 17

Went out to Hamworthy this morning and had photo taken with rest of crew of "A" by Alan (the official photographer from Kodak House). Saw the gang, had morning tea, and as there was nothing doing, thumbed a van and got a ride back to town. Played Snooker with Roy and won easily. Played Draughts with Bill Mabe and bought and posted some

Xmas Cards. Sent Cable to Auntie Mary. Stayed in all night, singing around piano. Paddy Druhan played. Had a couple of shandies. Seem to have lost taste for beer altogether.

No mail now since 7th November. Wrote to Eric and Joan and Mother this morning.

December 18

Spent this morning doing nothing except listen to the Wireless and working and a few crossword puzzles. This ennui is getting on my nerves. About 4.30 went into Bournemouth with Sid Miller – Harry's brother – and saw "They all Kissed the bride" – Joan Crawford and Melvin Douglas. Also a "Blondie" film. Enjoyed the programme no end. Home by 8.45 bus and had late tea and a couple of shandies at the mess with Brad and Les and Rickie. Rained all day. Hear Charlie Walker has gone for a Burton* over Germany. *[British slang meaning to be lost, destroyed, or to die.]

December 19

Arose at 10 a.m. – had breakfast at the "Snack Bar" then sat in the Lounge until dinner. Tucker* [Australian slang for food] is still very poor. Smed and I decorated the lounge in the afternoon in preparation for Xmas and it certainly looks swell. Cheese for tea, blast the stuff!

Met a naval P.O. after tea and brought him into the Mess for a jug or two; he wanted me to go to a dance, but I'm not in the mood for dancing these days. Lord knows why, but I think young Doreen has fallen for me; she came round to the Mess to inquire for me, but I got Steve to make some excuse for me, and slipped off to the Regent on my own. Saw "The Affairs of Jimmy Valentine" and a Soviet picture entitled "Defeat of the German Armies near Moscow"* – not bad. *[Also known as *Moscow Strikes Back*, this Soviet war documentary about the battle of Moscow, released in February 1942, was directed by Leonid Varlamov and Ilya Kopalin. It won an Academy Award.]

December 20

Got up for breakfast, but wished I hadn't. Went to 8 a.m. Mass, and found it didn't begin until 8.30 a.m. A few prayers for half an hour didn't do me any harm. Played some glug draughts until dinner and was beaten a couple of times. Had a "lush" dinner, and then went for a dinghy ride out to "D" and gave Sid Miller a hand with some difficulties he'd struck with his Radio. Surprised to find I still know enough to help somebody. After tea, I went with Les Eaton and Bunny to the "Shah of Persia" and finished up at the Mess. Told Ray Connolly's classic "Ghost Story" to an enthralled audience of the boys and their girls by firelight. Sang and had a good time. – To bed now as tired as billy-o, Diary, you old thing – you!

December 21

Got out of bed about 11.30 a.m. – Certainly am getting very lazy these days. After dinner I went to the slip and shot a line to six Aussie reporters who were gleaning gen on the Squadron. Les Eaton and I thumbed a ride home in a van and after having a bath I wrote Molly a letter. Gee! I miss her! After tea I yarned with a few of the lads down in the lounge and sang a few questionable parodies to the playing of Paddy Druhan. "Curly" (so called because he is bald) Brill, Mo's double, sang a very funny one on the "Lambeth Walk." Gale warning chased Les Wilson and a few of the other lads out to the kites. "Duty hands" for Xmas is causing a lot of anxiety.

Ed, on left, with mates outside the Mess

356

Letter #51

Bournemouth, Poole, 21 Dec. 1942. 2½ penny King George stamp. Received 17.3.43

December 21, 1942

My Sweetheart,

Life still goes on its monotonous way. Reading back my Diary for the last few weeks I can find nothing of interest in it at all. I wish they'd hurry up and let me know my fate. The only letter I've received for over six weeks now, was one I posted to myself. Don't think I've gone off my nut, dear. Actually this letter was my bankbook which I had to send, with an addressed envelope, to the head office for adding!

I have been to a lot of pictures lately, but the quality of the shows has been generally awful. The local flea-circus has been showing such things as old-time English productions (you know what they were like) and cowboy thrillers.

In at Bournemouth last Friday I saw one that I thought was fair – Joan Crawford and Melvin Douglas in "They all Kissed the Bride." [Joan Crawford's famous line "When I want a sneak, I'll hire the best and get a Jap" drew the biggest laugh from 1942 audiences. The line, now considered offensive, was cut from later prints.]

Preparations are being made for a regular "do" at the Mess next Thursday night – Christmas Eve. I think it will be a swell evening. Smed and I spent yesterday afternoon decorating the Lounge and the dance floor with coloured streamers, holly, etc. and it is a picture. We are quite proud of our efforts. I wish you were here, darling, so that I could invite you along.

We are having turkey, ham and pork for Xmas dinner. My mouth is watering in anticipation already. For breakfast we are to have bacon and fresh eggs. It will be some treat!

Six reporters of various Aussie papers called on us for an interview this afternoon, so my name should be gracing the Truth next week or so. We all "shot them a bit of a line." Speaking of line-shooting – I think the best I've ever heard was shot by a friend of mine (slightly inebriated) to a too persistent London news vendor. "What, buy a paper?" he said, "Listen! We don't buy the news – we make it!" The paper seller was rocked for quite a while by this.

How are things with you, dear? I hope the thing that you mentioned as worrying you in your last letter has stopped doing so, by now. Lord! I

357

wish I were back home with you! I still include the "special intention" you asked me to pray for in my prayers, sweet.

I went to 8 o'clock Mass yesterday, but found that, owing to the blackout and the fact that the sun doesn't put in an appearance until 8.20, that it didn't start till 8.30. So I had a good half hour alone, except for one or two people, in the dark Church to do some really good praying. You can guess what my main prayer was!

Last night, feeling completely "browned off," I allowed Les Eaton to inveigle me into going along with him and having a few jugs. I think it's about the first beer I've tasted for six weeks or more. Returning to the Mess about 9.30, we found a crowd of the boys and their girls in the Lounge. I put out the lights and with the room lit only by the flickering firelight, I told Ghost stories, ranging from Fisher's Ghost to Ray Connolly's classic, for about an hour. Then one of the girls played the piano and sang until about one o'clock. It was quite a nice night. I wish you'd been there.

The official R.A.A.F. photographer and Cartoonist was at the camp the other day and he took photos of all the boys and drew sketches of some of us. The Squadron is certainly receiving some attention from the news-hounds.

Well, Love, that's about all the news I can think of of any interest, so I'll finish off now. Please keep loving me and praying for me. I need you more than anything this world can offer. I always will. I adore you,

Ed xxxxx

P.S. Love me?   Ed x

Brisbane *Truth* 27.12.42

SUB. PATROLS, FERRY TRIPS

(From C. H. Bateson, formerly of Brisbane "Truth.")

London, Saturday. – Although there are a number of Queenslanders serving in the R.A.A.F. Anzac Squadron, now operating from a base which is reminiscent of an Australian scene, not many of them have seen much action.

For the majority life has been one long succession of routine anti-submarine patrols, interspersed with ferrying trips to Gibraltar, and only now and again has one of the Sunderlands belonging to this squadron attacked a U-boat or enemy merchantman, or had a running encounter with Hun aircraft.

Sergeant Air-Gunner John Gamble, of Red Hill, was aboard a Sunderland which attacked a 3500 ton armed merchantman. Said he: "We stooged round a bit, waiting to attack the Hun, who was sending up plenty of flack, but although he was pretty accurate, we weren't hit. Then we went in to attack; our bombs went very close, and I saw two fall half a ship's length ahead, and another two the same distance behind him. I reckon we shook 'em very badly with those explosions.

Sergeant Air-Gunner Les Wilson, of Murwillumbah, was also on this trip. He is one of the most experienced air-gunners with the squadron.

Sergeant Ed. Gallagher of New Farm, who came originally from Townsville, has something like 800 operational hours to his credit, of which he put up 500 with the first R.A.A.F. Sunderland Squadron. Now he has been taken off operations, and is awaiting a fresh posting. He's hoping it will be to Australia.

December 22

Went out to Hamworthy this morning. Saw Doc., but no news has yet come through. Handed in a pair of shoes to be mended. We were paid after lunch and I put a few quid in the bank. Read until tea, and afterwards Les Eaton and I went up to the "Sloop" where we met a few of the lads. I drank shandies until closing time then returned to the Mess. Had a jug with Ricky Laltam in his room.

Was given the enclosed drawing of the "King of the Gremlins." – Wonder who first thought of the term "gremlin." I remember I always had one slung on the old Marconi, when I was flying, and he certainly didn't bring us any bad luck.

December 23

Spent the day between P. and H. [Poole and Hamworthy] – Hear Cookie tried to give me a job to do on Friday but was circumvented by Geo. Read. After tea I went with Les, Ricky, and Les Eaton to the Sloop and drank shandies till 10 a.m. Then I returned to the Mess and 2.a.m. found me playing Chess with George.

December 24

Rose for breakfast as I heard there were eggs on the menu. After breakfast I went out to H. and nearly worked a flip on E.J. The party at night was a wow! I had a grand time. Quite a good crowd of people were there. Re met Sam Woods my old 10 Sqdn. Skipper. He has been posted to 461 as Station Master, in place of Raban. Sam is a S/Ldr. Now.

In bed at 4 a.m. – Lord, what a hang-over I have today! Off beer again – for good this time.

December 25

Rose at 8 a.m. – Went to Mass then back to the Mess and to bed. Hangover has developed into the worst cold I've had for years. Everyone seems to be quiet and subdued tonight.

Dinner today was good. – Turkey and pork washed down by beer. I took over the Orderley Room from 12 to 2 to allow the airmen to enjoy their Xmas dinner together and finished up nearly missing out on my own. Sgt. W.A.A.F.s sat with us. Seem a nice lot of girls. One of them is playing piano at the moment. I am supposed to be singing, but my throat is raw.

December 26

Slept in again. This arvo Steve and I went into Bournemouth and saw Don Ameché and Alice Faye in "Night in Rio," and Joan Blondell and Melvin Douglas in "Good Girls go to Paris."

Arriving back at the Mess about 10 p.m. I found Tubby Sullivan had returned from leave and a sing-song was in progress. Tubby informed me he has bought a book on Chess and it has improved him out of sight. Played him until 3 a.m. and found this was correct for he cleaned me up. Have the devil of a cold. Still no mail!

December 27

Mass at 8.30 a.m. Stayed in Mess all day. Cold is very annoying. Played Tubby Chess after tea and I beat him. He lent me his book and it is very interesting. Some good instructive games – especially one played by Napoleon. Some visitors came in and Tubby played the piano. In bed at midnight. Alec and Ron should be back from leave tonight, but there is no sign of them.

December 28

Played Alan Snooker and Chess this morning. Bought some dope for my cold.

Played Chess with Tubby all afternoon and again after tea. Drank a few noggins of ale. Lord! What a life! No mail received since 5th November, or thereabouts. I wonder what has happened?

December 29

Getting near the end of the year now. A few letters arrived today, at last! Wrote home to Molly and Mother.

Letter from Maud Millican of the G.P.O. Brisbane brought me bad news of Dave Poulsen's being missing at Milne Bay. Wonder how other boys are getting on? Played Chess and Snooker most of the day.

Letter #53

Stamped: Bournemouth Poole, Dec 30, 1942. Received 17.3.43.

December 28, 1942

My own Darling,

Christmas has come and gone again, making two I've spent away from you in this cold land – two that I grudge with all the feeling I can muster; I hope it is the last one that will ever find us apart. We have never yet spent a Christmas together, have we, dear? Remember 1940? You were with the folks at Yandina, while I, like a dill, was lapping up beer and disporting on the beach at Bribie Island with Nev and the boys.

I felt very lonely this Christmas, dear. No mail or anything arrived to offer consolation; in fact, until today, when I got two letters – one from Dad, and one from a girl at the G.P.O., none has arrived since the first of last November. Something must be holding mine up, for most of the lads' mail is coming over regularly. I always seem to be unlucky. Old Margaret the Corporal in charge of the W.A.A.F.s who look after our Mess took pity on my lack of letters, and, for fun, posted me a Xmas card from a neighbouring town. I thought it was very nice of her. She is a dear old soul.

There was a great dance at the Mess on Xmas Eve. Nearly everyone was at least slightly pickled. I got to bed about 4 a.m. I still don't know how I got up for Mass in the morning. I must have looked like a slice of Death warmed up, to the people there. I've landed a lovely cold out of my effort. My dressing table looks like a Chemist's window, with all the bottles of patent medicines I've bought to try to cure it.

There's to be even a better "do" on New Year's Eve. I think I'll go away for the night.

On Christmas Day, in order to let the Airmen and W.A.A.F.s enjoy their dinner, we sergeants and the officers took over their jobs and served them. It is the usual thing on this day. I had charge of the Orderly Room. We had our dinner about 2.30, and it was a good 'un. Turkey, Pork, Roast Potatoes, Plum-pudding, etc. Best feed I've had since I left Aussie.

My old Skipper, Sam Wood, of 10 Squadron has been made "Stationmaster" (Flight Commander) of this Squadron, and we had a few beers together on Xmas Eve to celebrate our re-union. He's a good chap. Has been made a Squadron Leader and won a D.F.C. lately. Deserves it, if anyone ever did.

Last Saturday Johnnie Stevens and I went into B. for a few hours to see a show, but every theatre was packed out except one, and I had to be contented with seeing a film I saw on the boat coming across the Pacific – "Night in Rio" – Don Ameche and Alice Faye. I'd seen the other one, too, years ago. Joan Blondell in "Good Girls go to Paris."

Returning to the Mess about 10 p.m. I found my old cobber and Chess opponent – Tubby Sullivan – had returned from leave, and was playing the piano for a crowd of the lads and their girls and a few W.A.A.F. Sergeants. My cold prevented my joining in the singing, but Tubby insisted in playing me Chess until 1 a.m.

Since then I've hardly left the Mess, being determined to get rid of this cold. I went up to the Institute this morning and played a few games of Snooker, at which much practice is making me fairly proficient.

The letter from Maud Millican I got this morning contained some bad news. An old pal of mine, – Dave Poulsen, who went to the "Terrace" with me, and later worked with me in the G.P.O. in Sydney and Brisbane, has been posted missing in New Guinea. He was always one of my best cobbers. I hope he's O.K.

Dad's letter included one from Rita who waxes eloquent of your charms, sweet. You seem to have made quite a hit with that youngest sister of mine. Not that I needed to be told how lovely you are.

I'm thinking of asking for a couple of days off over the New Year. May take a run up to London. Then again, probably I won't.

It's very cold, now. If you go outside at night, if you don't wear gloves, your hands will nearly drop off; and your feet, after a while, they feel like two blocks of ice. I saw my first snow, today, for this winter. Last winter I saw no snow at all, which may be hard to believe, but is a fact. The south coast of England doesn't have much snow.

I wish I were home with you, darling! I love you so! I'd give anything I have, just to be with you long enough to tell you this with my lips instead of with the poor substitute of pen and ink. Please keep loving me, no matter what happens, for, if you should ever cease to care for me, as I know you do, I think it would mean the end of everything for me.

Remember me to your Mother and Dad and the rest of the family, please, dear. I've sent them a cable for Xmas, which I hope has arrived. I couldn't remember your Dad's initials. I adore you, dear; – please pray for me; – you are always in my prayers.

Ed xxxxx

P.S. Love me? Ed x

BRIS. MEN IN CAPTURE OF BLOCKADE-RUNNER

LONDON, January 6 (AAP): Two Brisbane men were members of the crew of an Australian Sunderland which guided a cruiser through shocking weather conditions to intercept a German blockade-runner in the Atlantic.

The men were Sergeant L. G. Heal, wireless operator, and Sergeant J. E. Jackson, air gunner, both of Brisbane.

Describing the action, the captain of the Sunderland, Flying Officer K. C. Beeton, of Adelaide, said that a Coastal Command Wellington had spotted the blockade-runner and attacked in bad weather without success. Beeton said he was then sent out to find the ship.

"We searched in the worst flying conditions I have ever experienced, with low clouds, high wind and rain. We took off in the morning but had not found the ship in the afternoon and were thinking of giving up when we received a message to search a new area, where we encountered a cruiser which inquired if we had seen the ship.

"We replied 'No' but found the ship 10 to 15 minutes later making about 10 knots in the heavy seas. We returned to the cruiser and gave the position by signal lamp, and the cruiser shot off in pursuit.

"She was a magnificent sight full-out with the seas breaking over the bridge. We had now over-stayed our patrol time, but calculated if the wind did not change we could co-operate further, so flew a parallel track to the cruiser, dropping smoke-floats to give her a straight course.

"Unfortunately we couldn't take her right there to see the kill because our petrol was running low and the wind changed dead against us.

"I will never forget the trip home. With adverse winds and shortage of petrol we had to hit the base dead accurately or go down into the raging sea.

"Flying Officer Bowley, 21, of South Australia, who was navigator, had his head down at the desk working like a nigger. We made it, thanks to Bowley."

Telegraph.

364

December 30

Was shifted out of the Mess today to a Billet in Sheldown Rd. Seems quite a swell joint. Drank beer and played Chess all the afternoon and evening. Letter received from Joan, obviously posted previous to the one I received the day before. Slept at new billet. Slept well too. Find I'm inclined to like the old bed too much lately.

December 31

Dance at Mess tonight. – New Year's Eve! Lord! What a time was had by all. Got back to my billet at 4 a.m. Brought some chap from Bournemouth to stay with me as it was too far for him to walk to where he wanted to go. Steve and his G.F. had awful row which I vainly tried to mend. Kissed about 50 girls at midnight. Whacko! Joan's birthday today. Hope she is well and safe – also Eric.

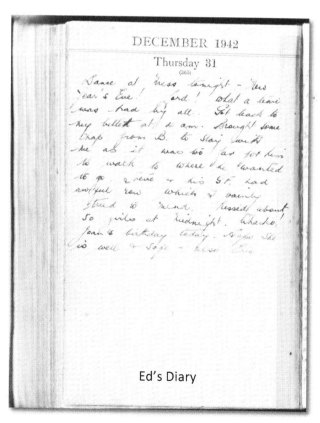

Ed's Diary

Preface to Year 1943

The year 1942 was for me full of wild excitements, hedged with periods of utter boredom and quietness – at times even sadness. I saw quite a lot of action with both 10 and 461 Squadrons, skittled, or helped to skittle, a few Jerries, which is a good thing. Saw many parts of England, and spent a glorious week in Ireland, at the Government's expense. I made many new friends, but lost quite a few old ones. Bertie Gall, Billy Isle, George Bentley, "Maizey," Ted Tailor, Ash Mears, Dave Poulsen, "Brad," "Bullsie," "Dentie," "Wang" Osborne, Oscar Wientholm, Davy Bell, Roy Chinnery, and Blue Eva are only a few who "failed to return." Wherever they are, I hope they are happy. They deserve to be, for despite the few human foibles they may have possessed, they were all good fellows, and grand pals.

I spent a fair bit of time in London, and at the "Boomerang" club in Australia House, I re-met many an old friend.

Discovered a lovely little inn in Fleet Street – The Cogers – which should be renamed "Little Australia," for it is the favourite hotel of all Aussies who get to London.

I met some delightful English people, among whom Mr. and I Aikman of "Darney Dene" Flackwell Heath, Bucks. Will always remain as a reminder of ideal Hospitality.

Towards the end of the year, a sudden dizzy spell accompanied by severe headaches put me out of the flying game. It is thought that they are the result of a bit of a crack up early in the year, when I was laid out for a few days. I spent some time in Hospital at Southampton, but no-one could discover anything particularly wrong with me.

However I was permanently taken off flying, and am now awaiting the result of a Medical Board. With luck, I should be home early this coming year, which will be marvellous. I'd give up all the thrills and fun and experiences I've found in this country if I could be home tomorrow.

This does not mean that I do not like England. In fact, I love it! I've enjoyed every moment I have spent here, and have made a resolution that I must return some day. But I'm lonely without Molly.

Look out, 1943, – here I come!

January 1, 1943

New Year's Day Eh? Diary? A day for the forming of resolutions. Have made a few but am not sanguine about my chances of keeping them. Know myself too well.

What a head I had when I arose at 12 noon, washed and sent my guest off home. Mad with myself for having missed Mass, but slept like a log until noon, having no-one to wake me. Will go tomorrow to try to make up for today.

Hope this year finds me home with Molly and the folks. Maybe I'll be a married man ere next New Year's Day. Like the idea, Diary?

January 2

Rose early and got to 8.30 a.m. Mass. Not many people there. Played Tubby Chess nearly all day and during the evening. Find quite a number of people are interested in the game now. We always have an audience while we're playing. Taught a few the rudiments.

Tubby and I are fairly good now. Think few people would beat us.

Had a few jugs at the Mess and retired early to bed.

January 3

Mass at 8.30 a.m. then played a few games of Snooker. This afternoon I went down to Hamworthy to see how things were there.

Tonight was guest night at the Mess. Tubby's and my song is going well, now. The Chorus has been completed and I have written the words for the verse while Tubby already has a grand theme for that part. I'll give you the words, Diary.

Verse:

I wandered last night where the breezes play
In the tree cloaked lane by the bay;
And I thought your love was a dying flame,
'Till I heard the breeze whisper your name, – Dear.

Chorus:

I was alone, under the stars, last night;
Watching the leaves pattern the pale moonlight:
I heard the breeze, breathing songs to the trees,
– Stories from over the Seas, – Dear :
– It whispered of you, low in the list'ning lane,
– Deep in my heart, I caught the sweet refrain;
I know now that our love will always be bright,
– The East Wind told me, last night.

January 4

Everyone at the mess last night said that our song is as good as any they have heard. The tune is certainly very lovely – a Jazz Waltz – my favourite tempo.

Today our lounge was occupied by the billeting mob, and we had no chance to get on with the job. Tubby and I played Chess all day. I never seem to win a game lately. He's too darn hot.

January 5

Somewhat similar day to yesterday. Did practically nothing all day except play chess and try to keep warm. The weather is bitterly cold with gales blowing up very frequently. Tried to collect my shoes, but they weren't ready yet.

January 6

George Read tells me that Woodsie has caught up with me, at last. It seems that my period of holiday is over at last. He asked Doc. Wilson if I was fit for duty yet, and the Doc. Said "yes – everything except flying." So I'm Duty N.C.O. tomorrow. See that there are two parcels awaiting me at the Orderley Room.

January 7

Well, things change! I'm going to Oxford tomorrow!

Took over the duties of Duty N.C.O. this morning from Alan Mayne and collected my two parcels – one from Molly and one from Mother. They contained some lovely things. About 2.30 I got a ring from Cpl. Styles who informed me that I am catching the 8.15 train to London in the morning and proceeding thence to the Military Hospital for Head Injuries at Oxford. [For the duration of World War II, St. Hugh's College (a University of Oxford women's college), was requisitioned and became a military hospital specializing in head injuries.]

368

I collected my pay and got Alan Pavey to be Duty N.C.O. Some blow for Woodsie!

Played Tubby Chess and retired early to bed.

January 8

Caught the train this morning and arrived in London at 11.30. At Paddington I got on a train for Oxford and I'm now in a nice room in the hospital. This, before the war, was a Catholic Convent for girls and seems a good place. Have met some nice sisters and nurses. Expect to be X Rayed tomorrow.

Thought I was only going to be here for a day, but fear this was wrong.

Met the M.O. who is a good chap. Had a long yarn tonight with him.

January 9

Had an E.E.G. this morning. This is a machine which records the electric impulses of the brain. The nurse affixed a contraption like a permanent waving machine to my head and switched on several knobs. Then a pen traced a wavy line on a long strip of paper.

Rested this afternoon and read a book or two. There is a sister here who is loveliness itself.

Had another long yarn with the M.O.

January 10

Was X ray'd this morning. Took about six or seven photos of my skull. Mass this morning in the little chapel in the hospital.

This is a lazy life.

I went for a stroll round the district this afternoon. There was a very heavy fog and a slight drizzle.

January 11

Saw the M.O. today. He tells me I'm being sent to a civvy hospital today for further X rays. (I'm writing this Tuesday morning.)

The apparatus they have here is not elaborate enough.

Loafed all day in bed as I was given a Lumbar Puncture in the morning and if I get up too soon after it I'd have had a bad headache. The L.P. was pretty grim!

January 12

Went to the Radcliffe Hospital in an ambulance this morning where some expert took about a dozen photos of my head. I feel guilty over their taking all the trouble with me when I feel perfectly O.K.

My back is very stiff from yesterday's L.P.

January 13

Had another E.E.G. this morning. Did a bit of P.T. to liven myself up a bit.

This E.E.G. lasted nearly an hour this time and the pen covered yards of paper. Saw the Major I.C. of the Hospital this morning who put me through the same examination as the M.O.

January 14

Saw Air Commodore Simon this morning and he seems a very nice chap. Asked me a few questions then fell to examining the various reports re my case!

Had another thoroughly lazy day. Getting fed up with this place, although it is very nice. My back is still a little sore.

January 15

Saw a board consisting of a number of Specialists this morning and went into Oxford this afternoon. Strolled down past the "Mitre" to the Thames, then back over the town. It is lovely old city. Seems Hallowed, somehow, as if the learning of ages rested like a weight on its shoulders.

Sent a couple of cables to Molly and Mother.

Some of the old buildings are certainly steeped in Age.

January 16

The M.O. saw me again this morning as usual but could give me no news regarding my case as a decision has not been reached yet.

Spent the day reading etc. Wish I could get back to camp.

January 17

Caught the bus back into town this afternoon and wandered round the place, drinking in its quaintness and beauty.

370

Mass was again celebrated in the lovely little chapel. The Priest seems a decent young chap.

January 18

The M.O. saw me this morning and told me that he was afraid that I was going to be boarded out and sent back to Aussie. All the tests except the x-rays have shown me to be perfectly O.K., but the Rays have revealed a slight abnormality of the blood vessels in a certain part of my brain, which might have conceivably caused the fainting spell I'm supposed to have experienced last September. Strain, such as flying, he says, might aggravate the condition which is apparently getting better, so it would not be fair to me to allow me to continue! (Never knew the A.F. was ever solicitous re a chap's future life.) He says that if I take things quietly now, I should be O.K. for the rest of my life. This, he says, is not the opinion of all the Specialists, for some of them maintain that there is nothing wrong with me at all, but the majority are of the opinion that I should be boarded out.

January 19

Was given leave today (but told I'd have to pay my own way) to go back to Poole for a night. Have to be back by 10 p.m. tomorrow. Spent the evening with the boys over a few jugs. Rung up Bullsie and had a long yarn. Fixed up with Paddy Kirke re my kit.

Saw Reading* and had a few jugs there while awaiting a connection this morning. Had dinner at some restaurant there. *[Reading is about 43 km southeast of Oxford, and about 126 km northeast of Poole.]

January 20

Went to the Orderley Room this morning and managed to wangle a ticket to Oxford. Collected my pay and said Good-bye to the boys. Packed my old tin trunk full of personal kit, and struggled back to Oxford with it via Waterloo and Paddington.

Found the Hospital much as I had left it.

Met some nice nurse from the Radcliffe on the Oxford train.

January 21

Sister told me this morning that I was going to London to see the C.M.B. on Saturday. To them I will have to make my plea to be kept in the Air Force. Gave some asparagus which had arrived in one of my parcels to the Sisters, also a tin of Peaches and Cream.

January 22

Went for a stroll this afternoon around the University parks with Jean, one of the nurses from the "Radcliffe." She seems a very nice girl, and, for some unknown reason, she is apparently fond of me. Going to London, first thing in the morning.

Got a letter tonight from Jean. She is keen.

January 23

Arrived in London about 10 a.m. Went to the C.M.B. in Goodge Place. Saw a Wing Commander there who, although very sympathetic, said he was afraid that I would have to be discharged from the services altogether. I kicked up such a row that they have arranged for me to stay in London until Monday, when Air Commodore Simons is coming down from Oxford.

Met Smithy, the Doc., Gascoyne and others at "The Cogers."

Took my bag (what a weight!) out to the "Chevrons" Club, where I have booked a room.

Met Paddy Druhan, who shocked me by telling me that "A" has gone for a row.* Don't know who was aboard, but I suppose Bulsie, Dent, Harry, Alan, Brad, Jock S., Roy Tucker, Moore, and Ricky's followers were lost. God! What a hell of a thing War is! Bulsie and his merry band were men. – Funny, you know, but for this business I'd have been with 'em. Paddy & Ron Mackie and I did a pub crawl, Leicester Sq. way.
*[Sunderland T9085 UT-A, a 461 Squadron Aircraft, went missing over the Bay of Biscay on 21/1/1943. The Aircraft took off from Hamworthy (Poole) at 1208 hours on an operational flight. The last and only signal from the aircraft, received at 1459 hours, was an SOS. The crew consisted of: Flt. Lt. B. Buls, Flying Officer H. Osborne, Pilot Officer J. Moore, P/O N. Dent, Sgt. Roy Tucker, Sgt. J. Gill, Sgt. Owen Filmer, Sgt. N. Hart, Sgt. Percy Evans, A/C R. Elrick, and Flt. Sgt. E. Bradley.]

January 24

Met Ron at the Boomerang Club, after Mass this morning, and we bussed it out to Aldgate, thence to Forest Gate where we looked up Les Bail's favourite pub, "The Freemason's Arms." Found it didn't open till 12.30 and had dinner while we were waiting at the local Police Stn's Canteen. The prop. of the Pub was pleased to hear from Les and we had a few jugs. Returned to Aussie House where we met Sid Miller and Bert Ross. Hadn't seen Herb since B'mouth days in '41. Sid tells me Harry, Alan, Jock, Ricky and Whitie are O.K. Bulsie had almost a new crew with him.

Glad to know Ricky & Harry are O.K., but Filmer, Hart and Percy Evans, who took their places, were good chaps. Trained to East Croydon from Victoria and met Paddy's host and hostess, – Gordon, Lorna and Emmi (a Swiss girl). Home to bed at 11 p.m.

HMAS AUSTRALIA SNATCHED AIRMEN FROM RAGING SEAS

LONDON, January 14 (AAP): The dramatic story of how HMAS Australia rescued the crew of a Sunderland flying boat from the Atlantic while an 80 mile-an-hour gale whipped up waves 20 feet high has now been disclosed.

It is told in "Coastal Command," which is the latest official war book dealing with this vital phase of the RAF's activity.

The Sunderland had been drifting almost nine hours in the full gale. When it landed it drifted so violently that the crew were terribly sea sick.

The Australia was attracted to the scene when it heard faint radio signals. The Sunderland then signalled, "Hurry, cracking up." The Sunderland disintegrated as the Australia came in sight.

The 19 members of the crew were bobbing up in waves as high as the warship's bridge, so 13 sailors went overboard, attached lines, and picked up nine of the airmen, who had been 50 minutes in the sea. The other separated by long, tedious flights, four members of the crew were lost.

Such dramatic episodes are often when the crews must constantly fight off boredom, which lowers the

efficiency of the patrol, perhaps enabling a U-boat or raider to slip by unnoticed.

The book states that the Coastal Command escorted almost 5,000 convoys, attacked 557 U-boats, and flew 55million miles between the outbreak of the war and September 30, 1942. The book does not specify individual feats, but it is interested in Australia and New Zealand, because so many of their airmen are operating

with the Coastal Command from the Arctic Circle to Africa.

The Coastal Command's chief enemy is not the Axis forces, but the treacherous weather, many good stories of which are told in the book, such as a hurricane which blew six Whitleys about an aerodrome although six 300 lb blocks of concrete were attached to each.

Fog and clouds – sometimes with a 700-foot iceberg jutting into them – are among the nightmares.

HMAS AUSTRALIA

"Telegraph" 15/1/43

January 25

Took my bags to Waterloo about dinner. Went from one doctor to another this morning; had about the same tests as I had when I first applied for the R.A.A.F. Told me at 12 to come back at 3. This was when I collected my bags from the "Chevrons" Club. Walked from Waterloo to the "Boomerang" Club where I had dinner and met Ron, Jackie Bell and Johnny Gamble. Went to the "Cogers", and Mooney's.

Back at C.M.B. and about 6.15 they informed me that they had altered their decision about me, and were going to keep me on, only for ground duties.

Caught a train for East Croydon and had a jug or two there then went out to Lorna's where I played Bridge (Three handed) with Gordon and Emmi until Paddy and Lorna returned from the pictures. Stayed the night with Paddy.

January 26

Came up to London about 12 with Lorna and Paddy. Had a coffee at Stewarts' Restaurant opposite Victoria Stn. Then took bus to the Boomerang Club where I had dinner.

Caught the 1.30 train from Waterloo and arrived back at camp about 5 p.m. Rang George Read at Orderly Room to let 'em know I was back.

Met Tubby and had a few jugs and a game of chess. Slept in Brad's bed at the Mess. Wonder if he's O.K. or not?

January 27

Called on the Doc. And told him the results of the C.M.B.

Saw Woodsie and he promised me some leave, but first I've been given a job which will last some days.

The Adj. was very affable and is trying to get me a commission. Was driven by him to Selsdown where I found Whitie packing and listing Bulsie and the boys' kits. It's a sad and rotten job.

Had a few jugs at the mess this evening.

January 28

Spent the day with Whitie on the job of the lads' kits.

Played a few games of draughts and had a few jugs at the Mess with Tubby and some of the lads.

Alan Mayne is in hospital but should be out tomorrow.

January 29

Still in the same job, but it's just about finished now. Should be over tomorrow. Took their valuables and personal kit up to the Stores and Orderley room this afternoon. Found my kit there too. Tubby came back about 9.30 a.m. and we had a couple of jugs. Have shifted to his room, now.

January 30

Went up to Orderley Room this morning, and saw Woodsie who gave me 10 days leave, which is a good thing.

Collected my pay and played Chess with Tubby this afternoon.

Got Tubby in the mood tonight and we put our first tune "East Wind" on paper. Tubby also composed the chorus of another and much better one.

About 10.30 the Group Captain called in and had a couple of jugs with us. Was very interested in our songs. Is a great chap.

Bought a jug of ale and Tubby and I played Chess till about 2 a.m.

January 31

Slept in this morning. Margaret gave me a late breakfast, and I went to High Mass at 11 a.m. Had about the best dinner I've had in the mess.

My train for London was due to leave at 3.17, and I rang Lorna and told her I'd be along after tea. She had invited me to stay with Gordon and her. Arrived at Waterloo at dark and had tea at Lyon's in the Strand, with some little Canadian A.T.S. girl I'd picked up somewhere or other. Said "Goodbye" to her at Charing Cross and finished up at East Croydon. Lily (Lorna) is ill in bed. Says it's the result of a hang-over plus 'flu.

February 1, 43

Emmi bought me my breakfast in bed this morning, lazy blighter that I am. Got up about 11 a.m. Day was wet, blowy and altogether English. Had a really restful day.

Hardly saw Lorna all day. She doesn't look too good at all.

February 2

The day dawned a little brighter than it has for some time, now, and I went to London, arriving at Victoria about mid-day.

Took 38 Bus to Piccadilly and had a few jugs there at both the little pub next to the Windmill and Mooney's.

Walked down Hay Market to Cousin's and thence to Leicester Square via the Long Bar.

Finished at the Windmill where I saw a show which was a bit better than usual

Home about 8 p.m.

Sunday Mail, 31/1/43

"Dark, massive, Squadron-Leader S.R.C. Wood, D.F.C., of Toorak has been appointed deputy-commander of an Australian Flying Boat Squadron formed in Britain on Anzac Day, 1942.

The squadron recently received the D.F.C. from the King, the result of a Bay of Biscay battle, in which it simultaneously engaged a U-boat and a Fockewulf deep-sea raider.

Squadron-Leader Wood should strengthen the new R.A.A.F. Sunderland Squadron which already has earned a fine reputation in Coastal Command operations in the Bay of Biscay and elsewhere.

Replacement of other senior R.A.F. squadron leaders by Australians is believed to be imminent. Squadron-leader Wood is the 13th R.A.A.F. member promoted as squadron-leader while serving in Britain."

February 3

Went out after dinner to get a haircut but found it was half-day. Struck on an old Qantas Pilot in a pub and he invited me to a hotel he owned.

Had a few drinks with him and his wife. He used to live in Hickey St. New Farm. Name – Fred Bohne.

Took Emmi out after tea and we went to the "Swan" and the "Blue Anchor." Both nice places.

February 4

Into London. Met Jack Bell and his pilot (Yank). Had a few with Evie at the Cogers.

Had a haircut, "Dinger" and the "Yank" went to a News Theatre in the Strand.

Had tea, then wandered up to Piccadilly, and thence back to the Cecil in the Strand. Thence to Mooney's over the road, and to the Strand Palace, the New Savoy and finally Charing X Station, where I caught my train home. Had argument (friendly) in the train re England and Aussie.

Home to bed by 10.30.

February 5

Got up late and after dinner made the acquaintance of a B.Y.T* at the Swan. Walked over the town of Croydon. Not a bad place. Am having a quiet night tonight. Lorna has just told me that Bill Dulley is coming down. Be good to see old Bill again. * [Bright Young Thing]

I remember drinking an ale with him at his house in New Farm on his wedding afternoon.

Later: Bill arrived about 10.30, having got lost. We are going to Lorna's sister's for the week-end. It's in Kent, and Lorna says I'll like it immensely.

February 6

Up early and by car with Gordon, Lily and Bill to a village where we caught a train to Tunbridge Wells. The weather was very bad and quite spoiled the scenery; from Tunbridge Wells, after a couple of jugs, we caught a bus which, after ¾ of an hour's journey, brought us to Goudhurst. The weather was steadily improving.

The couple of pots was having an effect (physical) before we got to G'hurst, and I just made it!

Stopped at the "Vine" for a few before going to "Hughenden" – Lorna's sister's place.

February 7

Went to Mass with Doris at 8.30. Lazed about during the morning playing the radiogram and reading. They have a marvellous collection of records.

Gordon, Bill, and the two girls and I visited the "Vine" for an appetiser before dinner, and after – (for no reason at all.)

Mary Philpott, (Gordon's secretary) arrived after dinner and she, Gordon, and I went for a hike. Saw some lovely scenery. Wandered through orchards and hop fields. Kent surely deserves the epithet "Garden of England." I'd love to visit here in the Spring or Summer time.

After tea we had a short session with Bill, Jess, his wife (another Doris), Reg and others of the villagers, all of whom went out of their way to make us feel "at home." I thoroughly enjoyed the day. Bill and I are staying till Tuesday when I have to go back to Camp, curse it! Bill is coming down next week-end, the lucky hound!

February 8

Gordon and Mary had to go back to work first thing in the morning. Bill and I slept in till 11 a.m. Lorna and Doris gave us our breakfasts in bed. Gee! They're great!

I wandered over the road for a quick'un. My discomfort in the bus last Saturday has resulted in the term "Gallageritis." I'll always remember Goudhurst, Doris and Mark. Met a Mr. J.P. Long, a grand chap, who is here auditing some company's books. A good chap and quite a character. He seems to have taken quite a liking to us. Had a few with him.

Bill, Lorna, Doris, J.P. and myself had a small party at the "Star" and the Vine tonight. Met the crowd again. I've never felt so badly about going back to camp before. I love this place! Paddy D. rang and informed Lorna that he and I had been promoted to F/Sgt. [Flight Sergeant]

February 9

Bill and Lorna and I left Goudhurst this afternoon. Had a few last drinks with J.P. and some of the boys. Felt very sad at leaving Goudhurst. We are spending the night in London and have put up at the "Norfolk" near Aussie House having been unable to get into the "Strand" A pretty crook place though 12/- per night.

Lily left us at H. to go to Sanderstead. Bill and I are going to have a few drinks tonight and then early to bed.

Later: Alas! For good intentions! We started off at the Cogers with Evie and then worked up Fleet St. and the Strand to finish on closing time at Charing X. Thence we went to the "Strand Palace" where we met "Dinger" Bell and Freddy Manger. The latter gave me a good tip which has filled me with excitement! He said, when I told him how mad I was at having to go back tomorrow, "why don't you ring up and ask for more?" Am going to ring first thing in the morning. Cookie is acting Flt. Commander so I should be O.K.

February 10

Rang first thing, but to my disappointment, could not contact Cookie. However I got him about 12.30 and Whacko! He told me I could stay away until Sunday! Oh! Lordie! Rang Lorna and told her my good luck and she is just as excited as I am.

Went to "Windmill" with Bill and thoroughly enjoyed the show. Rang Doris from East Croydon and she sounded very pleased, but told me she had a bad cold. Staying at Gordon's for the night and tomorrow. On Friday off to Goudhurst again! Wow!

Doris rang about 10 p.m. and tricked me by pretending to be someone else, the blighter. Is looking forward to our visit.

February 11

Went up to London and wandered around Oxford Circus and Bond St. Bought a record of the "Nun's Chorus" and a book "Seven Pilots" which is all about 10 Squadron – not even the names having been changed – for Doris. Bill and I gave Lily and Gordon a book in appreciation of their kindness and I thought I should give Doris something for putting us up and treating us so kindly.

Back to Goudhurst tomorrow and am I happy! Should be back in Camp now, but for meeting Freddy. Lorna, Gordon, Bill, Emmi and I went to one of the local inns tonight; met some friends of Gordon's – Wendy and Doug. – and afterwards Bill, Gordon, and I had a "yarn session."

February 12

Down at Goudhurst and "Hughenden" again where Doris received us with open arms. – Said she had missed us. Started off early this morning and arrived here about 11 a.m. by the same route as last Saturday. Gordon is not coming down until tomorrow.

Re-met all the old acquaintances and they were very surprised, and I think, pleased to see me so soon. Gee! I'm happy down here! Mark and his microphone are in great form. Also "D.D."

February 13

Had a few in the "Vine" with Jess. After dinner I met Gordon there on his way down. The others weren't expecting him so soon and I played a joke on Doris by telling her I had an old tramp outside who wanted a meal. She was surprised, though not fooled by me, to see Gordon round the corner of the house.

Had a party after tea. Also a few jugs. In the afternoon Doris and Mark took me along to Church and I enjoyed the walk no end.

I like Doris a lot.

Poor old Bill left for camp at 8 p.m. Gee! He was crooked. He has asked me to see Douglas for him re his transfer to 461 Sqdn.

February 14

I was supposed to be back at camp tonight, but said "curse it!" and decided to go "A.W.O.L." Spent the day with Gordon. We had a few at

Dinner and a last session at the "Vine" and the "Star" with Jess, his wife and the crowd.

Afterwards we went to Jess's place where we had supper of ham and some of their famous pickled onions.

Went to 10.30 mass with Doris. Gee! I'm sad tonight, Diary. I never want to leave this place. Think D. is pretty sad too.

Will close off now as have to be up very early.

February 15

Got up early. Said sad farewell to Lorna, Doris and Gordon and caught the 7.55 train to London. Mark walked to the Station with me to see me off. Good kid. Arrived London 9.30 and caught the 11.30 for camp. Walked around Fleet St. while I was waiting.

Nothing doing down here. Two letters from Molly, – Whacko! First for 8 weeks. She's lovely! Cable from Aileen signed "Aileen Moores." Great news! Never knew anything about this, but am very glad! Wish I were back at Goudhurst.

Saw film – "Jungle Book" with Paddy Druhan this evening.

Brisbane Truth   14/2/43

Fit and well again after a spell in hospital, Sergeant Air-Gunner Ed. Gallagher, of New Farm, has now rejoined his R.A.A.F. Sunderland Squadron, after ten day's leave, put in in Kent and Surrey. With over 800 operational hours to his credit, he expects shortly to be posted as an instructor, and hopes it will ultimately lead to his being transferred to Australia.

A number of Sunderland boys have already returned home, after having flown a million miles – roughly 9 thousand operational hours – in the Atlantic and the Bay of Biscay.

Letter # 61

From Bournemouth Poole, 1.30 pm. 16 Feb. 1943   2½-penny King George blue stamp. Rec'd. May 10, 1943.

AUS/405206, FLT/SGT GALLAGHER E.B., R.A.A.F., England

February 15, 1943

My own Darling,

Here I am, back at camp again, after the most glorious leave I've ever spent in this country. Needless to say I'm feeling very sore at having to return, but really, I shouldn't grumble, because I was due back last Thursday.

Awaiting me on my arrival, as you can see from the top, was my long expected Flight Sergeant's crown, and better still, three letters from you! A great surprise was the mention in one of your letters about Aileen. You said "after her wedding." This was the first I'd heard about any wedding. I suppose Ralph is the lucky man?

These letters and the few I got about New Year are the only mail I've received since November 5th.

My back has quite recovered now, except for a very slight twinge, now and then. I wonder how long it will be before I'm home, now?

You know, Darling, I should be heartily ashamed of myself for not having written for nearly a fortnight, but, to tell you the truth, I was so flat out on my leave that I never thought of writing, – which does not mean that I never thought of you! – You know, I did, all the time.

I must tell you about my leave. I went to a young couple who have a lovely house in East Croydon, and they treated me like a king. I have never been so spoiled in all my life! I wish you'd drop them a line, dear. I told them about you, and I know they'd appreciate a letter from you. The address is I G. Wilks, 60 Norfolk Ave., Sanderstead, Surrey.

I was never allowed to get up for breakfast, and they absolutely refused to allow me to spend any money. I was taken to a little village in Kent – Goudhurst, where a sister of Mrs. Wilks has a guest house that was built in the 16th Century. It is a lovely place. The sister is very lovely, too, but don't get jealous, dear, she's married.

The villagers took me to their hearts, and went far out of their way to make my stay happy; they succeeded so well that I refused to go back to camp when my time was up, and stayed a few days more. I've never been so happy since I saw you last, darling mine!

Re your letters: No, I haven't heard from Alice since I left Aussie. She owes me a few letters. And I haven't met Margot's boy-friend yet; I may run into him one of these days; I hope I do.

When I was in Goudhurst I went to Mass and paid a visit at a quaint old church in the village. Mrs. Wilks' sister is a convert and she took me along. Her husband is an R.C. – and a Sergeant in the army, somewhere or other.

Got a letter from Joan, too, today, telling me how happy she and Eric are. Gee! I envy them. However, I should be home soon and then we'll see what real Happiness is!

I'm a bit tired after my long journey today, so I'm off to bed soon. Please give my love to your family and the crowd, Love, and remember, I love you more than all the world.

Ed xxxxxxx

P.S. Love me?   Ed x

February 16

Went out to camp this morning. Nothing was said about my being A.W.O.L. Didn't expect any trouble. Met Snowy Couldrey and Alan Petherick and Lucky Long from 10 Sqdn. Snowy is only visiting but the others have been posted here. Also Tommy Egerton. Soon all 10 Sqdn will be here if things keep going this way.

Had a few with Snow and Paddy this evening at the "London" and the Mess.

February 17

Snow still here, but he went to his billet early tonight. The day was fairly uneventful. Tried to find out if we were to be paid our back money for our Crowns on Friday or not, but was unsuccessful. Early to bed.

February 18

Played snooker with Alan this morning and was in remarkably good form. Got several breaks of 25 and more. Poor old Al didn't get a look in.

Had another quiet night. Dot – the Flight Sgt. W.A.A.F. in the mess – is leaving Saturday morning. She was here tonight and is very crooked on having to leave. We'll miss her a lot as she's a very nice person.

February 19

Pay-day today, which was a good thing. I got twenty pound extra back-pay, which is a better thing. Banked eighteen pound and sent Bill the two pound ten shillings I borrowed last Wednesday. Cabled Molly and Mother. Wish I could get some mail!

What a dance at the Mess! Good Lord! Rang Goudhurst, just to see how things were there. Wish I were back there.

Went to the "George" with Terry Paget and a new arrival, "Bluey" Trotter, an electrician, thence to the "Sloop," back to the "George" and finished at the Mess at 3 a.m. Steve had a run-in with the Adjutant, who is apparently hot-headed after a few jugs. Col Steeley had filled his cup with beer and he wasn't amused (like Queen Vic.).

February 20

Rose at 11 a.m. with a lovely head! For-swore beer, but had a few with Bluey Trotter tonight. Got into a game of "Pontoon" and won a bob or two. To bed late again.

February 21

Despite late hour I was in bed last night, I got up for early Mass, then went down to "L." Met W.O. Dyball who asked me if I'd like a job in the W.T. Section. I agreed. Anything to pass the time.

Fresh Eggs for breakfast! – and bacon!

Visitors night in the Mess, but no-one there except Pam and I Kirke, and the two W.A.A.F. Sgts.

Bill Mabe has asked me if I'd like to take over the "L" end of the Flight Office. I think I'd like this better than W.T. work.

February 22

No mail yet! Wonder what has happened to the folks at T'ville. Molly is the only one who ever writes to me these days. Gee! I love her. Wish they'd hurry up and send me home. Have been put in charge of the Comforts here, and we're expecting a lot soon. Quiet night, with nothing exceptional. Have put on my crowns, and am pleased I have something to distinguish me from the erks at B'mth.

February 23

Took the afternoon off and went into B'mouth. Met Winkie Yule there. He's stationed quite near here. Saw a show at the Regent, – pretty good, it was. "My Sister Eileen," – Rosalind Russell. Gee! She's like Joan!

Went to the "Norfolk" and shot a line to some erks, and to the "Bath." Caught bus to Poole, where I visited the "Tatnam" for the first time. It's a nice little pub.

February 24

Poor old Curley Brill was recalled from leave, and returned tonight very sour with the world. We went to the "Tatnam," where I met "Bluey" Trotter, and a civvy. Have just left Blue who returned home to the civvy's place on his invitation. The Civvy is a nasty piece of work, I think, and I tried unsuccessfully to dissuade Blue from going. Jacko Jackson was here for a few hours today, having brought back Paddy and the boys of "K." Still the same old Jack, and he was as pleased to see me as I was to see him. I like him the best of all the lads of 11 Course.

February 25

Started new job in charge of the Flight Office today. Fairly interesting, I think. Something like Jack Forbes' in 10 Sqdn.

384

I went to a show with Bob Dibble this evening and saw two good pictures. "The Devil with Hitler," and Humphrey Bogart in some show or other whose name I forget. – Pretty good.

February 26

On new job again. Have the hang of things pretty well, now. There's not a lot to do.

Went to the "Sloop" and the "Shar" tonight, but only had one jug in each. Played "Slippery Sam" till 1 a.m., and won.

February 27

Worked all day on the new job. After tea met Mick Jackson, whom I last saw in Parkes, where he re-mustered to an observer. He has only just arrived in this country. I'm ashamed to say I was glad to find he is still only a Sgt. He was a bit put out to find Paddy and I are F/Sgts. I thought he'd be a cert. to get a Commission. Lord! He's insufferable enough now! How'd he be with a com?!

Met a naval officer from Adelaide and we had a session at the "Shar" and the "Sloop." Seems a good chap. I've given him the spare bed in my room for tonight to save him a long walk to his billet at "H."

February 28

Was unable to get to Mass this morning. Worked fairly hard all day, and tonight, went for a stroll round the town. Tubby is not back here yet, as there's not much doing these days.

Woodsie told me today that they were going to nip the £2/5/- I was paid while on leave for flying crew allowance, off me. Drat 'em.

Bournemouth Poole, 4 p.m., 1 March, 1943. One shilling brown stamp, and 3-pence purple stamp. Opened by censor 162. Rec'd 29.4.43 "By Air Mail Via U.S.A." in Ed's handwriting.

AUS/405206, F/St. Gallagher, E.B., 461 Sqdn., R.A.A.F., England

February 28, 1943

My Darling,

It will be your Birthday in three days, but for the third time in succession I won't be able to celebrate with you. Sometimes, when I think of all the time that people like Len and Sheila, Joan and Eric, and Aileen and Ralph have enjoyed together, – which we should have been able to enjoy too, but for this darned war, I get really down in the dumps. But though I know that the time we've lost has gone forever, dear, I'll try to make up for the waste, when I return; I thought, when I first left Aussie, that the fierce longing I had to return to you would at least be dulled by time. I was wrong; that longing has so increased, now, that it has become the only important thing of my life. I would do anything, – lie, steal, beg, or borrow – so long as it would bring me home to you. I love you so.

I just met an old Parkes acquaintance whom I have not seen since I left there; he has just arrived in this country and was able to give me the latest news re conditions in Aussie. Apparently the Yanks are not very popular. Strange how nobody has much time for them. I think it's because they talk too much and do so little.

I met a Naval officer last night, and he finished up sleeping in a spare bed in my room. This morning found us with lovely hangovers, so I've sworn off the beer again for good. I wonder how long this resolution will last. I've been given a job of work lately that keeps me very busy from about 7 a.m. so I missed mass this morning, as the first is at 8.30. I'll try to get along to Benediction tonight to make up for it.

The weather has been perfect of late; in fact, you'd think Spring had arrived. I wish you could see how lovely this country is just now. Only for the fact that you are in Aussie, I don't think I'd ever leave here if days were always as good as this.

The boys are outside my window, potting at clay-pigeons with shot-guns. The C.O. is there as well, and I see has just got five out of five. I must have a go. – Have had a go, and got three out of five, which is good for me. It's just dinner, so I'll knock off for a while.

Am at the Mess, now, – listening to the gramophone. Bing is just singing "Sweet Lelani," which brings me memories of home. Ann

Shelton has just finished singing "Nightingale," a pretty number. I must try to get a record of Donald Novis singing "Diane."

I'm ringing up the people I spent my last leave with, in a few minutes. I wish I could ring you like I used to on Sunday nights from Parkes and Evans Head. It would be more than a large slice of Heaven to hear your voice again, Darling. It used to be a wonderful thrill to hear you say "I love you," even when we were only a few hundred miles apart, and when I knew I'd be able to see you, and hold you in my arms in a matter of weeks or even days, you can imagine how I'd feel if I could hear you now! Gee! I love you! Please keep loving me, my dearest.

How are your Mother and Dad and the rest of the family? I hope Alice is well again. Like you, I have been worried about her. Please give them my love. I don't know if I told you I got their telegram at Xmas. It was very nice of them.

I hear that Brisbane is very much changed these days. The Censor tore out a whole page of your last letter, when you started to describe the changes, but I've met a lot of Brisbane lads who've only left Aussie lately, and they've given me most of the news.

Well, I'll finish off now. Please give my regards to all the crowd, dear. Pray for me, that I'll soon be home safe with you. I love you more than I can ever tell. You're the loveliest girl in the world, I adore you.

Ed xxxxxxx

P.S. Love me?   Ed x

March 1, 43

Same old day. Morry, the Mess caterer and I went for a walk down to the "Tatnam," and from thence went to the "Sloop," – quite a long hike. Won a few bob at "Pontoon" before turning in.

March 2

Had the day off and went into Bournemouth with Reg Bateup. Walked all over town trying to buy a fountain pen and a Gramophone Record. Visited the Norfolk and "won" a packet of "Lucky Strikes." Then had a look at the "Odeon" but didn't like the programme so I took Reg to play billiards, which I won.

Thence we went to "Wests" where we saw "Destry Rides Again" – Marlene Dietrich and James Stewart.

Afterwards to the "Central" where I met Mick Jackson, Dusty Miller, and a few others.

Home to the mess where I was in bed fairly early.

March 3

Work again – the job is fairly interesting, and keeps me hopping now and then.

Tonight I went for a stroll round the village. The days are lengthening out now. It's quite bright at 7 p.m. and the weather is lovely.

Molly's Birthday today. Been thinking of her all day. Gee! I miss her. I'd give everything I have, just to be with her, now!

March 4

Nothing to relate. No mail from home. Some from Lorna and Doris in reply to mine thanking them for the nice time they'd given me at Sanderstead and Goudhurst.

Rang them both. Trunks here are 1s/4 to anywhere in England after 7 p.m. Had a yarn. Gordon and Lorna have been down at Goudhurst, where Gordon did a spot of fishing.

March 5

Mess Dance. Another wild night. Doug Bowden, the Aussie Lieutenant, came along. He seemed to enjoy himself immensely.

Got pleasant surprise when I received my full pay today. It appears that I was deprived of the £2/15/0 when they paid me back-pay on my F/Sgt. Things are not so bad, after all.

Had a few with the "Doc" tonight, and he has just informed me that an order has come out, whereby I am to be sent back to Aussie, and given my discharge. Whacko! I wonder how the old G.P.O is doing?

March 6

Fairly busy day. No hangover for a change after a Mess Dance. Went down town with Les Eaton, Webbie, and Leo. Visited a few of the joints in High Street, and had a good night.

Ran into an argument with two of the Pongos on my return to the Mess. They give me the "horribles."

"E" of 10 was here today and I re-met many old pals – "Butch," "Happy" Adams, "Lucky," and others.

March 7

I'm becoming a heathen, I fear. Couldn't get to Mass again. Went to Benediction tonight to make up for it. Thinking of Molly tonight. Gee! I miss her.

Lorna rang me tonight to see how I was doing. Decent of her. Tubby came back tonight and we had one or two to celebrate.

March 8

Not much doing all day. Was kept busy handing out comforts to the boys. Hampers have arrived.

Doug Bowden turned up tonight and Paddy. Tubby, he and I had a great old sing-song round the piano. Played Chess until 2 a.m., and won. Made some pretty good moves.

March 9

Worked fairly hard all day. Rang Doris tonight and she has asked me to come to Goudhurst for the 48 hours leave I'm after. Think I will go. – Went out with Doug Trotter down High St., then along Wimbourne Rd. Had fish and chips supper and then to bed, – early for a change.

March 10

Saw Woodsie today and got next Sat. and Sun. off; also Monday by a bit

389

of engineering. Sure am looking forward to the week-end. Fairly busy in many ways. The C.O. held a parade here today and spoke well on the growth of this Station. I agree with him that it is the "Goods." Had a quiet night tonight.

March 11

Not much to write about today. Rang Goudhurst after tea and told them that I'd be down on Saturday.

Played Chess with Tubby and won two out of three. Spent a quiet night, and a fairly dry one.

March 12

Tubby and Maurice had decided on tonight as the night for our celebration, and although I am off the liquor, I couldn't let old Morrie down. About seven we set out, accompanied by Paddy, Jack Russell and Wal Mackie. First to the "Angel" where Tubby played a somewhat tinny piano beautifully, – thence to the little pub "over the road" and so on, – playing and singing at each one. It was quite a night, and we finished up with a grand finale at the Mess. Old Morrie is a good sort. Very genuine chap, and seems to have taken quite a fancy to me. Had a hot bath and shave before retiring, which should save me some time in the morning.

March 13

Arose with a bit of a hang-over and caught the 8.16 for London. Quite a good train and I was soon at the old berg. On the train met an ex-Aussie, who seemed a very decent chap. Had a couple of "Worthingtons" as a "pick-me-up" on Waterloo Station with him.

Caught a train at W'loo Junction for Tunbridge Wells, where I arrived about 1.30. Luckily the bus was a bit late, so I "made" it, and arrived at G'hurst after a lovely drive at 2.15. Was welcomed with open arms by Doris and Helen. Gee! I was glad to see them! Weather is lovely.

Tonight we had a dinner party and I re-met the old acquaintances from the "Star." – We went to the "Vine" and had a few jugs with all my old friends including Jess and Mrs. Apps and Reg and Charlie, etc. Gordon rang up today, and I hear that he is coming down with Lily, Mary and Phil and Kevin tomorrow for my birthday.

March 14

Went over to the "Vine" at dinner on way home from late mass. Met a few of the crowd. Then Gordon, Lorna, Mary, Phil and Kevin arrived from Sanderstead. Had a quiet afternoon, then, but after dinner the party began. I've never enjoyed a birthday so much.

Mrs. B. invited us into the back parlour of the "Vine" and there we celebrated until 2 a.m. – yet no-one was full. Jess and his wife were in great form.

I'm very crooked about having to go back to camp tomorrow. Darn everything.

March 15

Had final jug at the Vine at lunch with all the crowd. Phil and I had intended catching the 2 p.m. bus but a friend of Gordon's offered us a lift. At first he only intended taking us as far as Tunbridge Wells, but, in the finish we found ourselves in Bromley.

I'll never forget the drive! The chap was a mine of information and gave us all the history of the countryside, with its huge estates and ancient buildings as we drove past. The weather was perfect.

Arrived back in camp about 9.30 p.m. and felt very sorry for myself. Bill Mabe is away and Frank has been very busy.

March 16

Doris and Lorna were coming down here, next week-end, but as Paddy is almost certain to be away, and I heard today that I have to go to Southampton tomorrow to see a specialist, (the result of my persistent advocation of the fact that there is nothing wrong with me) – we decided to put the week-end off. I was in bed early tonight in preparation for tomorrow.

March 17

Caught 9.47 train for S'ampton, and saw the specialist (a nice chap) this afternoon. My journey "was not really necessary" as he only gave me the same as the others. – No Good! – I think I'll resign myself to the inevitable, now.

Anyway, I suppose it'll be good to get back into "civvies," and, best of all, – I'll see Molly again! Spent the night in S'ampton.

March 18

Arrived back in camp this arvo. Saw the Doc. And told him the result of yesterday's interview. He didn't seem surprised. I feel very crook tonight, – think it must have been something I ate this morning. Am off to bed.

March 19

Awoke this morning feeling terrible. Tried to do a bit of work, but finished off passing out, – just like a baby. Curley and Johnny Lewis carried me upstairs and put me to bed. Johnny rang for the Doc and an ambulance.

However by the time it arrived I was feeling much better, and refused to go in to dock. Was O.K. by tea, (having got rid of most of whatever was making me ill) and went to sleep about 7 p.m. – thus missing the fortnightly dance. – And saving a few quid.

March 20

To work this morning, feeling very stiff and sore, but otherwise well. Had a very quiet day and night. Read and played cards until about 10 p.m. and then to bed. Wish I would get some mail from Molly and home.

Bournemouth Poole 2   8.45 p.m., 21 March 1943,   2 x 1 penny red stamps, one green ½ penny stamp.   Rec'd   5/5/43. Letterhead: A.C.F. W.A. DIVISION. Envelope marked: KEEP YOUR MOVEMENTS SECRET

MOVEMENTS OF QUEENSLANDERS

(From C. H. Bateson.)

LONDON, Sat. — Sergeant Air-Gunner Bill Dulley, son of a well-known New Farm newsagent, has been attached to the Training Command ever since he arrived in Britain 17 months ago, and is carrying out training work for the Coastal Command.

FIT and well again after a spell in hospital, Sergeant Air-Gunner Ed. Gallagher, of New Farm, has now rejoined his R.A.A.F. Sunderland Squadron, after ten days' leave, put in in Kent and Surrey. With over 800 operational hours to his credit, he expects shortly to be posted as an instructor, and hopes it will ultimately lead to his being transferred to Australia.

A number of Sunderland boys have already returned home, after having flown a million miles—roughly a thousand operational hours—in the Atlantic and the Bay of Biscay.

Waiting a posting to the O.T.U. is Sgt. Pilot Jack Walsh, of Eidsvold. He arrived in Britain last November, and expects to go on Beaufighter night fighters.

"When I pass out of the O.T.U. I am hoping I will be posted to an R.A.A.F. Beaufighter Squadron," he said. "I would prefer to be with the Aussie crews."

Coming over here as an Ordinary Seaman under the Junior Yachtsmen's Scheme, Jack Horn, of Newmarket, now sports the single gold ring of a Sub-Lieutenant.

"Truth" 14/2/43

AUS / 405206   F/S Gallagher E.B.,   R.A.A.F.   Base   P/O Kodak Hse, London

March 20, 1943

My own Darling,

It is so long since I have heard from you, or from anyone else at home, that I am almost afraid to look in the letter-rack these days. I know there will be nothing there for me! All I pray for these days is to hear from you, and see in your own dear handwriting that you still love.

Contrary to a report in a Brisbane "Truth" of last December, which Les Wilson has just shown me, I have not been "fit and well," although it's true I'm hoping, though not daring to expect, that I'll soon be back in Aussie. As a matter of fact I only got out of hospital yesterday. Don't be scared, though, love. I went in on my own request, to undergo another examination to determine if I am fit for aircrew. It was a hopeless job. It appears as if I'll never fly again.

Don't be scared, however, my dearest, that you'll be marrying a crock, when I get back. There's nothing at all the matter with me except that I'm not allowed to fly again. So don't start worrying about me. I was only in the hospital for 48 hours.

I had a marvellous birthday, sweet. I Vinchill, who found out the date through Paddy Druhan, invited me up to Goudhurst again, and the

whole village helped me to celebrate. On Sunday I And Mr. Wilks and some of the boys and girls I know in East Croydon arrived at "Hughenden." The local innkeeper and his wife (who think the sun shines out of me for some queer reason) kept their house open until 2 a.m. – Lord, what a party! I Wilks gave me a lovely pair of leather gloves and I Vinchill presented me with two volumes of poetry. They are grand people. You know, darling mine, if I didn't love you, or rather, if you didn't hold all my heart, I think I could fall for those two young women.

As you can see, I'm hard at work again in my job as N.C.O. 1/C Flight Office! This is not a very onerous occupation, and suits a gentleman of my indolent nature perfectly.

It's funny, dear, but now that there is a distinct chance of my leaving this England soon, I have only just begun to realise how much I love it. It has grown on me, I think. When we are married, and have a little cash, I think we'll take a trip out here. I know you'll like the place.

That's enough about me. How are you and all the folks? I hope that you are all well. You can have no idea how much I have been worrying – not hearing from anyone. Last letter I got you mentioned Alice's not being well. I hope she is quite her old self again, long ere now. Please give everyone my love, and tell 'em how much I am looking forward to seeing them, and soon.

Hope there are not too many Yanks in Brisbane. I hate the breed, as does nearly everyone else. Even if they didn't talk so much they'd be futile. Of course the rabble they sent overseas are not representative of the true American. The Americans, well-to-do and middle-class, that I met in the U.S.A. and Honolulu, were very nice people.

Spring will soon be here in England, and I hope in one way, though in all others I'm dying to get home to you, that I'll see another English Springtime. I'll never try to describe one, they beggar description.

Well, dearest, I'll do a spot of work now. Please keep loving me, and praying for me. You are all I know that is worthwhile in this world, and, no matter what happens, I will always adore you.

Ed xxxxx

PS: Love me?   Ed   x

March 21

Busy day on the job. Met some chaps from B'mouth and showed them over "E." "Charlie" W/O – Played cards – "Crib" with Paddy against Reg and Tubby. Rang Goudhurst about 7.30 but they were out. Tried again about 10.15 and had chat with Doris. They may be here the week-end after next.

March 22

On Job all day. Started a new system, which, I think will be very good. Procured map of the Harbour and indicated positions of buoys. With different colour system of tiny flags I can indicate the position of each aircraft, whether it is S. or U/S and, if the latter, what is wrong with it.

Played cards until fairly late.

B.O.A.C. A/C went for Burton this morning. A few lads skittled.

March 23

Much the same as yesterday. Doug Trotter and I went for a stroll round town tonight, but I was in bed fairly early.

A few of the lads playing "Pontoon" attempted to draw me into a game, but there was nothing doing as far as I was concerned.

It seems as if a rift has occurred between Bill M. and his lady-love, – Pam.

March 24

Busy all day. Woodsie and Tommy Egerton seem pleased with the new system that I have inaugurated.

A few of 10 Sqdn Kites were here on detachment and I re-met many of the lads. It seems Jacko and the boys are all well.

Had a few jugs with old Maurice in the mess and played cards. Won about £1.

March 25

Same old hum-drum existence. Went into B. tonight and had a few jugs at some of the old familiar places. The days are getting very long, now. What a marvellous winter it has been! I have yet to see snow in this land, which is almost unbelievable. In bed early.

March 26

Went to a show with Doug Trotter and some of the lads after tea. Saw – at Regent – "King Solomon's Mines" (Paul Robeson) and enjoyed it immensely.

Had a few at the mess and so to bed. – Hope I dream of Molly. Wish I were home with her!

March 27

Nothing much to relate. Flat out all day and went to bed early after a spot of reading and writing.

March 28

Got to Mass this morning and felt very pleased with myself. When I arrived at my office I found that my hour or so's absence had passed unnoticed so I think I'll duck off every Sunday in future. The "daily statement" was a bit late, but I don't think anyone was very worried. Wrote some letters and played cards after tea. Tubby is away, so I miss my Chess.

March 29

Same hum-drum existence. Tommy Egerton is acting Flight Commander. Woodsie must be on leave. Put a few more quid in the bank. Went to a show with some of the lads today, after tea. Not bad.

March 30

News comes dropping. – Tommy Egerton let slip to me something today that I'm not supposed to know. – I'm leaving here on Friday! – Going to Bournemouth, on the first leg of a trip to Aussie! Whoopee! I'll be seeing Molly and the folks, again in a short time!   Cant' think of anything to write tonight Diary! – too excited.

March 31

Spent today trying to get my clearances from this station, as a new instruction arrived at camp hastening my departure by one day. – I'm to be in B'the on Thursday instead of Friday.

A whole new crew arrived today. – Seem a decent mob, and the old lads gave me a heck of a send-off tonight. Orderly room told me officially what I wasn't supposed to know yesterday.

Collected my pay 'n everything.

April 1, 1943

Got my laundry and shoes this morning, then Lance Woodlands and one of the lads took me to the Tatnam for a parting drink.

Lance helped me carry my bags to the bus. Arrived in B'th and spent much time and sweat and taxi-fares in finding where I had to go to. Got settled at last. Have to rise at 5.30 to catch train to London, whence I race across to Euston. – Tomorrow will be a busy day!

April 2

Arose at the offensive hour of 5.30 and caught train to London. On train met two other Aussies, Peter Henderson and Ken Creek, both on their way home. Got to London with just an hour to get from W'loo to Euston, and had to call at Kodak House on the way to get clearances and collect embarkation money. – Should have seen looks on faces of Aussies there, who were at the Post Office giving changes of addresses, when we told the official there to return any mail for us to Aussie!

Caught train at E. and after a lot of mucking about, arrived in B. [Brighton] about 6 p.m.

Have been put in a nice billet there.

Walked around B. tonight with Peter and Ken. It's a lively place!

April 3

Mucked about all day fixing things up at B. Poor old Peter's sailing has been cancelled and he is supposed to return to camp tonight, but has gone on strike and is waiting for tomorrow. Met Jack Culph, another Aussie on his way home. Had good feed tonight, – so much so that I hope I'm not ill from over-eating. This B. is the playground of England. You'd never know there was a war on here. Met some good N.Z.'s on their way home.

April 4

Found a little church and went to Mass this morning. Don't know how I got up after last night, – hardly seemed to have got to bed at all.

Fooled around all day doing nothing.

Bit of a pub crawl tonight, and got to bed fairly full. Gee! I'm excited! Think I'd be full even without a drop of beer!

April 5

News today! We're off at 4.30 a.m. tomorrow by train for a destination unstated to catch a vessel (unnamed) that's sailing Lord knows where.

Had a heck of a celebration tonight. Finished at some dive where we had chicken for supper.

Don't know how we'd have awoken this morning if the land-lady's daughter hadn't aroused us, so I'm blessed if I know how we're going to get up at four tomorrow!

Think I'll have to stay up all night.

April 6

Got up O.K. this morning despite my fears, and entrained for "G" [probably Gravesend] where we arrived this arvo.

Find myself tonight on board the "E" [RMS Queen Elizabeth]. Don't know if we're going to sail for U.S.A. or Canada, but sure hope it's the former. Don't like Canada, or its inhabitants!

Think we're leaving tonight or tomorrow morning.

April 7

Sailed today. Think this is going to be one hell of a trip. There's eight of us crowded in a cabin built for one! The air is foul, and there's more bull aboard than in an I.T.S. However, I'm on my way home! Lord how I've hoped and prayed and waited for this for 18 months. To see Molly again, Diary, I'd crawl back the whole way, so why should I grumble! The tucker is not too bad, however. – Rather good, in fact.

It's strange, looking over the side, and reflecting that every wave we pass brings me nearer to home, and everything that it means.

April 8

Life is very dreary on board. Nothing to do, read or write about. – The days are very long. Had a slight attack today, and am feeling very ill tonight. The sea is fairly calm. An old "Sunder-bomber" has been looking after us all day. Wonder if it's one of 10's or 461's – Don't suppose so.

Gee! I'm glad I'm here and not up in it. I can't express to you, Diary, old thing, how I feel, now that I am on my way home! I sometimes think I'm dreaming. But no dream could be half so good as this reality!

398

April 9

Still at sea. This is a heck of a voyage, despite the fact that it is such a famous ship. Nothing to do and all day to do it in.

Bought some cigars for Dad. Played Poker and won a couple of bob. Ken is in hospital with the 'flu.

April 10

Just another day at sea, but another day nearer to Molly and home!

Played cards. Had a haircut. Read a couple of books that I managed to scrounge. Fed up with this boat, – its stench and discomfort particularly. Are landing at N.Y., but Lord knows what will happen to us there. Hope we stay there a few days. Should berth on Monday.

April 11

Still at sea. No Padre on board so no mass. – Started a 500 School with Ron, Jack, and Jock. – Played and drank soft drink (as this boat is dry) all day. – Meals not the best. Have seen nothing of an exciting nature all the time since we left England. – But every day brings me nearer home. Wonder how everyone is there?

April 12

The grey Atlantic is still about us, – a little rougher last night and this morning than heretofore. Saw some of the great (?) U/S. Air Force today.

Can almost feel that Land is near. Should be in N.Y. tonight.

Expect will wake up tomorrow and find myself at the Quayside. Have been playing 500 and Poker all day.

April 13

Awoke this morning to find us at anchor in the Harbour. Lord! What a sight! Away in the distance I could see the Statue of Liberty and nearer on the Stbd. Bow the skyscrapers of which I've heard so much. Busy ferries ply back and forth, dwarfed by our size, filled with people waving to us. As the tide rose we upped anchor and about 2 p.m. were moored alongside the wharf. The next wharf sported the ill-fated "Normandy"* a sorry sight. Mad as hatters because we can't get off, and are not getting back our £10. About 6.30 staggered to a ferry which took us to Pennsylvania Station. Are ensconced in a magnificent railway carriage (1st Class) on our way to Canada. Glorious to see the lights of all colours blazing away. Have the urge to yell "What about that Blackout?" Have very comfortable bed which is being made up by a nigger porter, – very typical. *[During World War II, the French ocean-liner Normandie was seized by the United States' authorities at New York and renamed USS Lafayette. In 1942, the liner caught fire while being converted to a troopship, capsized and sank at the New York Passenger Ship Terminal. Although salvaged at great expense, restoration was deemed too costly and she was scrapped in October 1946.]

April 14

Awoke this morning and had breakfast of eggs, tomatoes and ham. – Played cards and looked at glorious scenery all day. Arrived at Moncton about 2 a.m. Had a good meal there of eggs, bacon and tomatoes. This is a heck of a place, I think. Real mixture of Canadian & R.A.F. – Baloney. Why the dickens did they bring us here?

April 15

Were mucked about all day getting needles jabbed in the arm, etc. Appears there is an outbreak of Scarlet Fever in this dump. Why the heck did they bring us here!

Had a jug or two at the canteen. (They have a wet canteen on the Station.)

Were paid £25 today.

April 16

Had a look at the Sergeant's Mess tonight and played a game of snooker. The mess is very well appointed. Tom and Bruce had a run-in with some W.O. who made disparaging remarks about Bruce's C.G.M.* No sign yet of our £10.

*[The *Conspicuous Gallantry Medal* was, until 1993, a military decoration awarded to personnel of the British Armed Forces and the Merchant Navy, as well as to personnel of other Commonwealth countries, below commissioned rank, for conspicuous gallantry in action against the enemy at sea or in the air.]

April 17

Went into the town of Moncton and bought several pairs of silk stockings and pair of slippers for Molly. No "Rayon" or "Nylon" procurable in Canada, though!

Wandered around all day; the town seems as much a dump as the camp, although we had a good feed for a dollar.

April 18

Mass at the camp at 9 a.m. Went into town after dinner, and wandered around. We're to get leave on Tuesday for a week. Jack and I are going to St. John (perhaps!).

Tonight went to a dance at the Sgt's Mess. Tom had a fight with some bloke who was a bit under the weather. Stupid of him. There was a dance on at which some of the B.Y.T.'s of Moncton attended.

Went to Benediction in town and unluckily struck a French Church. Tom wanted to walk out half-way through. The ceremony was very strange.

April 19

Got our £10 back today ($44.40). Jack and I have decided now to stay in Moncton instead of going to St. John, of which we hear no very good reports. Pen, Jack and I were going to stay at Shediac, on the advice of the Anglican Padre, with a Mrs. Gundary, but she was full-up. Are going to put up in Moncton at the Salvation Army Hostel.

April 20

On account of the bust-up last Sunday night, we have been forbidden the Sgt's Mess. Don't think this is legal, but don't care much as it was on the nose. Commenced our leave, today, but decided to wait till Thursday; – trying to arrange some place at which to stay.

April 21

Did nothing all day but have finally decided on the Salvo. Hostel in Moncton.

April 22

Put up at the Hostel this morning and very nice it is, too! Had good feed there. Pen, Jack and Tom and I have a room together.

Still amazed at the lack of Blackout. Wandered around town all day, and went to a show at night. Saw "The Black Swan" (Tyrone Power) at the "Imperial" (Shades of old Lutwyche!). Had a fair supper at the Hostel.

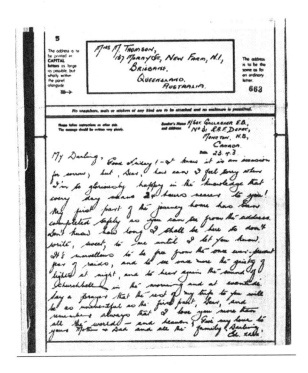

April 23

This is a good place to stay at! Breakfast is from 8-11, Dinner 12-3, and supper 4-11. Needless to say we breakfast at 10.50.

Today Jack and I went shopping. Bought some cosmetics and more stockings. They're a mob of robbers in this town. Have the idea I've been taken down the right and left! Hope Molly likes the stockings. I'm a hell of a picker and not sure of the size!

Am nearly living on eggs these days. What a contrast to England. Am getting a bit sick of them.

April 24

Another day of wandering. Tried to see the "bore" for which the Bay of Fundy (into which the Petitcodiac flows) is famous, but missed it. There is a tremendous tide-drop though. Pen, Jack and I lined up in the queue outside the Liquor Store and bought some hooch. Had a party tonight. Tom and Jock Pye are doing a bit of a like with a couple of girls, so missed the party

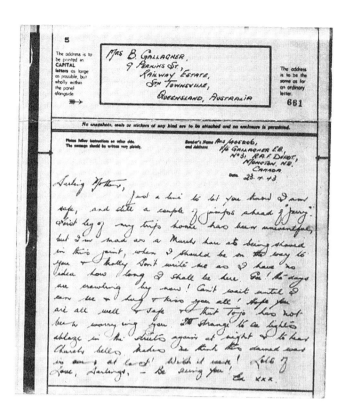

April 25

Had one of my famous turns early this morning and frightened heck out of Jack, Tom, and Pen. Came out of it O.K. but have been feeling terrible all day. Stayed in bed until this arvo.

These turns are getting more frequent. Will have to see the M.O. about them. I feel like a bit of Death wrapped up when I recover! Damn everything!

Went for a long walk with Tom this evening. Must have walked about 7 or 8 miles in all. Saw the famous "Magnetic Hill"* but like Queen Vic, was "not amused." *[Magnetic Hill, on the northern edge of Moncton, is an example of a gravity hill—the layout of the surrounding land produces an optical illusion where a very slight downhill slope appears to be an uphill slope.]

April 26

Caught a bus this noon to Shediac – just to have a look at the place. Were not very impressed until, walking down the road disconsolately, we were

403

hailed by a chap. He introduced himself as Alan Tate, brought us inside and introduced his sister and a chap named Stewart McDougall – the local chemist. Gee! The three are swell people! They have a few R.A.F. lads staying with them. Alan took us boys for a drive some miles (past I Gundary's) to a I, where the boys had a marvellous feed of oysters. Had a wonderful day!

April 27

Stewart called for Jack and I this morning and took us for a drive of nearly 100 miles through wonderfully interesting and beautiful country, on his business round. Altogether had a grand day. Saw Sackville where Mt. Allison 'Varsity is built, Amherst, and other townships and villages – all of historic interest. Met a lot of people who were friends of Stewart's. Back in camp about midnight.

April 28

Was pretty ill all day from another of those damned attacks. Beginning to fear all kinds of things wrong with me. Wonder if I have a piece of bone pressing on my brain? Drat that silly bump I got last year. Hope this is the last of the damned things. Don't want to go back to Molly a dratted crock! – I won't – anyhow!

April 29

Bit of a party at the canteen tonight. – Wrote a few sonnets to Molly, but thought none of them any good, so tore 'em up. Strangely enough, dreamt of Pat, Aileen and Joan last night. Hope they are all well and safe. Have palled up more with Jock Pye, Jack Culph, and Tom Rutherford, than with any of the others. They are swell chaps.

April 30

Slept and read all day. This inaction is driving me crazy! I should be on my way home! I've dreamt and prayed for over 18 months now of this – being on my way home to Molly, Mother and Dad and the girls and the folks, and this senseless stay in Canada is almost more than I can bear! I'm fed up! Not hearing anything from home is rotten too! But I've wired them not to write. It would be senseless, anyway – their writing. I may be on my way again tomorrow! (I hope!)

May 1, 1943

Strolled into town, and wandered around the shops. Had a few milk shakes. (There are no hotels in this province.) Home early to bed.

May 2

Went to 9 o'clock Mass on the station with Tom. Must go to Communion next Sunday. It's about time! This afternoon Tom and Jock and I caught the bus for Shediac. Stewart took us to his Drug store and we had a yarn for some time. Met Jack's girl-friend Marion and her sister.

Wrote Sonnet for the Tates with which they are very pleased. Have acquired the rep. of a sonneteer. Had dinner with Alan and Eleanor. Returned to camp about 12 p.m.

May 3

Nowt to relate. Cards and 500 all day. Drat this place!

May 4

Did nothing all day except read and play 500; but at 5.30 Tom Rutherford and I were picked up by Alan Tate, Miss Tate, and her sister and driven to Sackville.

Here we met a very pretty girl – Alan's niece, Ellen – and two young chaps from the Mt. Allison 'Varsity with whom we had a grand tea (Goose, etc.) at a lovely old inn called "Marshland's Inn." [Marshlands Inn at 55 Bridge Street in Sackville was built in 1854. It has served many visiting celebrities, including Queen Elizabeth II.]

Later we were shown over the Varsity and went for a stroll. Had lovely time. The Tates are certainly grand people!

To Friends At Shediac, N.B., Canada

Octave

I will remember, in the years unborn,

When Age has dulled my mem'ry with the glass

Of sweet forgetfulness – wide fields of golden grass,

– Brown carpets flecked with magic, when the morn

Smiles on the waking East, – tall whisp'ring trees,

Swaying their branches softly in a breeze

As gentle as a kiss, – and rainbow skies,

That cloak the western hills when daylight dies.

Sestette

I will forget those shuddering nights of fear,

When Heaven rained Hell, – and only will I hear

Your song-birds in the dawn, – and only know as now,

The soft-cool kiss of real-rain on my brow:

And, in the end, should Death's shade steal these few

Loved memories, – dear friends, – I will remember you!

May 5

Did nothing all day except play "500" and eat.
Tonight I had a session at the canteen and got mildly pie-eyed. Can't place too much blame on myself, though. This place is giving me the willies! Will go off my rocker if we're kept here too long.

May 6

Went into town this afternoon and bought some more stockings and sent a cable to Mother for Mother's Day next Sunday. Played a couple of games of "500" with Jock and Ron and Jack. Started off to go to the camp cinema this afternoon and was frightened off by the length of the queue. I got back from town by cab in time for tea. Have felt crook all day, with splitting headache.

Bit of a session with Jock and Pen tonight – but not much. Have just had a lovely shower.

May 7

Went to the camp cinema tonight and saw "Lady Be Good" – Robert Young, Eleanor Powell and Ann Southern. Not a bad show.

Bit worried about a uniform I handed in to be dry-cleaned last Thursday, of which there is no sign as yet. Wish we'd get away from this joint. They're treating us like A.C. Plonks. Am going to whinge like heck about it when I get the chance!

Had one glass of ale tonight after the show with Jock and Dave and the boys. Have decided to go to Shediac on Sunday.

May 8

The Uniform turned up, at last. Went into Moncton with Jack and Bruce where I sent a cable to Molly. Jack bought a suitcase and I tried vainly to get some laundry from a Chow. Had one or two jugs with Jock, Pen and some of the lads. Poor old Tom got very bad news from his wife in England. Rang the Tate family and told 'em we'd be down to Shediac tomorrow. Hope the weather's as fine as it was today.

May 9

Went to 9.30 Mass. Found a strange thing. There's Mass every day on the Station at 17.15! Never heard of Mass in the afternoon before! Must go along every day from now on.

Caught the Shediac Bus at 12 noon and arrived at the Tates about 1300.

Had a marvellous dinner of chicken. Mr. Tate drove us to witness an R.C. (French) ceremony. It was the blessing of the fishing boats. There, also, we bought some lobsters. Thence we drove through Shediac to a little Indian village about 20 miles away, where Mr. Tate brought us into the loveliest little Catholic Church I've ever seen!

Had a grand tea of lobster (or rather the others did.) They went to the Anglican Service and Tom and I went for a long walk.

We were very sorry to leave on the 2200 bus.

May 10

Nothing of note all day, except went to Mass with Tom and Alby this afternoon. Had a jug or two with Jock, Dave and the boys this evening at the Wet Canteen. Hear that the transient Sergeant's Mess is opening tomorrow or Wednesday.

May 11

Tom has been frantic the last few days over his wife and expected child in England. Learned today that the N.Z.'s are leaving tomorrow. We four Aussies are being left behind. Loud curses, etc. from us.

Tom and I went into town for a few presents to take home. Said Good-bye to the N.Z.'s over a few beers tonight.

May 12

Found today that N.Z.'s are not going till tomorrow, so tonight Tom and I took a run down to Shediac to enable him to say "So Long" to the Taits. Had a lovely tea down there and a long yarn with Alan and Eleanor.

May 13

Tom and the boys left today, much to their joy, but our sorrow. They were a grand crowd of chaps.

Jack and I put in for a 48 over next week-end, and are going to stay at Shediac. Visited the new Sergeant's Mess tonight and played snooker with Jack. It's a lovely place!

May 14

Could not go down to Shediac as intended tonight as received word from Alan that they would all be away at Sackville visiting a sick relative. Are going down tomorrow morning. Did some washing tonight instead.

May 15

Ironed first thing this morning. Bought a good fountain pen for Molly and then caught bus for Shediac. Met Alan and Stewart.

Played bowls with Stewart and had lovely tea at Cocaine. The boys had lobster and I had Ham, Eggs and chips.

Met Eleanor on her return to Shediac from Sackville, and then at 11.30 had another game of Bowls with Marion, Stewart and Jack. Had bad attack about 1 a.m. of my old trouble, curse it!

May 16

Managed to struggle up for 8 a.m. Mass at little French Church, although I felt terrible. Rested afterwards till 11 a.m., then Jack and I took Terry for a walk to the Log Cabin, on the waterfront.

Read all the afternoon and returned to camp about 11.30 p.m. very, (though pleasantly) tired. Had glorious week-end!

May 17

No news of our going yet. Spent a very uneventful day, and this evening visited the new Sergeant's mess and played Snooker over a few beers, with Jack and Curly.

Getting fed up with this joint. Sent a wire to Molly, Mother and to Lorna and the boys at Poole.

May 18

Had a very bad attack this morning which laid me flat all day. Feel awful.

Went to mass this arvo. Am very worried about myself. I'm lucky to have Alby Creek to look after me, when I pass out like this. He's a grand medical orderly, and a swell guy. He advises me to go and see the M.O. I think I will. Very shaky on my pins.

May 19

Went to the camp cinema tonight and saw a terrible show – Basil Rathbone in "Sherlock Holmes." Nearly went to sleep. Still feel not so good. Drat everything. Rumours that some of the boys may be leaving soon. Called on the M.O. today and he said to come on sick-parade tomorrow.

May 20

Went on Sick Parade and was shoved into hospital. Feel fairly well today and a bit at a loss on my back. Meals are pretty good and have a few nice sisters to look after me. Read all day.

May 21

Heck of a lot of excitement today! About 9.30 the M.O. comes round and tells me to get my things and go like billy-o as I was leaving M.

Collected my clothes, got dressed, then joined Alby and the boys who were waiting to be paid. Got $65, paraded at 2 p.m. and boarded train at 2.40 p.m. Alan, Eleanor and Stewart were there to say "Cheerio." Jolly decent of them to come all the way from Shediac. Grand scouts all of them. Even "Terry" was there. Stewart told us that he had a grand week-end's fishing prepared for Jack and I tomorrow. Almost sorry to be leaving, but Lord, <u>how</u> glad to be on the way home at last!

May 22

Aboard train travelling steadily south. Spent three hours in Boston early, and changed our Canadian dough into Yankee. Tasted best beer I've ever known since leaving B'ne. The beer taverns stay open from <u>10 a.m.</u> to <u>4 a.m.</u> It's a bit crook on Sunday mornings, for they close at 3 a.m.! Reached N. York about 3 p.m. and were wafted to Fort Hamilton* where we were locked in. Of course, this didn't mean a thing to us 15!

Jack and Ken and I were the first over the fence, and what a time we had! Found the Aussie sailors we met on the "Lizzie" and had a bath in their room. Wandered all over Broadway. Saw the Empire Bldg., into Carnegie Hall, the Aussie Club, in fact, everywhere. The subways are lousy. Will never understand how I got back to F. H., but know I lost Jack and Ken and picked up Alby and Curly. The most crowded day of my life! *[In the two World Wars, Fort Hamilton served as a major embarkation and separation center. It is located in the southwestern corner of Brooklyn near the Verrazano-Narrows Bridge. It is the only active military base in metropolitan New York City.]

May 23

Hardly seemed to have touched the pillow when I was aroused, flung (with my bags) on a truck, and driven to a wharf where we staggered aboard a tug. This wafted us to a liner (with the same initials as myself) and before long we were breasting the mighty sea. Found myself assigned a fair cabin and the meals are good.

Hate sea travel – too monotonous – though this trip is not so bad as heretofore, since I am on my way home!

May 24

Still suffering the effects of last Saturday night, but slowly recovering. Nothing but eat, sleep, play "bridge" or read.

May 25

Same as yesterday, – dull monotony, – but in the right direction.

May 26

One of my "turns," darn it! Alby was handy, though.

May 27

Feel "not-so-hot" – but recovering. Read and played cards. Saw flying fish, porpoises, etc. Thought a lot of home.

May 28

Deck games, reading etc. – nothing to relate. Much guessing as to time of arrival in Panama.

May 29

Same as the rest. Nothing to relate.

May 30

Sighted land this morning, and this afternoon wharfed at Colon. Surrounding scenery very tropical and very beautiful. Got ashore tonight and stocked up with cigarettes, etc. Saw over towns of Colon and Cristobal. Had great fun with Alby and Ken. Drank a few beers. Everything very primitive. A night to be remembered! Back on board by 2 a.m.

May 31

Pulled away from wharf early this morning and went through first part of canal. Very interesting and very beautiful. Reached a lovely lake*, part of way through, about 80' above sea level, and lay at anchor until night. After night fall we continued our way through the Canal, and I was very sorry, for much of its beauty was hidden by the darkness of Night.
*[Gatún Lake was artificially formed by the building of the Gatún Dam on the Rio Chagres]

June 1 1943

Out on the good old Pacific again for the first time in nearly two years! Never thought I would ever see this Ocean again, and now that I am on it, all sorts of worries beset my mind. It would be awful if I should never see Molly or the folks again, now, after coming so far! You know, Diary, looking back, I see that I never really expected to survive this War! I would never allow myself to dwell on the subject, but back in my mind, I felt that I had said "Good-bye" to everyone I loved for the last time. Now that I have really begun to hope again, I'm terribly frightened of everything that might go wrong. Please God, nothing will!

June 2

Cards, Reading, Sleeping and tons of Sea! Spare me from Ocean travelling! I detest it. Are making for N.Z. Wish we'd hurry up and get there!

June 3

Same as yesterday, except I chucked one of my turns! Had Ship's doctor and everyone there. However I recovered. The "Quack" has given me some pills and medicine to take; the medicine is b.a.! – Horrible muck.

June 4

Pretty crook all day, after yesterday's episode. Rested all day.

June 5

Read and played Cards. I think Alby and I must be the unluckiest "Bridge" partnership that has ever been! We NEVER hold good cards. I've never seen such a run of Bad luck in my life as we have suffered.

Getting nearer home – whacko!!!

June 6

Same as yesterday, except that for a change – Alby and I won. *Mirabile 412ictum!* The same old monotonous Pacific. Slight rain at p.m. for a variation.

June 7

Sunbaked and read detective stories all morning and slept on deck all afternoon. Played cards with Alby against Brad and Ken, but was soundly trounced. Every day brings us nearer home. Clocks are being put back 24 mins. Every midnight now. Must be going more westerly. Wish a miracle would happen and tomorrow would find me home. I wonder what Molly is doing? Missing me a bit, I hope.

June 8

Weather has been absolutely glorious, all day. Never seen anything better. Read, slept and played cards all day, as usual. Someone started a silly rumour today that the Huns had used poison gas on England. I was terribly worried for all my good friends there, but it turned out to be baloney. Roosevelt had merely mentioned in his speech what would happen to Jerry, if he did use Gas! And some glug had got it wrong. God! I hope it is never used! It would be simply terrible! I can't bear even to dwell on the subject. Surely Man will never be so inhuman to man.

June 9

Much the same as yesterday. Read, slept and played cards this morning, when I was interrupted by one of my damned attacks. Feel pretty crook as usual after it, and will be in bed early. Weather still good, but much colder.

June 10

Getting fed up to the teeth with this trip. Still feel rotten after yesterday's effort. Just as if I had a heck of a hang-over. Lay in bed most of the day. Played cards tonight until about 10.30.

June 11

Same as yesterday. Nothing to relate. Cards, sleep, and books. Am Duty N.C.O. tomorrow.

Brisbane "Telegraph" 11/6/43

WAR CASUALTIES

Flight Sergeant J.E. [Jacko] Jackson, eldest son of Mr. and I E. Jackson, 111 Latrobe Terrace, Paddington, is reported missing on an anti-submarine patrol in the Bay of Biscay. He was a member of the crew of a Coastal Command Sunderland flying boat serving as wireless air gunner.

June 12

Started off being Duty N.C.O. but was interrupted about 10.30 a.m. by another of those damned turns. Woke up at 11.30 a.m. in bed, having been carried there by Alby and Ken. Curse everything.

Weather very squally. Ship pitching and tossing like mad. Feel pretty crook after the turn, as usual and this lurching and bouncing is not improving things. Wish I were home. Have been thinking a lot of Molly and the folks today. Gee, I'm getting impatient to see them!

June 13

Weather still "on the nose." Ship copping hell out of huge seas! Only another week to go before we reach N.Z. Wish it were Sydney or rather Brisbane!

Find I'm not so liable to sea-sickness as I feared. Fed up with everything!

June 14

Barometer still falling and wind and seas increasing to gale strength. All deck games, etc. off. Seas breaking over bows and upper deck. Not feeling too good but not sea-sick. Read and generally rested all day. Getting closer and closer to home and everything it means. I wonder if I shall get leave straight away when I get to Aussie. I intend to put in for some as soon as is possible. Saw the M.O. today and got some more medicine off him. He says I must take things very quietly – not even any pictures!

June 15

Boat tossed like a cork all day and especially tonight. Never seen anything so rough! Some of the lads were genuinely scared going to bed. Slept like a log myself. Gee! This tub rolls. Sometimes it seemed as if the darned thing was going to turn turtle. Very surprised that I wasn't seasick, though must confess I was a bit squirmy. Wish this voyage were over! It was uncomfortable dining today. Sometimes all the dishes, etc. flew all over the table and some of the diners finished up in heaps on the floor. Hope this is over by tomorrow. Am getting fed up with this dashed weather!

June 16

Things still very rough today, though the gale has somewhat abated. Had a bit of a stroll round the decks today and managed to sneak a few minutes sun. Had a bit of a turn this afternoon and don't think this weather is doing me any good. Read and rested most of the afternoon. Went to bed early. Only a couple more days left for N.Z.

June 17

Got up about 6.50 this morning, and did a tour round the deck. Seems that the early rising hour has done me good. Played Bridge with Alby,

Arthur and Ken this morning. Funny, there's no tomorrow, or rather tomorrow's Saturday, not Friday! We are crossing the Date-line.

Loafed this afternoon and played bridge after tea. In bed early again tonight. Am I looking forward to about a fortnight from now!

June 18

This day has been missed right out of my life. It simply did not exist. – I might just as well have gone to bed last night and slept for 36 hours.

June 19

Went to bed last night (Thursday 17th) and woke up this morning. The day has been omitted because we crossed the International Date Line. Played Cards this morning and roamed around the deck. The day is gloriously fine, and the sea much calmer, though a strong wind is blowing. I bet the days pass terribly slowly until I am in Queensland again.

End of Diary entries

Flying Hours Log kept at back of Diary

415

Letter from New Zealand 28/6/1943, Postage & Revenue New Zealand 5-penny blue stamp with picture of Marlin jumping and Maori detail on edge. Opened by Examiner D.D.A. 107

EB Gallagher c/o I E. Pilkington, 157 Campbell Rd., Onehunga, Auckland, N.Z.

June 27, 1943

My own Darling,

Now that the time draws near when I will be able to see and hear you again after so long, I find myself in a perfect frenzy of impatience. Oh! Sweetheart, I love you! When I look back and count the days that have grown into months, and the months that have grown into years since last I was able to hold you in my arms, sometimes I wonder how I have been able to bear it! I nearly went mad, in Canada, when they held us up for weeks, and now that it appears that I may be stuck here for Lord knows how long, I'm beginning to froth at the mouth. If I could only ring you up, or somehow hear your voice!

Auckland has been very kind to us. Alby Creek, who is a friend I made on the voyage, and I have been made the guests of a I Pilkington who has been kindness itself to us. We've just got home from a drive all over the surrounding countryside. (She has a "Gas-Producer"* on her car) and our stay is being made very pleasant, but I wish they'd hurry up and send us on! Alby is a Corporal in the Medical Section, and he has assigned himself the job of looking after me. (Don't worry Dear – there's nothing much wrong with me, except this awful longing for you!) Alby is a good chap. He's from Adelaide, and he's been very decent to me. I don't know how I'd have got on without him. He's a very good R.C., too, and has made me stick to the straight and narrow. *[To address the shortage of petrol and rationing during WW2, Australian inventors came up with a conversion kit to run vehicles on the gas produced from burning charcoal]

I've had a marvellous trip, and some grand experiences to tell you of; incidentally, Love, I've managed to pick up those things you asked me to get; hope you like 'em.

I hope your Mother and Dad and Al and the others are all well. It will be great to see them all again. It's terribly hard to bear, not hearing from anyone at home, especially you, for so long! I hope the Cables and Airgraphs I've been sending from every place I've touched have all arrived safely. I wonder if I'll be able to get leave as soon as I arrive in Aussie? I'll go mad and bite someone or something if I don't! I don't know what is to become of me when I get home. I wonder if they'll keep me on as an instructor or if I'll be discharged and go back to the

G.P.O.? Frankly, I hope it's the latter. Lately I've begun to incline to agree with the quacks and the lads who have told me that I've done more than my share in this war. I have more operational hours than anyone else I have met who have been in England as long as I have, and I feel both physically and morally tired – washed out, in fact, and, I think I need a long, long rest! This spell away from flying that I've just had on this trip has freshened me up considerably, and already I feel like a new man. Only these attacks I have now and then – the aftermath of that darned concussion – worry me. But I find that if I take things very quietly, and keep right off drink or high excitements, that I have no trouble. I haven't had a glass of beer for months, now, and feel a lot better for the lack of it.

I hope all the Mulls and the lads are well. It will be grand seeing them all again. I can laugh at it all, now, Darling mine, but, when I left Brisbane that day, I felt that never again would I be coming back. It was a silly way to think, but I didn't give myself one chance in ten of surviving.

God has been very good to me. You and Mother must have prayed a lot for me. I shall have to spend the rest of my life being thankful.

Well, bed is calling and I'm a bit fagged after today's drive, so Goodnight, Darling. I hope it's only a matter of days before I can ring you (at least) and that you still love me, – because I adore you, – I always have, and I always will.

Ed xxxxx

P.S. Love me? Ed x

Epilogue

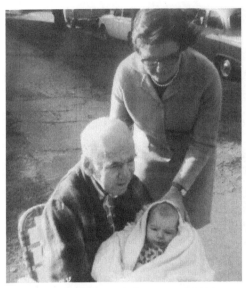

Ed and Molly with first grandchild, Luke Timmermans.

Ed married Molly on November 13, 1943 at the Holy Spirit Church in New Farm. Still with the Air Force, they first lived at the RAAF Station Sandgate until they built a house in 1947 at 23 Grays Road in Gaythorne, a suburb in Brisbane's northwest. They had three children, Bernard, born in 1944, Patricia (Tricia), born in 1946, and Ann, born in 1948. After he left the RAAF, Ed took a position in the Department of the Army, however, as time passed, the head injury sustained on February 20, 1942 resulted in more frequent seizures, and he eventually became a permanent patient in 1956 at Greenslopes Hospital, and later at Wacol, in Brisbane. As head injuries were a relatively new area medically, many experimental treatments, including electroconvulsive therapy (E.C.T.), were tried to reduce the frequency of the seizures.

Molly cared for Ed as well as she could, while bringing up the three children. He was 71 when he died at the Lillian Cooper Nursing Home, which overlooks the Brisbane River in Kangaroo Point. In his funeral Mass eulogy on August 16, 1986, Brisbane's Archbishop, Francis Rush, commented that he had learned from Ed's diary that he was a "very normal Australian, fun loving with a strong sense of duty and an acute sensitivity to all that is good and beautiful. He longed for the end of the War and his marriage to Molly Thomson. His gentle love pervades every page of the Diary."

Molly died, while still living in Gaythorne, on March 18, 1997 in the Holy Spirit Hospital, Brisbane, where she had volunteered for many years. She is buried beside Ed in the Pinaroo Cemetery in Aspley, Brisbane.

November 13, 1943
Wedding of Edward Gallagher to Mary Thomson
Brisbane, Queensland

Appendix

Various Letters to and from Family

Letter from Ed's Mother, Elizabeth (Lilly) Gallagher:

Railway Reserve,

9 Perkins St. West,

Sth Townsville.

14th September, 1940

Dear Ed,

   I miss you more each day. Poor old dad is no good about the house, all he is good for is digging holes and putting in shrubs. We haven't any window blinds up yet.

   I miss you singing around the house. I hope you keep it up.

   Longing to see you soon.

   Lots of love

   Mother xxxxx

Letter written by Ed to his father, Bernard Joseph Gallagher, who was the Comptroller of Railways stationed in Townsville in the war years—it could still (almost) serve today as a London travel guide.

AUS 405206 Sgt. Gallagher, E.B. RAAF, c/o R.A.F. Records Office, Gloucester, England

9/12/41

Dear Dad,

I've just had one of the most glorious weeks of my life! Words fail when you try to describe London; it simply beggars description. First there is its vastness. When you remember that nearly twice the population of Australia lives there, you get some idea. Try to imagine the heart of Sydney stretching over the whole of the area of Brisbane and you begin to get the idea. Jack and I were lost from the time we arrived to the time we left; only the courtesy of London's policemen, and the helpfulness of its citizens got us anywhere. It is so long since the last big raid, and so quickly has the damage been cleared that one has to go looking for it to find signs of the "invader." People go about their business as if their thoughts were furthest from war, and everyone is smiling and cheerful.

Repeated enquiries brought our footsteps to St. Pauls – one of Wren's masterpieces – built after the destruction of the older one in 1666 (in the Great Fire). We saw the graves of Wren, Nelson, Wellington, Reynolds, and scores of others. It is an awe-inspiring thing to walk through the Crypt, down stairs worn away by feet through the ages.

I can see this letter will have to be sent ordinary mail, or it will cost me a fortune.

Then we hopped on a bus bound for Trafalgar Square, and walked through the "Mall," along St. James Park, beside St. James Palace, to Buckingham Palace. Here we tried to sneak in, but were repulsed laughingly by a policeman, who told us the only way we could get in was by winning a D.F.C. or something. He yarned to us about the Raids as if they were portions of a Cricket Match. We stumbled on along Constitution Hill to Hyde Park, then retraced our steps along Piccadilly to Piccadilly Circus, where we ate and saw a stage show.

When we came out we found everything completely black. They don't know what a Black-out is where I am. London, in a pea soup fog, in a Black-out, is dark! – And How! – We bumped people and posts but our noses finally found a pub where we consumed a few jugs. This English beer is good! The Hotels open from 10 to 3, and from 5.30 to 11 p.m. – I've never seen a drunk in England. Of course, the usual "Ladies of the Street" were everywhere. "Stay the night with me Sergeant," is heard everywhere. Despite these charmers, Jack and I, with the assistance of many a "John" found our way back to our lodgings.

Next morning, at ten, it was still as dark as night. Another pea-souper! We began our campaign by calling at Australia House, where they made us very welcome and gave me a huge map of London. Jack and I decided to try to make our wanderings systematic, but later found this impossible. We just wandered where our feet and the buses took us.

We were sadly disappointed in Waterloo Bridge, made famous by the film of the same name; it was pulled down in 1924, and only a temporary structure remains, pending the construction of a new one.

We hurried through Waterloo, then across Westminster Bridge, by the Houses of Parliament and Downing Street, where we were stopped from getting too close by a friendly policeman, and ended at Westminster Abbey. You will understand my thrill, Dad, on entering this lovely building, when you realise it dates back to circa 800. It was intended first as a Mausoleum by Henry III. Here are buried all the Kings of England up to George II and all have been crowned there. All the most famous poets lie in "Poets' Corner." I could have spent hours there. Jack and I wandered through forbidden paths to a very old part, considered "unsafe." I saw an inscription "Dunstan" – the date was illegible. St. Dunstan was one of the Bishops of this church! I could have wandered round for hours, trying to decipher old inscriptions most of which were quaint, both in their remarks about the departed and the old English of pre-Elizabethan times. We saw the "Horse Guards," then made our way along the bank of the Thames, past Cleopatra's Needle to the Strand.

Fleet Street is a continuation of the Strand, and it is full of newspaper offices. I found it interesting to walk along. By this time it was nearly dark, and so we had tea, then wandered around in the Black-out, having an occasional drink at one of the many pubs, until we ended back at home.

On Wednesday, we set out early, intending to do great deeds. We started at Piccadilly Circus Underground Station, visited the Royal Academy then continued along Regent Street, to Oxford Street, and thence to the British Museum. Unfortunately it was closed, and all its treasures are stored away. We had dinner at some little old world hotel; all these hotels have lunch bars and drink bars adjoining so that you can order a couple of pots and your dinner at the same time – (like the old counter lunches in Sydney only more elaborate) – take it to a table and eat at your leisure. The food is generally better and cheaper than at the

Restaurants.

Then by bus to Marble Arch at the entrance to Hyde Park. We saw the "Serpentine", Kensington Gardens and its famous Albert Memorial, back through Rotten Row to the top of Constitution Hill, where we got a bus to Piccadilly Circus, where we carried out our desire to see a show at the famous Windmill Theatre. It was great. I don't think I've had a better time at a show for years – and Jack thinks the same.

On Thursday we went to the Tower, but found we could only be admitted with an arranged party. One of the famous Beef-eaters repulsed us with dignity, so we walked around the huge moat and across Tower Bridge which was obligingly raised to allow a steamer to pass.

We saw, however, just across from the tower the place where so many of our famous people parted company with their heads. It was strange to smoke a cigarette on the spot where Charles and many of his friends "bared their necks for the blow" and to tread the same worn cobblestones. Its claim to fame, now, is that it is one of those places (like the Sydney Domain) where half-wits spruik to an amused audience. We saw the Royal Mint, then walked through Eastcheap, Cannon St., and Ludgate Hill, to Fleet Street, where some obliging old chap picked us up in a huge limousine and drove us along Fleet Street and thence half round London. He was a great old chap – (I suspect he is Sir Something Somebody) and he pointed out some very interesting parts which I now forget as I had no time to take my usual notes. I remember Regents Park, Euston, Marylebone Station, Primrose Hill and Lords!

Excuse the break, Dad, but some of the boys dropped in and dragged me out for a night-cap. – They have just got the news that we are to get leave for seven days again!! From 22nd to 29th December I am to go to Lady Someone or other's place (of course they would forget the name!) with Jack Jackson and Arthur Smiles and the place is somewhere in Devon. I hope we don't repeat the performance of some of the boys who were put up by wealthy people during the week we went to London. They went out shooting, but saw no ducks until on the way home. They blazed away, but on returning, found they'd shot the tame ducks belonging to the house! Let no more be said!

Where am I in London? Oh! Yes! On Friday we saw over Madame Tussauds. It was an interesting and informative tour. I think we spent four hours going over it, and, even then we only saw about half because it was burnt out during a raid. I saw Don Bradman, looking extraordinarily life-like in wax. The Chamber of Horrors is breathtaking. All the most horrible tortures, and middle-age and 18th and 19th century executions are portrayed there in the most life-like forms. I, and you, especially, could write the world's best thriller there. No one is supposed

424

ever to have spent a night there alone. Fortified by some of the best Bass, Jack and I offered to take on the bet, but were refused! Thank heavens!

Soho is London's Kings Cross. It is full of the world's most famous night clubs. Jack and I, mainly for the experience, visited one or two, found all tame, and went home to bed, fairly early. On Saturday morning we raced up to Australia House early and managed to get included in a tour of the Tower of London. Gee! Dad! I wish you'd have been with me, instead of Jack. Jack is a good pal, but not the kindred spirit that you are. We'd have laid the plot of many a good yarn there. First we were received by a Beef-eater, in all his finery, then conducted across the "Byward Gate" – (i.e. across the moat) and saw how the gate (the porticullis) falls.

Just across the moat is an excavation made to allow people to see the foundations laid by the Romans about the first century! – It seemed strange to me, Dad, to know I was treading the same ground that Roman Centurions once trod. Just above us was the famous Bloody Tower, and the room in which Queen Elizabeth had been kept during the last years of the reign of her sister – Mary – I don't know whether you can grasp the feeling of awe, I felt when I knew I was treading the same ground her feet had trod, – maybe I had touched the same corner stone as Elizabeth – or Raleigh, or Anne Boleyn.

I saw the room and the chapel dedicated (in a fit of remorse) to Thomas A'Beckett by Henry VII (????) – my history is a bit onkus. – I saw the last burial place of all the people executed on Tower Green, – Anne Boleyn, – Jane Grey, – Essex, – saw the Wakefield Tower where the Crown Jewels were kept and followed the route taken by Colonel Blood when he swiped them. – Dad! I'll have to see you to tell you all the things I saw, and to make you feel the awe I felt. English novelists and poets are second rate! – If I had the opportunity of spending time in places such as this, I could write poetry and books that would thrill the world – and no kidding! Gosh! Dad! – the plots that came to my mind, and the atmosphere!

You and I must spend six months in London when this war is over, even if we have to beggar ourselves to do it, – so long as we leave Mother and the girls O.K. I'd live on 10 shillings a week to have the opportunity of seizing upon this atmosphere, to write. You know, Dad! I still have that feeling – maybe, if I have the time, and the leisure, during this war, I'll write something worthwhile! After our visit – (it's hard to stop writing about it, Dad, but I realise I'd need a thousand pages before I started) we wandered round Piccadilly again. We were determined to have have one drink at the Ritz before leaving London, so, bold as brass, we sauntered in, dodged hangers-on, etc., who wanted to either throw us out, or take our coats, and found ourselves in the midst of gilded

425

aristocracy. Making our way to the bar, Jack, in an Oxford Accent, asked for beer!!!! Imagine the horrified looks. None being forthcoming, to cover this unfortunate lapse, I said, "Two Black and Whites, please!" I produced a Five pound note (the last) and tipped the barman two shillings. After we'd consumed these at leisure, Jack, producing another five pound, ordered two more, and tipped the awe struck waiter another two shillings. Everyone was happy.

Next day saw us reluctantly catch our train for "home." I'd like to spend years in London, Dad – with you. We'd visit all the places we've read so much about – catch the "Victoria 9:30" (remember that book?) – cross "Waterloo Bridge" – do everything we ever wanted to do (and we could, in London) and come home, (and with Mollie to take down in Shorthand and type) and write Best-Sellers by the dozen. Gee! I missed you in London!

Lots of love, Dad, and give Mother and Mollie and Rita a special hug and kiss from me, – I miss you all, much more than I can say. Pray for me, and get Uncle Ed to pray for me.

Lots of love, Ed.

Letter from Ed's younger sister, Mollie, on the birth of his son, Bernard.

9 Little Perkins Street, W., Railway Reserve, South Townsville. N.Q.

11th *October, 1944.*

Darling Eddie and Molly,

You have no idea how thrilled we all are up this way. Dad and Mother are feeling very proud and pleased, and we can get anything we want just by calling them "Grand-dad" or "Grand-Mother".

How are you, Molly? I bet you're feeling very happy. I'd give anything to be down in Brisbane at this moment.

We had some boys out home on Tuesday night and Dad and they celebrated the arrival of his Grand-son. They got through a bottle of gin and were very happy, at least until the next morning.

Is Molly's mother still with you? It must have been a relief to Molly to have her with her.

What are you going to call the son and heir? Is it going to be Francis as Molly wanted? Dad and Mother rather like Kevin John. I like Terry. Don't you think Terry Gallagher would sound super? Rather Irish, though.

Mother is going to book a call through to you tonight, I think but we are a bit dubious about when to ring. Hope we can make it.

I have been working for a week now, and I rather like it. Not much work at the moment of writing, so I am making use of the opportunity and sending you this note.

Pardon the typing but I am working with my head cocked over my shoulder all the time in case anyone spots me.

Take care of yourself, all three of you, and once more congratulations, and very many thanks for making me an Aunty. I love it.

Lots of love to you both from

Mother, Dad, Rita and Mollie.

427

Home

16.10.44

Darlingest Angel,

Gee! I adore you! – But ain't I a Glom! – I've never even heard of it, (and if I had heard of it I'd have laughed like hell!). Fancy contracting Mumps!!! (of all things) while your wife's producing the son and heir! Oh Lord! I'll never live down the disgrace if I live to be age of Nestor. I'll be afraid to show my head anywhere; pointing fingers will follow me everywhere and sneering voices will chant "There goes fat-face Gallagher, – you know – the bloke who caught the Mumps when his son was born!"

Speaking of fat faces, mine's like a damn balloon; – and it's as sore as billy-o! When you joked about husbands being put to bed with Neuritis when the wife was confined, I bet you never visualised this! – nor did I. No more kids if this is what happens every time.

I called on Gril Shelshear on Sunday morning but he only agreed that I was suffering from a strained ligament, – the result of my "turn" on Friday. It was so darned sore on Sunday night that I went to the Ambulance this morning. The chap there said it looked more like a swollen gland than a ligament and advised me to call on the "Quack" at Rosemount – as soon as possible. This I did and was informed that I had "Mumps"! – Wouldn't it???

As the Rosemount bloke couldn't treat me I called in on Guy Shelshear on the way home (never again) and was given a prescription and fourteen days off work. So here I am in bed, being bullied by your Mother, and nearly going crazy because I can't go in to see you and the little bit of loveliness. Gosh! I'm unlucky! And, Darling, I miss you terribly.

Your letter that I got yesterday was wonderfully cheering. I'm looking forward to the next one. I nearly go dotty, lying here, wanting awfully to be with you. Even when you've finished with the Hospital, though, I'll have to keep out of your road until all traces of these damn things have gone. Which reminds me I've given Mother instructions not to go too close to you or the little fellow. She told me that Jean had what she thinks were "Mumps" just before she came up here. I've threatened to screw Mum's neck if it was she I caught them off. To tell the truth, I don't know who else it could be, especially if Jean had them! So don't take any risks, Angel. –

Poor old Mum is downstairs stuck into the washing at the

moment. She just came up to deliver a few curses on the dusty North-easter that's howling.

Mr. Conlon called in and we had quite a long chat yesterday evening. (I began this letter last night and am continuing this morning. – This may explain some of its disjointedness.) He's a very decent chap. It's rotten, though, this missing you two, so much. Three letters arrived yesterday – I had intended bringing them to you yesterday afternoon, after my visit to Rosemount. But the Doc's diagnosis put the Kybosh on that, – though he did say that "Mumps" are not so awfully infectious.

Well, I'd better shut up. I could ramble on for hours and hours. Give "his Nibs" a kiss for me, Love, and miss me a lot. I love you more than all the world, and I miss you more (Oh! Much More!) than I would Heaven.

> *I adore you,*

> *Ed. Xxxxx*

X (One (<u>No</u> <u>Germs</u>) for "B.")

P.S. Love me?

> *Ed X*

Ed's children

Tricia, Ann, and Bernard as teens — at about the age when Ed was hospitalized permanently. They grew up at 23 Grays Road, Gaythorne, and went to school at Mitchelton Convent School, and St. Joseph's College, Gregory Terrace, and All Hallows School, in Brisbane.

Bernard is the parish priest at St. Mary's Church, Beaudesert, Queensland, Tricia (Timmermans) has three children (Luke, Mary-Louise and Daniel) and lives in Victoria, British Columbia, Canada, and Ann (O'Rourke) has seven children (Kate, Meg, Liam, Joanne, Tom, Claire and Sarah) and lives in St. Lucia, Brisbane.

Background Airforce History

When war was declared in 1939, approximately 450 Australian pilots were serving with the Royal Air Force (RAF) in the United Kingdom (UK). Personnel from No 10 Squadron, Royal Australian Air Force (RAAF) were en route to the UK to take delivery of nine Short Sunderland flying boats. They remained in Britain for the duration of the War operating with RAF Coastal Command; they earned an outstanding reputation.

Representatives of Great Britain, Canada, Australia and New Zealand reached agreement at Ottawa, Canada, on 27 November 1939 to participate in the Empire Air Training Scheme (EATS). This project was to train aircrew for service with the Royal Air Force. For the Aussies, basic training was completed in Australia before undertaking advanced training in Canada. Six hundred and seventy four personnel also received training in Rhodesia (now Zimbabwe) before service with the RAF.

The first 34 Australians graduated from RAAF Service Flying Training Schools on 18 November 1940, with a further 37,000 aircrew eventually trained in Australia. To meet their commitment, the RAAF established two Air Navigation Schools, 3 Air Observers Schools, 3 Bombing and Gunnery Schools, 12 Elementary Flying Training Schools, 6 Initial Flying Training Schools and 8 Service Flying Training Schools. In addition, 7 Schools of Technical Training and other specialised technical schools were established to train ground crews in the maintenance of aircraft and equipment.

Source: Royal Australian Air Force History: www.airforce.gov.au

10 Squadron

Number 10 Squadron was formed at Point Cook, Victoria on 1 July 1939. A contingent of officers and airmen immediately proceeded to Great Britain to collect the squadron's Short S25 Sunderland Mk 1 flying boats. The aircraft were to be used for reconnaissance duties along the eastern seaboard of Australia. After the outbreak of World War Two, and in response to a request from the Dominions Office, the Australian Government agreed to leave the contingent and its aircraft in the UK. A further contingent of men were sent from Australia and, in November 1939, No. 10 Squadron became the first RAAF Unit (and the first Commonwealth Squadron) to commence active service in the war. The Squadron operated from RAF Stations Pembroke Dock and Plymouth until October 1945 when it disbanded. 10 Squadron reformed in Townsville to operate GAF Lincoln aircraft, conducting maritime surveillance and later also search and rescue across the north of Australia

Source:http://www.airforce.gov.au/raafmuseum/research/units/10sqn.htm

461 Squadron

461 Squadron formed in England in April 1942 (on ANZAC Day). Patrols commenced in July, and by September eight German U-boats had been attacked with several of the submarines sustaining damage. By May 1943, a Squadron Sunderland sank the first of what were to be many U-boats destroyed during the year.

The threat posed to the slow flying Sunderlands from agile enemy fighters led 461 Squadron ground staff to modify their Sunderlands with twin gun nose turrets and galley mounted machine guns. These modified aircraft were known as flying hedgehogs by their German adversaries, and were to prove so effective that they were later adopted throughout the RAF.

One of 461 Squadron's modified Sunderland's was attacked by eight Ju88 fighters over the Bay of Biscay. In the epic battle which followed, three fighters were destroyed, and the remainder forced to abandon the combat with damage. The bullet riddled flying boat, with five wounded crewmen on board limped to the Cornish Coast and made a force landing in the shallows.

1944 saw 461 Squadron operating in a new role – that of night strike using radar equipment and 'leigh' lights. As well as this role, anti-submarine patrols remained the most important activity, with the squadron sinking three more submarines in 1944.

By 1945 the Sunderlands had been fitted with sonobuoy submarine detection equipment, however, even with this new technology, German U-boats remained difficult to detect. In the last six months of the war the squadron was unable to add to its tally of German submarines. 461 Squadron disbanded at Pembroke Dock on 20 June 1945.

Source:
http://www.airforce.gov.au/raafmuseum/research/units/461sqn.htm

An Interesting Coincidence
According to rafcommands.com, No. 461 Squadron is known for one of the strange coincidences of the war. On 30 July 1943, the crew on Sunderland U/461 sank U-Boat U-461.

Dr.   CASH ACCOUNT AND BILL BOOK.   Cr.

Date	Where	Day		Night		Date	Where	Day		Night	
								Hrs	Min	Hrs	
	Bt./Fwd.	279	20	101	55	461 Sqdn		393	20	127	
16.4.42	Bombing	2	50				Bt. Fwd	393	20	127	
"	Gunnery	3	45			29.5.42	Mt.B-P.D.	1	00		
17.4.42	"	3	15			"	P.D-MtB	1	20		
18.4.42	P.D-MtB&Nav	7	30			30.5.42	MtB-Scillis	1	00		
19.4.42	A/Sub Sweep	9	05	2	05	" Scill-MtB	1	00		
22.4.42	MtB-Gib.	10	20			31.5.42 Nav. Ex.	5	55		
23.4.42	Gib-MtB	7	00	3	45	4.6.42 " "	7	50		
13.5.42	A/S Strike	8	15	3	15	5.6.42 MtB-P.D.	1	40		
15.6.42	Test Flip	1	05			" Ngt. C&B.	—	—	5	45
16.5.42	A/Ship Strike	8	40	2	20	6.6.42 C&B.	1	15		
19.5.42	Test Flip	1	35			" Ngt. C&B	0	15	6	15
20.5.42	Convoy	8	10	4	40	7.6.42 " "			5	00
21.5.42	C. and B.	3	55			8.6.42 P.D-MtB	0	55		
22.5.42	A/S Sweep	8	15	3	15	10.6.42 MtB-P.D.	1	40		
23.5.42	C and B.	2	05			" Ngt. C&B	·	05	6	10
24.5.42	Convoy	10	50			12.6.42 Test Flip	1	40		
26.5.42	A/S Patrol	6	20	5	20	" C&B	2	20		
27.5.42	Test Flip	0	20			8.6.42 Ngt C&B			4	20
"	" "	1	05			15.6.42 Gunnery	3	45		
28.5.42	A/S Patrol	9	40	1	20	16.6.42 Test Flip	1	40		
28.5.42	Was Last					" Ngt C&B.			3	45
	Trip with 10 Sqdn.					17.6.42 A.B-P.D.	0	50		
	Total English Flng.					" P.T MtB	1	25		
	Hours to Date.	393	20	127	55	20.6.42 MtB-P.D	1	30		
	Total Ops Hrs.	295	35	124	15	22.6.42 Bombing	3	05		
	No Ops Sorties	36				" Gunnery	3	30		
	Grand Total:- (with Aust Hrs.)	443	40	127	55	23.6.42 "	3	25		
						" Bombing	2	50		
						24.6.42 "	2	05		
	C./Fwd —	393	20	127	55	C/Fwd.	446	20	159	10

Flying Log

433

Dr. CASH ACCOUNT AND BILL BOOK. Cr.

Date	Where	Day Hrs	Day Min	Night Hrs	Night Min	Date	Where	Day Hrs	Day Min	Night Hrs	Night Min
	Br/Fwd	446	20	159	10		Br/Fwd	597	50	164	50
14.6.42	Gunnery	3	40			5/8/42	Testing	2	15		
15.6.42	"	2	50			6/8/42	Rescue	9	30	1	40
"	Bombing	2	55			9/8/42	A/S/P.	11	20	1	20
16.6.42	"	3	10			10/8/42	C+B.	2	15		
"	Gunnery	3	00			11/8/42	A/S/P	8	40	3	35
17.6.42	P.D-MTB.	1	05			13/8/42	"	12	10		
5.7.42	Belfast-P.D.	3	50			14/8/42	C+B.	3	15		
7.7.42	Test at P.D	1	20			28/8/42	A/S/P	9	40	2	05
"	P.D-MTB.	1	35			"	P.D-MTB	1	60		
8.7.42	Rescue	10	35			29/8/42	MTB-Gib	11	00		
9.7.42	MTB-P.D.	1	55			30/8/42	Med.	9	15	1	40
11.7.42	Test at P.D.	3	20			31/8/42	Gib-MTB	10	55		
"	U/S Stood Inn.	0	40			1/9/42	A/Ship Str.	11	15		
14.7.42	P.D-MTB	1	25			3/9/42	A/S/P	11	40	1	00
"	Test. U.T.A.	1	00			5/9/42	A/Ship St.	11	15	2	30
15.7.42	A/S/P.	13	20			6/9/42	MTB-P.	1	45		
16.7.42	"	12	55			10/9/42	Test Stran.	2	20		
16.7.42	Test Fair	2	00			"	Stran-P.	4	20		
18.7.42	A/S/P.	12	50			12/9/42	A/S/P.	10	05	2	10
20.7.42	Convoy.	13	10				Total Hrs				
22.7.42	A/S/P.	8	25	4	30		in England	742	35	180	50
23.7.42	Testing	3	05				Hrs. in Aust.	50	20		
24.7.42	Aboard A/S/P	3	55				Grand Total	792	55	180	50
26.7.42	A/Ship/Str	11	45				Ops. Hrs 461Sq	237	20	21	40
30.7.42	Test.	1	10				Ops Hrs 10 Sqd	295	35	124	15
31.7.42	A/Sub/Str	11	50				Non Op 461 Sq	111	55	31	15
1.8.42	C+B	2	55				Non Op 10 Sq	97	45	3	40
3.8.42	A/S/P.	11	50	1	10		Eng. Total	742	35	180	50
	C/Fwd.	597	50	164	50		No. Op Sort. 10	36		58	
							" " " 461	22			

Ed's Medals

R.A.A.F. Form P./T. 88.
(R.A.F. Form 580)

ROYAL AUSTRALIAN AIR FORCE
CERTIFICATE OF THE SERVICE AND DISCHARGE OF

The corner of this Certificate to be cut off if the man is discharged with a "bad" character, or with disgrace, or if specially directed by the Air Board.

Surname ___GALLAGHER___

Christian Name ___Edward Bernard___ Official No. ___405206___ aus

Date of Birth ___14/3/15___ Age on Entry into R.A.A.F. ___25___ years ___326___ days.

Place of Birth (Town) ___BRISBANE___, (District and State) ___QUEENSLAND___

Occupation in Civil Life ___Clerk___

Trade in Royal Australian Air Force ___Aircrew V___

Religious Denomination ___Roman Catholic___

Signature on Transfer to the Reserve or Discharge ___

Current Engagement in R.A.A.F.—
(a) State whether in Active or Reserve. ___Active___

Prior Engagement in H.M. Forces.

(b) Period :	Date current engagement commenced.	Age at this Date.	Terms of Enlistment	Service (Navy, Army, or Air Force) Unit.	Period. From	Period. To	Rank on Discharge.
	2/2/41	25	Duration War & up to 12 mths after				

(c) Date of Actual entry into { Permanent Force
{ Citizen Force ___2/2/41___

(d) Re-engaged for ___ years on ___

Date transferred to Royal Australian Air Force Reserve. ___ Date recalled from Royal Australian Air Force Reserve. ___

Name, Address, and Relationship of Person (or Persons) to be informed of Casualties (to be entered in pencil):—
Mr BERNARD GALLAGHER - Father
14 PERKINS ST, RAILWAY RESERVE
SOUTH TOWNSVILLE, QUEENSLAND

PARTICULARS AS TO MARRIAGE.

Full Christian Names and Surname of Woman and whether Spinster or Widow.	Place and Date of Marriage.	Present Address of Wife.	No. and date of Part II order promulgating.	Initials of Officer verifying entry.

Description of Person.	Height. Feet.	Height. Inches.	Chest. Inches.	Colour of Hair.	Colour of Eyes.	Colour of Complex'n.	Marks, Wounds or Scars.
On Enlistment 2.2-41	5	7	30/32	Light Brown	Blue	Fair	Nil
On Re-engagement							
" "							
" "							
" "							
" "							
Discharge							

Further Description, if necessary :—

DISCHARGE PARTICULARS :—

Date ___ Address on Discharge ___

Total Service ___ (Years) ___ (Days).

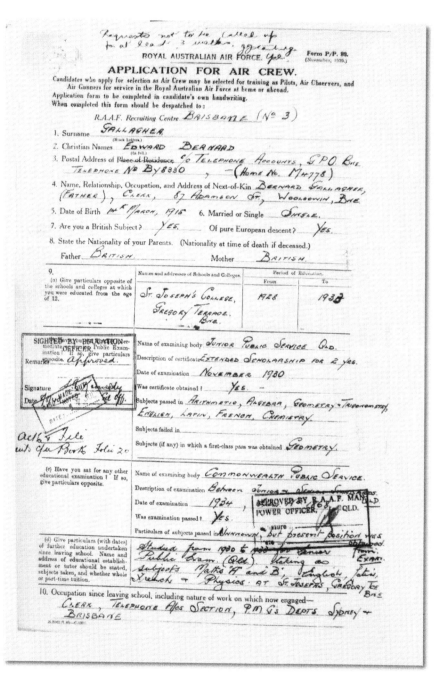

Requests not to be called up
for at least 2 weeks approving

ROYAL AUSTRALIAN AIR FORCE. 402

Form P/P. 80.
(November, 1939.)

APPLICATION FOR AIR CREW.

Candidates who apply for selection as Air Crew may be selected for training as Pilots, Air Observers, and Air Gunners for service in the Royal Australian Air Force at home or abroad.

Application form to be completed in candidate's own handwriting.

When completed this form should be despatched to:

R.A.A.F. Recruiting Centre BRISBANE (N° 3)

1. Surname GALLAGHER
   (Block letters.)
2. Christian Names EDWARD BERNARD
   (in full.)
3. Postal Address of Place of Residence C/o TELEPHONE ACCOUNTS, G.P.O. BNE.
   TELEPHONE N° B.Y.8330, — (Home No. M4778)
4. Name, Relationship, Occupation, and Address of Next-of-Kin BERNARD GALLAGHER,
   (FATHER), CLERK, 87 ADAMSON ST, WOOLOOWIN, BNE.
5. Date of Birth 1st MARCH, 1915. 6. Married or Single SINGLE.
7. Are you a British Subject? YES. Of pure European descent? YES.
8. State the Nationality of your Parents. (Nationality at time of death if deceased.)

   Father BRITISH. Mother BRITISH.

9. (a) Give particulars opposite of the schools and college at which you were educated from the age of 12.	Names and addresses of Schools and Colleges.	Period of Education.	
		From	To
	ST. JOSEPH'S COLLEGE, GREGORY TERRACE, BNE.	1928	1933

SIGHTED BY EDUCATION OFFICER
(b) State your Intermediate Public Examination? If so, give particulars
Remarks opposite. approved.

Signature [illegible]
Date [illegible]

act & file
with the Book folio 20

Name of examining body JUNIOR PUBLIC SERVICE QLD.
Description of certificate EXTENDED SCHOLARSHIP FOR 2 yrs.
Date of examination NOVEMBER 1930
Was certificate obtained? YES. —
Subjects passed in ARITHMETIC, ALGEBRA, GEOMETRY-TRIGONOMETRY, ENGLISH, LATIN, FRENCH, CHEMISTRY
Subjects failed in
Subjects (if any) in which a first-class pass was obtained GEOMETRY.

(c) Have you sat for any other educational examination? If so, give particulars opposite.	Name of examining body COMMONWEALTH PUBLIC SERVICE.
	Description of examination Between Junior — [illegible]
	Date of examination 1934,
	Was examination passed? YES.
	Particulars of subjects passed in Unknown, but present position was [illegible]

APPROVED BY R.A.A.F. MAN POWER OFFICER 63 QLD.

(d) Give particulars (with dates) of further education undertaken since leaving school. Name and address of educational establishment or tutor should be stated, subjects taken, and whether whole or part-time tuition.	Studied from 1930 to [illegible] for Senior Public Exam (Qld) taking as subjects Maths I and II, English, Latin, French + Physics at St. Joseph's, Gregory Te., Bne.

10. Occupation since leaving school, including nature of work on which now engaged—
    CLERK, TELEPHONE A/cs SECTION, P.M.G's DEPTS SYDNEY + BRISBANE

Enlistment Papers

437

OATH.

I, **Edward Bernard GALLAGHER** swear that I will well and truly serve Our Sovereign Lord the King as a member of the Air Force Reserve of the Commonwealth of Australia, and that I will resist His Majesty's enemies and cause His Majesty's Peace to be kept and maintained, and that I will in all matters appertaining to my service faithfully discharge my duty according to law. So help me God!

AFFIRMATION.

I, , solemnly and sincerely affirm and declare that I will well and truly serve Our Sovereign Lord the King as a member of the Air Force Reserve of the Commonwealth of Australia, and that I will resist His Majesty's enemies and cause His Majesty's Peace to be kept and maintained, and that I will in all matters appertaining to my service faithfully discharge my duty according to law.

Sworn
~~Declared~~ before me at   **Brisbane,**

in the State of   Queensland

this   **Seventeenth**   day of   *(Signature of Person enrolled.)*

September   One

thousand nine hundred and   **Forty**

Name
†*(Signature of Officer or Justice of the Peace administering the oath or taking the declaration.)*

Address   **No. 3 R.A.A.F. Recruiting Centre, Brisbane.**

Edward Bernard GALLAGHER   has been passed by me this day and posted

to Class   **AIR CREW**   of the Reserve.

Official Number R.

Date **17th September, 1940.**

FOR AIR MEMBER.   FOR PERSONNEL.   Wing Commander

RE-ENROLMENT.

I, No. R. (Rank) (Name)

at present serving in the Reserve enrolled on (date)

desiring to re-enroll in the Air Force Reserve for a period of four years from

  do hereby declare that I agree to re-enroll and to well and truly serve Our Sovereign Lord the King in the Air Force Reserve of the Commonwealth of Australia for the term of four years from (date), or until sooner lawfully discharged, dismissed, or removed; and that I will resist His Majesty's enemies and cause His Majesty's Peace to be kept and maintained; and that I will in all matters appertaining to my service faithfully discharge my duty according to law.

Signature of Reservist

Signed at

in the State of this

  day of 19

before me.   *(Signature)*

* A person who objects to taking the oath may make the affirmation. Cross out form not used. All amendments must be initialed by the Officer or J.P. witnessing the Affirmation.
† "Justice of the Peace" means a Stipendiary or Police or Special Magistrate, or some Magistrate of the State who is specially authorized by the Governor-General to administer the oath.
** Rank and appointment.

The Diane Watt Connection

Diane Holmes grew up in Gaythorne, Brisbane with her brother Donald and their parents, Mabel and Harry Watt. From the late forties to the early sixties, Diane and Donny, whose back fence touched the Gallagher's back fence, played regularly with us Gallagher kids, Bernard, Tricia and Ann. We lost contact when Diane headed to England in the sixties, but renewed friendships many years later. After reading about the movie *Coastal Command* in Dad's diary, and knowing Diane was married to a movie maker (Andrew Holmes), I emailed Diane to ask if she might know where I could find a copy of this movie. I was dumbfounded when she phoned me to tell me that not only did she know where I might get a copy of the movie, but that she had one, because, unbelievably, Andrew's father, Jack Holmes, had directed it. I visited Diane in Hampstead (London) when doing research for this book, and watched the movie. And there was Ed acting, just as he described it in his letter to Mum on February 20, 1942: "*... how would you like to keep a straight face if someone, especially a tried and trusted Squadron Leader, were to say to you, "Glub. Blurb. Horseradishes, Cauliflowers, Blah. Blah. Lollies and Peanuts."* Yes, really Dad, how would you!

Dear Tricia, Ann and Bernard,

It's spooky how we are somehow all linked together by the most incredible coincidence of this film. I remember Bernard, when you were here [Hampstead, UK] the first time; you traced your father's wartime postings in the West Country. It's strange that Andrew never thought to mention the film his father made about Sunderlands during the War. Well, I guess it's not that unusual for who would have thought that there could be any connection between the Holmes and the Gallaghers. I still can't get my head around the fact that Jack Holmes and Eddie Gallagher met and worked together all those years ago!

There is a booklet that accompanied the Coastal Command video, which gives details about the origins of the Crown Film Unit that Andrew's dad, Jack Holmes, joined in 1933. The unit was the brainchild of John Grierson, and included well-respected names in the documentary world such as Harry Watt, (no relation) Humphrey Jennings, etc. Coastal Command was released in October 1942 and was described by the Star as "one of the finest films of the war". There was a publicity sheet that accompanied the film on its release, which describes the "operational excitement of another Sunderland". This aircraft (your father's) served with No.10 Squadron, RAAF, and in June 1940 its crew sighted 20 survivors of a torpedoed ship in the Atlantic and brought a vessel to effect their rescue. Later it was again instrumental in saving two boatloads of survivors from another ship, and this aircraft had occasion that same year to alight in the Atlantic to pick up 21 survivors. The flying boat's captain, a Squadron Leader from Campderdown, Victoria, made a landing in difficult conditions, and took off again with his extra load in a rapidly rising sea. This was a risky undertaking, as the Sunderland had not been designed to land on a running ocean; the underside of the hull was only three-sixteenths of an inch thick. Both P9606 and P9605 could be this aircraft; both had been with No. 10 Squadron RAAF, although the former had only been with the unit for two months at the beginning of 1940, whereas the latter remained with it. However P9606 served with No. 201 Squadron for the remainder of that year, and into 1941, carrying out Atlantic patrols. Do you want me to buy you a copy (only PAL available) and send it to you? I will be happy to do so.

Lots of love

Diane

I found a copy of Coastal Command on YouTube, where you may see and hear the Coastal Command crews (including, briefly, Ed) going about their courageous day-to-day attempts to find U-boats, and keep the enemy at bay: http://www.youtube.com/watch?v=BssQCDqZXek
It is available on DVD (which also includes "The Story of the Black Cats" showing missions by Catalina crews in the Pacific) at: www.periscopefilm.com

Ed is on the left in these clips

RAAF MEN FOR FILM "Telegraph" Special London, March 25 (1943)

An Australian Spitfire squadron based in the south of England has been selected to provide players and the background for a new Crown Film Unit production, the shooting of which, subject to the exigencies of service, will begin almost immediately.

Squadron Leader Jack R. Ratten, a Tasmanian, who is well known in mining circles in Queensland, Pilot Officers R.H.S. Ewins of Ballarat, and E.A.R. Esau of 363 Annerley Road, South Brisbane, and Sergeants F.K. Halcombe of North Adelaide, and R.G. Clemesha, of Vaucluse, will appear in the more prominent parts with the whole squadron making up messroom and other aerodrome scenes.

The film will be Crown Unit's fourth in co-operation with the Ministry of Information, the others being "Target for Tonight," "Coastal Command," and "Fires Were Started."

The latter records the work of the national fire service and opens in London on April 12. Australia's senior Sunderland Squadron already has figured in "Coastal Command." The captain and first pilot of one of the Sunderlands filmed were Wing-Commander O.L.G. Douglas of Sydney, who is now commanding another Australian Sunderland squadron, and Flight Lieutenant H.D. White, of Adelaide.

When 204 Squadron left for North Africa they were replaced on April 1st 1940 by Number 10 Royal Australian Air Force Squadron, who not only stayed for the remainder of the War but were set to become Mount Batten's most famous occupants. A fascinating and detailed account of their wartime exploits hunting German U-boats has been told by Dennis Teague in his book "Strike First: They shall not pass unseen". By the time they left the base in October 1945, so Dennis Teague relates, they had flown 4,553,860 nautical miles, undertaken 3,177 operational flights, sunk 5 submarines, received 25 Distinguished Flying Crosses (DFC), one DFC with Bar, 9 Distinguished Flying Medals (DFM), 1 British Empire Medal (BEM) and had 36 'mentioned in despatches'. Before they left England they were awarded a Crest by His Majesty King George VI with the motto 'Strike First'.

Sonnets

To Molly – 7th July, 1941

Stark loneliness has lingered by my bed

To mock a tardy dawn, when solitude

Has been my night-long guest, and Mem'ry's brood

The children of my brain: and I have fled

Its bleak-dead company, yet still have known

Its cold clutch at my heart amid a whirl

Of gay society; and many a girl

Has leant upon my arm, – yet I have been alone.

And I had sought, with mad, vain leaps of mind,

Beyond the ends of life, yet could not find

One avenue of rest, one place to hide

Deep from myself, – when you walked by my side.

And while, within my heart, I hold your own,

And you but pray for me, – I shall not walk alone.

Reality

Octave

Sometimes it seems that all this Loveliness,

– This tapestry that changes in the West

When Evening cloaks the hills, – this Happiness

That makes the songs of birds, – Life's joyous zest,

– The fragrance of a Rose, – is but a dream

That stays no longer than the moon's swift flights

Through rifts in wind-swept clouds, or dews that gleam,

Low hidden in the grass on Summer nights.

Sestette

And in this world of mystic fancies filled

With dreams, – where heavy-scented flowers steal

My soul, – like nectars by the Gods distilled,

Sweet hours spent with you alone seem real:

– And may that last dream – Death – one gift allow

That I deem real, – your lips upon my brow!

22/5/42   Mt. Batten   EBG

Dreams

Sleep softly, dear, within your quiet room,

And mayhap dream of me, – and through the gloom

My Love will guard you, till the Dawn's first ray

Awakes, and let no anxious yesterday

Disturb your dreaming heart. – All unaware

I'll smoothe away the night's last ling'ring care,

And bend above the bed where lightly lies

Your dear dark hair, – and kiss your drowsy eyes.

– Thus are the nights with me: My last half-thought

Of you, ere Slumber steals my soul, is brought

Unbroken to a dream so crystal clear

I deem it real; and then your voice I hear,

More silent than the swallow's quiet flight

Through jewelled leaves, – whisp'ring "My Love, – Good-Night!"

Mt Batten – "Pockley's Corner", England-Spain. R.B.U. 9.3.42

A Friend's Smile

Dear friend, – when wearied with this life my soul

Seeks some sweet refuge where it may console

Itself against the sneers of an unfeeling world,

– Against the gibes that thoughtlessly are hurled

By those I count among my dearest friends;

– When sorrows sear my heart, and all in vain,

I search through Pleasure's halls to dull the pain,

– Haply I think of you, – and sadness ends.

When all the world seems canopied with shade;

– When all the joys I grasp at seem to fade.

Like fleeting dreams, and fading leave my soul

Lost in the maze of an ungained goal,

– 'Tis then I turn to you, and in a while,

All sorrow seems a spell, – broke by your smile.

Pembroke Dock (England),   A.S. Strike.   5/3/42   EBG

To M. – Plymouth – 1942

When Night is near, before sleep steals my brain,

Like some soft-footed thief, – I lie awake

Awhile, half-dreaming of the day's sweet gain,

And bitter loss'; but Dearest when I take

The laughter from the grief, I fret to find

The tears of vanished moments far outweigh

The joys; – that some dear friendship's loss, through blind

Unreasoning, has draped the world in grey.

But if, – sometime between the Dawn and Dark,

We two have met, – and mayhap we have walked

Down flower-edged paths of some secluded park;

– And you have smiled at me, as soft we talked,

– Then can I smile, and deem the day well spent,

And close my eyes, and dreamless sleep – content.

Angle Bay (Eng.)   3.2.42

447

Envy

Octave

Oft-times I envy other men their wealth,

– Their skill at sports, – their luck in games of chance,

Others their power, some their better health;

– This man his looks and that his swift advance

In worldly state; and, Dearest, when I fret,

– By hopeless wish dismayed, – when : my poor gain

Torments my weary soul, and I regret

What might have been, – then living seems in vain.

Sestette

While other men by Fortune seem endowed,

And I, her fool, stand by like one forgot,

I murmur 'gainst the fate that holds me bowed

With weight of woe, and scorn my paltry lot.

– But, Dear, when sweet remembrances recall

That You love me, – I'm richer than them all!

Anti-Sub Patrol from P.D.   *28/1/42*

Always

Octave

Not only in the hours of dreaming night

Are you with me: Not only when the light

Of mystic moonbeams sets my thoughts to rove

On Mem'ries wings, to times when you and love

Were near, to hold within my trembling arm

   –   All wordless with the wonder of your charm,
Does your dear presence linger in my heart,

– Thrilling my soul with you, – though leagues apart.

Sestette

Not only when the soft winds weave a spell,

To breathe your name within my yearning ear,

Am I with you: But as the long-dead shell

Still knows the surge of seas, – your voice is ever near:

– Not only neath the moon, – beneath the sun,

But always, on you Dear, my soul's thoughts run!

449

If I Should Lose You

Octave

I thought, were I to lose you, dear, the sky

Would merge its blue-depth in a cloud-bound hell,

– The breeze of morning, whispering softly by

The flowers, nodding in a dew-hung dell,

Would in a Tempest rage, and fill the world

With seething voices; – that the stars on high

Would from their settings in the blue be hurled,

While, dim-low o'er the earth, the moon would die.

Sestette

But, I was wrong: Nothing has seemed to wane!

 – The day is still as fair, the nights still gleam
With gems. Still do I eat, and drink, and dream,

And seem to smile. Regret has sought in vain

To force my eyes one burning tear to shed.

– Nor did I die: – Yet, Darling, I am dead!

November 20, 1943

Octave

When I recall those happy hours we shared

In sweet soft-talks, and silences more sweet

Than words, the thoughts I dared

Not speak, – yet longed to say, – unbidden fleet

In sorrowful procession through my mind.

Then do I long for those lost hours again

That I might urge my trembling lips to find

The force I lacked to speak my heart's dear pain.

Sestette

Yet, still, my inmost soul could not be bared

By words, – poor bondlings of the earthy brain:

Nor could I tell you, Darling, how I cared

In sonnets, which the Masters sang in vain

But when, into mine own, your Dear eyes glow,

No words I'll need, for you, my Love, will know!

20.11.43

Dreaming

Octave

Dreaming, while night-winds kissed the restless trees,

I dreamt that in some garden fair I lay,

Watching the silver-sheen of moonbeams play

Through fountains quivering gently in the breeze :

I thought that all the beauty in the world

Was there, among the flowers lightly furled

In sleep; – that all the love, the peace, the grace

Of Life was born within that quiet place.

Sestette

But, then, I heard light feet caress the grass,

And saw a moon-bathed figure softly pass

The drowsy roses, bright with diamond dew,

And bend o'er me, and smile, – and it was you!

And, dear, the mystic light that lingered there

Grew dim beside that smile, – the plot seemed bare.

Octave

Where once Atlantis stood, the gloomy deeps

Of restless ocean stir, and in the dust

Of long-lost Ophir's street, the Jackal sleeps:

– Thus Time, with grasping claw outstretched, thrust

Strong citadel and city 'neath its tread,

And, in the chronicle of mighty loads,

Left naught but rows of painted faces, – dead,

With maces broke, and rust-encased swords.

Sestette

All things, of Man's endeavour built, decay,

And dying, of their passing leave no sign,

Save where the Master's hand assigns the clay

A lasting beauty, – tinged with the Divine:

And, Dear, when all things else we loved are gone,

Our Love, – deep born of God, – will linger on!

Quasi-Sonnet: Reverie

Darkened launches steal like shadows

Down the reaches of the river,

Sending ripples to the shallows

Underneath the restless trees.

Latticed gleams of liquid silver

Through the swaying branches quiver

Changing patterns with each whisper

Of the sighing evening breeze.

I dream of white sails, homeward bound, and

evenings of long ago,

With sweet old songs, and laughters gay,

and lovers whisp'ring low,

'Neath a sky as bright, with a wind as light

blurring a mirrored face,

– Chasing a running wavelet over a sandy race:

And I think of some who sang with me, as

we heeled with the dipping trees

– Loved for a day, – now forgotten, like

popular melodies.

Your Eyes

When, like the fragrance of the sweet musk-rose,

Your beauty fades, – then still will I love thee;

And still to me your loveliness will be

Fresh as the newest flower that shyly blows

Upon a bank in some fair country lane,

Where trees sway softly in a morning breeze,

– Where songs of birds, and murmurings of bees

Mingle with prattling brooks – new fed by rain.

The beauty of the sun in western skies

Lingers a while, then swiftly fades and dies,

Leaving the way for darkness and the night.

But Age, and even Death possess no might

To dim within my soul that softest light,

The glory in the magic of your eyes.

(The soft and glowing splendour of your eyes.)

To Dal on her Wedding Day

The newest Rose today first kiss'd the morn

Close where you walked, – breathing an incense rare

Fragrant with all the freshness of the dawn

In homage to the magic of your hair.

And since Apollo's chariot woke the day

He shone for you, and lingered for a while

At Dusk, – to leave one glorious crimson ray

To delve the shy – sweet mystery of your smile.

The Songs the birds sing to the Evening Star,

Some Angel wrote, – flouting all heaven's laws

To praise the Charm that Age can never mar

Nor Death destroy, – the beauty that is yours –

Yet I, ambitious fool, with earthy words,

And awkward, ill-made verse, – would match the birds!

[Dick and Dal Webb lived next door to Ed and Molly at 27 Grays Road, Gaythorne in Brisbane.]

Sonnet. – To M. – 10.9.40

When, in some future time, I lie in wait

For Death's chill hand to still my last faint sigh,

– Seeking to drown my fears, my soul I'll sate

With dear remembrances of days gone by;

– And through my mind will fleet a passing show

Of faces half-forgot, – while in mine ears

Again, as in a shell, I'll dimly know

The surge of voices, – muffled by the years.

And mayhap, of these mem'ries, some will glow

Within my heart, like starlight after rain;

While others, burning, – passing grim and slow,

Will rend my soul with an exquisite pain:

– But these will pass, – as darting shadows flee

Across the moon, – if I but think of thee.

On Someone's Twenty-Fourth Birthday

Octave

The years have gone, and Dear, each fleeting day

An Angel must have spent in toil,

To form the charm that age can never spoil,

The Beauty that is yours: to make the gay

Shy sweetness of your smile, – your dear dark hair.

The tenderness that lingers in the blue

Deep heaven of your eyes: – In breathless care

To shape the sweet perfection that is you!

Sestette

Yet still the passing years will but adorn

The loveliness that's yours this August day;

And when, in other ages yet unborn,

Back to youth's rose-strewn paths your mem'ries stray,

You'll find that life had just flung wide the door,

In that dear time, when you were twenty-four!

Sestette 2: On Someone's Twenty-first Birthday.

And still the passing years will but adorn

The grace and loveliness you have today;

And when, in other ages yet unborn,

Back to youth's rose-strewn paths your mem'ries stray,

You'll find that life and love had just begun

In that dear time, when you were twenty-one!

To M. — 23.3.41

I dread the dragging hours of endless night,

When sleep seems further than the stars, – and you

A million leagues beyond their dimmest light.

– When restless yearning for the peace I knew

When you were near, delays the dreary morn;

And false half-sleep defeats, with wishful dreams,

My dear-sought rest, – tormenting, 'till the dawn,

My weary soul with myriad wondrous schemes.

– Mad schemes (I know them mad the while) that fleet

Like shadows through my brain. – Vain plans to flee,

With duty flung to winds, and once more see

The magic in your eyes; and know the beat

Of your dear heart on mine; – the dancing gleams

In your dark hair: – And morning mocks my dreams.

South-Wind — To M.T. while in England.

Sometimes I wonder if this same shy breeze,

That whispers by my window at the close

Of day, – breathing soft Southern fantasies

To dreaming shrubs of May and scented Rose,

Has lingered on its way to touch your hair,

– To kiss your brow, – for deep in it I find

A fragrance rarer than the May, – more fair

Than Rose, – and I grow jealous of the wind!

Half-hidden where the drowsy Laurels turn

Their green arms to the moon, I strive to hear,

– Low murmured to the Jasmine and the Fern,

– A word of you, not meant for mortal ear:

– But mockingly the siblants seem to tease

My soul, – and I grow jealous of the trees!

Pembroke Dock, 31/12/41

Sonnet No. 175 Oxford. 12/1/43

Variation on "To M. 5.4.41 Parkes, N.S.W.

   –   Because I love her."

Octave

When, in the silent hours of drowsy night,

I lie awake, half dreaming, while the light

Of magic moonbeams makes sweet mysteries

The places where it falls, – sometimes through the trees

That mask the gleaming pathway, low I hear

The East wind whispering its tales of Fear

And Courage to the world, – singing of wrongs,

Of Joy and Life and Love, in old, sweet songs.

Sestette

And when I know this same cloud-sailing moon

Has smiled on you, – this wind has sung its tune

In your dear ear, – has kissed your hair,

And set caressing fingers on the fair

Enchantment of your brow, – dark envies seize

My Soul, – and I grow jealous of the moon and breeze.

Made in the USA
Charleston, SC
19 September 2013